Wiley Finance Series

For other titles in the Wiley Finance Series
please see www.wileyeurope.com/finance

D1437293

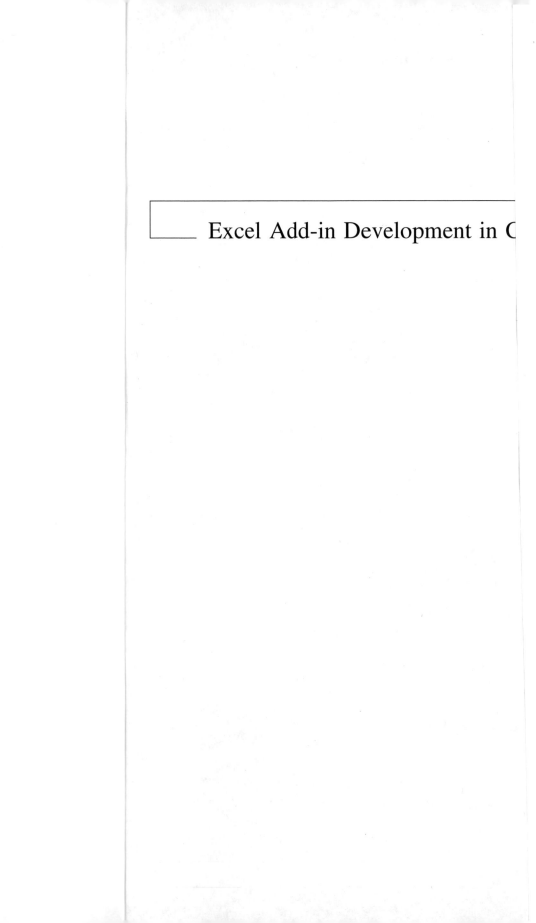

Excel Add-in Development in C

Excel Add-in Development in C/C++

Applications in Finance

Steve Dalton

John Wiley & Sons, Ltd

Copyright © 2005   John Wiley & Sons Ltd, The Atrium, Southern Gate, Chichester,
                          West Sussex PO19 8SQ, England

                          Telephone (+44) 1243 779777

Email (for orders and customer service enquiries): cs-books@wiley.co.uk
Visit our Home Page on www.wileyeurope.com or www.wiley.com

All Rights Reserved. No part of this publication may be reproduced, stored in a retrieval system or
transmitted in any form or by any means, electronic, mechanical, photocopying, recording, scanning or
otherwise, except under the terms of the Copyright, Designs and Patents Act 1988 or under the terms of a
licence issued by the Copyright Licensing Agency Ltd, 90 Tottenham Court Road, London W1T 4LP, UK,
without the permission in writing of the Publisher. Requests to the Publisher should be addressed to the
Permissions Department, John Wiley & Sons Ltd, The Atrium, Southern Gate, Chichester, West Sussex PO19
8SQ, England, or emailed to permreq@wiley.co.uk, or faxed to (+44) 1243 770620.

Designations used by companies to distinguish their products are often claimed as trademarks. All brand
names and product names used in this book are trade names, service marks, trademarks or registered
trademarks of their respective owners. The Publisher is not associated with any product or vendor mentioned
in this book.

This publication is designed to provide accurate and authoritative information in regard to the subject matter
covered. It is sold on the understanding that the Publisher is not engaged in rendering professional services. If
professional advice or other expert assistance is required, the services of a competent professional should be
sought.

Other Wiley Editorial Offices

John Wiley & Sons Inc., 111 River Street, Hoboken, NJ 07030, USA

Jossey-Bass, 989 Market Street, San Francisco, CA 94103-1741, USA

Wiley-VCH Verlag GmbH, Boschstr. 12, D-69469 Weinheim, Germany

John Wiley & Sons Australia Ltd, 33 Park Road, Milton, Queensland 4064, Australia

John Wiley & Sons (Asia) Pte Ltd, 2 Clementi Loop #02-01, Jin Xing Distripark, Singapore 129809

John Wiley & Sons Canada Ltd, 22 Worcester Road, Etobicoke, Ontario, Canada M9W 1L1

Wiley also publishes its books in a variety of electronic formats. Some content that appears
in print may not be available in electronic books.

Library of Congress Cataloging-in-Publication Data

Dalton, Steve.
    Excel add-in development in C/C++ : applications in finance / Steve Dalton.
        p. cm.
    Includes bibliographical references and index.
    ISBN 0-470-02469-0
  1. Microsoft Excel (Computer file) 2. Business – Computer programs. 3. C (Computer program
language) 4. C++ (Computer program language) 5. Computer software – Development. I. Title.
    HF5548.4.M523D35 2004
    005.54 – dc22   2004016908

British Library Cataloguing in Publication Data

A catalogue record for this book is available from the British Library

ISBN 0-470-02469-0

Typeset in 10/12pt Times by Laserwords Private Limited, Chennai, India
Printed and bound in Great Britain by Antony Rowe Ltd, Chippenham, Wiltshire
This book is printed on acid-free paper responsibly manufactured from sustainable forestry
in which at least two trees are planted for each one used for paper production.

Contents

API what does it mean

= application program
     interface

1

Preface

This book is intended to provide the reader with a guide to the issues involved with creating powerful and reliable add-ins for Excel. With years of use, many people build up the experience and understanding needed to create custom functions for Excel in C and C++. However, given the very limited books and resources available, this can be a largely trial-and-error process. The motivation in writing this book is to create something I wish I had had through the years: a coherent explanation of the relevant technology, what steps to follow, what pitfalls to avoid, and a good reference guide. With these things at your side, writing C/C++ DLL and XLL resources can be almost as easy as writing them in Visual Basic, but yields the enormous performance benefit of compiled C/C++ and the Excel C API.

In setting goals for this book, I was particularly inspired by two excellent books that I have grown to admire more and more over the years, as they have repeatedly proven their worth; *The C Programming Language* (Kernighan and Ritchie) and *Numerical Recipes in C* (Press, Teukolsky, Vetterling and Flannery), albeit that the style of C-coding of the latter can be somewhat dense. If this book achieves a fraction of the usefulness of either of these then you will, I hope, be happy to own it and I will be happy to have written it.

This book is intended for anyone with at least solid C and/or C++ foundation skills, a good working knowledge of Excel, a little experience with VBA (though not necessary) and the need to make Excel do things it doesn't really want to do, or do them faster, more cleanly, more flexibly. A reasonable grasp of basic software development concepts and techniques is assumed. (Section 1.1 *Typographical and code conventions used in this book*, on page 1, provides more detail of the coding style of the examples given.)

The example add-in project included on the CD ROM is intended to demonstrate some of the most important or difficult concepts described in the book, as well as the possibilities that are opened up when you can really play with Excel. These reflect my professional background in the financial markets, although if you are not of that world, you should still find that the techniques described are very widely applicable.

There is an enormous amount of material that could have been included in a book on this subject that has either been pared down to the briefest of coverage or omitted completely. I fully accept that there will be those who, perhaps rightly, feel that certain things should have been covered in a book that boasts such a title, and I can only apologise. Any future editions will, I hope, provide an opportunity to rectify the most heinous and unpopular of these shortcomings.

The first spreadsheet application I encountered was a version of Visicalc in 1984 that ran on a 64K RAM Atari games console. It was dizzyingly slow and I had no practical use for it at the time. Nevertheless, all the essential elements of a modern spreadsheet application were there. Like the bicycle, many improvements have been made since the very early versions but the basic design was virtually right first time. Spreadsheet users have continued to find applications well beyond the intentions of early designers. It's a safe bet that spreadsheets will be an important tool for many decades to come. It's also safe to say that, for some people, what comes out of the box will never be enough. This book is for those people.

Acknowledgements

I would like to acknowledge and sincerely thank the following people: Alister Morton for first demystifying the C API for me many many years ago; Sean Storey for his help with certain C++ language and style points and for his general input and proof-reading; Fredrik Wahlgren for his very valuable help with the section on COM and automation, and for his general comments; Mike Trutt for his proof-reading and comments on writing style; Rob Bovey for his early comments and encouragement, and for his later help; Mike Clinch for his consistently good advice without which life would be very much more difficult; Les Clewlow and Chris Strickland for their perspective as authors and for their encouragement as friends and lastly, all those who've had to put up with me having one, rather boring and obsessive, topic of conversation for the time it has taken to complete this first edition.

not Visual Brain proper

My Cpp Function
names of XLL
XLL functions

explain
what W32
is

Introduction

1.1 TYPOGRAPHICAL AND CODE CONVENTIONS USED IN THIS BOOK

To distinguish between the text of the book, Visual Basic code, C/C++ code, and Excel worksheet functions, formulae and cell references, the following fonts are used throughout:

Excel functions and formulae	Arial
Windows application menus and control button text	Arial
Visual Basic code	Lucida Console
C/C++ code	Courier
Directory paths, file names and file masks	Courier

Passages of source code appear as boxed text in the appropriate font.

The spelling and grammar used throughout this book are British Isles English, with the occasional Microsoft extension such as *dialog*.

Examples of non-VB code are mostly in C++-flavoured C. That is, C written in C++ source modules so that some of the useful C++ features can be used including:

- the declaration of automatic variables anywhere in a function body;
- the use of the `bool` data type with associated `true` and `false` values;
- the use of call-by-reference arguments;
- C++ style comments.

C functions and variables are written in lower case with underscores to improve readability, for example, `c_thing`. In the few places C++ classes are used, class and instance names and member functions and variables are written in proper case, and in general, without underscores, for example, `CppThing`. Class member variables are prefixed with 'm_' to clarify class body code. Beyond this, no coding standard or variable naming convention is applied. Names of XLL functions, as registered with Excel, are generally in proper case with no underlines, to distinguish them from Excel's own uppercase function names, for example, `MyCppFunction`.

Where function names appear in the book text, they appear in the appropriate font with trailing parentheses but, in general, without their arguments. For example, a C/C++ function is written as `c_function()` or `CppFunction()` and an Excel worksheet function is written as Excel_Function(). VB functions may be written as VB_Function(), or simply `VB_Function` where the function takes no arguments, consistent with VB syntax.

Code examples mostly rely on the Standard C Library functions rather than, say, the C++ Standard Template Library or other C++ language artefacts. Memory allocation and release use `malloc()`, `calloc()` and `free()`, rather than `new` and `delete` or the Win32 global memory functions. (There are one or two exceptions to this.) This is not because the choice of the C functions is considered better, but because it is a simple common denominator. It is assumed that any competent programmer can alter the examples given to suit their own preferences. String manipulation is generally done with the standard C library functions such as strchr(), rather than the C++ String class. (There is some discussion of BSTR strings and the functions that handle them, where the topic is interoperability of C/C++ DLLs and VB.)

The standard C library sprintf() function is used for formatted output to string buffers, despite the fact that it is not type-safe and risks buffer overrun. (The book avoids the use of any other standard input/output routines.)

The object oriented features of C++ have mostly been restricted to two classes. The first is the cpp_xloper, which wraps the basic Excel storage unit (the xloper) and greatly simplifies the use of the C API. The second is the xlName which greatly simplifies the use of named ranges. (Strictly speaking, defined names can refer to more than just ranges of cells.) There are, of course, many places where an add-in programmer might find object-abstraction useful, or the functionality of the classes provided in this book lacking; the choice of how to code your add-in is entirely yours.

C++ *throw and catch* exception handling are not used or discussed, although it is expected that any competent C++ programmer might, quite rightly, want to use these. Their omission is intended to keep the Excel-related points as the main focus.

Many other C++ features are avoided in order to make the code examples accessible to those with little C++ experience: namespaces, class inheritance and friends, streams and templates. These are all things that an experienced C++ programmer will be able to include in their own code with no problem, and are not needed in order to address the issues of interfacing with Excel.

The C++ terms *member variable* and *member function*, and their VB analogues (*property* and *method*, are generally used in the appropriate context, except where readability is improved.

1.2   WHAT TOOLS AND RESOURCES ARE REQUIRED TO WRITE ADD-INS

Licensed copies of a 32-bit version of Excel and a 32-bit Windows OS are both assumed. (16-bit systems are not covered in this book). In addition, and depending on how and what you want to develop, other software tools may be required, and are described in this section. Table 1.1 summarises the resources needed for the various levels of capability, starting with the simplest.

Table 1.1 Resources required for add-in development

What you want to develop	Required resources	Where to get them
VBA macros and add-ins	VBA (for Excel)	Supplied with Excel
Win32 DLLs whose functions can be accessed via VBA	VBA A compiler capable of building a Win32 DLL from the chosen source language (which does not have to be C or C++)	Supplied with Excel Various commercial and shareware/freeware sources

Table 1.1 (*continued*)

C/C++ Win32 DLLs whose functions can be accessed via VB and that can control Excel using OLE/COM Automation	VBA A C/C++ compiler capable of building Win32 DLLs, and that has the necessary library and header file resources for OLE/COM Automation	Supplied with Excel Various commercial and shareware/freeware sources. Microsoft IDEs provide these resources. (See below for details.)
C/C++ Win32 DLLs that can access the Excel C API whose functions can be accessed directly by Excel without the use of VBA.	A C/C++ compiler capable of building Win32 DLLs. The C API library and header files. A copy of the XLM (Excel 4 macro language) help file. (Not strictly required but a very useful resource.)	Various commercial and shareware/freeware sources. Downloadable free from Microsoft at the time of writing. (See below for details.) Static library also shipped with Excel.
.NET add-ins and controllers.	Excel 2002 or later. A C/C++/C# compiler capable of building .NET components for Microsoft Office applications.	

At the time of writing, a good starting point for locating Microsoft downloads is www.microsoft.com/downloads/search.asp.

1.2.1 VBA macros and add-ins

VBA is supplied and installed as part of all 32-bit versions of Excel. If you only want to write add-ins in VB, then that's all you need. The fact that you are reading this book already suggests you want to do more than just use VB.

1.2.2 C/C++ DLL add-ins

It is, of course, possible to create Win32 DLLs using a variety of languages other than C and C++. You may, for example, be far more comfortable with Pascal. Provided that you can create standard DLLs you can access the exposed functions in Excel via VB. If this is all you want to be able to do, then all you need is a compiler for your chosen language that can build DLLs.

Chapter 4 *Creating a 32-bit Windows (Win32) DLL using Visual C++ 6.0 or Visual Studio .NET*, page 75, contains step-by-step examples of the use of Microsoft's *Visual Studio C++ version 6.0 Standard Edition* and *Visual Studio C++ .NET 2003* integrated development environments (IDEs). The examples demonstrate compiler and project settings and show how to debug the DLL from within Excel. No prior knowledge of these IDEs is required. (Standard Win32 DLLs are among the simplest things to create.) Other IDEs, or even simple command-line compilers, could be used, although it is beyond the scope of this book to provide examples or comparisons.

1.2.3   C/C++ DLLs that can access the C API and XLL add-ins

If you want your DLL to be able to access the C API, then you need a C or C++ compiler, as well as the C API library and header file. The C API functions and the definitions of the data types that Excel uses are contained in the library and header files `xlcall32.lib` and `xlcall.h`. Both of these are contained in a sample project, downloadable from Microsoft at the time of writing, free of charge, at download.microsoft.com/download/platformsdk/sample27/1/NT4/EN-US/Frmwrk32.exe. It is also possible to link Excel's library in its DLL form, `xlcall32.dll`, in your DLL project, removing the need to obtain the static `.lib` version. This file is created as part of a standard Excel installation. Another approach is to create the `.lib` file from the `.dll` file, as discussed in section 5.1.

This framework project is also included with Microsoft's *Excel 97 Developer's Kit* (1997, Microsoft Press) on its accompanying CD-ROM. The book contains a great deal of useful reference data, and describes the framework project in detail, something beyond the scope of this book. It is perhaps a little short on practical guidance, but owning a copy is nevertheless recommended. At time of writing, this book is now out of print, but still available on the Microsoft Developer Network (MSDN) website at msdn.microsoft.com/library/default.asp?url =/library/officedev/office97/edkfrnt.htm.

An XLL add-in is a DLL that exports a set of interface functions to help Excel load and manage the add-in directly. These functions, in turn, need to be able to access Excel's functionality via the C API, if only to be able to register the exported functions and commands. Only when registered can they be accessed directly from the worksheet (if functions) or via menus and toolbars (if commands). The C API is based on the XLM (Excel 4 macro language). This book provides guidance on the most relevant C API functions in Chapter 8. However, for a full description of all the C API's XLM equivalents you should ideally have a copy of the XLM help file, which is typically named `Macrofun.hlp`. This is, at the time of writing, downloadable in the form of a self-extracting executable from Microsoft at download.microsoft.com/download/excel97win/utility4/1/WIN98/EN-US/Macrofun.exe.

1.2.4   C/C++/C# .NET add-ins

This book does not cover .NET and C#. These technologies are an important part of Microsoft's vision for the future. The resources required to apply these technologies are Visual Studio .NET and a .NET-compatible version of Excel, i.e., Excel 2002 and later. The principle purpose of this book is to bring the power of compiled C and C++ to Excel users, rather than to be a manual for implementing these new technologies.

1.3   TO WHICH VERSIONS OF EXCEL DOES THIS BOOK APPLY?

Table 1.2 shows the marketing names and the underlying version numbers to which this book applies. Excel screenshots in this book (worksheets, dialogs, etc.) are all those of Excel 2000. Most of the interface differences between versions 2000 and 2003 (the latest at the time of writing) are quite superficial. The workbooks on the CD ROM are Excel 2000 format. (Contact ccppaddin@eigensys.com if you require 97 format files.)

Table 1.2 Excel version numbers

Product marketing name	Version number
Excel 97 (SR-1, SR-2)	8
Excel 2000	9
Excel 2002	10
Excel 2003	11

1.4   ABOUT ADD-INS

An add-in is simply a code resource that can be attached to a standard application to enhance its functionality. Excel is supplied with a number of add-ins that can be installed according to the user's preference and need. Some provide specialist functions not needed by the average user, such as the Analysis ToolPak (sic), and some that provide complex additional functionality such as the Solver add-in.

Add-ins come in two main flavours: interpreted macros and compiled code resources. Version 4 of Excel introduced macro sheets which could contain macros written in the Excel macro language (XLM). These comprised columns of instructions and calculations that either led to a result being returned to the caller, if functions, or that performed some action such as formatting a cell, if commands. Macro sheets could be part of a workbook or saved and loaded separately so as to be accessible to any workbook. Despite their flexibility they were relatively slow and did not promote sensible structured coding. In fact they encouraged the exact opposite given that, for example, they could modify themselves whilst executing.

Version 5 introduced Visual Basic worksheets. This enabled coding of functions and commands as before but promoted better coding practices and made implementation of algorithms from other languages easier. Excel 97 replaced these VB-sheets with Visual Basic for Applications and the Visual Basic Editor (VBE) – a comprehensive IDE complete with context-sensitive object-oriented help, pre-compiler, debugger and so on.

Macros, be they XLM or VB, are interpreted. When run, the interpreter reads each line one-by-one, makes sense of it while checking for errors in syntax, compiles it and only then executes the instructions. Despite the fact that VBA does some of this work in advance, this is a slow process. The VBA approach avoids the need for tools to create fully pre-compiled code making the creation of add-ins possible for the non-expert programmer. VBA makes Excel application objects accessible and is therefore the obvious choice for a host of user-defined commands and functions where speed of development rather than speed of execution is the prime concern. Additionally, Microsoft have not updated the C API since the release of Excel 97 and only support XLM for backwards compatibility. New functionality and objects added since this release are only available to applications that can access Excel's COM-exposed objects. This is not too serious as the type of functionality added is that which it is most appropriate to access from VBA (or VB), rather than via the C API, anyway.

The other main flavour of add-in is the pre-compiled code resource which has none of the execution overhead of interpreted languages and is therefore extremely fast by comparison. The cost is the need to use and so understand, another development language, and another compiler or IDE. In essence, this is no harder than using VBA and the VB editor. The additional requirement is to know what Excel expects from and provides to anything calling itself an Excel add-in. In other words, you need to understand the Excel interface. The two interfaces that have been available over recent years are the C API and COM (the Common Object Model) also known as Automation). COM provides access to Excel's exposed objects, their methods and properties. VBA itself is a COM Automation application. Section 9.5 *Accessing Excel functionality using COM/OLE Automation*, on page 295, discusses some very basic COM concepts.

VB macros can be saved as Excel add-ins with very little effort but the resulting code is still slower than, say, compiled C add-ins. (Some performance comparisons are given in section 9.2 *Relative performance of VB, C/C++: Tests and results* on page 289). Despite the rapid development and flexibility of VB, it lacks some of the key language concepts present in C and C++, in particular, pointers. These can sometimes be critical to the efficient implementation of certain algorithms. One example of where this is especially true is with the manipulation of strings.

The advent of .NET changes a number of things. For example, VB code resources can be compiled and the functions contained made accessible directly from a worksheet, at least in Excel 2002 and later. C, C++ and C# resources can similarly be accessed directly from a worksheet without the need to use the C API.

1.5   WHY IS THIS BOOK NEEDED?

For anyone who decides that VBA just isn't up to the task for their application or who wants to decide the best way to make an existing C or C++ code resource available within Excel, just the task of weighing up all the options can at first seem daunting. There is at the time of writing *no* published text written specifically to help someone make this decision and then follow it through with practical step-by-step guidance. There are a number of commercial products that enable developers to access the power of the Excel via C API indirectly, through some sort of managed environment and set of classes. These are beyond the scope of this book, but do make sense for certain kinds of project.

The Excel C API is documented in Microsoft's *Excel 97 Developer's Kit* (1997, Microsoft Press), out of print at the time of writing. *This* book tries to complement that text as far as possible, providing information and guidance that it lacks. Where they overlap, this book tries to present information in a way that makes the subject as easy as possible to grasp. The *Developer's Kit* is a revision of an earlier version written for the 16-bit Excel 95, and contains much that was only relevant to developers making a transition from 16-bit to 32-bit. It provides a very comprehensive reference to the Microsoft BIFF (binary interchange file format) which is, however, of little use to most add-in writers.

Writing Win32 DLLs is fairly straightforward, but it is easy to get the impression that it is highly technical and complex. This is partly because available literature and articles often contain much that is no longer current (say relating to 16-bit versions of Windows), or because they concentrate heavily on 16- to 32-bit transition issues, or are simply badly written. Having said that, there are a few complexities and these need to be understood by anyone whose add-ins need to be robust and reliable. Overcoming the complexities to speed up the creation of fast-execution add-ins in C and C++ is what *this* book is all about.

1.6   HOW THIS BOOK IS ORGANISED

The book is organised into the following chapters:

Chapter 2 *Excel Functionality*
Basic things that you need to know about Excel, data types, terminology, recalculation logic and so on. Knowing these things is an important prerequisite to understanding subsequent chapters.

Chapter 3 *Using VBA*
Basic things about using VBA: creating commands and functions; accessing DLL functions via VB; VB data types; arrays and user-defined data structures, and how to pass them to DLLs and return them to Excel.

Chapter 4 *Creating a 32-bit Windows (Win32) DLL Using Visual C++ 6.0*
How to create a simple Win32 DLL, in VC or VC++ .NET, and export the functions so they can be accessed by VB for example. Lays the foundation for the creation of XLLs – DLLs whose functions can be accessed directly by Excel.

Chapter 5 *Turning DLLs into XLLs: The Add-in Manager Interface*
How to turn a DLL into an add-in that Excel can load using the add-in manager: an XLL. The functions that Excel needs to find in the DLL. How to make DLL functions accessible directly from the worksheet.

Chapter 6 *Passing Data between Excel and the DLL*
The data structures used by the Excel C API. Converting between these data structures and C/C++ data types. Getting data from and returning data to Excel.

Chapter 7 *Memory Management*
Stack limitations and how to avoid memory leaks and crashes. Communication between Excel and the DLL regarding responsibility for memory release.

Chapter 8 *Accessing Excel Functionality Using the C API*
The C interface equivalent to the XLM macro language and how to use it in a DLL. Information about some of the more useful functions and their parameters. Working with named ranges, menus, toolbars and C API dialogs. Trapping events within a DLL.

Chapter 9 *Miscellaneous Topics*
Timing function execution speed. A brief look at how to access Excel's objects and their methods and properties using IDispatch and COM. Keeping track of cells. Multitasking, multi-threading and asynchronous calls into a DLL add-in. Setting up timed calls to commands.

Chapter 10 *Example Add-ins and Financial Applications*
Examples that show how the previous chapters can be applied to financial applications such as, for example, Monte Carlo simulation.

1.7 SCOPE AND LIMITATIONS

The early chapters are intended to give just enough Excel and VBA background for the later chapters. There are literally dozens of books about Excel and VBA ranging from those whose titles are intended to coerce even the most timid out of the shadows, to those with titles designed to make them a must-buy for MBA students, such as '*Essential Power Excel Tips For Captains Of Industry And Entrepreneurs*'. (At the time of writing, this was a fictitious book title.) There are, of course, many well-written and comprehensive reference books on Excel and VBA. There are also a number of good specialist books for people who need to know how best to use Excel for a specific discipline, such as statistical analysis, for example.

The book is primarily focused on writing add-in worksheet functions. The reasons for this are gone into in later sections, such as section 2.8 *Commands versus functions in Excel* on page 19. One reason is that commands often rely on the creation of user-defined dialogs, which is a task far better suited to VBA. Even if the functionality that your command needs is already written in C/C++ code in a DLL, it can still easily be accessed from VB. Another reason is that, in general, commands do not have the same speed of execution requirements as worksheet functions – one of the main reasons for using a C/C++ DLL for functions.

Commands are covered to a certain extent, nevertheless. They can be a useful part of a well planned interface to a DLL. Knowing how to create and access them without the use of VB is important. Knowing how to create menus and menu items is important if you want DLL commands to be accessed in a seamless way. Chapter 8 *Accessing Excel Functionality Using the C API* on page 169 covers these topics.

The Excel COM interface is largely beyond the scope of this book, mainly to keep the book focused on the writing of high performance worksheet function, which COM does not help with. The other main reason is that if you need functionality that COM provides and the C API does not, for example, access to certain Excel objects, you are probably better off using VBA.

This book is not intended to be industry-specific or profession-specific except in the final chapter where applications of particular interest in certain areas of finance are discussed. It should be noted that the book is not intended to be a finance text book and deliberately avoids laborious explanations of things that finance professionals will know perfectly well. Nor are examples intended to necessarily cover all of what is a very broad field. It is hoped that readers will see enough parallel with their own field to be able to apply earlier sections of the book to their own problems without too much consternation.

2
Excel Functionality

2.1 OVERVIEW OF EXCEL DATA ORGANISATION

Excel organises data, formulae and other objects into a 2-dimensional grid of cells ($65,536 = 2^{16}$ rows by $256 = 2^8$ columns), one grid per worksheet, with as many sheets per workbook as system resources allow. Each cell can contain several different types of data as well as format information and embedded comments. (A workbook can also contain VB code modules associated with a particular worksheet object or the workbook object.)

Excel, like all Microsoft Office applications, provides two types of command-access objects: menu bars and toolbars. There are many other Windows objects, but cells, worksheets, workbooks and command-access objects are of most interest to an add-in developer. The hierarchy of these objects, simply represented, is as follows:

Table 2.1 Simple representation of primary Excel objects

Application: Excel				
Workbooks			Menu bars	Toolbars
Worksheets and other sheet types			Menus	Toolbar buttons
Ranges of cells and individual cells	Charts, drawings and other Excel and non-Excel objects	Control objects (Command buttons, etc.)	Menu items	
			Sub-menu items	

2.2 A1 VERSUS R1C1 CELL REFERENCES

Excel supports two styles of cell reference, both used for display and input. The default (and by far most commonly used) is the A1 style where the alphabetic part of the reference represents the column (from A to IV) and the numeric part represents the row (from 1 to 65,536). The other is referred to as the R1C1 style. The main reason spending any time discussing these is that some of the C API functions require or return range addresses in one form only. Some of Excel's VBA functionality also requires R1C1 notation, for example, when setting graph source-data ranges. Table 2.2 summarises both styles.

Table 2.2 A1 and R1C1 style comparisons

	A1 style	R1C1 style
Row-column order	Column then row	Row then column
Top row in sheet	1	R1
Bottom row in sheet	65536	R65536

(continued overleaf)

Table 2.2 (*continued*)

	A1 style	R1C1 style
Left-most column in sheet	A	C1
Right-most column in sheet	IV	C256
Relative reference style as shown by formula =A2 entered into cell B1.	=A2	=R[1]C[-1]
Absolute reference style as shown by formula =$A$2 entered into cell B1.	=$A$2	=R2C1
Mixed reference style as shown by formula =A$2 entered into cell B1.	=$A$2	=R2C[-1]
Relative reference in same row or column as shown by formula =A2 entered into cells B2 and A1.	=A2	=RC[1] (in cell A1) =R[-1]C (in cell B2)

Note: The index in square brackets in relative references in R1C1 style can be any number from −65,535 to +65,535 inclusive.

2.3   CELL CONTENTS

Internally, a cell within Excel has a great deal of data associated with it. This includes the display format, attached comments (notes), protection status, etc. The two most important properties for someone wishing to write functions are:

1. The cell's formula – a text string that Excel parses to an internal compiled form, and which is then used to re-evaluate the cell in a recalculation.
2. The cell's value – if the cell contains a formula, the result of its evaluation, otherwise the data that was entered directly by the user or an Excel command or macro.

2.4   WORKSHEET DATA TYPES AND LIMITS

From a spreadsheet user's perspective, the *type* of value of any non-empty cell (or group of cells in the case of an array) will always be one of the following:

- a number (floating point);
- a Boolean value (TRUE or FALSE);
- a character string;
- an Excel-specific error code;
- an array comprised, in general, of a mixture of the above types.

Excel will always evaluate a cell formula to one of these data types. Sometimes the function in the cell will return something other than one of these, such as a range reference, but Excel will then evaluate this to one of these types.

The formatting applied to a cell can, of course, make the appearance of a number it contains very different. A number may appear as a date, a time, a percentage, a currency amount, in scientific notation or as a formatted fraction. Note that Excel doesn't distinguish between integer and floating-point numbers on a worksheet. A function that takes integer arguments, such as DATE(*year, month, day*), will truncate any non-whole number argument rather than complain about the number type.

The limits on each of the above five data types are as follows:

Table 2.3 Worksheet data types and limits

Number	Floating point range: $\pm x$ where $1.0 \times 10^{-307} \le \|x\| < 1.0 \times 10^{+308}$ *(Max values of x may display as $\pm 1.0E+308$.)*
	Floating point accuracy: 15 decimal places displayed. Sometimes 16 places are stored internally depending on binary representation of mantissa. Integer (stored by Excel as floating point): $\pm i$ where $0 \le \|i\| \le 1,000,000,000,000,000 \ (10^{15})$ *(Outside these bounds, floating point representations truncate lowest order digits.)* Notes: 1. Certain number formats have narrower limits than these, e.g., dates and times. 2. *Integer* division is, in fact, floating point division and may, in extreme cases, yield non-integer results where the true result should be an integer.
Boolean	TRUE FALSE
Character string	Maximum length: $32,767 = 2^{15} - 1$ Minimum length: Zero (Empty string: = " ") Allowable characters: • ASCII codes: 1 to 255 inclusive *(Note: Only codes 32 and above print on screen.)* Notes: Only 1,024 characters can be displayed in a cell, but all 32,767 are displayed in the formula bar. The C API is limited to a maximum string length of 255.
Excel error	#NULL! #DIV/0! #VALUE! #REF! #NAME? #NUM! #N/A
Array	A one- or two-dimensional collection of mixed-type elements that can be any one of the above types.

(continued overleaf)

Table 2.3 (*continued*)

Literal arrays are enclosed in curly braces { and }, row-by-row (sometimes referred to as row-major). Row elements are delimited by commas, and rows themselves are delimited by semi-colons. For example, {1, "A"; TRUE, NA()} represents the 2×2 matrix $$\begin{bmatrix} 1 & A \\ TRUE & \#N/A \end{bmatrix}$$

2.5   EXCEL INPUT PARSER

When a user types input to a cell in Excel and commits the data (by pressing enter, tab or selecting another cell), Excel performs several operations in the order outlined below. In essence, it is attempting to guess what kind of input the user was providing, and then tries to interpret accordingly. Understanding the order in which Excel does these things may help you when creating your own functions or commands.

1. If the input starts with a string prefix (a single quote mark) Excel places all of the input characters in the cell *as typed*, with no modification. (The string prefix is not displayed.) If the input begins with =, + or -, it assumes a formula and uses its formula parser to check the syntax. An error dialog appears if the formula does not make sense. Otherwise Excel will try and figure out if the user typed something that looked like a date, a time, a currency amount, a percentage, or just a number. If none of these, it reverts to considering the input as a string and places it in the cell unchanged.

   Note: This tendency to recognise dates and times before text can be quite annoying, especially if you intended to input a string such as the ratio "2:1". Excel will change the format of the cell to a time format and convert the input to the numeric value 0.084027777 (the fraction of the day that has passed at 02:10 a.m.). Having to remember to prefix such inputs with a single quote mark can be frustrating.

2. Where the input is seen as a possible formula, Excel attempts to identify, convert and evaluate function arguments and nested functions starting with the innermost, i.e., most nested. Cell references and ranges are converted to values, which are then converted to the right data types if necessary and so on. Where a token that is not recognised as a function or defined name is encountered, the conversion and evaluation fails with a #NAME? error. Otherwise defined names are converted just as the cells or expressions they represent would be.

3. Once the input has been accepted, Excel attempts to recalculate those things that depend on the new input. If the input was a number and cell previously contained a number, Excel will only recalculate if the value has changed. If a new formula has been entered with references to new inputs, Excel verifies that no circular references have been created by this new formula. If a cell does depend on inputs which themselves depend on the value of this cell, Excel complains.

4. Depending on the optional Excel or cell format settings, Excel may resize the column width or row height.

2.6   DATA TYPE CONVERSION

Excel always attempts to convert data from one type to another where required. This section explains when Excel tries to do this, and when it is and is not successful.

2.6.1   The unary = operator

It may seem too obvious to mention, but the $=$ sign at the start of a cell or array formula is a unary operator that evaluates whatever appears to its right. The result will always be one of the four basic types: a number, a string, a Boolean true/false, or an error. Cell references are converted to the *values* of the cells they refer to. Formulae are evaluated to the outermost function's return value or the lowest-precedence operator result. This process results in an error value if a function could not be called or an operator could not be applied. (Conversion of cell references is covered in more detail below.)

2.6.2   The unary − operator (negation)

The unary negation operator, or more simply the minus sign, converts the operand immediately to its right to a number and then negates its value. Boolean true and false are converted to 1 and 0. A double negation will therefore convert text representations of numbers to real numbers, as does the VALUE() function. Both produce a #VALUE! error if the conversion fails.

2.6.3   Number-arithmetic binary operators: + - */^

Where Excel is evaluating a cell that contains any of the number-arithmetic binary operators, strings will be converted to numbers where possible, i.e., where they are in one of the number formats that Excel recognises. (This includes date and time formats where the resulting number after conversion is the date-time serial number.)

2.6.4   Percentage operator: %

The unary percentage operator – the *divide by 100* operator – acts on the operand immediately to its left. It has the highest operator precedence so that $=1/2\%$ will evaluate to 50 not to 0.005. Excel attempts to convert this operand to a number where it is not already one. As with the number arithmetic binary operators, all recognised number formats will be converted, so that, perhaps bizarrely, the formula ="1-Jul-2002 12:37:03"% evaluates to 374.385 rather than to an error. (Note that in this example Excel converts the date string to a number and then applies the % operator.) The equally strange formula =TRUE% evaluates to 0.01.

2.6.5   String concatenation operator: &

Where the string concatenation operator & is used, Excel will convert numbers to strings in a default number format, unrelated to any display format, with as much precision as required to represent the number accurately, up to the maximum precision supported.

2.6.6   Boolean binary operators: =,<, >,<=, >=,<>

Where these operators are acting on strings, evaluations are case-insensitive. (The Excel function EXACT() performs a case-sensitive equality test.) In fact, Excel converts upper case A-Z to lower case before making the comparison, as can be seen from the 3rd and 4th examples in Table 2.4:

Table 2.4 Case-insensitive string comparisons

Formula...	...evaluates to:
="A"="a"	TRUE
="a">"Z"	FALSE
="Z">"["	TRUE
=CHAR(90)>CHAR(91)	TRUE

Apart from string case conversion, Excel does not convert operands for these operators. Table 2.5 shows some examples of the consequences:

Table 2.5 Mixed-type comparisons

Formula...	...evaluates to:
=123="123"	FALSE
=123>"121"	FALSE
=123<>"123"	TRUE
=TRUE ="TRUE"	FALSE

2.6.7 Conversion of single-cell references

Excel will convert a single-cell reference to the value of the cell referred to, unless it is being passed to a function that expects a reference as its parameter rather than a value. (Later chapters go into detail on such functions, but a simple example is ROW(), which extracts and returns the row number of a cell reference.) If an operator or function using the reference requires a different data type than that of the reference's value, then Excel will also attempt to convert to the required type. (See next section for more detail.) For example, if a cell contains the formula =SUM(A1,B1), with A1 containing the number 123 and B2 the string "456", Excel will convert the reference A1 to the value of that cell, 123, and the reference B1 to the string "456" and then to the argument type expected by SUM(), the number 456, leading finally to a result of 579.

2.6.8 Conversion of multi-cell range references

Some functions will work equally well with single cell references and range references, for example, SUM(A1,B1,C1) gives the same result as SUM(A1:C1). In the latter case, the SUM() function converts the range A1:C1 to a mixed type array of values and then iterates through that converting and summing values where possible. The work of handling the range argument is done within the code of the SUM() function.

However, there are cases where Excel needs to convert a range argument before calling a function or applying an operator. Here the behaviour is a little more complex. Table 2.6 shows how Excel copes with range arguments in combination with a simple arithmetic operation, plus one in this case. (The strings in row 3 indicate the formulae entered in the cells immediately below.) Clearly *range* $+1$ is a meaningless operation without *range* being converted or interpreted somehow.

Table 2.6 Range reference argument conversion examples

	B	C	D	E	F
3	Static values	{=B4:B8+1}	{=SUM(B4:B8+1)}	=SUM($B$4:$B$8+1)	=$B$4:$B$8+1
4	1	2	20	2	2
5	2	3	20	3	3
6	3	4	20	4	4
7	4	5	20	5	5
8	5	6	20	6	6
9		#N/A	20	#VALUE!	#VALUE!

In column C, *range* $+1$ is entered as an array formula (see section 2.9.2 on page 21). Excel interprets this as an instruction to add 1 to each of the cells in the input range, and place the results one-by-one into the corresponding cells in the output range. Where there is no corresponding output cell, Excel places #N/A. Essentially, B3:B8+1 is converted to an array which is then mapped onto the array formula's range. What Excel is doing is treating the range as if it were a matrix and interpreting the operation 'add 1' as an instruction to add one to each element of the matrix.

In column D, Excel again performs the same matrix operation when confronted with B3:B4+1, and passes the resulting matrix to SUM() which then adds the elements and returns a single value. The formula is entered as an array formula and therefore this single value gets copied to every cell under the array. (Note that the formula =SUM(B4:B8,1) would have yielded 16, not 20.) Had the formula not been entered as an array formula, the behaviour would have been very different, as shown in columns E and F.

In columns E and F, the respective formula is duplicated in each of the cells in rows 4 to 9. (The absolute reference $ signs do not effect the way the cells are evaluated.) The perhaps surprising thing is that Excel returns a result that is different depending on the *location* of the cell as well as the formula within it. This is a unique behaviour in Excel. Excel converts the range reference to a single cell reference that corresponds to the location of the calling cell. For example, cell F4 is calculated as if the reference were to cell B4; cell F5 as if it were to cell B5, and so on. There is no corresponding cell in the input range for cells E9 and F9 so Excel returns #VALUE! to indicate that it could not convert the range argument.

2.6.9 Conversion of defined range names

Where a cell formula contains a token that cannot be interpreted as a constant (either numeric or string within double-quotes) or a cell reference, Excel searches for a named range on the current sheet and then the current workbook. (See below for an explanation of the term *current*.)

Names can be specified in any of the following forms:

- [Book1.xls]Sheet1!*Name*
- Sheet1!*Name* – where the workbook is taken to be the current workbook
- *Name* – where the workbook and sheet are the current ones.

If the sheet is specified, Excel will search for the name's definition on that sheet. If a workbook and sheet name are specified, Excel will search in that workbook and sheet. If the name is found, it is replaced by its definition (typically a reference to cells in a workbook), then converted to a value or array of values if necessary, following the same rules as outlined above. Note that if the name refers to a multi-cell range, this is interpreted and converted as described above in section 2.6.9.

2.6.10 Explicit type conversion functions: N(), T(), TEXT(), VALUE()

Explicit type conversion is possible with the functions VALUE() and TEXT() with the advantage that TEXT() provides control over the text format where an implicit conversion does not. Type conversion can also be constrained with the functions N() and T(). Table 2.7 summarises the action of these functions on the basic data types:

Table 2.7 Explicit worksheet data type conversion

	Input argument type			
	Number	String	Boolean	Error
N()	Returns the (unformatted) number.	Returns zero.	N(TRUE) → 1 N(FALSE) → 0	Returns the Excel error unchanged.
T()	Returns empty string.	Returns the string.	Returns empty string.	
TEXT()	Returns a string of the number in the given format.	Converts to a number then back to a string in the given format. If the conversion fails, returns #VALUE!	Converts to "TRUE" or "FALSE" regardless of the given format.	
VALUE()	Returns the (unformatted) number.	Converts to a number. If the conversion fails, returns #VALUE!	Returns #VALUE!	

Other type conversion functions are also provided by Excel, i.e., DATEVALUE() which converts a date string to a serial date-time number and TIMEVALUE() which converts a time string to a serial date-time number.

2.6.11 Worksheet function argument type conversion

Excel will attempt to convert arguments being passed to functions, regardless of whether they are Excel's built-in worksheet functions, a third party's add-in functions or user-defined VB functions. Worksheet functions can take as arguments any combination of the following:

1. a single literal value;
2. an array of literal values;
3. a reference to a single cell;
4. a reference to a rectangular range of cells.

In the first two cases, the values themselves can be any one of the basic Excel data types (see *Worksheet data types and limits* above for more detail).

Excel attempts to convert from the supplied type to the function's required type. (Chapter 8 *Accessing Excel Functionality Using the C API*, on page 169, explains how to construct and declare functions whose arguments are to be passed *as is, without conversion.*) Where Excel cannot convert an argument to the declared type, the function is evaluated to #VALUE!. Note that Excel does not call the code of the underlying function if this happens.

Consider a function that takes an array of values. Suppose it is passed a reference to a rectangular range: Excel will convert the range to an array of the values that those cells contain. However, in contrast to single-cell references, Excel will not convert the types of those values. For example, the formula =SUM({123,"123"}) (note the curly braces which surround a literal array in Excel) evaluates to the number 123 since the second value in the array is not converted from a string to a number. The formula =SUM(123,"123"), however, evaluates to 246 as Excel is quite happy to convert the string argument "123" to the number 123 before passing it to SUM(). The reason for this is that such functions are declared as taking an Excel array type in which each element can be any one of a number of basic data types, regardless of the types of the other elements. Excel cannot know what types the function ideally wants and leaves any element conversion to the function itself.

Note that some functions can accept one of a number of types, for example, in the function IF(*test, if true, if false*), the second and third arguments can be any type and are passed and returned unconverted depending on the outcome of the test. The fact that range references are not converted prior to IF() being called is most easily evidenced with a formula such as =ROWS(IF(A1,B1:B2,C1:C3)), which will return either the value 2 or 3 depending on the value of A1.

Table 2.8 details the conversions that Excel attempts to make (if necessary) in passing arguments to worksheet functions:

Table 2.8 Worksheet function argument type conversion

Supplied argument	Excel will attempt, if required, to convert to...
Number	Integer Floating point → Integer (by truncation of digits after the decimal point) (Converse does not apply, as all worksheet numbers are floating point.) String In default number format with as much precision as required to represent the number up to the maximum precision supported by Excel. Boolean Zero → FALSE

(continued overleaf)

Table 2.8 (*continued*)

Supplied argument	Excel will attempt, if required, to convert to...
	Non-zero → TRUE
String	Number Must be any one of Excel's known number formats including date, time, etc. Boolean Must be 'true' or 'false' (not case-sensitive).
Boolean	Number True → 1 False → 0 (Conversion not always performed). String True → "TRUE" False → "FALSE"
Single cell reference	1st step: Value of cell referred to. 2nd step: Number → Integer, String or Boolean String → Number or Boolean Boolean → Number or String
Multiple cell reference	Array (Note: each element in the array has the same data type as the corresponding cell's value).

2.6.12 Operator evaluation precedence

Table 2.9 Operator evaluation precedence

Operators (operation)	Notes
Name lookup and substitution	
Reference-to-value and type conversion	
() and worksheet functions	Evaluated left to right
%, unary −	
^	=4^50% evaluates to 2
*/	
Binary +−	
&	=4+2&1+5="66" evaluates to TRUE
Binary =, <, >, <=, >=, <>	Evaluated left to right

2.7 EXCEL TERMINOLOGY: ACTIVE AND CURRENT

Excel functions that provide information about a cell, a range of cells or a sheet in a workbook often make a distinction between the workbook, sheet or cell that the user is currently looking at, and the workbook, sheet or cell from which the function was called.[1] The same is true of commands that affect a workbook or one of its constituents. The terms *active* and *current* are used to make the distinction, which can be quite confusing. Here is a clear definition:

Table 2.10 Active versus current terminology

Term	Definition
Active workbook	The one that the user is currently looking at. If Excel does not have focus then the active workbook is the one that was visible when Excel last had focus.
Active sheet	The one that the user is currently looking at. If Excel does not have focus then the active sheet is the one that was visible when Excel last had focus. The active sheet is always in the active workbook.
Active cell	The one into which input would be placed if the user started typing. This cell may not be visible if the user has scrolled off to one side. If Excel does not have focus then the active cell is that cell on the sheet that was active when Excel last had focus. The active cell is always on the active sheet.
Current workbook	The one that is currently being recalculated by Excel. The active and the current workbook may or may not be the same at any given moment.
Current sheet	The one that is currently being recalculated. The active and the current sheet may or may not be the same at any given moment. The current sheet is always in the current workbook.
Current cell	The one which is currently being evaluated. The active and the current cell may or may not be the same at any given moment. They will be the same if the calculation of the cell results from, say, the user entering new contents to the cell. The current cell is always on the current sheet.

2.8 COMMANDS VERSUS FUNCTIONS IN EXCEL

There is an important distinction in Excel between functions, represented by formulae in worksheet cells that may or may not take arguments but *always* return a value, and commands which are equivalent to a user doing something. For example, NOW() is a function: it returns a number representing the date and time right now. In contrast, the action taken by Excel to format a cell when a user presses a formatting icon on a toolbar is a command.

---

[1] There are other components that can be active, e.g., components of a chart that have been selected, which are not covered here.

Commands are allowed to do just about anything in Excel. Functions are given far less freedom. VB functions are given a little more freedom than DLL add-ins. (Some of the details of the differences between these two are discussed in the later chapters on VB and C/C++.) It is easy to see why there needs to be some difference between functions and commands: it would be a bad thing to allow a function in a worksheet cell to *press* the undo icon whenever it was calculated. On the other hand, allowing a user-defined command to do this is perfectly reasonable.

Most (but not all) of this book is concerned with writing functions rather than commands simply because commands are better written in VB and may well require dialog boxes and such things to interact with the user. Chapter 3 *Using VBA* on page 41 does talk about VB commands, but not in great detail; there are plenty of books which talk at great length about these things. Later chapters concerning the C API do talk about commands, but the focus is on worksheet functions.

Table 2.11 gives a non-exhaustive summary of the things that commands can do that functions can't.

Table 2.11 Capabilities of commands versus functions

Action	Command	Function
Open or close a workbook	Yes	No
Create or delete a worksheet	Yes	No
Change the current selection	Yes	No
Change the format of a cell, worksheet or other object	Yes	No
Take arguments when called	No	Yes
Return a value to the caller	No	Yes
Access a cell value (not via an argument)	Yes	C API: Sometimes[2] VBA: Yes
Change a cell value	Yes	Only the calling cell or array and only by return value
Read/write files	Yes	Yes
Start another application or thread	Yes	Yes
Set up event-driven Windows call-backs	Yes	Yes
Call a command-equivalent Excel 4 macro, C API function, or Excel object method	Yes	No

[2] Worksheet functions are more limited than macro sheet functions in their ability to access the values of other cells not passed in as arguments. For more details on this subject see section 8.5.4 *Giving functions macro sheet function permissions* on page 188.

2.9   TYPES OF WORKSHEET FUNCTION

This book assumes a frequent-user level of familiarity with Windows, Windows applications, Excel and its user interface. This section assumes that readers are familiar with the most common commands, menus, functions, how to use them, how to use Excel help and so on. This section says nothing about these standard features, but instead discusses how functions fall into certain types. When considering writing your own, it is important to be clear about what kind of function you are creating.

2.9.1   Function purpose and return type

Individual worksheet cells are either empty or are *evaluated* to one of four different data types:

- Numbers;
- Boolean (TRUE/FALSE);
- Strings;
- Error values.

(See section 2.4 *Worksheet data types and limits* on page 10.) Functions, however, can evaluate to arrays and range references as well as to these four types. (The functions INDIRECT(), OFFSET() and ADDRESS(), for example, all return references.)

Functions that return references are generally only of use when used to create range (or array) arguments to be passed to other functions. They are not usually intended as the end-product of a calculation. Where such a function returns a single cell reference, Excel will attempt to convert to a value, in the same way that =A1 on its own in a cell will be reduced to the value of A1. The formula =A1:A3 on its own in a cell will produce a #VALUE! error, unless it is entered as an array formula into one or more cells (see next section).

As shown by examples later in this book, you can create functions that *do* useful things, without needing to return anything important, except perhaps a value that tells you if they completed the task successfully or not. A simple example might be a function that writes to a data file whenever a certain piece of information changes.

In thinking about what you want your own functions to do, you should be clear about the purpose of the function and therefore of its return type and return values, before you start to code it.

2.9.2   Array formulae – The Ctrl-Shift-Enter keystroke

Functions can return single values or arrays of values, and many can return either. For example, the matrix formula, MMULT(), returns an array whose size depends on the sizes of the input arrays. Such functions need to be called from a range rather than from a single cell, in order to return all their results to the worksheet.

To enter an array formula you need to use the *Ctrl-Shift-Enter* keystroke. Instead of the usual *Enter* to commit a formula to a single cell, *Ctrl-Shift-Enter* instructs Excel to accept the formula as an array formula into the selected group of cells, not just the active cell. The resulting cell formula is displayed in the formula bar as usual but enclosed within curly braces, e.g., {=MMULT(A1:D4,F1:I4)}. The array formula can then only be modified as a whole. Excel will complain if you attempt to edit or move part of an array, or if you try to insert or delete rows or columns within it.

The all-or-nothing edit feature of array formulae makes them useful for helping to protect calculations from being accidentally overwritten. The worksheet protection feature of Excel is stronger. It allows precise control over what can be modified with password protection. However, it also disables other features that you might want to be accessible, such as the collapse and expansion of grouped rows and columns. Array formulae provide a half-way house alternative.

Functions and operators that usually take single cell references can also be passed range arguments in array formulae. How Excel deals with these is covered above in section 2.6.8.

2.9.3   Required, optional and missing arguments and variable argument lists

Some functions take a fixed number of arguments, all of which need to be supplied otherwise an error will be returned, for example DATE(). Some take required and optional arguments, for example, VLOOKUP(). Some take a variable number such as SUM(). A few functions have more than one form of argument-list, such as INDEX(), equivalent to the concept of overloading in C++.

With C/C++ DLL functions, Excel handles variable length argument lists by always passing an argument, regardless of whether the user provided one. A special *missing* data type is passed. If the argument can take different types, say, a string or a number, the function can be declared in such a way that Excel will pass a general data type. It is then up to the function's code whether to execute or fail with the arguments as provided. This and related subjects are covered in detail in Chapter 6 *Passing Data between Excel and the DLL* on page 105.

2.10   COMPLEX FUNCTIONS AND COMMANDS

2.10.1   Data Tables

Data Tables provide a very useful way of creating dynamic tables without having to replicate the calculations for each cell in the table. Once the calculation has been set up for a single result cell (not in the table), a table of results for a range of inputs is produced. Excel plugs your inputs in one-by-one and then places the resulting value in the Data Table. Data Tables can be based on one input to produce a single row or column of results, or on two inputs to produce a 2-dimensional table.

Tables are set up with the Data/Table. . . command, invoking a simple wizard that prompts you to specify the input row and/or column for the table. This book doesn't go into any detail (refer to Excel's help to find out more), but it is worth considering what they are. If you look at the formula that Excel puts in part of the table where the results are placed, you will see that there is an array formula {=TABLE(. . .)}. On the face of it, therefore, it looks like a Data Table is just another function entered as an array formula. It gives the appearance of being recalculated like a function, except that Excel enables you to turn the automatic recalculation of tables off using Tools/Options. . ./Calculation.

However: you can't edit and re-enter the cells under the TABLE() function, even if you have changed nothing; the Paste Function dialog does not recognise TABLE() as a valid function; you can't move the cells that are immediately above or to the left of the cells occupied by the TABLE() function; you can't set up a table other than with the Data Table wizard.

The best way to think of a Data Table is as a completely different type of object that allows a complex set of calculations in the worksheet to be treated as a user-defined function in this very specific way. An example of where use of a Data Table might be preferable to writing a VB or C/C++ function might be the calculation of net income after tax. This depends on many pieces of information, such as gross income, tax allowances, taxation bands, marital status, etc. Coding all this into a user-defined function may be difficult, take an unjustifiably long time, involve the passing of a large number of arguments, and might be hard to debug. A well laid-out spreadsheet calculation, complete with descriptive labels for the inputs, and a Data Table, provide an excellent way of creating a source for a lookup function.

One thing to watch is that Excel does not detect circular references resulting from the input calculation depending on the table itself. In other words, it will allow them. Every time the table is recalculated, the circular reference will feed back one more time. There's no reason someone in their right mind would want to do this, of course, but be warned.

Warning: Data Tables can recalculate much more slowly than repeated calculation of cells. Excel's recalculation logic can also be a little hard to fathom with large Data Tables – it's not always clear when the calculation is complete.

2.10.2   Goal Seek and Solver Add-in

Excel provides two ways of solving for particular static cell values that produce a certain value in another cell. These are both *commands*, not functions, so you cannot automatically re-solve when something in your sheet changes. To achieve this you would need to write a user-defined function that will implement some kind of solver. The simplest of Excel's solvers is the Goal Seek (Tools/Goal seek...) which invokes the following dialog, and provides a way of solving for one final numerical value given one numerical input.

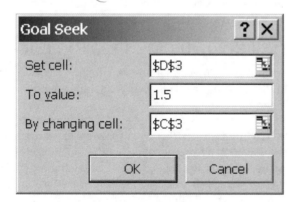

Figure 2.1   Excel's Goal Seek dialog

The second and more powerful method is the Solver Add-in, supplied with Excel and accessible through the Tools/Solver... menu command once the add-in has been installed.

The dialog that appears is shown in Figure 2.2.

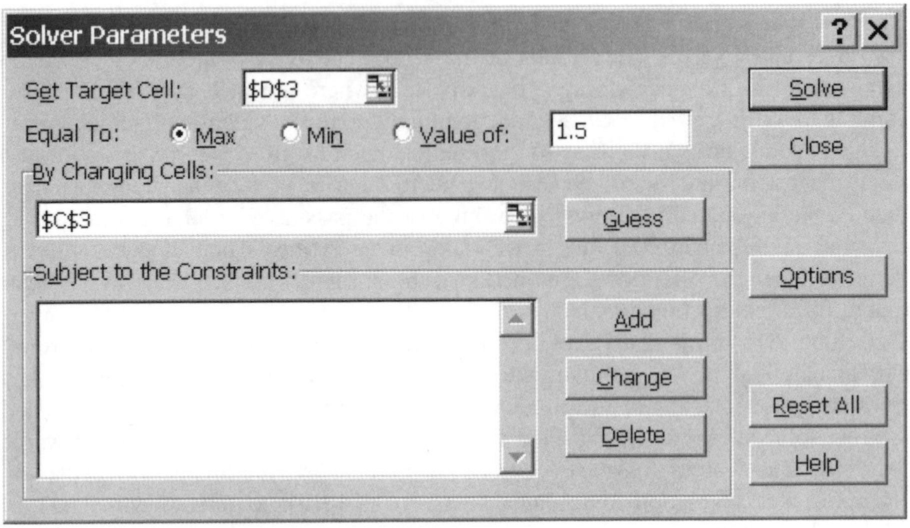

Figure 2.2   Excel's Solver add-in dialog

This is a far more flexible solver, capable of solving for a number of inputs to get to the desired single cell value, maximum or minimum. The user can also set constraints to avoid unwanted *solutions* and options that dictate the behaviour of the algorithm. Section 10.12 *Calibration*, on page 381, talks more about this very powerful tool.

The complexities governing when solutions converge, when they are unlikely to, when there may be multiple solutions, and to which one you are most likely to converge, are beyond the scope of this book. (Excel provides help for the solver via the Tools/Solver... dialog's Help button.) If you intend to rely on a solver for something important you either need to know that your function is very well behaved or that you understand its behaviour well enough to know when it will be reliable.

2.11   EXCEL RECALCULATION LOGIC

The first thing to say on this often very subtle and complex subject is that there is much more that can be said than is said here. This section attempts to provide some basic insight and a foundation for further reading.

Excel recalculates by creating lists of cells which determine the order in which things should be calculated. Excel constructs this by inspecting the formulae in cells to determine their precedents, establishing precedent/dependent relationships for all cells. Once constructed, cells in the lists thus generated are marked for recalculation whenever a precedent cell has either changed or has itself been marked for recalculation. Once this is done Excel recalculates these cells in the order determined by the list.

After an edit to one or more formulae, lists may need to be reconstructed. However, most of the time edits are made to *static* cells that do not contain formulae and are not therefore dependent on anything. This means that Excel does not usually have to do this work whenever there is new input.

As this section shows, this system is not infallible. Care must be taken in certain circumstances, and certain practices should be avoided altogether. (VB code and spreadsheet examples are contained in the spreadsheet `Recalc_Examples.xls` on the CD ROM.) Further, more technically in-depth reading on the subject of this section is available on Microsoft's website.

2.11.1   Marking dependents for recalculation

Excel's method, outlined above, results in a rather brute-force recalculation of dependents regardless of whether the *value* of one the cells in a list has changed. Excel simply marks all dependents as needing to be recalculated in one pass, and then in the second pass recalculates them. This may well be the optimum strategy over all, but it's worth bearing in mind when writing and using functions that may have long recalculation times. Consider the following cells:

Cell	Formula
B3	=NOW()
B4	=INT(B3)
B5	=NumCalls_1(B4)

The VB macro `NumCalls_1()`, listed below, returns a number that is incremented with every call, effectively counting the times B5 is recalculated. (For more information on creating VB macro functions, see Chapter 3 *Using VBA* on page 41).

```
Dim CallCount1 As Integer ' Scope is this VB module only

Function NumCalls_1(d As Double) As Integer

    CallCount1 = CallCount1 + 1
    NumCalls_1 = CallCount1

End Function
```

Pressing {F9} will cause Excel to mark cell B3, containing the volatile function NOW(), for recalculation (see section 2.11.3 *Volatile functions* below). Its dependent, B4, and then B4's dependent, B5, also get marked as needing recalculation. Excel then recalculates all three in that order. In this example, the value of B4 will only change once a day so Excel shouldn't need to recalculate B5 in most cases. But, Excel doesn't take that into consideration when deciding to mark B5 for recalculation, so it gets called all the same. With every press of {F9} the value in B5 will increment.

A more efficient method might *appear* to be only to mark cells as needing recalculation if one or more of their precedents' *values* had changed. However, this would involve Excel changing the list of cells-to-be-recalculated after the evaluation of each and every cell. This might well end up in a drastically less efficient algorithm – something critics often overlook.

Where a number is directly entered into a cell, Excel is a little more discerning about triggering a recalculation of dependents: if the number is re-entered unchanged, Excel will not bother. On the other hand, if a string is re-entered unchanged, Excel *does* recalculate dependents.

2.11.2   Triggering functions to be called by Excel – the trigger argument

There are times when you want things to be calculated in a very specific order, or for something to be triggered by the change in value of some cell or other. Of course, Excel does this automatically, you might say. True, but the trigger is the change in value of some input to the calculation. This is fine as long as you *only* want that to be the trigger. What if you want something else to be the trigger? What if the function you want to trigger doesn't need any arguments? For example, what if you want to have a cell that shows the time that another cell's value last changed so that an observer can see how fresh the information is?

The solution is simple: the trigger argument. This is a dummy argument that is of absolutely no use to the function being triggered other than to force Excel to call it. (Section 9.1 *Timing function execution in VB and C/C++* on page 285 relies heavily on this idea.) The VB function NumCalls_1() in the above section uses the argument solely to trigger Excel to call the code.

In the case of wanting to record the time a static numeric cell's value changes, a simple VB function like this would have the desired effect:

```
Function Get_Time(trigger As Double) As Double

    Get_Time = Now

End Function
```

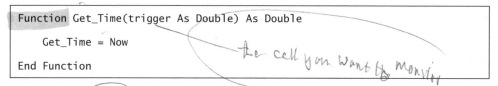
the cell you want to monitor

The argument trigger is not used in the calculation which simply returns the current date and time as the number of days from 1st January 1900 inclusive by calling VB's Now function. It just ensures the calculation is done whenever the static trigger changes value (or when Excel decides it needs to do a brute-force recalculation of everything on the sheet).[3]

The concept of a trigger argument can, of course, usefully be applied to C/C++ add-in functions too, and is extensively used in later sections of this book.

2.11.3   Volatile functions

Excel supports the concept of a *volatile* function, one whose value cannot be assumed to be the same from one moment to the next even if none of its arguments (if it takes any) has changed. Excel re-evaluates cells containing volatile functions, along with all dependents, every time it recalculates, usually any time *anything* in the workbook changes, or when the user presses {F9}.

It is easy to create user-defined functions that are optionally volatile (see the VB macro NumCalls_1() in the above section), by using a built-in volatile function as a trigger argument. Additionally, VB and the C API both support ways to tell Excel that an add-in function should be treated as volatile. With VB, Excel only learns this when it first calls the function. With the C API a function can be registered as volatile before its first call.

Among the standard worksheet functions, there are five volatile functions:

- NOW();
- TODAY();   *Volatile functions*

---

[3] If the trigger were itself the result of a formula, this function might be called even when the *value* of the trigger had not changed. See section 2.11.5 *User-defined functions (VB Macros) and add-in functions* on page 25.

- RAND();
- OFFSET(*reference, rows, column, [height], [width]*);
- INDIRECT().

NOW() returns the current date and time, something which is, in the author's experience, always changing. TODAY() is simply equivalent to INT(NOW()) and used not to exist. RAND() returns a different pseudo-random number every time it is recalculated. These three functions clearly deserve the volatile status Excel gives them. OFFSET() returns a range reference, relative to the supplied range reference, whose size, shape and relative position are determined by the other arguments. OFFSET()'s case for volatile status is a little less obvious. The reason, simply stated, is that Excel cannot easily figure out from the arguments given whether the *contents* of the resulting range have changed, even if the range itself hasn't, so it assumes they always have, to be on the safe side.

The function INDIRECT() causes Excel to reconstruct its precedent/dependant tree with every recalculation in order to maintain its integrity.

Volatile functions have good and bad points. Where you want to force a function that is not volatile to be recalculated, the low-cost (in CPU terms) volatile functions NOW() and RAND() act as very effective triggers. The down-side is that they *and all their dependants and their dependants' dependants* are recalculated every time anything changes. This is true even if the value of the dependants themselves haven't changed – see the VB macro function NumCalls_1() in the section immediately above. Where OFFSET() and other volatile functions are used extensively, they can lead to very slow and inefficient spreadsheets.

2.11.4 Cross-worksheet dependencies – Excel 97/2000 versus 2002/2003

Excel 97 and 2000

Excel 97 and 2000 construct a single list for each worksheet and then recalculate the sheets in alphabetical order. As a result, inter-sheet dependencies can cause Excel to recalculate very inefficiently.

For example, suppose a simple workbook only contains the following non-empty cells, with the following formulae and values. (The VB macro NumCalls_4(), which returns an incremented counter every time it is called, is a clone of NumCalls_1() which described in section 2.11.1 above.)

Sheet1:

Cell	Formula	Value
C11	=NumCalls_4(NOW()+Sheet2!B3)	1

Sheet2:

Cell	Formula	Value
B3	=B4/2	1
B4		2

Excel is, of course, aware of the dependency of Sheet1!C11 on Sheet2!B3 but they both appear in different lists. Excel's *thought* process goes something like this:

1. Something has changed and I need to recalculate.

2. The first sheet in alphabetical order is Sheet1 so I'll recalculate this first.
3. Cell Sheet1!C11 contains a volatile function so I'll mark it, and any dependents, for recalculation, then recalculate them.
4. The second sheet in alphabetical order is Sheet2 so I'll recalculate this next.
5. Cell Sheet2!B4 has changed so I'll mark its dependents for recalculation, then recalculate them.
6. Now I can see that Sheet2!B3 has changed, which is a precedent for a cell in Sheet1, so I must go back and calculate Sheet1 again.
7. Cell Sheet1!C11 not only contains a volatile function, but is dependent on a cell in Sheet2 that has changed, so I'll mark it, and any dependents, for recalculation, then recalculate them.

In this simple example, cell Sheet1!C11 only depends on Sheet2!B3 and the result of the volatile NOW() function. Nothing else depends on Sheet1!C11, so the fact that it gets recalculated twice when Sheet2!B4 changes is a fairly small inefficiency. However, if Sheet2!B3 also depended on some other cell in Sheet1 then it is possible that it and all its dependents could be recalculated twice – and that would be very bad.

If cell Sheet2!B4 is edited to take the value 4, then Excel will start to recalculate the workbook starting with Sheet1. It will recognise that Sheet1!C11 needs recalculating as it depends on the volatile NOW() function, but it will not yet know that the contents of Sheet2!B3 are out of date. Once it is finished with Sheet1, halfway through workbook recalculation, both sheets will look like this:

Sheet1:

Cell	Formula	Value
C11	=NumCalls_4(NOW()+Sheet2!B3)	2

Sheet2:

Cell	Formula	Value
B3	=B4/2	1
B4		4

Now Excel will recalculate Sheet2!B3, which it has marked for recalculation as a result of Sheet2!B4 changing. At this point Sheet2 looks like this:

Sheet2:

Cell	Formula	Display
B3	=B4/2	2
B4		4

Finally Excel will, again, mark Sheet1!C11 as needing recalculation as a result of Sheet2!B3 changing, and recalculate Sheet1, re-evaluating Sheet1!C11 for the second time including the call to NOW() and to NumCalls_4(). After this Sheet1 will look like this:

Sheet1:

Cell	Formula	Display
C11	=NumCalls_4(NOW()+Sheet2!B3)	3

If NumCalls_4() were doing a lot of work, or Sheet1!C11 was a precedent for a large number of calculations on Sheet1 (or other sheets) then the inefficiency could be costly.

One way around this is to place cells that are likely to drive calculations in other sheets, in worksheets with alphabetically lower names (e.g., rename Sheet2 as A_Sheet2), and those with cells that depend heavily on cells in other sheets with alphabetically higher (e.g., rename Sheet1 as Z_Sheet1).

It is, of course, possible to create deliberately a workbook that really capitalises on this inefficiency and results in a truly horrible recalculation time. This is left as an exercise to the reader. (See section 2.15 *Good spreadsheet design and practice* on page 35.)

Excel 2002/2003

The above problem is fixed in Excel 2002 and 2003 by there being just one tree for the entire workbook. In the above example, Excel would have figured out that it needed to recalculate Sheet2!B3 before Sheet1!C11. When Sheet2!B4 is changed, Sheet1!C11 is only recalculated once. However, unless you know your spreadsheet will only be run in Excel 2002 and later, it's best to heed the alphabetical worksheet naming advice and minimise cross-spreadsheet dependencies particularly in large and complex workbooks.

2.11.5   User-defined functions (VB Macros) and add-in functions

Excel's very useful INDIRECT() function creates a reference to a range indirectly, i.e., using a string representation of the range address. From one recalculation to the next, the value of the arguments can change and therefore the line of dependency can also change. Excel copes fine with this uncertainty. With every recalculation it checks if the line of dependency needs altering.

However, where a macro or DLL function does a similar thing, Excel can run into trouble. The problem for Excel is that VB functions and DLL add-in functions are able to reference the values of cells other than those that are passed in as arguments and therefore can hide the true line of dependency.

Consider the following example spreadsheet containing these cells, entered in the order they appear:

Cell	Formula	Value/Display	Comment
B4		1	Static numeric value
B5	=NOW()	14:03:02	Volatile input to B6
B6	=RecalcExample1(B5)	1	Call to VB function

An associated VB module contains the macro RecalcExample1() defined as follows:

```
Function RecalcExample1(r As Range) As Double

    RecalcExample1 = Range("B4").Value

End Function
```

Editing the cell B4 to 2, in all of Excel 97/2000/2002/2003, will leave the spreadsheet looking like this:

Cell	Formula	Value/Display	Comment
B4		2	New numeric value
B5	=NOW()	14:05:12	Updated input to B6
B6	=RecalcExample1(B5)	1	Call to VB function

In other words, Excel has failed to detect the dependency of RecalcExample1() on B4. The argument passed to RecalcExample1() in this case is volatile so you might expect the function to be called whenever there is a recalculation. However, the macro is declared as taking a *range* as an argument, which itself is not volatile. Therefore Excel does not mark B6 for recalculation and the cell does not reflect the change in value of B4. If cell B5 is edited, say by pressing {F2} then {Enter}, then B6 is recalculated once, but then reverts to the same blindness to changes in B4's value.

Now consider the following cells and macro in the same test sheet:

Cell	Formula	Value/Display	Comment
C4		1	Static numeric value
C5	=NOW()	14:12:13	Volatile input to C6
C6	=RecalcExample2(C5)	1	Call to VB function

Now consider the following the macro RecalcExample2() defined as follows:

```
Function RecalcExample2(d As Double) As Double

    RecalcExample2 = Range("C4").Value

End Function
```

Editing the cell C4 to 2 (in Excel 2000) will leave the spreadsheet looking like this:

Cell	Formula	Value/Display	Comment
C4		2	New numeric value
C5	=NOW()	14:14:11	Updated input to C6
C6	=RecalcExample2(C5)	2	Call to VB function

In this case Excel has updated the value of C6. However, Excel has not detected the dependency of RecalcExample2() on C4. The argument passed to RecalcExample2() is volatile and the macro takes a double as an argument (rather than a range as in the previous example), therefore Excel marks it for recalculation and the cell ends up reflecting the change in value of C4. If C5 had not contained a volatile number, the dependency of C6 on C4 would still have been missed.

Because Excel is effectively blind to VB functions accessing cells not passed to it as arguments, it is a good idea to avoid doing this. In any case, it's an ugly coding practice and should therefore be rejected purely on aesthetic grounds. There are perfectly legitimate uses of Range().value in VB, but you should watch out for this kind of behaviour.

Excel behaves a little (but not much) better with DLL functions called directly from the worksheet. The workbook Recalc_Examples.xls contains a reference to an example add-in function called C_INDIRECT1(*trigger, row, column*) which takes a trigger argument, the column (A = 1, B = 2, ...) and the row of the cell to be referenced indirectly by the DLL add-in. This function reads the value of the cell indicated by the row and column arguments, tries to convert this to a number which it then returns if successful. (The source for the function is contained in the example project on the CD ROM and is accessible by loading the Example.xll add-in.)

It is easy to see that Excel will have a problem making the association between values for row and column of a cell and the value of the cell to which they refer. Where the trigger is volatile, the function gets called in any case, so the return value will reflect any change in the indirect source cell's value. If the row and column arguments are replaced with ROW(*source cell*) and COLUMN(*source cell*), Excel makes the connection and changes are reflected, regardless of whether the trigger is volatile or not.

Where the cell reference is passed to the DLL function as a range, as is the case with C_INDIRECT2(*trigger, ref*) in the example add-in – analogous to the VB macro RecalcExample1() – Excel manages to keep track of the dependency, something that VB fails to do.

The advice is simple: avoid referencing cells indirectly in this way in worksheet functions. You very rarely need to do this. If you think you do, then perhaps you need to rethink how you're organising your data.

2.11.6 Data Table recalculation

See section 2.10.1 *Data Tables* on page 22 for more about Data Tables and how Excel treats them differently.

2.12   THE ADD-IN MANAGER

The Add-in Manager is that part of the Excel application that loads, manages and unloads functions and commands supplied in add-ins. It recognises three kinds of add-ins:

- standard Win32 DLLs that contain a number of expected interface functions;
- compiled VB modules;
- Excel 4 Macros (XLM) modules (for backwards-compatibility).

(DLLs can be written in C/C++ or other languages such as Pascal.)

The file extensions expected for these types are `*.XLA` for VB module add-ins and `*.XLL` for DLL add-ins. Any file name and extension can be used, as Excel will recognise (or reject) the file type on opening it. (See section 3.9 *Creating VB add-ins (XLA files)* on page 72 for a brief description of how to create XLA add-ins.)

For XLL add-ins written in C and C++, there are a number of other things the programmer has to do to enable the Add-in Manager to load, access and then remove, the functions and commands they contain. Chapter 5 *Turning DLLs into XLLs: The Add-in Manager Interface*, on page 95, describes the interface functions the add-in must provide to be enable Excel to do these things.

2.13   LOADING AND UNLOADING ADD-INS

Excel ships with a number of *standard* add-in packages, a description of which is beyond the scope of this book. The Tools/Add-ins... dialog (see Figure 2.3) lists all the add-ins that Excel is aware of in that session, with those that are active having their check-boxes set. Making a known add-in active is simply a case of checking the box. If Excel doesn't know of an add-in's existence yet, it is simply a question of *browsing* to locate the file.

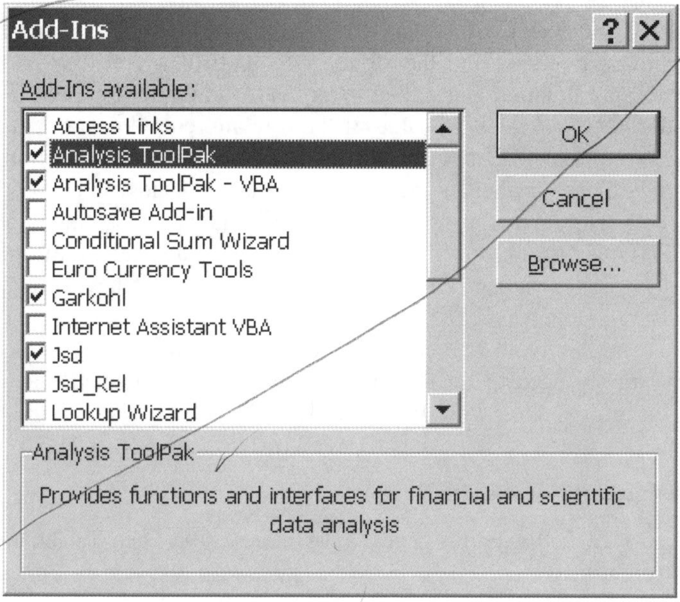

Figure 2.3   Excel's Add-in Manager dialog

Excel's known list of add-ins is stored in the Windows Registry. Add-ins remain listed even if the add-in is unselected – even if Excel is closed and restarted. To remove the add-in from the list completely you must delete, move or rename the DLL file, restart Excel, then try to select the add-in in the Add-in Manager dialog. At this point Excel will alert you that the add-in no longer exists and ask you if you would like it removed from the list.[4]

2.13.1 Add-in information

The Add-in Manager dialog (see Figure 2.3) displays a short description of the contents of the add-in to help the user decide if they want or need to install it. Chapter 5 *Turning DLLs into XLLs: The Add-in Manager Interface*, on page 95, explains how to include and make available this piece of information for your own add-ins.

2.14   PASTE FUNCTION DIALOG

Hand-in-hand with the Add-in Manager is the Paste Function dialog (sometimes known as the *Function Wizard*). The feature is invoked either through the Insert/Function... menu or via the '*fx*' icon on a toolbar. If invoked when the active cell is empty, the following dialog appears (in Excel 2000) allowing you to select a function by category or from a list of all registered functions. If invoked while the active cell contains a function, the argument construction dialog box appears – see section 2.14.3 below.

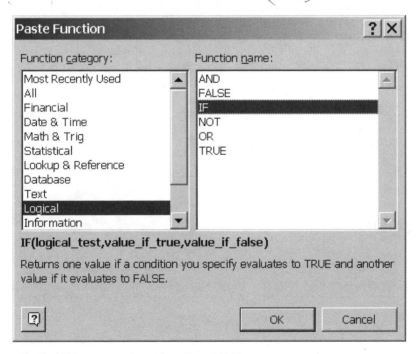

Figure 2.4   Excel's Paste Function dialog (Excel 2000)

---

[4] You can edit the registry, something you should not attempt unless you really know what you are doing. The consequences can be catastrophic.

2.14.1   Function category

In the left-hand list box are all the function categories, the top two being special categories with obvious meanings. All functions are otherwise listed under one and only one specific category. Many of these categories are hard-coded Excel standards. Add-ins can add functions to existing categories or can create their own, or do both. If functions have been defined in a VB module or have been loaded by the Add-in Manager from an XLA add-in file, then the category UDF (in Excel 2000) or User Defined (in Excel 2002 and later) appears and the functions are listed under that.

2.14.2   Function name, argument list and description

Selecting a category will cause all the functions in that category to be listed in alphabetical order in the right-hand list box. The figure shows the Logical category selected and all six logical functions. Selecting a function name causes the name as it appears in the spreadsheet, a named comma-separated argument list and a description of the function to be displayed below the list boxes. In the above example the arguments and function description for the IF() function are shown.

2.14.3   Argument construction dialog

Pressing OK in the Paste Function dialog causes the argument construction dialog to appear for the highlighted function. Invoking the Paste Function command on an active cell containing a function has the same effect. The figure below shows this for the IF() function. Where invoked on an empty cell the dialog is blank. Where invoked on an existing formula, the fields are populated with the expressions read from the cell's formula.

This dialog has a number of important features that should be understood by anyone wanting to enable users to access their own add-in functions in this way. These are highlighted in the following diagram which shows the Excel 2000 dialog.

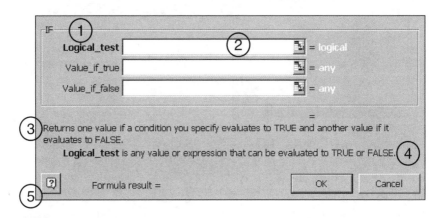

Figure 2.5   Paste Function argument construction dialog (Excel 2000)

(1) Argument name – from the argument list in the Paste Function dialog. (Bold type indicates a required argument; normal type, an optional one.)
(2) Argument expression text box – into which the user enters the expression that Excel evaluates in preparation for the function call.

(3) Function description – as shown in the Paste Function dialog.

(4) Argument description – for the currently selected argument, providing a brief explanation of the argument purpose, limits, etc.

(5) A context-specific help icon – used to get help specific to this function. In Excel 2002
and 2003, the help button is replaced with a text hyperlink.

The dialog also provides helpful information relating to the values that the argument
expressions evaluate to and the interim function result. (Note that Excel attempts to
evaluate the function after each argument has been entered.) If the function is a built-
in volatile function, the word volatile appears after the equals just above the function
description.

Once all required arguments have been provided, pressing OK will commit the function,
with all its argument expressions as they appear in the dialog, to the active cell or cells.

Section 8.5 *Registering and un-registering DLL (XLL) functions*, on page 185, explains
in detail how to register DLL functions that the Paste Function dialogs can work with. In
other words, how to provide Excel with the above information for your own functions.

2.15   GOOD SPREADSHEET DESIGN AND PRACTICE

2.15.1   Filename, sheet title and name, version and revision history

Ever since the demise of DOS 8.3 format filenames, it has been possible to give documents
more descriptive names. This is a good thing. Having to open old documents because you
can't remember what they did is a real waste of time. You should add a version number
(e.g., v1-1, using a dash instead of a dot to avoid confusion with the filename/extension
separator), particularly where a document may go through many revisions or is used
by others.

In addition to the filename version, you should consider including version information
in the worksheets themselves, especially where workbooks are used by many people.
These could be for each sheet, for the whole workbook or whatever is appropriate, but at
least should include an overall workbook version number matching the filename version.

A revision history (the date; who made the changes; what changes were made) is easy
to create and maintain and can save a lot of time and confusion. For complex workbooks,
creating a revision history worksheet at the front of the workbook with all this information
for easy reference can save a great deal of time and heartache later.

You should consider giving every sheet a descriptive title in cell A1, in a good sized font
so that you can't help but know what you're looking at. Using the *Freeze Panes* feature
(Window/Freeze Panes) is a good idea, so that the title, and any other useful information,
is visible in cases where the data extends deep into the spreadsheet.

Naming sheets descriptively is also easy (double-click on the tab's name) and pays divi-
dends. For display reasons these may need to be abbreviated where there are many tabs. Be
careful with the alphabetical order of sheet names where there are cross-worksheet links.
(See section 2.11.4 *Cross-worksheet dependencies – Excel 97/2000 versus 2002/2003* on
page 27 for an explanation.)

2.15.2   Magic numbers

Magic numbers are static numbers that appear in calculations or in their own cells without
much, if any, explanation. They are a *very* bad thing. Sometimes you may feel that

numbers need no explanation, such as there being 24 hours in a day, but err on the side of caution. It is not obvious that the number 86,400 is the number of seconds in a day, for example. A simple comment attached to the cell might be all that's needed to avoid later confusion or wasted time spent decrypting and verifying the number.

Putting magic numbers into calculations themselves, rather than accessing by reference to a cell that contains them, is generally to be avoided, even though this leads to a slightly more efficient recalculation. They are hidden from view and awkward to change if the assumptions that underpin them change. There may also be many less-obvious places where the number occurs, perhaps as a result of cell copying, and all occurrences might not be found when making changes.

Where magic numbers represent assumptions, these should be clearly annotated and should ideally be grouped with other related assumptions in the worksheet (or even workbook) so that they are easy to review and modify.

2.15.3   Data organisation and design guidelines

Data in a spreadsheet can be categorised as follows:

- Variable input data to be changed by the user, an external dynamic data source, the system clock or other source of system data.
- Fixed input (constant) data to be changed only rarely, representing assumptions, numerical coefficients, data from a particular publication or source that must be reproduced faithfully, etc.
- Static data, typically labels, that make the spreadsheet readable and navigable and provide users with help, instructions and information about the contents and algorithms.
- Calculated data resulting from the action of a function or command.

There might also be cells containing functions whose values are largely irrelevant but that perform some useful action when they are re-evaluated, for example, writing to a log file when something changes.

Here are some guidelines for creating spreadsheets that are easy to navigate, maintain and understand:

1. Provide version and revision data (including name and contact details of the author(s) if the workbook is to be used by others).
2. Group related assumptions and magic numbers together and provide clear comments with references to other documents if necessary.
3. Group external links together, especially where they come from the same source, and make it clear that they are external with comments.
4. Avoid too much complexity on a single worksheet. Where a worksheet is becoming over-complex, split it in two being careful to make the split in such a way that cross-worksheet links are minimised and that these links are clearly commented in both sheets.
5. Avoid too much data on a single worksheet. Too much may be difficult to define – a very large but simple table would be fine, but 100 small clusters of only loosely related data and formulae are probably not.
6. Avoid excessive and unnecessary formula repetition, and repetition of expressions within a single formula.

7. Avoid over-complex formulae. Even where repetition within the formula isn't a concern, consider breaking large formulae down into several stages. Large and complex formulae are not only difficult to read and understand later, but make spreadsheets harder to debug.
8. Use named ranges. This not only makes formulae that reference the data more readable and easier to understand but also makes accessing the data in VB or a C/C++ add-in easier and the resulting code independent of certain spreadsheet changes.
9. Use formatting (fonts, borders, shading and text colours) not only to clarify the readability, but also to make a consistent distinction between, say, variable inputs, external dynamic data and 'static' assumption data.
10. Use hyperlinks (press Ctrl-K) to navigate from one part of a large book to another.

2.15.4 Formula repetition

Excel is a faithful servant. It will do what you tell it to do without question and, more significantly, without optimisation. A cell formula such as

=IF(VLOOKUP(W5,B3:B10,1)<SUM(A3:A10),VLOOKUP(W5,B3:B10,1)+SUM(A3:A10),
VLOOKUP(W5,B3:B10,1)-SUM(A3:A10))

will cause Excel to evaluate the VLOOKUP() and SUM() functions twice each. It has no ability to see that the same result is going to be used several times. (You can easily verify this kind of behaviour using a VB macro such as NumCalls_1() listed in section 2.11.1 on page 25). The obvious solution is to split the formula into 3 cells, the first containing VLOOKUP(), the second containing SUM() and the third containing IF() with references to the other two cells.

Repetitions may not be so obvious as this and do not all need to be removed. Sometimes the action of a fairly complex formula is clearer to see when it contains simple repetitions rather than references to cells somewhere far away in the workbook.

Generally speaking, trying to do things in a minimum number of cells can lead to over-complex formulae that are difficult to debug and can lead to calculation repetition. You should err on the side of using more cells, not fewer. Where this interferes with the view you are trying to create for the user (or yourself), use the row/column hide feature or the Data/Group and Outline/Group feature to conceal the interim calculations, or move the interim calculations to another part of the *same* worksheet.

2.15.5 Efficient lookups: MATCH(), INDEX() and OFFSET() versus VLOOKUP()

One of the most commonly used and useful features of spreadsheets is the *lookup*. For the basics of what a lookup is, how it works and the variations read Excel's help. In using lookups it is important to understand the relative costs, in terms of recalculation time, of the various strategies for pulling values out of large tables of data.

Tables of data usually stretch down rather than across. We think in terms of adding lines at the bottom of a table of data rather than adding columns to the right. We read documents line-by-line, and so on. This bias is, of course, reflected in the fact that Excel has 256 times as many rows than columns. Consequently, most lookup operations involve searching a vertical column of data, typically using VLOOKUP(). However, it is easy to create situations where the use of this function becomes very inefficient.

Take, for example, the following task: to extract 3 pieces of data from the row in the table shown below where the left-most column contains the number 11. (See Vlookup_Match_Example.xls on the CD ROM.)

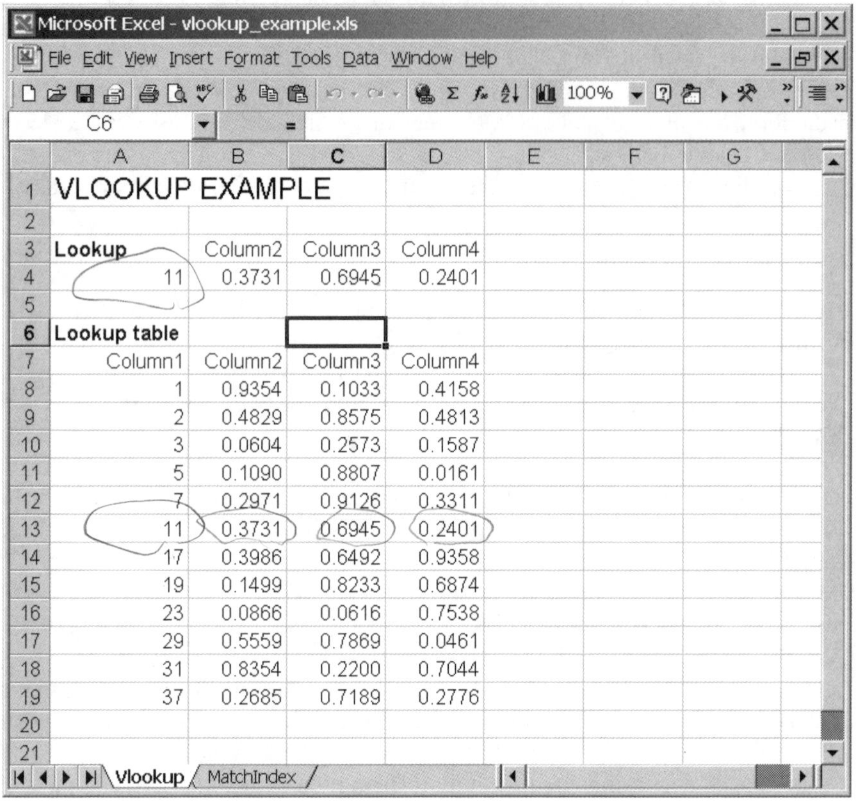

Figure 2.6   VLOOKUP example worksheet

This is easily achieved, as shown, with the following three formulae:

Cell	Formula
B4	=VLOOKUP(A4,A8:D19,2)
C4	=VLOOKUP(A4,A8:D19,3)
D4	=VLOOKUP(A4,A8:D19,4)

At first glance there seems to be no formula repetition, so no problem. In fact, Excel has had to do the same thing three times: search down column A looking for the number 11. In a small table this isn't a big problem, but in a large table with hundreds or thousands of entries this becomes a lot of work. The solution is to use the functions MATCH() and INDEX() in combination as shown here.

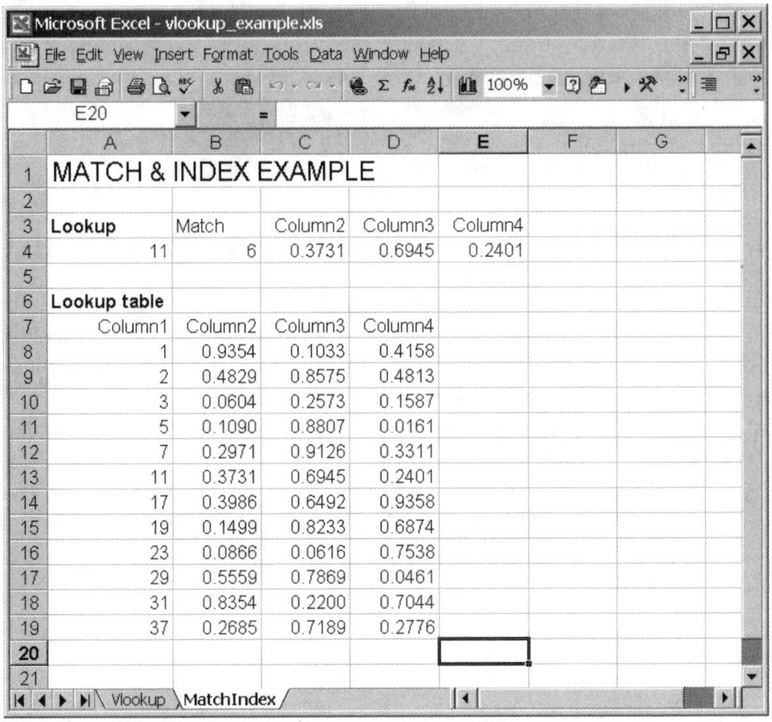

	A	B	C	D	E	F	G
1	MATCH & INDEX EXAMPLE						
2							
3	**Lookup**	Match	Column2	Column3	Column4		
4	11	6	0.3731	0.6945	0.2401		
5							
6	**Lookup table**						
7	Column1	Column2	Column3	Column4			
8	1	0.9354	0.1033	0.4158			
9	2	0.4829	0.8575	0.4813			
10	3	0.0604	0.2573	0.1587			
11	5	0.1090	0.8807	0.0161			
12	7	0.2971	0.9126	0.3311			
13	11	0.3731	0.6945	0.2401			
14	17	0.3986	0.6492	0.9358			
15	19	0.1499	0.8233	0.6874			
16	23	0.0866	0.0616	0.7538			
17	29	0.5559	0.7869	0.0461			
18	31	0.8354	0.2200	0.7044			
19	37	0.2685	0.7189	0.2776			
20							
21							

Figure 2.7 MATCH & INDEX example worksheet

The MATCH() function does the part that Excel would otherwise repeat, determining the correct row in the table. Once done, the required values can be extracted with the very efficient INDEX() function. This will be close to three times faster than the VLOOKUP()-only solution for large tables. The resulting formulae look like this:

Cell	Formula
B4	=MATCH(A4,A8:D19,0)
C4	=INDEX(B8:B19,B4)
D4	=INDEX(C8:C19,B4)
E4	=INDEX(D8:D19,B4)

Note: An additional benefit of MATCH() and INDEX() over VLOOKUP(), where you know the lookup value is in the table and can safely pass zero as the 3rd parameter, is that it doesn't require the lookup column to be ordered. Also, Excel will happily find a string not just a number. In this example, INDEX() takes a more precise reference to the source column. If a column is inserted, MATCH() and INDEX() won't care whereas the formulae in the VLOOKUP() example will all need to be edited.

The OFFSET() function is similar to INDEX() except that it returns a reference to a cell or range of cells rather than a value of a single cell. This gives it more power than INDEX() but at a cost: it is a volatile function. (See section 2.11.3 on page 26.) Excel can't know from one call to the next what range will result, and needs to recalculate each time. Therefore OFFSET() should never be used when INDEX() will do. Trying to get around this with INDIRECT() will not work, as this function too is volatile.

2.16 SOME PROBLEMS WITH VERY LARGE SPREADSHEETS

Despite being a wonderful tool for a surprisingly broad range of data analysis tasks, Excel does have its limits. This is most obvious when it comes to memory utilisation in very large workbooks. Excel can become alarmingly slow, and even unstable, when asked to perform routine operations on large groups of cells. Even the act of deleting a large block of cells in a workbook that is straining the memory resources of the host machine, can take tens of minutes to complete. If Excel runs out of memory for the *undo* information, it may alert the user that the operation cannot continue with undo. Even then, it still may fail and Excel might even crash. Excel's often graceless handling of out-of-memory conditions is one of its (very few) weaknesses, one which Microsoft improves with every new release.

2.17 CONCLUSION

For *normal* use you don't need to worry about some of the subtle complexities that this chapter tries to shed light on. Where the demands are more rigorous, however, the need to be aware of the most efficient way to use Excel and how to avoid some of its recalculation problems becomes more important. It can even be critical to the spreadsheet doing properly what you want it to.

3

Using VBA

This chapter provides only a brief introduction to using VBA to create commands and functions. It is not intended to be a detailed how-to guide to VB in Excel. It touches briefly on:

- the creation of VB commands and macro functions;
- passing data between VBA and Excel;
- accessing DLL functions from VBA;
- passing data between VBA and a DLL.

For those who want to know more about VB, VBA and the subjects raised in this chapter, some VB-related titles are included in the book list at the end of the book.

If you don't want to bother with the *Add-in Manager* and *Paste Function* dialog in Excel, then you can access all of your C/C++ code from VBA and this chapter explains how. It describes what you need to know to be able to access your DLL code and how to pass and convert arguments and return types.

VBA is a very powerful application enabling complex things to be done very easily. But this book is intentionally about doing things that are beyond the scope or performance of VB. If you want to know more about VBA's capabilities, experiment. The VB editor is easy to use, especially to anyone with experience of, say, Visual C++, and the Tools/Macro/Record New Macro... menu option provides a great *how-to* guide for writing commands and is some help with code you might want to include in a function.

Section 3.8 on page 71 includes a VB-specific discussion of the differences between commands and functions. Sections 2.8 *Commands versus functions in Excel*, on page 19, and 8.1.1 *Commands, worksheet functions and macro sheet functions*, on page 170, together provide a more general discussion of this topic.

3.1 OPENING THE VB EDITOR

There are several ways of bringing up the VB editor:

- through the Tools/Macro/Visual Basic Editor;
- with the keyboard short-cut {Shift F11} ;
- by installing the VB Editor command icon onto a toolbar via the Tools/Customise dialog.

The third option is recommended, since, once done, it saves a lot of time, although the keyboard short-cut is quick if you can remember it.

If you have done this with a blank spreadsheet, you should then see something like this:

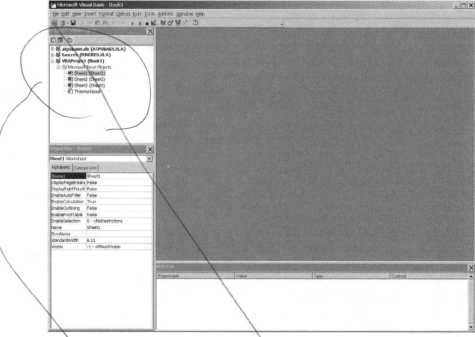

Figure 3.1 The Visual Basic Editor interface

In the above example, you will see several documents referred to in the top left-hand pane (the *Project Explorer* window). The first two in this screen shot belong to standard add-ins that have been loaded by Excel, and the third belongs to the default-named workbook, Book1, that Excel created on being opened.

For each sheet in Book1 there is a corresponding object listed. There is also an object associated with the entire workbook. Each of these has an associated VB code container which can be opened and edited by double-clicking on the object's name in the Project Explorer window. The top right pane, which contains the VB source editor, then displays whatever VB code is associated with that object. For a new spreadsheet, these VB code modules are empty.

3.2 USING VBA TO CREATE NEW COMMANDS

Commands can be associated with individual worksheets or with the entire workbook. To be accessible in the right place – to have the right scope – VB code for these must be placed in the appropriate VB code object. A command that is coded in the Sheet3 code object will not run successfully if invoked from another sheet. If you only intend it to be invoked from Sheet1, then code it into Sheet1. If you want it to be accessible in all sheets in the workbook, place it in the Workbook code module.

3.2.1 Recording VB macro commands

This is the easiest way to create simple commands and to learn how to use the Excel VB objects to do things in your own commands. The Tools/Macro/Record new macro... command is all you need to remember. The following dialog enables you to tell Excel and the VBE where to place the code it generates and what to call it. It also places a handy little comment into the code.

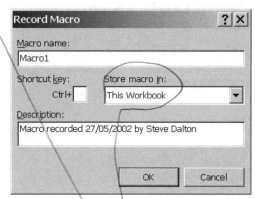

Figure 3.2   VBA Record Macro dialog

If you elect to place the code in This Workbook (as shown) you will see that a new folder appears called *Modules*, containing a new code module, by default called Module1. Double-clicking on the name Module1 will cause the editor to display the code, something like this:

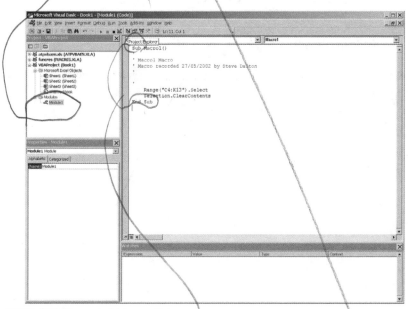

Figure 3.3   VBE Recorded Macro dialog

The command code procedure is in a Sub/End Sub code block declaration. It has no return type or return value and takes no arguments. If you want to communicate something to the user, such as success or failure, your command will have to open an alert or dialog box containing what you want to convey or write directly to a predetermined cell or named range.

You can, of course, create your own code modules and add your own Sub/End Sub commands manually.

3.3 ASSIGNING VB COMMAND MACROS TO CONTROL OBJECTS IN A WORKSHEET

Control objects include:

- checkboxes;
- text boxes;
- command buttons;
- option buttons (radio buttons);
- list boxes;
- combo boxes (text box with list box);
- toggle buttons;
- spin buttons;
- scroll bars;

... and many others.

Each one of these objects can be placed into a worksheet using the *Control Toolbox* toolbar. They all have events and properties associated with them and can have code associated with those events. For example, creating a command button, which would be given the default name *CommandButton1*, and then right-clicking and selecting *Edit code* will cause the VBE to appear with an empty command code declaration placed within the container worksheet's VB code object, like this:

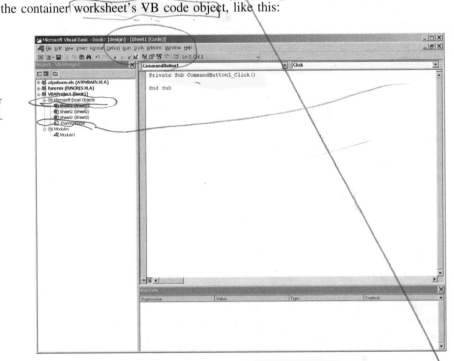

Figure 3.4 VBE worksheet code showing command button event trap

Above the code editor pane are two list boxes, one showing the object to which the event applies, in this case *CommandButton1*, and the other the action, in this case *Click*. Changing the action will cause the VBE to create a new empty command with a declaration that reflects the selected action. The code these code blocks contain will then be invoked whenever the specified action occurs.

3.4 USING VBA TO TRAP EXCEL EVENTS

As shown above, the VB code associated with a worksheet can also contain code associated with events corresponding to the worksheet itself. Selecting Worksheet in the left-hand list box above the code editor pane will cause the VBE to create an empty code block such as this:

```
Private Sub Worksheet_SelectionChange(ByVal Target As Range)

End Sub
```

Whenever the cursor is in a piece of *worksheet* command code, the right-hand list box will give access to all the events associated with the worksheet object. As with control object actions, changing the action will cause the VBE to create a new empty command with a declaration that reflects the selected action. Similarly, in the *ThisWorkbook* code object, events relating to (or visible to) the entire workbook can be accessed and command code written that will be executed every time that event occurs.

Trapping Excel commands can be very useful, for example, enabling you to do things when:

* a workbook is closed;
* a worksheet is selected;
* a change is made;
* a single cell is selected or edited.

(To achieve the last example, you would need to create a trap for the whole worksheet and then inspect the argument.) What is important to remember is that code associated with a trapped Excel event is a *command*. You can call function code from a command but you cannot call a command from a worksheet function. Command code cannot return a value.

The code module associated with the workbook supports the following event traps in Excel 2000:

* Activate;
* AdddinInstall;
* AdddinUninstall;
* BeforeClose;
* BeforePrint;
* Deactivate;
* NewSheet;
* Open;

- SheetActivate;
- SheetBeforeDoubleClick;
- SheetBeforeRightClick;
- SheetCalculate;
- SheetChange;
- SheetDeactivate;
- SheetFollowHyperlink;
- SheetSelectionChange;
- WindowActivate;
- WindowDeactivate;
- WindowResize.

By Excel 2003, the following traps also exist:

- PivotTableCloseConnection;
- PivotTableOpenConnection;
- SheetPivotTableUpdate;
- Sync.

Each of these events is trapped by a subroutine in this module with the name `Workbook_*` where * is replaced by one of the above event names. For example, the following routine traps the recalculation of any and all sheets in the workbook.

```
Private Sub Workbook_SheetCalculate(ByVal Sh As Object)

End Sub
```

The code module associated with the worksheet supports the following subroutine traps:

- Activate;
- BeforeDoubleClick;
- BeforeRightClick;
- Calculate;
- Change;
- Deactivate;
- FollowHyperlink;
- SelectionChange.

By Excel 2003, the following trap also exists:

- PivotTableUpdate;

In other words, the sheet object supports the trapping of these events sheet-by-sheet. If you want to trap an event for all sheets, use the event trap in the workbook module. If you want to trap the event just in that sheet, use the event trap in the sheet module.

Similarly, user-form objects in VB support a number of trappable events accessed via routines in their associated code modules, as do other embedded objects in a workbook.

3.5   USING VBA TO CREATE NEW FUNCTIONS

Creating new functions is very straightforward. Code is declared and contained within a Function/End Function code block. This must be placed in a VB code module listed under *Modules* in the VBE in order for Excel to be able to recognise it as a user-defined worksheet function. Function code placed in the code module associated with a workbook or sheet will not be accessible from the worksheet. Creating a new code module is easily done by right-clicking on any of the objects in the VB project associated with the workbook (in the Workspace window: the left-most pane in the default view) and then selecting Insert.../Module. This causes the editor to create a new VB code module object in the workbook and opens it for editing in the edit window.

3.5.1   Function scope

Function code can, of course, be placed anywhere in any code module, but its scope will be limited to the VB project associated with the workbook. Other open workbooks will not be able to access the function.

Functions created in the code object associated with one of the workbook objects, such as a worksheet, work fine, but can only be called by command code or other function in *that* code object, and definitely not from the worksheet.

Commands within the project can also call the project's functions including those in code modules. (Remember, functions cannot call commands regardless of scope.)

VB functions and commands can be given greater scope by saving and loading them as an XLA add-in file. (See section 3.9 *Creating VB add-ins (XLA files)* on page 72 for a brief description of how to create XLA add-ins.) Once loaded, worksheet functions they contain can be accessed by any open workbook. Function scope can also be restricted by prefacing function names with the Private keyword.

There is more to function and variable scope than touched on here, including the Public and Private keywords and the Option Private Module statement. For more about these you should refer to VBA's help.

3.5.2   Declaring VB functions as volatile

It is often useful and sometimes necessary for a function to be called every time Excel recalculates rather than just when an input has changed. This requires that Excel be informed that the function is *volatile*. This is easily achieved in VBA by calling the application method Application.Volatile immediately after the dimensioning of variables. (Note: Excel does not know the function is to be treated as volatile until it has been called at least once.) The following VBA code shows an example.

```
Function Volatile_Fn_Example(trigger As Integer) As Double

    Dim val As Double

    Application.Volatile

    val = 2.123 ' arbitrary meaningless number for example only

    Volatile_Fn_Example = Now * val

End Function
```

This is a particularly important thing to do when using VB as a wrapper or interface to DLL functions that need to be treated as volatile, say, those that return some external dynamic information.

3.6   USING VBA AS AN INTERFACE TO EXTERNAL DLL ADD-INS

3.6.1   Declaring DLL functions in VB

Both functions and commands written in C/C++ (or other languages where code is compiled to a Win32 DLL) can be accessed directly in VB using the `Declare` statement whose syntax is as follows:

Syntax 1

```
[Public | Private] Declare Sub name Lib "libname" [Alias
"aliasname"] [([arglist])]
```

Syntax 2

```
[Public | Private] Declare Function name Lib "libname" [Alias
"aliasname"] [([arglist])] [As type]
```

Syntax 1 relates to commands; syntax 2, to functions. The optional `Public` and `Private` keywords specify the scope of the imported function – the entire VB project or just the VB module, respectively.

The *name* is the name you want to use within the VB code. If this is different from the name in the DLL then the `Alias "aliasname"` specifier must be used and should give the name of the function as exported in the DLL. If you want to access a DLL function by reference to an ordinal number in the DLL, then specify an alias name which is the ordinal prefixed by #.

If the imported function is to be treated as a volatile worksheet function, then the VBA wrapper function must invoke the method `Application.Volatile`.

3.6.2   Call-by-reference versus call-by-value

VB does not have the concept of pointers that exists in the world of C/C++. In the world of VB, functions can modify their arguments if they have been passed *by reference* using the `ByRef` keyword. In fact, this is the default behaviour for VB. In the example code below `go_double_me(2.1)` would return the value `4.2`.

```
Function double_me(ByRef d as Double) as Boolean

    d = d * 2
    double_me = True

End Function
```

```
Function go_double_me(d as Double) as Double
    Call double_me(d)
    go_double_me = d
End Function
```

As ByRef is the default in VB, this keyword can be removed with no change to the behaviour of the code. In contrast, substituting ByRef with ByVal would have the effect that go_double_me() would return exactly what was passed to it un-doubled. (Note the inclusion of the Call keyword, without which the function would be called as ByVal, but which also has the effect of suppressing the return value of the called function.)

In C the default is *call-by-value*, with *call-by-reference* achievable only with the use of pointers. In C++ there is also the option of passing reference arguments as well as pointers. C++ reference arguments (prefixed with an ampersand '&' in the function declaration) work in exactly the same way as VB's call-by-reference, allowing access to the value of the variable without the need to de-reference a pointer. This is all summarised in Table 3.1.

Table 3.1 Call by value versus by ref in VB, C and C++

	VB	C	C++
Call by ref	[ByRef] *arg* As *VB_type*	C_type *p_arg	CPP_type *p_arg CPP_type &arg
Call by value	ByVal *arg* As *VB_type*	C_type arg	CPP_type arg

When passing arguments to C/C++ DLL functions, care should be taken with certain data types. The VB String is passed as a pointer to a string structure when passed ByVal, and as a pointer to a pointer when passed ByRef. (See next section for more detail on String and other VB data types.)

3.6.3 Converting argument and return data types between VB and C/C++

By and large, VB uses similar native data types to C/C++, although there are some differences:

- VB integers are all signed 16-bit, equivalent to a C short.
- VB doesn't support pointers.

They also have much in common:

- VB allows definition of user-defined data types, using the Type statement, closely analogous to C's typedef struct.
- VB uses a number of OLE/COM data types such as Variant which are also defined for C/C++ in Windows in the OLE/COM header files.

These things are all discussed in the following sections. Table 3.2 below gives a summary of the data types in VB, their value ranges where appropriate, and the equivalent data types in C/C++.

Accuracy note

VB permits greater ranges of value of its variables than Excel does. In particular:

- The range of a VB Double is slightly greater than the range of an Excel number. (All Excel numbers are stored as 8-byte floating-point.)
- The VB Date type can represent dates as early as 1-Jan-0100 using negative serialised dates. Excel only allows serialised dates greater than or equal to zero.
- The VB Currency type – a scaled 64-bit integer – can achieve accuracy not matched in Excel.

The table in section 2.4 *Worksheet data types and limits* on page 10 provides details of Excel's data type range values.

3.6.4   VB data types and limits

VB in Excel provides access to a very large number of pre-defined object types relating to Excel, Microsoft Office, OLE Automation, etc. Only the following 12 (excluding user-defined types) are easily accessible to C/C++ functions called from VB. There is no easy way to pass a VB Range variable to a C/C++ DLL function. It's not impossible – you could assign it to a Variant argument and pass that, but you would then have to use the COM IDispatch interface to interrogate the object that the C VARIANT would contain. This starts to get complicated. Passing a range reference, for example, is far easier using the C API. But, be warned: the C API does not expose as many of Excel's objects and properties as VB.

Table 3.2 VB data types and limits, and their C/C++ equivalents

Visual Basic	Range in VB	C/C++
Byte	Min: 0 Max: $255 = 2^8 - 1$	unsigned char
Boolean	-1 (TRUE) 0 (FALSE)	signed short (16-bit)
Integer	Min: $-32,768 = -2^{15}$ Max: $+32,767 = 2^{15} - 1$	signed short (16-bit)
Long	Min: $-2,147,483,648 = -2^{31}$ Max: $+2,147,483,647 = 2^{31} - 1$	signed long (32-bit)

Currency	Min: $-922,337,203,685,477.5808$
	     $= -2^{63}/10,000$
	Max: $+922,337,203,685,477.5807$
	     $= (2^{63} - 1)/10,000$
		CY in <wtypes.h>
		= __int64 (scaled)
		
		(see below)

Table 3.2 (*continued*)

Single	Positive values Min: +1.401298e−45 Max: +3.402823e+38 Negative values Min: −1.401298e−45 Max: −3.402823e+38	float (4-byte)
Double	Positive values Min: +4.94065645841247e−324 Max: +1.79769313486232e+308 Negative values Min: −4.94065645841247e−324 Max: −1.79769313486231e+308	double (8-byte)

Date	Min: −657,434.0
	  (1-Jan-0100 00:00:00 a.m.)
	Max: ~2,958,465.999,999,94
	  (31-Dec-9999 23:59:59.995)
		DATE in <wtypes.h>
		= double (8-byte)
		(see below)

String		BSTR in <wtypes.h> (see below)
Variant		VARIANT in <oaidl.h> (see below)
Object type		(see below)
Array		(see below)
User-defined type		(see below)

3.6.5 VB/OLE Currency type

The VB/OLE Currency data type is passed to C/C++ as a structure of type CY, defined in the Windows header file <wtypes.h> as follows:

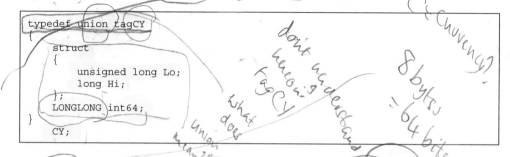

```
typedef union tagCY
{
    struct
    {
        unsigned long Lo;
        long Hi;
    };
    LONGLONG int64;
}
    CY;
```

The 64-bit integer structure LONGLONG is defined using the non-ANSI 64-bit integer type __int64 and represents non-integer numbers to 4 decimal places scaled up by a factor of 10,000. In Win32 environments, various operations and macro definitions are defined for __int64 variables in <winnt.h>, such as logical and arithmetic bit shifts. However, the simplest way to deal with this data type is to cast it to a double as in this example code. In theory, this conversion is at the expense of some accuracy. However, this is true only for values which are outside the range of Excel in the first place.

```
CY c = some_function_that_returns_a_CY(some_argument);
double d = (double)(c.int64) / 1e4; // Divide to undo the scaling
```

You will encounter this data type when your C/C++ DLL is passed an array of VARIANTS by VB created from an Excel Range object's Value property, where one or more cells in the Range have been formatted using the standard currency format for the regional settings in force at the time. This is mildly annoying: the value of a cell should be its underlying value regardless of the display format. (Excel and VB do a similar thing for worksheet cells formatted as dates.) If you are handling arrays of data originating in Excel worksheet ranges, you will need to deal with this data type. (See sections 3.6.9 *Variant data type* and 3.7 *Excel ranges, VB arrays, SafeArrays, array Variants* below for more detail and some example code.)

3.6.6 VB/OLE Strings

The VB String data type is an OLE data type defined for C/C++ as BSTR in <wtypes.h>. The BSTR is implemented as a *pointer* to a zero-terminated array of type unsigned short – a string of 16-bit wide characters. However, Excel passes and accepts null-terminated *byte*-strings. VBA for Excel understands this and stores the bytes of the string in the high and low bytes of the array pointed to by the BSTR.

For example, the text "Test string" passed from VB to a C/C++ function would be stored as shown in Table 3.3.

Table 3.3 Excel VBA string passed to C/C++: Example 1

Passed in as BSTR bstr	Value (unsigned short)	Value (byte string)
(*bstr)[0]	0x6554	((char *)(*bstr))[0] = 0x54 = 'T' ((char *)(*bstr))[1] = 0x65 = 'e'
(*bstr)[1]	0x7473	((char *)(*bstr))[2] = 0x73 = 's' ((char *)(*bstr))[3] = 0x74 = 't'
(*bstr)[2]	0x7320	((char *)(*bstr))[4] = 0x20 = ' ' ((char *)(*bstr))[5] = 0x73 = 's'
(*bstr)[3]	0x7274	((char *)(*bstr))[6] = 0x74 = 't' ((char *)(*bstr))[7] = 0x72 = 'r'

Table 3.3 (*continued*)

(*bstr)[4]	0x6e69	((char *)(*bstr))[8] = 0x69 = 'i' ((char *)(*bstr))[9] = 0x6e = 'n'
(*bstr)[5]	0x0067	((char *)(*bstr))[10] = 0x67 = 'g' ((char *)(*bstr))[11] = 0x00 = Null termination of ANSI byte string
(*bstr)[6]	0x0000	Zero termination of BSTR string

The text "Test" would be stored as shown in Table 3.4.

Table 3.4 Excel VBA string passed to C/C++: Example 2

Passed in as BSTR bstr	Value (unsigned short)	Value (byte string)
(*bstr)[0]	0x6554	((char *)(*bstr))[0] = 0x54 = 'T' ((char *)(*bstr))[1] = 0x65 = 'e'
(*bstr)[1]	0x7473	((char *)(*bstr))[2] = 0x73 = 's' ((char *)(*bstr))[3] = 0x74 = 't'
(*bstr)[2]	0x0000	Zero termination of BSTR string *and* null termination of ANSI byte string combined

How long is a piece of string? As can be seen from these two examples, string length is dependent on what you are thinking of as the string. OLE provides two functions for determining the length of a BSTR: SysStringLen() and SysStringByteLen(). They would return the following when applied to these example strings:

Table 3.5 BSTR string length comparisons

String	SysStringLen()	SysStringByteLen()	Bytes allocated
Test string	6	11	14
Test	2	4	6

For strings of bytes passed in a BSTR from VB you should use SysStringByteLen().

Warning: When VB passes strings to C/C++ via a Variant argument of type VT_BSTR, the string is *not* a byte-string, but a null-terminated string of unsigned shorts. Care must be taken to distinguish between these two cases, as different system functions are required to read and create these. (See section 3.6.10 *Variant types supported by VBA* on page 58.)

3.6.7 Passing strings to C/C++ functions from VB

When passed ByVal to C/C++ a VB String arrives as a BSTR. You could declare the argument as an unsigned short *. (Note that in doing this you would make your code dependent on the particular implementation of the BSTR type.) You can also declare your argument as char *, having the effect of casting the pointer directly to the memory allocated to the BSTR.

When passed ByRef a VB string arrives as a pointer to a BSTR, equivalent to a pointer to a pointer to an unsigned short, which you could declare as BSTR * or simply as unsigned short **. VB will always pass a non-null pointer to the BSTR. The pointer *that this points to* will be set to null if the string was declared in VB (using Dim) but not allocated a value. Consider the following piece of VB code:

```
' Argument is passed ByRef by default
Declare Function C_BSTR_Example1 Lib "example.xll" _
        (s As String) As Boolean

Function VB_BSTR_EXAMPLE(Trigger As Variant) As Boolean

    Dim s As String

' Call 1: String is dimensioned but not initialised
    C_BSTR_Example (s)

' Call 2: String is initialised to an empty string
    s = ""
    C_BSTR_Example (s)

' Call 3:
    s = "Test string"
    C_BSTR_Example (s)

    VB_BSTR_EXAMPLE = True

End Function
```

Suppose that the C/C++ function is prototyped as follows:

```
// Function definition corresponding to VB definition of
// Declare Function C_BSTR_Example1 ...(s As String) As Boolean,
// i.e. argument passed ByRef.

short __stdcall C_BSTR_Example1(BSTR *ptr_bstr)
{
    if(!ptr_bstr) // Should never be NULL, but...
        return 0; // Return VB False

    if(!*ptr_bstr) // Is string initialised?
        return 0; // Return VB False if not

    for(int i = 0; ; i++)
    {
        if(!((char *)(*ptr_bstr))[i])
            break;
    }
    return -1; // Return VB True
}
```

In call 1, `ptr_bstr` will have a non-null value so there is no need to check if `ptr_bstr` is NULL (unless you're particularly distrusting of VB or think that something less reliable might also call the function). On the other hand, the pointer pointed to by `ptr_bstr` *will* have a null value in this case, so in general there is a need to check if `*ptr_bstr` is NULL.

In call 2, the value `*ptr_bstr` will now be non-null as the VB `String` variable was assigned a value. However, as the string is an empty string, the first (and only) unsigned short will be the zero string-terminator. In other words the value `*ptr_bstr[0]`, or equivalently `**ptr_bstr`, will be zero in this case. It is entirely up to you if you check immediately for this condition or allow subsequently called functions that access the string to do the checking.

In call 3, not only has the VB variable been assigned a value, but it is a non-empty string and `*ptr_bstr` will, in this case, point to an array of unsigned shorts as detailed above.

As such strings are firstly UNICODE and secondly allocated in VB, care is needed on the C/C++ DLL side. OLE provides a number of functions that deal with BSTR variables, among them `SysAllocStringByteLen()`, `SysReAllocString()`, `SysReAllocStringLen()`, `SysFreeString()` and `SysStringLen()`.

If you want to store the strings beyond the current call to your DLL, you should make you own deep copies of them and store those, rather than store a shallow copy of the pointer. Otherwise, if and when the calling program frees the memory later, it would invalidate your pointer.

3.6.8 Returning strings to VB from a DLL

There are, of course, three ways to return any value to a calling program:

1. Modify the passed-in arguments (if you have access to them).
2. Via the function's return value.
3. Via some commonly accessible memory.

You should ignore the third option as the first two are by far the most sensible and both fairly straightforward.

In general, if you want to modify a passed-in argument in your C code, you should pass it `ByRef` (the default), i.e., accept a pointer that you can de-reference to change the value of the caller's variable. For the BSTR type, even though it is already a pointer you must still pass it as `ByRef` to be able to modify the passed in string. Also you <u>must</u> use the OLE functions to resize the string if you want to increase or decrease its length. Resizing frees the original memory and allocates some new space, but without causing the calling program (VB in this example) a problem, as it too uses the OLE interface. If you want something you can chop about and manipulate locally, however, you should simply make a deep copy of the string.

If you want to assign a new value to a passed-in argument, you <u>must</u> check first to see if it has been allocated, i.e., if the BSTR's value (a pointer) is not null, and free the memory with a call to `SysFreeString()` before overwriting the pointer value in order to prevent memory leaks.

The following code shows how to pass strings back from a C/C++ DLL to VB via a return value. The important point is the use of the OLE `SysAllocStringByteLen()`

function to allocate new space for the string. This enables VB to free the string when it is done with it.

```c
// Example code to create and return a BSTR to VB.
// Creates a string of the 1st 'n' A-Z characters.

BSTR __stdcall C_BSTR_Example2(short n) // C short=VB Integer(16-bit)
{
    if(n <= 0 || n > 26)
        return NULL;

// 1st argument is initialisation string, but we want
// to initialise this ourselves so pass NULL.   2nd
// argument is number of bytes in the byte-string NOT
// including the null termination space for which space is
// allocated and which is added by SysAllocStringByteLen()
//
// Returns NULL if unsuccessful at allocating memory, which
// must be freed by a call to SysFreeString().   In this
// example, freeing memory is left to the caller, i.e. VBA

    BSTR bstr = SysAllocStringByteLen(NULL, n);

    if(*bstr)
    {
        char c = 'A';

        for(int i = 0; i < n; )
            ((char *)(bstr))[i++] = c++;
    }
    return bstr;
}
```

Here is the VB declaration and an example of VB code that calls this. (Note the explicit inclusion of ByVal in the argument list.)

```vb
Declare Function C_BSTR_Example2 Lib "example.xll" _
        (ByVal n As Integer) As String

Function VB_BSTR_EXAMPLE2(Length As Integer) As String

    VB_BSTR_EXAMPLE2 = C_BSTR_Example2(Length)

End Function
```

VBA takes care of freeing the returned BSTR using the correct OLE Automation interface call. Even though it looks like the combination of these two pieces of code should result in a memory leak, it is, in fact, perfectly fine.

(Note: The Add-in Manager and the C API provide easier passing of strings between the spreadsheet and add-in than VB, as Excel passes strings as ANSI C null-terminated *byte* strings, enabling functions that are accessed directly from Excel to declare strings as char *. Responsibility for freeing up DLL-allocated string memory, however, reverts to the DLL programmer. See section 7.4 *Getting Excel to call back the DLL to free DLL-allocated memory* on page 166 for details.)

3.6.9   Variant data type

A Variant is a multi-type variable that can contain (or point to) a variety of different data types. It superficially makes all data types look the same enabling functions to be declared that take Variants as arguments or return them. Such functions can therefore process more than one, or even all, data types. In VB, it is the default data type for variables: the omission of the As *Type* data type specifier anywhere it might appear is equivalent to a declaration of As Variant.

It is good practice to declare all argument, return and variable types explicitly. The code is far more readable, errors in scope are also avoided and VB is not saddled with unnecessary type conversions. The Option Explicit statement at the top of a code module forces the programmer to do just this.

The OLE Variant is represented in VB by the Variant data type and in C/C++ by the VARIANT structure. When passed ByVal to C/C++ a Variant arrives as a VARIANT. The C structure can be thought of as containing two key (top-level) components:

- a VARTYPE vt (defined as an unsigned short in <wtypes.h>) containing a numeric code corresponding to the type of data the variant contains;
- a large union of all the data types (some of which are pointers) that the OLE Variant supports.

Here is a simple C/C++ example which, if exported from a DLL and declared in VB, would simply convert a VB Integer to a Variant of integer type:

```
VARIANT __stdcall int_to_variant(short val)
{
    VARIANT v;

// Good practice to initialise the variant structure first
    VariantInit (&v);

// This VARTYPE specifies a 2-byte signed integer (i.e. a short),
// equivalent to a VB Integer
    v.vt = VT_I2;

// Assign the passed-in value to the 'short' union member
    v.iVal = val;

    return v;
}
```

Variants are important in the context of this book insofar as they play an important role in the simplest way of passing of arrays of data from worksheet ranges to C/C++ DLLs via VB. (There are ways to do this that don't involve Variants.) They are also used to return variable-sized arrays of data from VB back to array formulae in the worksheet. (Use of Variants is the only way to do this.) The subject of passing arrays to and fro is covered in detail below in section 3.7 *Excel ranges, VB arrays, SafeArrays, array Variants* on page 64.

Variants are also useful in getting data from, and returning data to, cells in Excel where the type could be one of a number of things, say a string or a number.

The C API opens up some of Excel's internal data storage structures, by-passing the need for Variants. These structures do, nevertheless, have much in common with Variants. (See Chapter 6 *Passing Data between Excel and the DLL* on page 105.)

3.6.10   Variant types supported by VBA

Of the many data types supported by the OLE Variant, only the following are supported by VBA in Excel, and therefore only these need to be handled by a DLL function that is called from VBA.

Table 3.6 VBA – supported Variant types

Data type	VARTYPE	Numeric value	C union member
Empty	VT_EMPTY	0	(No associated data)
Long signed 32-bit integer	VT_I4	2	long lVal
Short signed 16-bit integer	VT_I2	3	short iVal
4-byte single-precision	VT_R4	4	float fltVal
8-byte double-precision	VT_R8	5	double dblVal
Currency	VT_CY	6	CY *pcyVal
Date	VT_DATE	7	DATE date (DATE is defined as double)
String	VT_BSTR	8	BSTR bstrVal
Object	VT_DISPATCH	9	IDispatch *pdispVal (See VB Object type below)
Error	VT_ERROR	10	ULONG ulVal (Easier to use than SCODE)
Boolean	VT_BOOL	11	short boolVal
Variant (see notes below)	VT_VARIANT | *	12	VARIANT *pvarVal or SAFEARRAY *parray
ByRef (see notes below)	VT_BYREF | *	16384 0x4000	Pointer to one of the above data types
Array (see notes below)	VT_ARRAY | *	8192 0x2000	SAFEARRAY *parray

Array and ByRef note

The VT_ARRAY and VT_BYREF bits are bit-wise or'd with the value of the associated data type. In a Variant array, therefore, the data type not only says that the Variant is an array but also what is the data type of the elements. If the Variant's data type is bit-wise or'd with the VT_BYREF bit, then the Variant contains a pointer to the given data type.

If both bits are set, then the array that the Variant contains is an array of pointers to the given data type.

Variant note

A Variant will only contain a Variant in conjunction with one or both of the VT_ARRAY and VT_BYREF bits. If the VT_BYREF bit is set then the pointer is accessed via the VARIANT *pvarVal data member. If it is the VT_ARRAY bit, then the Variant contains an array of Variants whose individual elements may be of mixed-type, and are accessed via the SAFEARRAY *parray data member. (See also note below.)

Array of Variants note

A Variant type of particular interest is a Variant containing an array of Variants. Such arrays are created when assigning a worksheet Range.Value property in VB to a Variant – one of the ways of passing an array originating in a range of worksheet cells to a C/C++ DLL. (See section 3.7 *Excel ranges, VB arrays, SafeArrays, array Variants* on page 64 for details.)

String note

When VB passes strings to C/C++ via a Variant argument of type VT_BSTR, the string is a string of unsigned shorts, i.e., UNICODE wide characters. Care must be taken to distinguish between this case and when VB passes a VB String, which is a BSTR interpreted as a byte-string. Different system functions are required to read and create each type of string. (See also section 3.6.6 *VB/OLE Strings* on page 52.) In the case of Variant strings, the functions SysStringLen() and SysAllocStringLen() should be used in place of SysStringByteLen() and SysAllocStringByteLen() respectively. The wide-char string to byte-string system conversion functions MultiByteToWideChar() and WideCharToMultiByte(), and their C library analogues mbstowcs() and wcstombs(), are also useful. (See the Variant conversion routines in the example project source file xloper.cpp, and also section 3.7 below.)

3.6.11 Variant types that Excel can pass to VB functions

Within Excel, VB functions declared with Variant arguments will be passed an even more limited subset by Excel worksheet formulae, namely:

Table 3.7 Variant types passed to VBA from Excel worksheets

VARTYPE	Arguments that will be passed as this type
VT_R8	All numbers, with the exception of those formatted as dates or in the currency format.
VT_BOOL	Excel's TRUE and FALSE values. <u>NOTE:</u> Excel converts TRUE and FALSE to the numbers 1 and 0 respectively, whereas the Variant stores these as − 1 and 0. Care should be taken where conversions are being made.

(*continued overleaf*)

Table 3.7 (*continued*)

VARTYPE	Arguments that will be passed as this type
VT_DATE	Any number formatted in one of Excel's date formats or date-time formats. (Numbers displayed with a time format are passed as VT_R8.)
VT_BSTR	All strings. (See note in above section.)
VT_DISPATCH	Ranges (single-cell and multi-cell).
VT_ARRAY | VT_VARIANT	Literal arrays.
VT_CY	Any number formatted in the currency format defined for the current regional settings.
VT_ERROR	All Excel error values.
VT_EMPTY	All empty cells or omitted arguments.

A VB function declared as follows will return the type of the Variant as a number, using the VB function VarType(), except that ranges are converted, rather than Var-Type returning VT_DISPATCH. Single cell ranges are converted to the data type of the cell's value. Multi-cell ranges are converted to arrays of Variants, type VT_ARRAY \| VT_VARIANT.

```
Function VariantType(v As Variant) As Integer

    VariantType = VarType(v)

End Function
```

The following VB function will similarly convert the Range to a Variant before calling VarType().

```
Function VariantRangeType(r As Range) As Integer

    VariantRangeType = VarType(r)

End Function
```

In both of these cases, the function VarType() is passing back the type of the Range object's Value property.

The following VB code, which declares and calls a simple DLL function that returns a Variant, does no such conversion of ranges references, and therefore would return the value 9 (VT_DISPATCH) for anything other than literal arguments. For example, a worksheet formula =VariantTypeC(A1) would return 9 regardless of the contents of cell A1.

```
Declare Function C_vt_type Lib "example.dll" _
    (ByRef arg As Variant) As Integer

Function VariantTypeC(v As Variant) As Double

    VariantTypeC = C_vt_type(v)

End Function
```

Where the intention of the DLL function is to operate on the *value* of the range passed in, it is therefore necessary to convert the Range to one or more values. The simplest way to achieve this is to detect that the passed-in Variant is a range and then convert it to an array Variant, like so:

```
Declare Function C_vt_fn Lib "example.dll" _
    (ByRef arg As Variant) As Integer

Function VariantFn(v As Variant) As Double

    If IsObject(v) Then
        VariantFn = C_vt_fn(v.Value)
    Else
        VariantFn = C_vt_fn(v)
    End If

End Function
```

It is then the task of the DLL code to determine if the passed-in Variant is a simple value or an array. Note that in the above case, single-cell references are converted to 1x1 arrays. (See section 3.7 *Excel ranges, VB arrays, SafeArrays, array Variants* on page 64 for more about arrays.)

Excel error values are most easily read from the `ulVal` property of the variant. The numerical value is equivalent to the 2,148,141,008 plus the error code used in the C API and defined in the header file `xlcall32.h`. Variants containing Excel error values can also be created in VB using the `CVerr()` VB function. Table 3.8 provides a comparison of the various representations.

Table 3.8 Excel error codes

Error	Variant `ulVal` value	C API value	`CVerr()` argument
#NULL!	2148141008	0	2000
#DIV/0!	2148141015	7	2007
#VALUE!	2148141023	15	2015
#REF!	2148141031	23	2023
#NAME?	2148141037	29	2029
#NUM!	2148141044	36	2036
#N/A	2148141050	42	2042

3.6.12   User-defined data types in VB

In C, a user-defined type is defined with a simple `typedef struct {...}` *name*; statement block. A virtually identical construct exists in VB: `Type` *name* `... End Type`. Care needs to be taken to ensure that the variables within the type definition blocks in C and VB are equivalent data types and in the same order. You don't need to give the variables or the structure itself the same names in both languages – all that is passed is a pointer to a block of memory that needs to be interpreted in the same way in both places.

Important note

VB aligns the elements of structures along 4-byte boundaries but the default for VC 6.0 and VC .NET is to align to an 8-byte boundary. To avoid run-time errors or what would look like corruption of data you need to use a `#pragma pack(4)` statement where the C structure is defined (the recommended approach), or change the project settings default using a "/Zp4" compiler command line flag.

Here are some examples of good and bad user-type definitions:

Table 3.9 VB user type and C typedef examples

VB	C	Comments

`Type VB_User_Type`
`    i as Integer`
`    d as Double`
`    s as String`
`End Type`
	`#pragma pack(4)`
	
	`typedef struct`
	`{`
	`    short iVal;`
	`    double dVal;`
	`    BSTR bstr;`
	`}`
	
	`    C_user_type;`
	
	`// restore default`
	`#pragma pack()`
		GOOD.
		
		Note the different names of the structure and the variables contained within it. Note also the `#pragma pack(4)` which *is* required in order to prevent run-time errors.

`Type User_Type`
`    i as Integer`
`    d as Double`
`    s as String`
`End Type`
	`typedef struct`
	`{`
	`    short iVal;`
	`    double dVal;`
	`    BSTR bstr;`
	`}`
	`    C_user_type;`
		BAD
		
		Missing `#pragma pack(4)` will cause the double and the string to be misaligned and cause a run-time error.

`Type User_Type`
`    i as Integer`
`End Type`
	`#pragma pack(4)`
	
	`typedef struct`
	`{`
	`    int i;`
	`}`
	`    C_user_type;`
	
	`#pragma pack()`
		BAD
		
		C/C++ `int` is a 32-bit variable. VB's `Integer` is 16-bit.

Table 3.9 (*continued*)

| Type User_Type
  i as Integer
  d as Double
End Type | `#pragma pack(4)`

`typedef struct`
`{`
   `double d;`
   `short i;`
`}`
   `C_user_type;`

`#pragma pack()` | BAD

Corresponding variables must be in the same order. |

User-defined types are best passed **ByRef** (the default) arriving at C/C++ as a pointer to the structure. Here is some example code, first the VB. . .

```
 Type VB_User_Type
     i As Integer
     d As Double
     s As String
 End Type

 Declare Function C_user_type_example Lib "example.dll" _
 (Arg As VB_User_Type) As Integer

 Function VB_USER_TYPE_TEST(i As Integer, d As Double, s As String) _
 As Integer

     Dim t As VB_User_Type

     t.i = i
     t.d = d
     t.s = s

     VB_USER_TYPE_TEST = C_user_type_example(t)

 End Function
```

. . . and the corresponding C/C++ code:

```
#pragma pack(4) // required to be consistent with VB

typedef struct
{
    short iVal;
    double dVal;
    BSTR bstr;
}
    C_user_type;

#pragma pack() // restore the default

short __stdcall C_user_type_example(C_user_type *arg)
{
    short retval;
```

```
if(arg == NULL)
   return 0;

retval = arg->iVal;
retval += (short)(arg->dVal);

if(arg->bstr)
   retval += SysStringByteLen(arg->bstr);

return retval;
}
```

This example code simply returns the sum of the integer argument, the integer part of the floating-point argument and, if it has been initialised, the byte-length of the BSTR.

3.6.13   VB object data type

VB objects are passed from VB to DLLs as *dispatch* pointers for use with the OLE 2 IDispatch interface. For example, range arguments passed to VB functions declared as taking Variants are of this type. If passed directly to DLL functions also declared as taking Variants, the DLL will have to understand the IDispatch interface in order to access the cell values. This can be avoided by converting ranges to array Variants as demonstrated in the example in section 3.6.11 above, and is discussed more in section 3.7 *Excel ranges, VB arrays, SafeArrays, array Variants* on page 64.

The OLE/COM IDispatch interface enables programs (known as *OLE Automation Controllers*) to access the objects of other applications. Although this is relevant to the general subject of writing add-ins for Excel, the scope of this book does not cover these topics and all the mechanisms that these things entail. The *Microsoft Excel 97 Developer's Kit* contains a chapter on doing just this as well as there being numerous other texts, and online help on MSDN.

3.7   EXCEL RANGES, VB ARRAYS, SAFEARRAYS, ARRAY VARIANTS

The usefulness of arrays, especially in passing blocks of data between Excel, VB and C/C++ (in both directions) makes them an important topic. There are a number of different ways in which each of Excel, VB and C/C++ treat arrays. This can lead to some confusion and complexity. This section aims to reduce this by providing an overview of the different ways arrays can be created and represented, and to recommend an approach that removes much of the complexity.

Firstly, it is helpful to simply list all of the various array types:

- Excel literal worksheet array: can contain all of the basic worksheet data types. (See section 2.4 *Worksheet data types and limits* on page 10 for more information.)
- Excel range reference: an Excel object that refers to a collection of cells, whose values can intuitively be thought of as matrices or vectors, although, strictly speaking, not really an array.

- VB array: OLE SafeArray type, used to represent an array whose elements are all of the same type, determined at declaration. Supports all the basic data types and Variants.
- VB array Variant: An OLE Variant that contains an array; not to be confused with an array of Variants. The array contained is of type SafeArray. Its elements can be of any type including Variants.
- C/C++ SafeArray: An OLE SafeArray, analogous to the VB array.
- C/C++ array Variant: An OLE Variant containing an OLE SafeArray, analogous to the VB array Variant.
- C/C++ array: A flexible memory block accessible with pointers and square-bracket indexing.

The goal of this section, consistent with the focus of the book, is to demonstrate how best to move data into and out of Excel worksheets, using user-defined functions. More specifically, the goal is to get arrays of worksheet data into a C/C++ DLL via VB and to return data back to the worksheet. The key to the whole issue is the array Variant for the following reasons:

1. It is supported in both VB and C/C++.
2. In C/C++ the contained SafeArray's data are easily accessed and converted.
3. It supports arrays of all the required types, including Variants so that it can represent mixed-type arrays of worksheet data. (See sections 3.6.10 *Variant types supported by VBA* and 3.6.11 *Variant types that Excel can pass to VB functions*.)
4. VB arrays are easily converted to array Variants.
5. Excel range objects are easily converted to array Variants.
6. Excel literal arrays are passed as array Variants to VB functions declared with Variant arguments.
7. Being an OLE data type, inter-process memory management is simplified.

Reason number 5 is perhaps the most important: the Range object is fairly easily handled in VB, but if passed directly to C/C++, its properties (specifically, cell contents) can only be accessed using the IDispatch interface. VB worksheet functions declared as taking Variant arguments can be passed either literal values and arrays, or ranges when called from the worksheet.

Here is an overview of the best steps to take in setting up VB and C/C++ functions that together are capable of taking and returning an array:

1. Declare the VB function as taking a Variant argument and returning a Variant. This ensures that literal values, literal arrays, single- and multi-cell ranges are all passed to the function and that an array Variant can be returned to Excel.
2. Detect passed-in range objects using the VB IsObject() function and convert them to array Variants. (See below for details.)
3. Declare C/C++ functions as taking Variant arguments and returning a Variant.
4. Pass the VB Variant, which may be a single value or an array Variant, through to the C/C++ function.
5. Let the C/C++ function detect whether or not it has been passed an array Variant.
6. Use the OLE SafeArray functions to access or convert the array Variant data. (See below for details.)
7. Use the OLE Variant and SafeArray functions to create a new array Variant and to populate its elements.

8. Return the array Variant to VB from C/C++.
9. Return the array Variant to Excel from VB.

The following sub-sections cover in more detail the various steps involved as well as providing more background information.

3.7.1   Declaring VB arrays and passing them back to Excel

VB arrays are fairly straightforward. They can be declared *statically* with statements such as these:

```
Dim integer_array(0 To 5) As Integer ' 6 elements, zero-indexed
Dim square_array(1 To 3, 1 To 3) As Double ' 9 elts, unit-indexed
Dim variant_array(1 to 4) As Variant ' 4 Variant elts
```

The Option Base statement at the top of the code module tells VB what the lower bound on an omitted array index should be for all arrays in that module. For example. . .

```
' Specify a default array lower bound of 1
Option Base 1
```

. . . then the array square_array above can, equivalently but more readably, be declared as follows:

```
Dim square_array(3, 3) As Double ' 9 elements, unit-indexed
```

Arrays can also be declared without dimensions and then re-dimensioned dynamically later. A data type must be specified at declaration and cannot be changed. Here's an example:

```
' Don't need to specify the number of or size of the dimensions
Dim array() As Double

' Allocate space for NumRows x NumCols elements
ReDim array(NumRows, NumCols)
```

Arrays can be declared with up to 60 dimensions, but for practical Excel add-in purposes, 1 or 2 is usually all you need given the two-dimensional nature of Excel worksheets.

Arrays are most easily returned to Excel as array Variants as shown in the following examples. The conversion from VB array to array Variant is implicit in the assignment of the array to the Variant return value. The type of the array elements is inherited from the data type of the VB array. Excel understands how to copy the contents of array Variants into the calling cell(s).

Note that these VB functions would need to be entered on the worksheet as array formulae. (See section 2.9.2 *Array formulae – The Ctrl-Shift-Enter keystroke* on page 21 for details of how to enter array formulae into a worksheet.) Note also that a 1-dimension VB array is interpreted by Excel as a single column vector, and that a 2-dimension array has its indices interpreted as row then column.

Returning a rectangular array

This example returns a 3x3 array of integers, populated row-by-row with the numbers 1 to 9.

```
Function VB_ARRAY_RETURN_EXAMPLE(trigger as Variant) As Variant

'    a(num rows, num columns)
     Dim a(1 To 3, 1 To 3) As Integer

'    Row 1
     a(1, 1) = 1
     a(1, 2) = 2
     a(1, 3) = 3

'    Row 2
     a(2, 1) = 4
     a(2, 2) = 5
     a(2, 3) = 6

'    Row 3
     a(3, 1) = 7
     a(3, 2) = 8
     a(3, 3) = 9

     VB_ARRAY_RETURN_EXAMPLE = a

End Function
```

Returning a row vector

To return a row vector, the array, if static, should be declared as in this example. Note that the base in this example is zero, not 1. It makes no difference to the worksheet cells what the base of the array is, provided that there are 3 elements.

```
Function VB_ROW_VECTOR(trigger As Variant) As Variant

     Dim a(0 To 2) As Integer

     a(0) = 1
     a(1) = 2
     a(2) = 3

     VB_ROW_VECTOR = a

End Function
```

Returning a column vector

To return a column vector, the array, if static, should be declared as in this example:

```
Function VB_COLUMN_VECTOR(trigger As Variant) As Variant

'    a(num rows, num columns)
     Dim a(1 To 3, 1 To 1) As Integer
```

```
    a(1, 1) = 1
    a(2, 1) = 2
    a(3, 1) = 3

    VB_COLUMN_VECTOR = a

End Function
```

3.7.2   Passing arrays and ranges from Excel to VB to C/C++

Arrays in Excel can either be literal arrays, e.g., {1,2,3;4,5,6}, or range references. A VB function must be declared as taking a Variant argument if it is to be able to accept either form of input. (Such functions can then also accept single cell references and single literal values too.)

Literal arrays are passed as array Variants with Variant elements. The sub-types are inherited from the types of the literal array elements. (Single literal values are passed as simple Variants whose sub-type is that of the literal value.)

Range references, including single cell references, are passed as object Variants of type VT_DISPATCH; easily detected using the function IsObject(). If these are to be passed on to a C/C++ DLL function, they are best converted to array Variants. This is most easily done using the Range object's Value property. The array's elements are initialised with the data from the cells. The elements of the array are type Variant, and their sub-type is inherited from the corresponding cell. Note that the sub-type of an array element is, in general, affected by the display format of a cell – see section 3.6.4 on page 50 for details.

The following code shows an example VB interface function that either passes a single Variant or an array Variant to a DLL function, depending on whether it was passed a range reference or a literal array or value. Note that a single-cell reference is converted to a 1x1 array.

```
Declare Function C_vt_function Lib "example.dll" _
        (ByRef arg As Variant) As Variant

Function VtFunction(v As Variant) As Variant

    If IsObject(v) Then
        VtFunction = C_vt_function(v.Value)
    Else
        VtFunction = C_vt_function(v)
    End If

End Function
```

The C/C++ DLL function would be prototyped as follows:

```
VARIANT __stdcall C_vt_function(VARIANT *pv);
```

A VB interface function declared as taking a range argument, would not be able to receive literal values from the worksheet. If this were not a problem, then the VB code might look like this, given that there is no need to call IsObject().

```
Function VtFunction(r As Range) As Variant

    VtFunction = C_vt_function(r.Value)

End Function
```

The following line would have resulted in a Variant of type VT_DISPATCH being passed to the DLL function.

```
    VtFunction = C_vt_function(r)
```

3.7.3   Converting array Variants to and from C/C++ types

Array Variants are Variants that contain an array. The array itself is an OLE data type called the SafeArray, declared as SAFEARRAY in the Windows header files. An understanding of the internal workings of the SAFEARRAY is not necessary to bridge between VB and C/C++. All that's required is a knowledge of some of the functions used to create them, obtain handles to their data, release data handles, find out their size (upper and lower bounds), find out what data-type the array contains, and, finally, destroy them.

The key functions, all accessible in C/C++ via the header windows.h, are:

```
SafeArrayCreate()

SafeArrayDestroy()

SafeArrayAccessData()

SafeArrayUnaccessData()

SafeArrayGetDim()

SafeArrayGetElemsize()

SafeArrayGetLBound()

SafeArrayGetUBound()

SafeArrayGetElement()

SafeArrayPutElement()
```

To convert an array Variant, the C/C++ DLL code needs to do the following:

- Determine that the Variant is an array by testing its type for the VT_ARRAY bit.
- Determine the element type by masking the VT_ARRAY bit from its type.
- Determine the number of dimensions using the SafeArray cDims property or by using the SafeArrayGetDim() function.
- Determine the size of the array using SafeArrayGetUBound() and SafeArrayGetLBound() for each dimension.
- Convert each array element from the possible Variant types that could originate from a worksheet cell to the desired data type(s).

To create an array Variant, the C/C++ DLL code needs to do the following:

- Call `SafeArrayCreate()`, having initialised an array of `SAFEARRAYBOUND` structures (one for each dimension), to obtain a pointer to the SafeArray.
- Initialise a `VARIANT` using `VariantInit()`.
- Assign the element type bit-wise or'd with `VT_ARRAY` to the Variant type.
- Assign the SafeArray pointer to the Variant `parray` data member.
- Set the array element data (and sub-types, if Variants).

The final points in each set of steps above can be done element-by-element using `SafeArrayGetElement()` and `SafeArrayPutElement()`, or, more efficiently, by accessing the whole array in one memory block using `SafeArrayAccessData()` and `SafeArrayUnaccessData()`. When accessing the whole block in one go, it should be borne in mind that SafeArrays store their elements column-by-column, in contrast to Excel's C API array types, the `xl_array` (see page 107) and the `xltypeMulti` xloper (see page 111), where the elements are stored row-by-row.

Array Variant arguments passed by reference can be modified in place, provided that the passed-in array is first released using `SafeArrayDestroy()` before being replaced with the array to be returned.

The `cpp_xloper` class converts Variants of any type to or from an equivalent xloper type. (See sections 6.2.3 *The xloper structure* on page 111, and 6.4 *A C++ class wrapper for the xloper – cpp_xloper* on page 121. See also the Variant conversion routines in the example project source file, `xloper.cpp`.) The following example code demonstrates this:

```
VARIANT __stdcall C_vt_array_example(VARIANT *pv)
{
    static VARIANT vt;
// Convert the passed-in Variant to an xloper within a cpp_xloper
    cpp_xloper Array(pv);

// Access the elements of the xloper array using the cpp_xloper
// accessor functions...

// Convert the xloper back to a Variant and return it
    Array.AsVariant(vt);
    return vt;
}
```

Note on memory management

One advantage of passing Variant SafeArrays back to VB is that VB can safely delete the array and free its resources, and will do this automatically once it has finished with it. Equally, if a passed-in array parameter is used as the means to return an array, and an array is already assigned to it, the DLL *must* delete the array using `SafeArrayDestroy()` before creating and returning a new one. (The freeing of memory passed back to Excel directly from an XLL is a little more complex – see Chapter 7 *Memory Management* on page 161 for details.)

3.7.4   Passing VB arrays to and from C/C++

You may want to pass a VB array directly to or from a DLL function. When passing a VB array to a DLL, the C/C++ function should be declared in the VB module as shown in the following example. (The `ByRef` keyword is not required as it is the default.)

```
Declare Function C_safearray_example "example.dll" _
        (ByRef arg() As Double) As Double
```

The corresponding C/C++ function would be prototyped as follows:

```
double __stdcall C_SafeArray_Example(SAFEARRAY **pp_Arg);
```

As you can see, the parameter `ByRef arg()` is delivered as a *pointer to a pointer* to a `SAFEARRAY`. Therefore it must be de-referenced once in all calls to functions that take pointers to SAFEARRAYs as arguments, for example, the OLE SafeArray functions.

When returning VB arrays (i.e., SafeArrays) from the DLL to VB, the process is similar to that outlined in the previous sections for array Variants. SafeArray arguments passed by reference can also be modified in place, provided that the passed-in array is first released using `SafeArrayDestroy()`.

In practice, once you have code that accepts and converts array Variants, it is simpler to first convert the VB array to array Variant. This is done by simple assignment of the array name to a Variant.

3.8   COMMANDS VERSUS FUNCTIONS IN VBA

Section 2.8 *Commands versus functions in Excel* on page 19 describes the differences between commands and functions within Excel. The differences between the parallel concepts of commands and functions in VBA are summarised in the Table 3.10.

Table 3.10 Commands versus functions in VBA

	Commands	Functions
Purpose	Code containing instructions to be executed in response to a user action or system event.	Code intended to process arguments and/or return some useful information. May be worksheet functions or VB functions.

VB code (see also sections below)	Macro command:
	`Sub CommandName(...)`
	`...`
	`End Sub`
	
	Command object event:
	`Sub CmdObjectName_event(...)`
	`...`
	`End Sub`
	
	Workbook/worksheet event action:
	`Sub ObjectName_event(...)`
	`...`
	`End Sub`
		`Function FunctionName(...)As_`
		`return_type`
		
		`...`
		
		`FunctionName = rtn_val`
		
		`End Function`

(continued overleaf)

Table 3.10 (*continued*)

	Commands	Functions
VB code location	Macro command: • Worksheet code object • Workbook code object • VB module in workbook • VB module outside workbook Command object event: • Code object of command object container Worksheet object event: • Worksheet code object Workbook object event: • Workbook code object	Worksheet function: • VB module in workbook • VB module outside workbook VB project function: • Worksheet code object • Workbook code object • VB module in workbook • VB module outside workbook

3.9   CREATING VB ADD-INS (XLA FILES)

VB macros can be saved as Excel add-ins simply by saving the workbook containing the VB modules as an XLA file, using the File/Save As... menu and selecting the file type of Microsoft Excel Add-in (*.xla). When the XLA is loaded, the Add-in Manager makes the functions and commands contained in the XLA file available. There are no special things that the VB programmer has to do for the Add-in Manager to be able to recognise and load the functions. Note that the resulting code runs no faster than regular VB modules – still slower than, say, a compiled C add-in.

3.10   VB VERSUS C/C++: SOME BASIC QUESTIONS

This chapter has outlined what you need to do in order to create custom worksheet functions and commands using only VB (as well as using VB as an interface to a C/C++ DLL). You might at this point ask yourself if you need to go any further in the direction of a full-blown C/C++ add-in. Breaking this down, the main questions to ask yourself before making this decision are:

1. Do I really need to write my own functions or are there Excel functions that, either on their own or in simple combination, will do what I need?
2. What Excel functionality/objects do I need to access: can I do this using the C API, or do I need to use VBA or the OLE interface?
3. Is execution speed important?
4. What kind of calculations or operations will my function(s) consist of and what kind of performance advantage can I expect?
5. Is development time important to me and what language skills do I have or have access to?
6. Is there existing source code that I want to reuse and how easily can it be ported to any of VB, C or C++?
7. Does my algorithm involve complex dynamic memory management or extensive use of pointers?

8. Who will need to be able to access or modify the resulting code?
9. Is the Paste Function (Function Wizard) important for the functions I want to create?
10. Do I need to write worksheet functions that might need a long time to execute, and so need to be done on a background thread by a remote application?

With regard to the second point, it should be noted that C API can only handle byte-counted strings with a maximum length of 255 characters. At one time, strings within Excel were limited to this length, but not any more. If you need to be able to process longer strings you will not be able to use the C API, but you will still be able to use your C/C++ routines accessing them via VB, as VB supports a BSTR string variable capable of supporting much longer strings.

This book cannot answer these questions for you, however, question 4 is addressed in section 9.2 *Relative performance of VB, C/C++: Tests and results* on page 289.

EXCEL

WIN32 DLL

cannot
call

back via

DLL

C API

loaded ?
registered ?
installed ?
activated ?
checked ?
linked ?

Creating a 32-bit Windows (Win32) DLL Using Visual C++ 6.0 or Visual Studio .NET

This chapter covers the steps involved in creating a stand-alone Win32 Dynamic-Link Library using Microsoft Visual C++. It explains, through the creation of an example project, how to create a DLL containing functions that can be accessed by VB without the need for the Excel C API library and header files. (Without these things, however, the DLL cannot call back into Excel via the C API.) Nevertheless, it is possible to create very powerful C/C++ add-ins with just these tools.

A full description of DLLs and all the associated Windows terminology is beyond the scope of this book. Instead, this section sets out all the things that someone who knows nothing about DLLs needs to know to create add-ins for Excel; starting with the basics.

4.1 WINDOWS LIBRARY BASICS

A library is a body of (compiled) code which is not in itself an executable application but provides some functionality and data to something that is. Libraries come in two flavours: static and dynamic-link. Static libraries (such as the C run-time library) are intended to be linked to an application when it is built, to become part of the resulting executable file. Such an application can be supplied to a user as just the executable file only. A dynamic-link library is loaded by the application when the application needs it, usually when the application starts up. An application that depends on functionality or data in a DLL must be shipped to a user as the executable file plus the DLL file for it to work. One DLL can load and dynamically link to another DLL.

The main advantage of a DLL is that applications that use it only need to have one copy of it somewhere on disk, and have much smaller executable files as a result. A developer can also update a DLL, perhaps fixing a bug or making it more efficient, without the need to update all the dependent applications, provided that the interface doesn't change.

4.2 DLL BASICS

The use of DLLs breaks into two fairly straightforward tasks:

- How to write a DLL that exports functions.
- How to access functions within a DLL.

DLLs contain executable code but are not executable files. They need to be linked to (or loaded by) an application before any of their code can be run. In the case of Excel, that linking is taken care of by Excel via the Add-in Manager or by VBA, depending on how you access the DLL's functions. (Chapter 5 *Turning DLLs into XLLs: The Add-in Manager interface*, on page 95, provides a full explanation of what the Add-In Manager does.)

If your DLL needs to access the C API it will either need to be linked statically at compile-time with Excel's 32-bit library, `xlcall32.lib`, or link dynamically with the DLL version, `xlcall.dll`, at run-time. The static library is downloadable from Microsoft in an example framework project. (See section 1.2 *What tools and resources are required to write add-ins* on page 2.) The dynamic-link version is supplied as part of a standard 32-bit Excel installation.

4.3   DLL MEMORY AND MULTIPLE DLL INSTANCES

When an application runs, Win32 assigns it a 32-bit linear address space known as its *process*. Applications cannot directly access memory outside their own process. A DLL when loaded must have its code and data assigned to some memory somewhere in the global heap (the operating system's available memory). When an application loads a DLL, the DLL's code is loaded into the global heap, so that it can be run, and space is allocated in the global heap for its data structures. Win32 then uses memory mapping to make these areas of memory appear as if they are in the application's process so that the application can access them.

If a second application subsequently loads the DLL, Win 32 doesn't bother to make another copy of the DLL code: it doesn't need to, as neither application can make changes to it. Both just need to read the instructions contained. Win32 simply maps the DLL code memory to both applications' processes. It does, however, allocate a second space for a private copy of the DLL's data structures and maps this copy to the second process only. This ensures that neither application can interfere with the DLL data of the other. (16-bit Windows' DLLs used a shared memory space making life very interesting indeed, but the world has moved on since then.)

What this means in practice is that DLL writers don't need to worry about static and global variables and data structures being accessed by more than one user of their DLL. Every instance of every application gets its own copy. Each copy of the DLL data is referred to as an instance of the DLL.

4.4   MULTI-THREADING

DLL writers *do* need to worry about the same running instance of an application calling their DLL many times from different threads. Take the following piece of C code for example:

```
int __stdcall get_num_calls(void)
{
    static int num_calls = 0;

    return ++num_calls;
}
```

The function returns an integer telling the caller how many times it has been called. The declaration of the automatic variable num_calls as static, ensures that the value persists from one call to the next. It also ensures that the memory for the variable is placed in the application's copy of the DLL's data memory. This means that the memory is private to the application so the function will only return the number of times it has been called by this application.

The problems arise when it may be possible for the application to call this function twice from different threads at the *same* time. The function both reads and modifies the value of the memory used for num_calls, so what if one thread is trying to write while the other is trying to read? The answer is that it's unpredictable. In practice, for a simple integer, this is not a problem. For larger data structures it could be a serious problem. The best way to avoid this unpredictability is the use of *critical sections*.

Windows provides a function GetCurrentThreadId() which returns the current thread's unique system-wide ID. This provides the developer with another way of making their code thread-safe, or altering its behaviour depending on which thread is currently executing.

4.5 COMPILED FUNCTION NAMES

4.5.1 Name decoration

When compilers compile source code they will, in general, change the names of the functions from their appearance in the source code. This usually means adding things to the beginning and/or end of the name and, in the case of Pascal compilers, changing the name to all uppercase. This is known as *name decoration* and it is important to understand something about the way C and C++ compilers do this so that the functions we want to be accessible in our DLL can be published in a way the application expects.[1]

The way the name is decorated depends on the language and how the compiler is instructed to make the function available, in other words the *calling convention*. (See below for more details on and comparisons of calling conventions.) For 32-bit Windows API function calls the convention for the decoration of C-compiled functions follows this standard convention:

A function called function_name becomes _function_name@n where n is the number of bytes taken up by all the arguments expressed as a decimal, with the bytes for each argument rounded up to the nearest multiple of four in Win32.

Note that the decorated name is independent of the return type. Note also that all pointers are 4 bytes wide in Win32, regardless of what they point to.

Expressed slightly differently, the C name decoration for Win API calls is:

- Prefix   _
- Suffix   @n where n = bytes stack space for arguments
- Case change   None

---

[1] The complexity of name decoration is avoided with the use of DEF files and C++ source code modules, see later in this chapter.

Table 4.1 gives some examples:

Table 4.1 Name decoration examples for C-compiled exports

C source code function definition	Decorated function name
void example1(char arg1)	_example1@4
void example2(short arg1)	_example2@4
void example3(long arg1)	_example3@4
void example4(float arg1)	_example4@4
void example5(double arg1)	_example5@8
void example6(void *arg1)	_example6@4
void example7(short arg1, double arg2)	_example7@12
void example8(short arg1, char arg2)	_example8@8

Win32 C++ compilers use a very different name-decoration scheme which is not described as, among other reasons, it's complicated. It can be avoided by making the compiler use the standard C convention using the `extern "C"` declaration, or by the use of DEF files. (See below for details of these last two approaches.)

4.5.2 The `extern "C"` declaration

The inclusion of the `extern "C"` declaration in the definition of a function in a C++ source file instructs the compiler to externalise the function name as if it were a C function. In other words, it gives it the standard C name decoration. An example declaration would be:

```
extern "C" double c_name_function(double arg)
{

}
```

An important point to note is that such a function must also be given an `extern "C"` declaration in all occurrences of a prototype, for example, in a header file. A number of function prototypes, and the functions and the code they contain, can all be enclosed in a single `extern "C"` statement block for convenience. For example, a header file might contain:

```
extern "C"
{
double c_name_function(double arg);
double another_c_name_function(double arg);
}

double cplusplus_name_function(double arg);
```

4.6   FUNCTION CALLING CONVENTIONS:
__cdecl, __stdcall, __fastcall

The Microsoft-specific keyword modifiers, __cdecl, __stdcall and __fastcall, are used in the declaration and prototyping of functions in C and C++. These modifiers tell the compiler how to retrieve arguments from the stack, how to return values and what cleaning up to do afterwards. The modifier should always come immediately before the function name itself and should appear in all function prototypes as well as the definition.

Win32 API applications and DLLs, as well as Visual Basic, all use the __stdcall calling convention whereas the ANSI standard for C/C++ is __cdecl. By default, VC compiles functions as __cdecl. This default can be overridden with the compiler option Gz. However, it's better to leave the default compiler settings alone and make any changes explicit in the code. Otherwise, you are setting a trap for you or someone else in the future, or creating the need for big warning comments in the code.

The modifier __fastcall enables the developer to request that the compiler use a faster way of communicating some or all of the arguments and it is included only for completeness. For example, the function declaration

```
void __fastcall fast_function(int i, int j)
```

would tell the compiler to pass the arguments via internal registers, if possible, rather than via the stack.

Table 4.2 summarises the differences between the three calling conventions. (It's really not necessary to remember or understand all of this to be able to write add-ins).

Table 4.2 Summary of calling conventions and name decoration

	__cdecl	__stdcall	__fastcall
Argument passing order	Right-to-left on the stack.	Right-to-left on the stack.	The first two DWORD (i.e. 4-byte) or smaller arguments are passed in registers ECX and EDX. All others are passed right-to-left on the stack.
Argument passing convention	By value except where a pointer or reference is used.	By value except where a pointer or reference is used.	By value except where a pointer or reference is used.
Variable argument lists	Supported	Not supported	Not supported
Responsibility for cleaning up the stack	Caller pops the passed arguments from the stack.	Called function pops its arguments from the stack.	Called function pops its arguments from the stack.
Name-decoration convention	**C functions:** **C++ fns declared as** extern "C": Prefix: _	**C functions:** **C++ fns declared as** extern "C": Prefix: _	Prefix: @ Suffix: @n n = bytes stack space for arguments

(continued overleaf)

Table 4.2 (*continued*)

	__cdecl	__stdcall	__fastcall
	Suffix: none Case change: none **C++ functions:** A proprietary name decoration scheme is used for Win32.	Suffix: @*n* *n* = bytes stack space for arguments Case change: none **C++ functions:** A proprietary name decoration scheme is used for Win32.	Case change: none
Compiler setting to make this the default:	/Gz	/Gd or omitted	/Gr

Note: The VB argument passing convention is to pass arguments *by reference* unless explicitly passed by value using the ByVal keyword. Calling C/C++ functions from VB that take pointers or references is achieved by default or with the explicit use of the ByRef keyword.

Note: The Windows header file <Windef.h> contains the following definitions which, some would say, you should use in order to make the code platform-independent. However, this book chooses not to use them so that code examples are more explicit.

```
#define WINAPI     __stdcall
#define WINAPIV    __cdecl
```

4.7 EXPORTING DLL FUNCTION NAMES

A DLL may contain many functions not all of which the developer wishes to be accessible to an application. The first thing to consider is how should functions be declared so that they can be called by a Windows application. The second thing to consider is how then to make those functions, and only those, visible to an application that loads the DLL.

On the first point, the declaration has to be consistent with the Windows API calling conventions, i.e., functions must be declared as __stdcall rather than __cdecl. For example, double __stdcall get_system_time_C(long trigger) can be used by the DLL's host application but long current_system_time(void) cannot. (Both these functions appear in the example DLL later in this chapter.)

On the second point, the DLL project must be built in such a way that the __stdcall functions you wish to export are listed in the DLL by the linker. There are two ways to do this:

1. list the function name in a definition (*.DEF) file, *OR*
2. use the __declspec(dllexport) keyword in the declaration.

In practice, the only reason to declare functions with __stdcall in your DLL is precisely because you intend to make them visible externally to a Windows application such as Excel.

4.7.1   Definition (*.DEF) files

A definition file is a plain text file containing a number of keyword statements followed by one or more pieces of information used by the linker during the creation of the DLL. The only keyword that needs to be covered here is EXPORTS. This precedes a list of the functions to be exported to the application. The general syntax of lines that follow an EXPORTS statement is:

```
entryname[=internalname] [@ordinal[NONAME]] [DATA] [PRIVATE]
```

Example 1

Consider the following function declaration in a C++ source file:

```
extern "C" double __stdcall get_system_time_C(long trigger);
```

Given the decoration of the function name, this would be represented in the definition file as follows:

```
EXPORTS
; (Comment) This function takes a single 'long' argument
   get_system_time_C=_get_system_time_C@4
```

In the above example, get_system_time_C is the entryname: the name you want the application to know the function by. In this example, the same undecorated name has been chosen as in the source code, but it could have been something completely different. The internalname is the decorated name. As the function is declared as both extern "C" and __stdcall it has been decorated as set out in the table in section 4.6 on page 79.

The keywords PRIVATE, DATA and @ordinal[NONAME] are not discussed as they are not critical to what we are trying to do here.

Example 2

We could also have declared the C++ function (in the C++ source code file) without the extern "C" like this:

```
double __stdcall get_system_time_C(long trigger);
```

The corresponding entry in the .DEF file would be:

```
EXPORTS
   get_system_time_C
```

In this case the linker does all the hard work. We have no extern "C" statement and no name decoration reflected in the DEF file. The linker makes sure on our behalf that the C++ decorated name is accessible using just the undecorated name.

Example 2 is the best way to make functions available, as it's the simplest. However, if you find that Excel cannot find your functions, you can use extern "C" and the decorated name in the DEF file as in Example 1.

The only other thing worth pointing out here is the very useful comment marker for .DEF files, a semi-colon, after which all characters up to the end of the line are ignored.

For example, the above DEF file could look like this:

```
EXPORTS
; My comment about the exported function can go here
; after a semi-colon...
    get_system_time_C ; ...plus more comments here
```

4.7.2   The __declspec(dllexport) keyword

The __declspec(dllexport) keyword can be used in the declaration of the function as follows:

```
__declspec(dllexport) double __stdcall get_system_time_C(long trigger)
{
}
```

The __declspec(dllexport) keyword must be placed at the extreme left of the declaration. Functions declared in this way do not need to be listed in a DEF file. However, if you want to avoid the function being made available with the C++ name decoration you would need to declare the function as follows:

```
extern "C" __declspec(dllexport) double __stdcall
get_system_time_C(long trigger)
{
}
```

The problem now is that the linker will make the function available as _get_system _time_C@4 and, if we are telling the application to look for a function called get_ system_time_C, it will not be able to find it. The two solutions are, therefore, to tell the application to look for the decorated name or to use a DEF file containing the decorated name.

NOTE: USING A DEF FILE MAKES THE SOURCE CODE CLEANER AND GIVES MORE CONTROL OVER THE NAME THAT'S ULTIMATELY PUBLISHED.

4.8   WHAT YOU NEED TO START DEVELOPING ADD-INS IN C/C++

This chapter shows the use of Microsoft Visual C++ 6.0 Standard Edition and Visual Studio .NET (in fact, Visual C++ .NET, which is a subset of VS .NET). Menu options and displays may vary from version to version, but for something as simple as the creation of DLLs, the steps are almost identical. This is all that's needed to create a DLL whose exported functions can be accessed via VB.

However, to create a DLL that can access Excel's functionality or whose functions you want to access directly from an Excel worksheet, you will need Excel's C API library and header file, or COM (see section 9.5). (See also section 4.12 below, and Chapter 5 *Turning DLLs into XLLs: The Add-in Manager interface* on page 94.)

4.9   CREATING A DLL USING VISUAL C++ 6.0

This section refers to Visual C++ 6.0 as VC. Visual Studio 6.0 has the same menus and dialogs. Section 4.10 on page 87 covers the same steps as this section, but for the Visual C++ .NET 2003 and Visual Studio .NET 2003 IDEs, which this book refers to as VC.NET to make the distinction between the two.

4.9.1   Creating the empty DLL project

This example goes step-by-step through the creation of a DLL called `GetTime.dll` which is referred to in the following chapter and expanded later on. It will export one function that, when called, will return the date and time in an Excel-compatible form to the nearest second.

The steps are:

1. Open the Visual C++ IDE.
2. Select File/New...
3. On the New dialog that appears select the Projects tab.
4. Select Win32 Dynamic-Link Library, enter a name for the project in the Project name: text box and select a location for the project as shown and press OK.

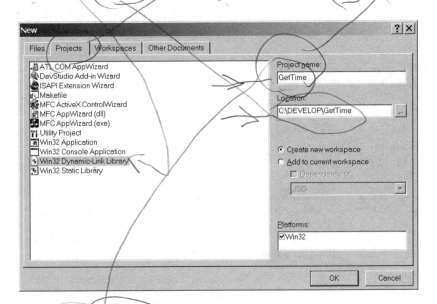

5. Select Create an empty DLL project on the following dialog and press Finish.
6. Select OK to clear the message dialog that tells you that the project will be created with no files.
7. Make sure the Workspace window is visible. (Select View/Workspace if it isn't.)
8. Expand the GetTime files folder.
9. Right-click on the Source Files sub-folder and select Add Files to Folder...
10. In the File name: text box type *GetTime.cpp*. [The Files of type: text box should now contain C++ Files (...).]

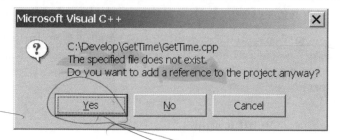

11. The following dialog will appear. Select Yes.
12. Expand the Source Files folder in the Workspace window and you will now see the new file listed.
13. Double-click on the icon immediately to the left of the file name *GetTime.cpp*. You will see the following dialog:

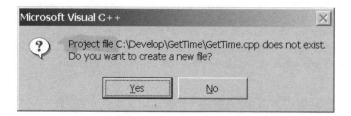

14. Select Yes.
15. Repeat steps 10 to 14 to create and add to Source Files a file called *GetTime.def*.

The project and the required files have now been created!

It has no code, of course, so all it's doing at this point is taking up disk space, but now you're ready to start writing code.

If you explore the directory in which you created the project you will see the following files listed:

`GetTime.cpp`	A C++ source file. This will contain our C or C++ source code. (Even if you only intend to write in C, using a *.cpp* file extension allows you to use some of the simple C++ extensions such as the `bool` data type.)
`GetTime.def`	A definition file. This text file will contain a reference to the function(s) we wish to make accessible to users of the DLL (Excel and VBA in this case).

You will also see a number of project files of the form `GetTime.*`.

4.9.2 Adding code to the project

To add code to a file simply double-click on the file name and VC will open the text file in the right hand pane. We will add some simple code that returns the system time, as reported by the C run-time functions, as a fraction of the day, and export this function via a DLL so that it can be called from VB. Of course, VB and Excel both have their own functions for doing this but there are two reasons for starting with this particular example: firstly, it introduces the idea of having to understand Excel's time (and date) representations, should you want to pass these between your DLL and Excel. Secondly, we want to be able to do some relative-performance tests, and this is the first step to a high-accuracy timing function.

For this example, add the following code to the file GetTime.cpp:

```
#include <windows.h>
#include <time.h>

#define SECS_PER_DAY (24 * 60 * 60)

//==========================================================
// Returns the time of day rounded down to the nearest second as
// number of seconds since the start of day.
//==========================================================
long current_system_time(void)
{
    time_t time_t_T;
    struct tm tm_T;

    time(&time_t_T);
    tm_T = *localtime(&time_t_T);

    return tm_T.tm_sec + 60 * (tm_T.tm_min + 24 * tm_T.tm_hour);
}
//==========================================================
// Returns the time of day rounded down to the nearest second as a
// fraction of 1 day, i.e. compatible with Excel time formatting.
//
// Wraps the function long current_system_time(void) providing a
// trigger for Excel using the standard calling convention for
// Win32 DLLs.
//==========================================================
double __stdcall get_system_time_C(long trigger)
{
    return current_system_time() / (double)SECS_PER_DAY;
}
```

The function long current_system_time(void) gets the system time as a time_t, converts it to a struct tm and then extracts the hour, minute and second. It then converts these to the number of seconds since the beginning of the day. This function is for internal use only within the DLL and is, therefore, not declared as __stdcall.

The function double __stdcall get_system_time_C(long trigger) takes the return value from long current_system_time(void) and returns this divided by the number of seconds in a day as a double. There are three things to note about this function:

1. The declaration includes the __stdcall calling convention. This function is going to be exported so we need to overwrite the default __cdecl so that it will work with the Windows API.
2. There is a trigger argument enabling us to link the calling of this function to the change in the value of a cell in an Excel spreadsheet. (See section 2.11.2 *Triggering functions to be called by Excel – The Trigger Argument* on page 26.)

3. The converted return value is now consistent with Excel's numeric time value storage.

Now we need to tell the linker to make our function visible to users of the DLL. To do this we simply need to add the following to the file GetTime.def:

```
EXPORTS
    get_system_time_C
```

That's it.

4.9.3 Compiling and debugging the DLL

In the set up of the DLL project, the IDE will have created two configurations: debug and release. By default, the debug configuration will be the active one. When you compile this project, VC will create output files in a debug sub-folder of the project folder called, not surprisingly, Debug. Changing the active configuration to *release* causes build output files to be written to the Release sub-folder. As the name suggests the debug configuration enables code execution to be halted at breakpoints, the contents of variables to be inspected, the step-by-step execution of code, etc.

Without getting into the details of the VC user interface, the Build menu contains the commands for compiling and linking the DLL and changing the active configuration. The Project menu provides access to a number of project related dialogs and commands. The only one that's important to mention here is Project/Settings, which displays the following dialog (when the Debug tab is selected, as in this case):

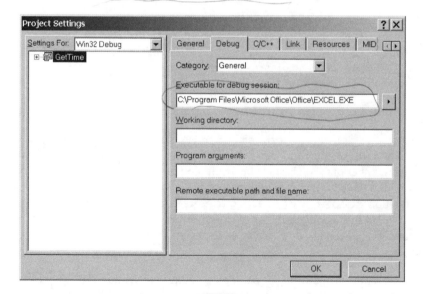

As you can see, these are the settings for the debug configuration. The full path and filename for Excel has been entered as the debug executable. Now, if you select Build/Start Debug.../Go, or press {F5}, VC will run Excel. If your project needs rebuilding because of changes you've made to source code, VC will ask you if you want to rebuild first.

So far all we've done is created a DLL project, written and exported a function and set up the debugger to run Excel. Now we need to create something that accesses the function. Later chapters describe how to use Excel's Add-in Manager and Paste Function wizard, but for now we'll just create a simple spreadsheet which calls our function from a VB module.

To follow the steps in the next section, you need to run Excel from VC by debugging the DLL. (Select Build/Start Debug. . ./Go or press {F5}.) This enables you to experiment by setting breakpoints in the DLL code.

You can also specify a spreadsheet that Excel is to load whenever you start a debug session. This example shows the name and location of a test spreadsheet called Get-TimeTest.xls entered into the Program arguments field. (Excel interprets a command line argument as an auto-load spreadsheet.)

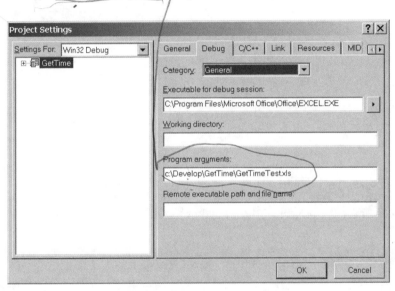

Next time Build/Start Debug. . ./Go is selected, or {F5} is pressed, VC will run Excel and load this test spreadsheet automatically. This is a great time-saver and helps anyone who might take over this project to see how the DLL was supposed to work.

4.10   CREATING A DLL USING VISUAL C++ .NET 2003

This section refers to Visual C++ .NET 2003 as VC.NET. Visual Studio .NET 2003 has the same menus and dialogs. Section 4.9 on page 83 covers the same steps as this section, but for the Visual C++ 6.0 and Visual Studio C++ 6.0 IDEs, which this section refers to as VC to make the distinction between the two.

4.10.1   Creating the empty DLL project

This example goes step-by-step through the creation of a DLL called NETGetTime.dll which is referred to in the following chapter and expanded later on. It will export one function that, when called, will return the date and time in an Excel-compatible form to the nearest second.

1. Open the Visual C++ .NET IDE which should appear something like this:

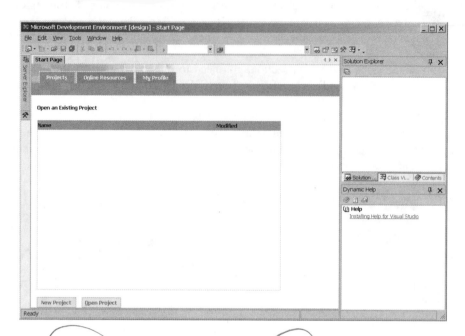

2. On the New Project dialog that appears, select the Win32 folder.
3. Select Win32 Project and enter a name for the project in the Name: text box and select a location for the project as shown and press OK.

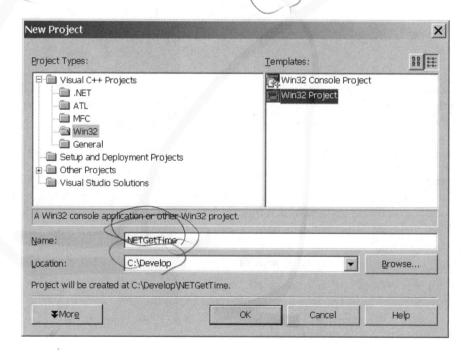

4. The following dialog will then appear:

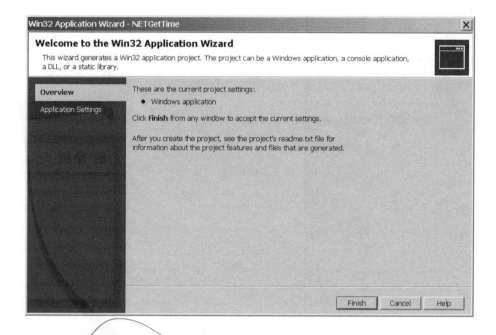

5. Select the Application Settings tab, after which the following dialog should appear:

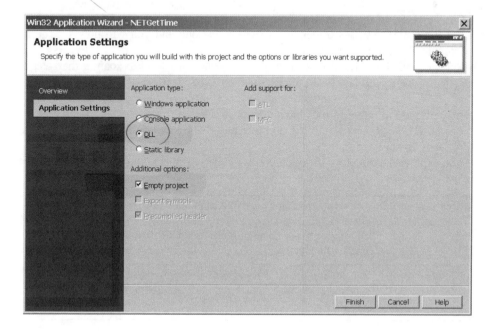

6. Select the <u>D</u>LL radio button, check the Empty Project checkbox and press Finish. You should now see something like this:

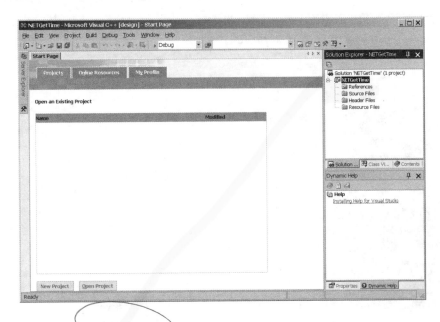

7. Make sure the Solution Explorer is visible. (Select <u>V</u>iew/Solution Explorer if it isn't.)
8. Expand the NETGetTime folder. *Name of Project*
9. Right-click on the Source Files sub-folder and select Add/Add new item...
10. In the Add New Item dialog, select the C++ File (.cpp) in the <u>T</u>emplates pane, type GetTime. in to the <u>N</u>ame text box.
11. Expand the Source Files folder in the Solution Explorer and you will now see the new (completely empty) file listed.
12. Repeat steps 9 to 11, selecting instead the Module Definition File (.def) in the <u>T</u>emplates pane, to create and add to Source Files a file called *GetTime.def*.

The project and the required files have now been created!

It has no code of course so all it's doing at this point is taking up disk space, but now you're ready to start writing code.

If you explore the directory in which you created the project, you will see the following files listed:

GetTime.cpp	A C++ source file. This will contain our C or C++ source code. (Even if you only intend to write in C, using a .*cpp* file extension allows you to use some of the simple C++ extensions such as the bool data type.)
GetTime.def	A definition file. This text file will contain a reference to the function(s) we wish to make accessible to users of the DLL (Excel and VBA in this case).

You will also see a number of project files of the form NETGetTime.*.

4.10.2   Adding code to the project

The process of adding code is essentially the same in VC as in VC.NET. Section 4.9.2 on page 84 goes through this for VC, adding two functions to GetTime.cpp and an exported function name to the DEF file. These functions are used in later parts of this book to run relative performance tests. If you are following these steps with VC.NET, you should go to section 4.9.2 and then come back to the following section to see how to compile and debug.

4.10.3   Compiling and debugging the DLL

In the set up of the DLL project, the IDE will have created two configurations: debug and release. By default, the debug configuration will be the active one. When you compile this project, VC.NET will create output files in a debug sub-folder of the project folder called, not surprisingly, Debug. Changing the active configuration to *release* causes build output files to be written to the Release sub-folder. As the name suggests, the debug configuration enables code execution to be halted at breakpoints, the contents of variables to be inspected and the step-by-step execution of code, etc.

Without getting into the details of the user interface, the Build menu contains the commands for compiling and linking the DLL and changing the active configuration. The Project menu provides access to a number of project related dialogs and commands. The only one worth mentioning here is the Project/NETGetTime Properties..., which displays the following dialog (with the Debug settings selected in this case):

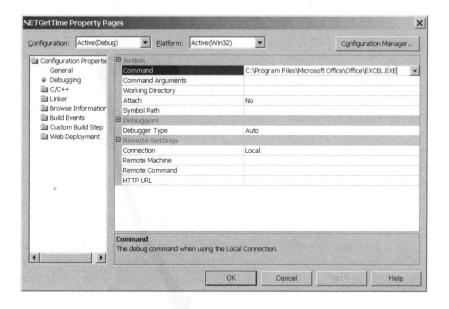

As you can see, these are the settings for the debug configuration. The full path and filename for Excel has been entered as the debug executable. Now, if you select Debug/Start, or press {F5}, VC.NET will run Excel. If your project needs rebuilding because of changes you've made to source code, VC.NET will ask you if you want to rebuild first.

So far all we've done is created a DLL project, written and exported a function and set up the debugger to run Excel. Now we need to create something that accesses the function. Later chapters describe how to use Excel's add-in manager and Paste Function wizard, but for now we'll just create a simple spreadsheet which calls our function from a VB module.

To follow the steps in the next section, you need to run Excel from VC.NET by debugging the DLL. (Select Build/Start Debug.../Go or press {F5}.) This enables you to experiment by setting breakpoints in the DLL code.

You can also specify a spreadsheet that Excel is to load whenever you start a debug session. This example shows the name and location of a test spreadsheet called Get-TimeTest.xls entered into the Command Arguments field. (Excel interprets a command line argument as an autoload spreadsheet.)

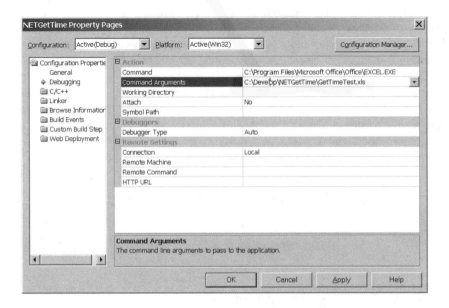

Next time Debug/Start is selected, or {F5} is pressed, VC.NET will run Excel and load this test spreadsheet automatically. This is a great time-saver and helps anyone who might take over this project to see how the DLL was supposed to work.

4.11   ACCESSING DLL FUNCTIONS FROM VB

VB provides a way of making DLL exports available in a VB module using the Declare statement. (See section 3.6 *Using VBA as an interface to external DLL add-ins* on page 48 for a detailed description.) In the case of the example in our add-in the declaration in our VB module would be:

```
Declare Function get_system_time_C Lib "GetTime.dll" _
    (ByVal trigger As Long) As Double
```

(Note the use of the line continuation character '_'.)

As described in Chapter 3 *Using VBA* on page 41, if you open a new VB module in `GetTimeTest.xls` and add the following code to it, you will have added two user-defined functions to Excel, Get_C_System_Time() and Get_VB_Time().

```
Declare Function get_system_time_C Lib "GetTime.dll" _
    (ByVal trigger As Long) As Double

Function Get_C_System_Time(trigger As Double) As Double

    Get_C_System_Time = get_system_time_C(0)

End Function

Function Get_VB_Time(trigger As Double) As Double

    Get_VB_Time = Now

End Function
```

(Note that the full path of the DLL is, in general, required in the VB `Declare` statements.)
Back in Excel, the following simple spreadsheet has been created:

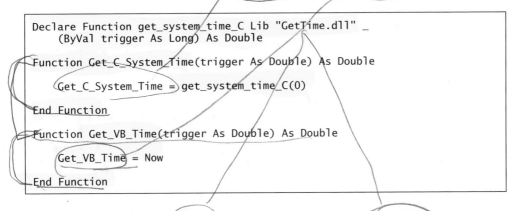

Cell	Formula
B4	=NOW()
B5	=Get_VB_Time(B4)
B6	=Get_C_System_Time(B4)

Here, cell B4 will recalculate whenever you force a recalculation by pressing {F9}, or when Excel would normally recalculate, say, if some other cell's value changes. (The

Now() function is *volatile* and is re-evaluated whenever Excel recalculates despite not depending on anything on the sheet.) The fact that B4 is a precedent for B5 and B6 triggers Excel to then re-evaluate these cells too. (See section 2.11.2 *Triggering functions to be called by Excel – The Trigger Argument* on page 26.)

Pressing {F9} will therefore force all three cells to recalculate and you will see that the C run-time functions and the VB Now function are in synch. You should also see that the NOW() function is also in synch but goes one better by showing 100 ths of a second increments. (This is discussed more in Chapter 9 where the relative execution speeds of VB and C/C++ are timed and compared.)

4.12   ACCESSING DLL FUNCTIONS FROM EXCEL

In order to access DLL functions directly from Excel, as either worksheet functions or commands, without the need for a VBA wrapper to the functions, you need to provide an interface – a set of functions – that Excel looks for when using the Add-in Manager to load the DLL. This is covered in detail in Chapter 5 *Turning DLLs into XLLs: The Add-in Manager Interface* as well as subsequent sections. The interface functions are intended to be used to provide Excel with information it needs about the DLL functions you are exporting so that it can integrate them – a process know as registration, covered in detail in section 8.5 *Registering and un-registering DLL (XLL) functions* on page 182.

Turning DLLs into XLLs: The Add-in Manager Interface

5.1 ADDING THE EXCEL LIBRARY AND HEADER FILES TO A DLL PROJECT

An XLL is simply a DLL that supports an interface through which Excel and the DLL can communicate effectively and safely. This communication is 2-way: the DLL must export a number of functions for Excel to call; the DLL needs access to functions through which it can call Excel. For the latter, the DLL requires access to an Excel library, xlcall32.lib (or its DLL equivalent), and a header file that defines the data structures and constant definitions and enumerations used by Excel. These two files can be sourced as described in section 1.2 *What tools and resources are required to write add-ins* on page 2. The DLL version of the library is installed automatically with every 32-bit Excel version.

The precise steps for adding these files to your project can vary from one compiler and IDE to another, especially when adding a static library to your build. In both VC6 and VC.NET the static library can be explicitly added via the project options settings. In VC6 it can, alternatively, be added to the build more directly as a source file.

Where dynamically loading xlcall32.dll, it is not necessary to include a reference to the file in the project settings – this is done in code using the Windows API LoadLibrary() or GetModuleHandle() functions. In fact, when doing this, any reference to the static library should be removed from the build.

Another approach is to create a static library from xlcall32.dll and a DEF file consistent with this.[1] An in-depth discussion of this is beyond the scope of this book, although an Internet search will yield much relevant material. Once the DEF file has been obtained or created, the static library can be made using the LIB.EXE utility supplied with Visual Studio as in the following command line example:

```
C:\>lib /def:xlcall32.def
```

A DEF file that contains the following lines will work subject to LIB.EXE being able to find a path to xlcall32.dll.

```
LIBRARY xlcall32.dll
EXPORTS
Excel4 @1 NONAME
Excel4v @2 NONAME
LPenHelper @3 NONAME
XLCallVer @4 NONAME
```

5.2 WHAT DOES THE ADD-IN MANAGER DO?

5.2.1 Loading and unloading installed add-ins

The Add-in Manager is responsible for loading, unloading and remembering which add-ins this installation of Excel has available to it. When an XLL (see below for more

---

[1] An example of a command line utility that creates a DEF file from a static library file is MakeDef.exe by George Hazan, freely available at time of writing via www.codeguru.com.

explanation of the term XLL) is loaded, either through the File/Open... command menu or via Tools/Add-ins... , the Add-in Manager adds it to its list of known add-ins.

Warning: In some versions of Excel, the Add-in Manager will also offer to make a copy of the XLL in a dedicated add-in directory. This is not necessary. In some versions, a bug prevents the updating of the XLL without physically finding and deleting this copy, so you should, in general, not let Excel do this.

5.2.2   Active and inactive add-ins

When an add-in is loaded for the first time it is *active,* in the sense that all the exposed functions, once registered properly, are available to the worksheet. The Add-in Manager allows the user to *deactivate* an add-in without unloading it by un-checking the checkbox by the add-in name, making its functions unavailable. (This is a useful feature when you have add-ins with conflicting function names, perhaps different versions of the same add-in.)

5.2.3   Deleted add-ins and loading of inactivate add-ins

On termination of an Excel session, the Add-in Manager makes a record of the all active add-ins in the registry so that when Excel subsequently loads, it knows where to find them. If a remembered DLL has been deleted from the disk, Excel will mark it as inactive and will not complain until the user attempts to activate it in the Add-in Manager dialog. At this point Excel will offer to delete it from its list.

If the Excel session in which the add-in is first loaded is terminated with the add-in inactive, Excel will not record the fact that the add-in was ever loaded and, in the next session, the add-in will need to be loaded from scratch to be accessible.

If the Excel session was terminated with the add-in active then a record is made in the registry. Even if subsequent sessions are terminated with the add-in inactive Excel will remember the add-in and its inactive state at the next session. The inactive add-in is still loaded into memory at start up of such a subsequent session. Excel will even interrogate it for information under certain circumstances, but will not give the DLL the opportunity to register its functions.

5.3   CREATING AN XLL: THE xlAuto INTERFACE FUNCTIONS

An XLL is a type of DLL that can be loaded into Excel either via the File/Open... command[2] menu or via Tools/Add-ins... or a command or macro that does the same thing. To be an XLL, that is to be able to take advantage of Excel's add-in management functionality, the DLL must contain and export a number of functions that Excel looks for. Through these the DLL can add its functionality to Excel's. This includes enabling Excel and the user to find functions via the Paste Function wizard, with its very useful argument-specific help text. (See section 2.14 *Paste Function dialog.*)

These functions, when called by Excel, give the add-in a chance to do things like allocate and initialise memory and data structures and *register* functions (i.e., tell Excel all about them), as well as the reverse of all these things at the appropriate time. They can also display messages to the user providing version or copyright information, for

---

[2] Excel 2000 and earlier versions only.

example. The DLL also needs to provide a function that enables the DLL and Excel to cooperate to manage memory, i.e., to clean up memory dynamically allocated in the DLL for data returned to Excel.

The functions that do all these things are:

- `xlAutoOpen`
- `xlAutoClose`
- `xlAutoAdd`
- `xlAutoRemove`
- `xlAddInManagerInfo`
- `xlAutoRegister`
- `xlAutoFree`

The following sections describe these functions, which can be omitted in most cases. (<u>Note:</u> These functions need to be exported, say, by inclusion in the DLL's .DEF file, in order to be accessible by Excel.)

5.4   WHEN AND IN WHAT ORDER DOES EXCEL CALL THE XLL INTERFACE FUNCTIONS?

Table 5.1 XLL interface function calling

Action	Functions called
User invokes Add-in Manager dialog for the first time in this Excel session. The add-in was loaded in previous session.	xlAddInManagerInfo
In the Add-in Manager dialog, the user deactivates (deselects) the add-in and then closes the dialog.	xlAutoRemove xlAutoClose
In the Add-in Manager dialog, the user activates the add-in and then closes the dialog.	xlAutoAdd xlAutoOpen
User loads the add-in for the first time.	xlAddInManagerInfo xlAutoAdd xlAutoOpen
User starts Excel with the add-in already installed in previous session.	xlAutoOpen
User closes Excel with the add-in installed but deactivated.	No calls made.
User closes Excel with the add-in installed and activated.	xlAutoClose xlAddInManagerInfo
User starts to close Excel but cancels when prompted to save their work. (See note below.)	xlAutoClose

Note: If the user starts to close Excel, causing a call to xlAutoClose, but then cancels when prompted to save their work, Excel does not then call any of the xlAuto functions to reinitialise the add-in. Even if xlAutoClose attempts to unregister the worksheet functions, a bug in the C API prevents this from being successful. Therefore Excel continues to run and the worksheet functions continue to work. The problems arise where, for example, memory or other resources are released in the call to xlAutoClose or where custom menus are removed. These disappear until reinstated with a call to xlAutoOpen.

Note: If the user deactivates an add-in in the Add-in Manager dialog, but reloads the same add-in (as if for the first time) before closing the dialog, Excel will call xlAutoAdd and xlAutoOpen without calling xlAutoRemove or xlAutoClose. This means the add-in re-initialises without first undoing the first initialisation, creating a risk that custom menus might be added twice, for example. To avoid adding menus twice it is necessary to check if the menu is already there.

Warning: Given the order of calling of these functions, care is required to ensure that no activities are attempted that require some set-up that has not yet taken place. For this reason it is advisable to place your initialisation code into a single function and check in all the required places that this initialisation has occurred, using a global variable. A satisfactory approach is to check in both xlAddInManagerInfo and xlAutoAdd, and to call xlAutoOpen explicitly if the add-in has not been initialised. As well as being the place where all the initialisation is managed from, xlAutoOpen should also detect if it has already been called so that things are not initialised multiple times.

5.5 XLL FUNCTIONS CALLED BY THE ADD-IN MANAGER AND EXCEL

5.5.1 xlAutoOpen

- int __stdcall xlAutoOpen(void);

Excel calls this function whenever Excel starts up or the add-in is loaded. Your DLL can do whatever initialisation you want it to do at this point. The most obvious task is the registration of worksheet functions, but other tasks (such as setting up of custom menus, initialisation of data structures, initialisation of background threads) are also best done here. (See Chapter 8 for details.)

The function should return 1 to indicate success.

Here is a simple example which uses a DLL function register_function() that registers a function with Excel that is exposed by the DLL according to an index number. Section 8.5 provides details.

```
bool xll_initialised = false;

int __stdcall xlAutoOpen(void)      // Register the functions
{
    if(xll_initialised)
        return 1;

    for(int i = 0 ; i < NUM_FUNCS; i++)
        register_function(i);
```

```
    xll_initialised = true;
    return 1;
}
```

5.5.2 xlAutoClose

• int __stdcall xlAutoClose(void);

Excel calls this function whenever Excel closes down or the add-in is unloaded. Your DLL can do whatever cleaning up you need to do at this point, but should un-register your worksheet functions and free memory at the very least. (See section 8.5 *Registering and un-registering DLL(XLL) functions* on page 182 below for more detail.)

The function should return 1 to indicate success.

Here is a simple example which uses a DLL function unregister_function() that un-registers a function exposed by the DLL, and previously registered with Excel, according to an index number.

```
int __stdcall xlAutoClose(void)
{
    if(!xll_initialised)
        return 1;

    for(int i = 0 ; i < NUM_FUNCS; i++)
        unregister_function(i)

    xll_initialised = false;
    return 1;
}
```

5.5.3 xlAutoAdd

• int __stdcall xlAutoAdd(void);

Excel calls this function when the add-in is either opened (as a document using File/Open...) or loaded via the Add-in Manager (Tools/Add ins...) or whenever any equivalent operation is carried out by a macro or other command. In both of these cases, Excel also calls xlAutoOpen() so this function does not need to register the DLL's exposed functions if that has been taken care of in xlAutoOpen(). Omitting this function has no adverse consequences provided that any necessary housekeeping is done by xlAutoOpen().

The function should return 1 to indicate success.

Here is a simple example which uses a DLL function new_xlstring() to create a byte-counted string which needs to be freed by the caller when no longer required.

```
int __stdcall xlAutoAdd(void)
{
    if(!xll_initialised)
        xlAutoOpen();

    xloper xStr, xInt;
```

```
    xStr.xltype = xltypeStr;
    xStr.val.str = new_xlstring("Version 1.0 has been loaded");

    xInt.xltype = xltypeInt;
    xInt.val.w = 2; // Dialog box type.

    Excel4(xlcAlert, NULL, 2, &xStr, &xInt);
// Free memory allocated by new_xlstring()
    free(xStr.val.str);
    return 1;
}
```

Using the C++ xloper class cpp_xloper, introduced in section 6.4, the above code can be rewritten as follows:

```
int __stdcall xlAutoAdd(void)
{
    cpp_xloper xStr("Version 1.0 has been loaded");
    cpp_xloper xInt(2); // Dialog box type.
    Excel4(xlcAlert, NULL, 2, &xStr, &xInt);
    return 1;
}
```

5.5.4 xlAutoRemove

- int __stdcall xlAutoRemove(void);

Excel calls this function when the add-in is deselected via the Add-in Manager dialog (Tools/Add-Ins...), or whenever any equivalent operation is carried out by a macro or other command. In this case, Excel also calls xlAutoClose() so this function does not need to un-register the DLL's exposed functions if that has been taken care of in xlAutoClose(). Omitting this function has no adverse consequences provided that any necessary housekeeping is done by xlAutoClose().

The function should return 1 for success.

The following example displays a message and uses a DLL function new_xlstring() to create a byte-counted string which needs to be freed by the caller when no longer required.

```
int __stdcall xlAutoRemove(void)
{
    xloper xStr, xInt;

    xStr.xltype = xltypeStr;
    xStr.val.str = new_xlstring("Version 1.0 has been removed");

    xInt.xltype = xltypeInt;
    xInt.val.w = 2; // Dialog box type.

    Excel4(xlcAlert, NULL, 2, &xStr, &xInt);
```

```
// Free memory allocated by new_xlstring()
    free(xStr.val.str);
    return 1;
}
```

Using the C++ `xloper` class `cpp_xloper`, introduced in section 6.4, the above code can be rewritten as follows:

```
int __stdcall xlAutoRemove(void)
{
    cpp_xloper xStr("Version 1.0 has been removed");
    cpp_xloper xInt(2); // Dialog box type.
    Excel4(xlcAlert, NULL, 2, &xStr, &xInt);
    return 1;
}
```

5.5.5 `xlAddInManagerInfo`

- `xloper * __stdcall xlAddInManagerInfo(xloper *);`

Excel calls this function the first time the Add-in Manager is invoked. It should return an `xloper` string with the full name of the add-in which is then displayed in the Add-in Manager dialog (Tools/Add-Ins...). (See example below.) If this function is omitted, the Add-in Manager dialog simply displays the DOS 8.3 filename of the add-in without the path or extension.

The function should return 1 to indicate success.

Here is a simple example which uses a DLL function `new_xlstring()` to create a byte-counted string that is marked for freeing once Excel has copied the value out.

```
xloper * __stdcall xlAddInManagerInfo(xloper *p_arg)
{
    if(!xll_initialised)
        xlAutoOpen();

    static xloper ret_oper;

    ret_oper.xltype = xltypeErr;
    ret_oper.val.err = xlerrValue;

    if(p_arg == NULL)
        return &ret_oper;

    if((p_arg->xltype == xltypeNum && p_arg->val.num == 1.0)
    || (p_arg->xltype == xltypeInt && p_arg->val.w == 1))
    {
// Return a dynamically allocated byte-counted string and tell Excel
// to call back into the DLL to free it once Excel has finished.
        ret_oper.xltype = xltypeStr | xlbitDLLFree;
        ret_oper.val.str = new_xlstring("My Add-in");
    }
    return &ret_oper;
}
```

Using the C++ xloper class `cpp_xloper`, introduced in section 6.4, the above code can be rewritten as follows:

```
xloper * __stdcall xlAddInManagerInfo(xloper *p_arg)
{
    if(!xll_initialised)
        xlAutoOpen();

    cpp_xloper Arg(p_arg);
    cpp_xloper RetVal;

    if(Arg == 1)
        RetVal = AddinName;
    else
        RetVal = (WORD)xlerrValue;

    return RetVal.ExtractXloper();
}
```

Invoking the Add-in Manager calls this function resulting in the following being displayed:

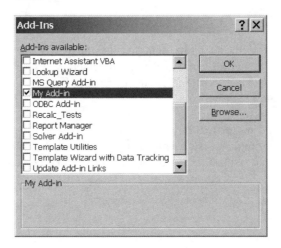

5.5.6 `xlAutoRegister`

• xloper * __stdcall xlAutoRegister(xloper *);

This function is only called from Excel 4 macro sheets when an executing macro encounters an instance of the REGISTER() macro sheet function where information about the types of arguments and return value of the function are not provided. xlAutoRegister() is passed the name of the function in question and should search for the function's arguments and then *register* the function properly, with all arguments specified. (See section 8.5 on page 182.) As macro sheets are deprecated, and outside the scope of this book, this function is not discussed any further. The function can safely either be omitted or can be a stub function returning a NULL pointer.

5.5.7 `xlAutoFree`

- `void __stdcall xlAutoFree(xloper *);`

Whenever Excel has been returned a pointer to an `xloper` by the DLL with the `xlbit-DLLFree` bit of the `xltype` field set, it calls this function passing back the same pointer. This enables the DLL to release any dynamically allocated memory that was associated with the `xloper`. Clearly the DLL can't free memory before the `return` statement, as Excel would not safely be able to copy out its contents. The `xlAutoFree()` function and the `xlbitDLLFree` bit are the solution to this problem. (See also Chapter 7 *Memory Management* on page 161 for more about when and how to set this bit.)

Returning pointers to `xlopers` with the `xlbitDLLFree` bit set is the only way to return DLL-allocated memory without springing a memory leak. The next-best solution is to allocate memory, assign it to a static pointer, and free it the next time the function gets called.

Typically, your DLL will need to contain this function when

- returning DLL-allocated `xloper` strings;
- returning DLL-allocated range references of the type `xltypeRef`;
- returning DLL-allocated arrays of `xlopers`. If the array contains string `xlopers` that refer to memory that needs to be freed then `xlAutoFree()` should do this too. (See example below.)

There are a few points to bear in mind when dealing with arrays:

- The array memory pointed to by an array `xloper` can be static or dynamically allocated. The `xlbitDLLFree` bit should only be set for arrays where the memory was dynamically allocated by the DLL.
- Array elements that are strings may be static, or may have had memory allocated for them by either the DLL or Excel.
- Excel will only call `xlAutoFree()` for an array that has the `xlbitDLLFree` bit set, which should be one that was dynamically allocated in the DLL.
- A static array containing dynamic memory strings will leak memory.
- A DLL-created dynamic array containing Excel-allocated strings requires that the `xlbitXLFree` bit be set for each string, and `xlAutoFree()` needs to detect this.
- You should not pass arrays of arrays, or arrays containing references, back to Excel: your implementation of `xlAutoFree()` does not need to check for this. (The example implementation below would, in fact, cope fine with this, but the inclusion of a reference in an array would confuse and possibly destabilise Excel.)

The following code provides an example implementation that checks for arrays, range references and strings – the three types that can be returned to Excel with memory still needing to be freed. The function can call itself recursively when freeing array elements. For this reason the function checks for an argument that has the `xlbitXLFree` bit set. Excel will never call this function for an `xloper` with this bit set, but this implementation copes with Excel-created strings in DLL-created arrays.

```
void __stdcall xlAutoFree(xloper *p_op)
{
    if(p_op->xltype & xltypeMulti)
    {
// Check if the elements need to be freed then check if the array
// itself needs to be freed.
        int size = p_op->val.array.rows * p_op->val.array.columns;
        xloper *p = p_op->val.array.lparray;

        for(; size-- > 0; p++)
            if(p->xltype & (xlbitDLLFree | xlbitXLFree))
                xlAutoFree(p);

        if(p_op->xltype & xlbitDLLFree)
            free(p_op->val.array.lparray);
    }
    else if(p_op->xltype == (xltypeStr | xlbitDLLFree))
    {
        free(p_op->val.str);
    }
    else if(p_op->xltype == (xltypeRef | xlbitDLLFree))
    {
        free(p_op->val.mref.lpmref);
    }
    else if(p_oper->xltype | xlbitXLFree)
    {
        Excel4(xlFree, 0, 1, p_op);
    }
}
```

Passing Data between Excel and the DLL

Where DLL functions are being accessed directly by Excel, you need to understand how to pass and return values. You need to think about the data types of both the arguments and return value(s). You need to know whether arguments are passed by reference, (by pointer, as the interface is C), or by value. You need to decide whether to return values via the function's return value or by modifying arguments passed in by reference. Where the data you want to pass or return is not one of the simple data types, you need to know about the data structures that Excel supports and when their use is most appropriate.

Finally, you need to know how to tell Excel about your exported functions and tell it all the above things about the arguments and return values. This point is covered in detail in section 8.5 *Registering and un-registering DLL (XLL) functions* on page 182. This chapter concentrates on the structures themselves.

6.1 HANDLING EXCEL'S INTERNAL DATA STRUCTURES: C OR C++?

The most flexible and important data structure used by Excel in the C API is defined as the xloper in the SDK header file. This 10-byte C structure, the union that it contains and the sub-structures in the union, are all described in detail in this chapter. An understanding of xlopers and, very importantly, how to handle the memory that can be pointed to by them is required to enable direct communication between the worksheet and the C/C++ DLL: all exported commands and worksheet functions need to be registered, something that involves calling a function in the C API using xlopers.

The handling of xlopers is something well suited to an object oriented (OO) approach. Whilst this book intentionally sticks with C-style coding in most places, the value of the OO features of C++ are important enough that an example of just such a class is valuable. The cpp_xloper class is described in section 6.4. Many of the code examples in subsequent sections and chapters use this class rather than xlopers. In some cases, examples using both approaches have been provided to show the contrast in the resulting code.

Where xlopers have been used rather than this class, this is either because the intention is to show the detailed workings of the xloper as clearly as possible, or because use of the class, with its overhead of constructor and destructor calls, would be overkill.

6.2 HOW EXCEL EXCHANGES WORKSHEET DATA WITH DLL ADD-IN FUNCTIONS

Where DLL functions take native C data type arguments such as ints, doubles and char * null-terminated strings, Excel will attempt to convert worksheet arguments as described in section 2.6 *Data type conversion* on page 12. Return values that are native data types are similarly converted to the types of data that worksheet cells can contain.

Excel can also pass arguments and accept return values via one of three pre-defined structures. In summary, this gives the DLL and Excel four ways to communicate:

1. Via native C/C++ data types, converted automatically by Excel.
2. Via a structure that describes and contains 2-dimensional arrays of 8-byte doubles, which this book refers to as an `xl_array`.
3. Via a structure that can represent the contents of any cell; numbers, strings, Boolean true or false, Excel error values and arrays, referred to as an `oper`.
4. Via a structure that can not only represent the contents of any cell, but also ranges and a few other things, named the `xloper` in the SDK header file. This structure is covered in depth in the next few sections.

Not all of the data types that the `xloper` can contain will be passed or returned in calls from a worksheet function. Some are only used internally, for example, when calling back into Excel from the DLL through the C API.

6.2.1   Native C/C++ data types

Excel will pass arguments and accept return values for all of the following native C/C++ data types, performing the necessary conversions either side of the call to the DLL.

- `[signed] short [int] (16-bit);`
- `[signed] short [int] * (16-bit);`
- `unsigned short [int] (16-bit = DWORD);`
- `[signed] [long] int (32-bit);`
- `[signed] [long] int * (32-bit);`
- `unsigned [long] int (32-bit);`
- `double;`
- `double *;`
- `[signed] char * (null-terminated string);`
- `unsigned char * (byte-counted string).`

Other types, e.g., `bool`, `char` and `float`, are not directly supported and declaring functions with types other than the above may have unpredictable consequences. Casting to one of the supported data types is, of course, a trivial solution, so in practice this should not be a limitation.

If Excel cannot convert an input value to the type specified then it will not call the function but will instead return a #VALUE! error to the calling cell(s). Excel does permit DLL functions to return values by modifying an argument passed by a pointer reference. The function must be registered in a way that tells Excel that this is how it works and, in most cases, must be declared as returning `void`. (See section 8.5 *Registering and un-registering DLL (XLL) functions* on page 182 for details.)

Note: Returning values by changing an argument will not alter the value of a cell from which that value originally came. The returned value will be deposited in the calling cell just as if it were returned with a `return` statement.

6.2.2   Excel floating-point array structure: xl_array

Excel supports a simple floating-point array structure which can be defined as follows and is passed to or returned from the DLL by pointer reference:

```
typedef struct
{
    WORD rows;
    WORD columns;
    double array[1]; // Start of array[rows * columns]
}
    xl_array;
```

In some texts this structure is called FP or _FP, but since the name is private to the DLL (and the structure is not defined in the SDK header file) it is up to you. The above name is more descriptive, and this is how the rest of the book refers to this structure.

Warning: Excel expects this structure to be packed such that array[1] is eight bytes after the start of the structure. This is consistent with the default packing of Visual Studio (6.0 and .NET), so there's no need to include #pragma pack() statements around its definition. You need to be careful when allocating memory, however, that you allocate 8 bytes plus the space for array[rows * columns]. Allocating 4 bytes plus the space for the array will lead to a block that is too small by 4 bytes. A too-small block will be overwritten when the last array element is assigned, leading to heap damage and destabilisation of Excel. (See the code for xl_array_example1() below).

Note: The array stores its elements row-by-row so should be read and written to accordingly. The element (r,c), where r and c count from zero, can be accessed by the expression array[r*rows + c]. The expression array[r][c] will produce a compiler error. A more efficient way of accessing the elements of such an array is to maintain a list of pointers to the beginning of each row and then access the elements by offsetting each start-of-row pointer. (*Numerical Recipes in C*, Chapter 1, contains very clear examples of this kind of thing.)

Later sections provide details of two (closely related) data structures, both capable of passing mixed-type arrays, the oper and the xloper. The xl_array structure has some advantages and some disadvantages relative to these.

Advantages:

- Memory management is easy, especially when returning an array via an argument modified in place. (See notes below.)
- Accessing the data is simple.

Disadvantages:

- xl_arrays can only contain numbers.
- If an input range contains something that Excel cannot convert to a number, Excel will not call the function, and will fail with a #VALUE! error. Excel will interpret empty cells as zero, and convert text that can be easily converted to a number. Excel <u>will not</u> convert Boolean or error values.
- Returning arrays via this type (other than via arguments modified in place) presents difficulties with the freeing of dynamically allocated memory. (See notes below.)
- This data type cannot be used for optional arguments. If an argument of this type is missing, Excel will not call the function, and will fail with a #VALUE! error.

Note: It is possible to declare and register a DLL function so that it returns an array of this type as an argument modified-in-place. The size of the array cannot be increased, however. The shape of the array can be changed as long as the overall size is not increased – see xl_array_example3() below. The size can also be reduced – see xl_array_example4() below. Returning values in this way will not alter the value of the cells in the input range. The returned values will be deposited in the calling cells as if the array had been returned via a return statement. (See section 8.5 *Registering and un-registering DLL (XLL) functions* on page 182 for details of how to tell Excel that your DLL function uses this data structure.)

Note: Freeing dynamic memory allocated by the DLL is a big problem when returning arrays using this type. You can declare a static pointer, initialise it to NULL and check it every time the function is called – see xl_array_example1() below. If it is not null, you can free the memory allocated during the last call before re-executing and re-allocating. This ensures that the DLL doesn't suffer from leakage, but it does suffer from retention. This might only be a problem for very large arrays. It is a problem that is solved with the use of xlopers. (See section 6.2.3 below and also Chapter 7 *Memory Management* on page 161 for more details.)

Examples

The following examples provide code for four exportable functions, one of which creates and returns an array of this type, the others returning an array via a passed-in array argument. Note the differences in memory management.

The first allocates memory for an array of the specified size, and assigns some simple values to it, and returns a pointer to it to Excel.

```
xl_array * __stdcall xl_array_example1(int rows, int columns)
{
    static xl_array *p_array = NULL;

    if(p_array) // free memory allocated on last call
    {
        free(p_array);
        p_array = NULL;
    }

    int size = rows * columns;

    if(size <= 0)
        return NULL;

    size_t mem_size = sizeof(xl_array) + (size-1) * sizeof(double);

    if((p_array = (xl_array *)malloc(mem_size)))
    {
        p_array->rows = rows;
        p_array->columns = columns;

        for(int i = 0; i < size; i++)
            p_array->array[i] = i / 100.0;
    }
    return p_array;
}
```

Note: If the memory were allocated with the following line of code, instead of as above, the memory block would be too small, and would be overrun when the last element of the array was assigned. Also, Excel would misread all the elements of the array, leading to unpredictable return values, invalid floating point numbers, and all kinds of mischief.

```
// Incorrect allocation statement!!!
p_array = (xl_array *)malloc(2*sizeof(WORD) + size*sizeof(double));
```

A related point is that it is not necessary to check both that a pointer to an xl_array and the address of the first data element are both valid or not NULL. If the pointer to the xl_array is valid then the address of the first element, which is contained in the structure, is also valid.

Warning: There is no way that a function that receives a pointer to an xl_array can check for itself that the size of the allocated memory is sufficient for all the elements implied by its rows and columns values. An incorrect allocation outside the DLL could cause Excel to crash.

The next example modifies the passed-in array's values but not its shape or size.

```
void __stdcall xl_array_example2(xl_array *p_array)
{
    if(!p_array || !p_array->rows
    || !p_array->columns || p_array->columns > 0x100)
        return;

    int size = p_array->rows * p_array->columns;

    for(int i = 0; i < size; i++)
        p_array->array[i] = i / 10.0;
}
```

The next example modifies the passed-in array's values and shape, but not its size.

```
void __stdcall xl_array_example3(xl_array *p_array)
{
    if(!p_array || !p_array->rows
    || !p_array->columns || p_array->columns > 0x100)
        return;

    int size = p_array->rows * p_array->columns;

// Change the shape of the array but not the size
    int temp = p_array->rows;
    p_array->rows = p_array->columns;
    p_array->columns = temp;

// Change the values in the array
    for(int i = 0; i < size; i++)
        p_array->array[i] /= 10.0;
}
```

The next example modifies the passed-in array's values and reduces its size.

```
void __stdcall xl_array_example4(xl_array *p_array)
{
    if(!p_array || !p_array->rows
    || !p_array->columns || p_array->columns > 0x100)
        return;

// Reduce the size of the array
    if(p_array->rows > 1)
        p_array->rows--;

    if(p_array->columns > 1)
        p_array->columns--;

    int size = p_array->rows * p_array->columns;

// Change the values in the array
    for(int i = 0; i < size; i++)
        p_array->array[i] /= 10.0;
}
```

In memory the structure is as follows, with the first double aligned to an 8-byte boundary:

1-2	3-4	4-8	9-16	17-24
WORD	WORD		double	[double...]

Provided that the values of the first two WORDs are initialised in a way that is consistent with the number of doubles, any structure that obeys this format can be passed to and from Excel as this data type.

For example:

```
typedef struct
{
    WORD rows;
    WORD columns;
    double top_left;
    double top_right;
    double bottom_left;
    double bottom_right;
}
    two_by_two_array;
```

If rows and columns are initialised to 2, this structure can be passed or received as if it were an xl_array. This could simplify and improve the readability of code that populates an array, in some cases.

Warning: The following structure definition and function are (perhaps obviously) incorrect. The code will compile without a problem, but Excel will not be able to read the returned values as it expects the structure to contain the first element of the array, not a pointer to it. A similar function that tried to interpret an `xl_array` passed from Excel as if it were an instance of this example, would encounter even worse problems as it attempted to read from invalid memory addresses.

```
typedef struct
{
   WORD rows;
   WORD columns;
   double *array; // Should be array[1];
}
   xl_array;  // OH NO IT ISN'T!!!

xl_array * __stdcall bad_xl_array_example(int rows, int columns)
{
   static xl_array rtn_array = {0,0, NULL};

   if(rtn_array.array) // free memory allocated on last call
   {
      free(rtn_array.array);
      rtn_array.array = NULL;
   }

   int size = rows * columns;

   if(size <= 0)
      return NULL;

   if(!(rtn_array.array = (double *)malloc(size*sizeof(double))))
   {
     rtn_array.rows = rows;
     rtn_array.columns = columns;

     for(int i = 0; i < size; i++)
        rtn_array.array[i] = i / 10.0;
   }
   return &rtn_array;
}
```

6.2.3 The `xloper` structure

Internally, the Excel C API uses a C structure, the `xloper`, for the highest (most general) representation of one or more cell's contents. In addition to being able to represent cell values and arrays, it can also represent references to single cells, single blocks of cells and multiple blocks of cells on a worksheet. There are also some C API-specific data types not supported as worksheet values or arguments to worksheet functions: the integer type, the XLM macro flow type and the binary data block type.

The `xloper` contains two parts:

- A 2-byte WORD indicating the data type of the `xloper`.
- An 8-byte C union interpreted according to the type of `xloper`.

The structure can be defined as follows and is passed to or returned from the DLL by reference, i.e., using pointers. The definition given here is functionally equivalent to the definition as it appears in the SDK header file, except for the removal of the XLM flow-control structure which is not within the scope of this book. The same member variable and structure names are also used. The detailed interpretation of all the elements and the definitions of the xlref and xlmref structures are contained in the following sections.

```
typedef struct _xloper
{
   union
   {
       double num;    // xltypeNum
       char *str;     // xltypeStr
       WORD _bool;    // xltypeBool
       WORD err;      // xltypeErr
       short int w;   // xltypeInt

       struct
       {
          struct _xloper *lparray;
          WORD rows;
          WORD columns;
       }
          array; // xltypeMulti

       struct
       {
          WORD count;    // Ignored, but set to 1 for safety!
          xlref ref;
       }
       sref;           // xltypeSRef

       struct
       {
          xlmref *lpmref;
          DWORD idSheet;
       }
          mref;       // xltypeRef

       // XLM flow control structure omitted.

       struct
       {
          union
          {
             BYTE far *lpbData; // data passed to XL
             HANDLE hdata; // data returned from XL
          }
             h;
          long cbData;
       }
       bigdata;       // xltypeBigData
   }
   val;

   WORD xltype;
}
   xloper;
```

The following table shows the values that the xltype field can take, as well as whether you can expect that Excel might pass one to your DLL function. The table also shows the values that can be passed via the oper structure covered in section 6.2.6 *The oper structure* on page 119. (Whether Excel passes xlopers or opers depends on the way the function arguments are registered with Excel. See section 8.5 *Registering and un-registering DLL (XLL) functions* on page 182 for details.)

Table 6.1 `xloper` types passed from worksheet to add-in

Constant as defined in `xlcall.h`	Hexadecimal representation	Passed from Excel worksheet to add-in as `xloper`:	Passed from Excel worksheet to add-in as oper (see page 119):
`xltypeNum`	0x0001	Yes	Yes
`xltypeStr`	0x0002	Yes	Yes
`xltypeBool`	0x0004	Yes	Yes
`xltypeRef`	0x0008	Yes	No
`xltypeErr`	0x0010	Yes	Yes
`xltypeMulti`	0x0040	Yes	Yes
`xltypeMissing`	0x0080	Yes	Yes
`xltypeNil`	0x0100	Yes[1]	Yes
`xltypeSRef`	0x0400	Yes	No
`xltypeInt`	0x0800	No	No
`xltypeBigData`	0x0802	N/A (see below)	

The following exportable example function returns information about all the `xloper` types that might be encountered in a call from a worksheet cell:

```
// Header contains definition of xloper and the constants for xltype
#include <xlcall.h>

char * __stdcall xloper_type_str(xloper *pxl)
{
    if(pxl == NULL)
        return NULL; // should never be passed in by Excel

    switch(pxl->xltype)
    {
        case xltypeNum:      return "0x0001 xltypeNum";
        case xltypeStr:      return "0x0002 xltypeStr";
        case xltypeBool:     return "0x0004 xltypeBool";
        case xltypeRef:      return "0x0008 xltypeRef";
        case xltypeSRef:     return "0x0400 xltypeSRef";
        case xltypeErr:      return "0x0010 xltypeErr";
        case xltypeMulti:    return "0x0040 xltypeMulti";
        case xltypeMissing:  return "0x0080 xltypeMissing";
        default:             return "Unexpected type";
    }
}
```

[1] Only as part of a literal array where a value is omitted, e.g., {1, , 3}.

The declaration of an argument as an `xloper` `*` tells Excel that the argument should be passed in without any of the conversions described in section 2.6.11 *Worksheet function argument type conversion*, page 16. This enables the function's code to deal directly with whatever was supplied in the worksheet. Excel will never pass a null pointer even if the argument was not supplied by the caller. An `xloper` is still passed but of type `xltypeMissing`. The check for a NULL argument in the above code is just good practice (because you never know).

The above function simply checks for the type of the `xloper`, represented in the `xltype` data member of the `xloper` structure, and returns a descriptive string containing the hexadecimal value and the corresponding defined constant. This function can only be called from a worksheet once it has been *registered* with Excel, a topic covered in detail in section 8.5 *Registering and un-registering DLL (XLL) functions* on page 182. The name with which the function is registered in the example project add-in is XloperTypeStr.

Table 6.2 shows some examples of calls to this function and returned values:

Table 6.2 `xloper` types as passed by Excel to the XLL

Worksheet cell formula	Returned value	Comment
=XloperTypeStr(2) =XloperTypeStr(2.1)	0x0001 xltypeNum	Same for integers and doubles.
=XloperTypeStr("2") =XloperTypeStr("")	0x0002 xltypeStr	
=XloperTypeStr(TRUE)	0x0004 xltypeBool	
=XloperTypeStr(Sheet2!A1) =XloperTypeStr(Sheet2!A1:A2)	0x0008 xltypeRef	Call is <u>not</u> made from Sheet2
=XloperTypeStr(A1) =XloperTypeStr(A1:A2) =XloperTypeStr(INDIRECT("A1:A2"))	0x0400 xltypeSRef	
=XloperTypeStr(NA()) =XloperTypeStr(1/0) =XloperTypeStr(#REF!) =XloperTypeStr(LOG(0))	0x0010 xltypeErr	
=XloperTypeStr({1,2,"3"})	0x0040 xltypeMulti	
=XloperTypeStr()	0x0080 xltypeMissing	

So, an `xloper` will always have two first-level components; a WORD `xltype` and a union `val`. The SDK header file provides definitions of constants for `xltype` and the following table gives some detail of the corresponding `val` union constituents.

Table 6.3 The `xloper` expanded

xltype constants	Value	Union members (val.*)
xltypeNum	0x0001	double num
xltypeStr	0x0002	unsigned char *str
xltypeBool	0x0004	WORD _bool
xltypeRef	0x0008	struct mref ↓ DWORD mref.idSheet xlmref *mref.lpmref ↓ WORD mref.lpmref->count xlref mref.lpmref->reftbl[1] ↓ WORD mref.lpmref->reftbl[].rwFirst WORD mref.lpmref->reftbl[].rwLast BYTE mref.lpmref->reftbl[].colFirst BYTE mref.lpmref->reftbl[].colLast with reftbl[]'s array index running from 0 to (count - 1) inclusive.
xltypeErr	0x0010	WORD err
xltypeFlow	0x0020	(Supports XLM flow-control, not covered in this book).
xltypeMulti	0x0040	struct array ↓ WORD array.rows WORD array.columns Xloper *array.lparray ↓ WORD array.lparray[].xltype union array.lparray[].val ... with lparray[]'s array index running from 0 to (val.array.rows * val.array.columns - 1) inclusive.
xltypeMissing	0x0080	No data associated with this xloper.
xltypeNil	0x0100	No data associated with this xloper.

(continued overleaf)

Table 6.3 (*continued*)

xltype constants	Value	Union members (val.*)
xltypeSRef	0x0400	struct sref ↓ WORD sref.count (always = 1) xlref sref.ref ↓ WORD sref.ref.rwFirst WORD sref.ref.rwLast BYTE sref.ref.colFirst BYTE sref.ref.colLast
xltypeInt	0x0800	signed int w
xltypeBigData	0x0802	struct bigdata ↓ long bigdata.cbData union bigdata.h ↓ BYTE *bigdata.h.lpbData HANDLE bigdata.h.hdata

In addition to the above values for data types, the following bits are used to signal to Excel that memory needs to be freed after the DLL passes control back to Excel. How and when these are used is covered in Chapter 7 *Memory Management* on page 161.

xlbitXLFree	0x1000
xlbitDLLFree	0x4000

Warning: An xloper should not have either of these bits set if it might be passed as an argument in a call to Excel4() or Excel4v(). This can confuse Excel as to the true type of the xloper and cause the function to fail with an xlretFailed error (=32).

Note: Setting xlbitXLFree on an xloper that is to be used for the return value for a call to Excel4(), prior to the call, will have no effect. The correct time to set this bit is:

- after the call that sets its value;
- after it might be passed as an argument in other calls to Excel4();
- before a pointer to it is returned to the worksheet.

For example, the following code will fail to ensure that the string allocated in the call to Excel4() gets freed properly, as the xltype field of ret_oper will be reset in a successful call. (See also Chapter 7 *Memory Management* on page 161.)

```
xloper * __stdcall bad_example(void)
{
    static xloper ret_oper;
    ret_oper.type |= xlbitXLFree; // WRONG: will get reset
    Excel4(xlGetName, &ret_oper, 0);
    return &ret_oper;
}
```

Warning: When testing the type of the `xloper` there are a few potential snares, as shown by the following code example:

```
int __stdcall xloper_type(xloper *p_op)
{
// Unsafe. Might be xltypeBigData == xltypeStr | xltypeInt
    if(p_op->xltype & xltypeStr)
        return xltypeStr;

// Unsafe. Might be xltypeBigData == xltypeStr | xltypeInt
    if(p_op->xltype & xltypeInt)
        return xltypeInt;

// Unsafe. Might be xltypeStr or xltypeInt
    if(p_op->xltype & xltypeBigData)
        return xltypeBigData;

// Unsafe. Might have xlbitXLFree or xlbitDLLFree set
    if(p_op->xltype == xltypeStr)
        return xltypeStr;

// Unsafe. Might have xlbitXLFree or xlbitDLLFree set
    if(p_op->xltype == xltypeMulti)
        return xltypeMulti;

// Unsafe. Might have xlbitXLFree or xlbitDLLFree set
    if(p_op->xltype == xltypeRef)
        return xltypeRef;

// Safe.
    if((p_op->xltype & xltypeBigData) == xltypeStr)
        return xltypeStr;

// Safe.
    if((p_op->xltype & ~(xlbitXLFree | xlbitDLLFree)) == xltypeRef)
        return xltypeRef;

    return 0; // not a valid xltype
}
```

Some of the above unsafe tests might be perfectly fine, of course, if you know that the type cannot be `xltypeBigData`, or can only be, say, `xltypeBigData` or `xltypeErr`, or that neither of the bits `xlbitXLFree` or `xlbitDLLFree` can be set. But you should be careful.

6.2.4 The `xlref` structure

The `xlref` structure is a simple structure defined in the SDK header file `xlcall.h` as follows:

```
typedef struct xlref
{
    WORD rwFirst;
    WORD rwLast;
    BYTE colFirst;
    BYTE colLast;
};
```

This structure is used by Excel to denote a rectangular block of cells somewhere on a worksheet. (Which worksheet is determined by the `xloper` that either contains or points to this structure.) Rows and columns are counted from zero, so that, for example, an `xlref` that described the range A1:C2 would have the following values set:

- `rwFirst = 0`
- `rwLast = 1`
- `colFirst = 0`
- `colLast = 2`

The `xlopers` that describe ranges on worksheets either contain an `xlref` (`xltypeSRef`) or point to a table of `xlrefs` (`xltypeRef`).

Warning: A range that covers an entire column on a worksheet (e.g. A:A in a cell formula, equivalent to A1:A65536) is, in theory, represented in this data type but, whether by design or flaw, will be given the `rwLast` value of `0x3fff` instead of `0xffff`. This limitation could cause serious bugs in your DLL if you are not aware of it. One possible reason for this seemingly strange behaviour is the fact that the array `xloper` type, the `xltypeMulti`, can only support 65,535 rows rather than 65,536.

6.2.5 The `xlmref` structure

The `xlmref` structure is simply an array of `xlrefs` (see above). The only place this is used is in an `xloper` of type `xltypeRef` which contains a pointer to an `xlmref`. It is defined in the SDK header file `xlcall.h` as follows:

```
typedef struct xmlref
{
    WORD count;
    xlref reftbl[1];     /* actually reftbl[count] */
};
```

Excel uses the `xlmref` in an `xltypeRef` `xloper` to encapsulate a single reference to multiple rectangular ranges of cells on a specified worksheet. A single rectangular block on a sheet may also be represented by an `xltypeRef` `xloper`, in which case the `xlmref count` is set to 1.

To allocate space for an `xlmref` representing, say, 10 rectangular blocks of cells (each described by an `xlref`), you would allocate space for one `xlmref` and nine `xlrefs` as the space for the first `xlref` is contained in the `xlmref`. In practice you would only rarely need to do this. A single `xlmref`, with its count set to 1, is all you need to describe a specific range of cells, and that is almost always sufficient.

If you are writing functions that you want to be able to handle such multiple block references, you will need to iterate through each `xlref`, to collect and analyse all the data.

6.2.6   The `oper` structure

Excel supports a simplified `xloper` structure, sometimes referred to as an `oper`. This can represent any of the data types that a worksheet cell can evaluate to: floating-point numbers, strings, Boolean true/false, and Excel errors. It can also represent empty cells, missing arguments and arrays whose elements are themselves `oper`s.

The structure can simply be defined as follows and is passed to or returned from the DLL by pointer reference:

```
typedef struct _oper
{
    union
    {
        double num;
        char *str;
        WORD _bool;
        WORD err;

        struct
        {
            struct _oper *lparray;
            WORD rows;
            WORD columns;
        }
            array;
    }
        val;

    WORD type;
}
    oper;
```

As you can see, this structure is a simply a slimmed-down `xloper`, missing the ability to represent true integers, worksheet ranges and XLM macro flow-control values. The values that the `type` field can take are identical to the corresponding values in the `xltype` field of the `xloper`. Its appearance in memory is identical to the `xloper` enabling `oper`s to be cast up to `xloper`s and `xloper`s to be cast down to `oper`s. You do need to be careful when casting down that the `type` field is one of the following:

- `xltypeNum`;
- `xltypeStr`;
- `xltypeBool`;
- `xltypeErr`;
- `xltypeMulti`;
- `xltypeNil`;
- `xltypeMissing`.

Both the xloper and the oper appear the same in memory, so functions prototyped as taking pointers to xlopers can be registered with Excel as taking pointers to opers. (See section 8.5.3 *Specifying argument and return types* on page 186.) This is a very useful technique. If Excel is passed a range in the function call, it will de-reference it for you. This can greatly simplify DLL code that does not need to know anything about the range, but is only concerned with the values within that range. Since an Excel-supplied oper can be treated as an xloper, there is even no need to define the oper structure anywhere in your code.

The following example shows a simple function that is a good candidate for being registered as taking an oper argument rather than an xloper.

```
char * __stdcall what_is_it(xloper *p_oper)
{
   switch(p_oper->xltype)
   {
   case xltypeStr:    return "It's a string";
   case xltypeNum:    return "It's a number";
   default:           return "It's something I can't handle";
   }
}
```

Note that the xltype field is equivalent to the type field described in the oper definition above, and that there's no need to refer to an oper structure. The function doesn't need to coerce a reference to either a string or a number – Excel will have already done this if required. The function just needs to see what type of *value* it was passed.

The following example shows a function that is not such a good candidate to be registered as taking an oper argument. The reason is that it performs a conversion using the xlCoerce function (see section 8.7.3 on page 201). If Excel has already had to convert from a range reference to an oper, a call to this function will end up doing two conversions. If registered as taking an xloper, Excel would pass a range reference unconverted and only one conversion would end up taking place.

```
xloper * __stdcall convert_it(xloper *p_oper, int to_a_number)
{
   static xloper ret_val;
   xloper targe_type;

   targe_type.xltype = xltypeInt;
   targe_type.val.w = (to_a_number ? xltypeNum : xltypeStr);

   Excel4(xlCoerce, &ret_val, 2, p_oper, &targe_type);

   return &ret_val;
}
```

Warning: Care should be taken when returning xlopers from functions registered with Excel as returning opers – returning a non-oper type could confuse Excel and cause problems. My recommendation would be always to register functions as returning xlopers. This not only avoids this problem, but helps with memory management.

6.3 DEFINING CONSTANT `xlopers`

Two of the `xloper` types do not take values, `xltypeMissing` and `xltypeNil`. A few others take just a limited number of values: `xltypeBool` takes just two; `xltypeErr`, seven. It is convenient and computationally very efficient to define a few constant values, and in particular pointers to these, that can be passed as arguments to `Excel4()` or can be returned by functions that return `xloper` pointers. The following code sample shows a definition of a structure that looks like an `xloper` in memory, but that can be initialised statically. It also contains some `xloper` pointer definitions that perform a cast on the address of instances of this structure so that they *look* like `xlopers`.

Many of the code examples later in this book use these definitions.

```
typedef struct
{
    WORD word1;
    WORD word2;
    WORD word3;
    WORD word4;
    WORD xltype;
}
    const_xloper;

const_xloper xloperBooleanTrue = {1, 0, 0, 0, xltypeBool};
const_xloper xloperBooleanFalse = {0, 0, 0, 0, xltypeBool};
const_xloper xloperMissing = {0, 0, 0, 0, xltypeMissing};
const_xloper xloperNil = {0, 0, 0, 0, xltypeNil};
const_xloper xloperErrNull = {0, 0, 0, 0, xltypeErr};
const_xloper xloperErrDiv0 = {7, 0, 0, 0, xltypeErr};
const_xloper xloperErrValue = {15, 0, 0, 0, xltypeErr};
const_xloper xloperErrRef = {23, 0, 0, 0, xltypeErr};
const_xloper xloperErrName = {29, 0, 0, 0, xltypeErr};
const_xloper xloperErrNum = {36, 0, 0, 0, xltypeErr};
const_xloper xloperErrNa = {42, 0, 0, 0, xltypeErr};

xloper *p_xlTrue = ((xloper *)&xloperBooleanTrue);
xloper *p_xlFalse = ((xloper *)&xloperBooleanFalse);
xloper *p_xlMissing = ((xloper *)&xloperMissing);
xloper *p_xlNil = ((xloper *)&xloperNil);
xloper *p_xlErrNull = ((xloper *)&xloperErrNull);
xloper *p_xlErrDiv0 = ((xloper *)&xloperErrDiv0);
xloper *p_xlErrValue = ((xloper *)&xloperErrValue);
xloper *p_xlErrRef = ((xloper *)&xloperErrRef);
xloper *p_xlErrName = ((xloper *)&xloperErrName);
xloper *p_xlErrNum = ((xloper *)&xloperErrNum);
xloper *p_xlErrNa = ((xloper *)&xloperErrNa);
```

6.4 A C++ CLASS WRAPPER FOR THE `xloper` – `cpp_xloper`

This book deliberately avoids being *about* object oriented (OO) programming so that it is completely accessible to those with C skills only or those with C resources they wish to use with Excel. However, wrapping `xlopers` up in a simple C++ class greatly simplifies their handling as the following sections aim to demonstrate.

The creation of a simple class to do this is, in itself, a helpful exercise in understanding `xloper` use, in particular the management of memory. The class code that follows is intentionally simple and so accessible to those with little or no C++ or OO experience. It is meant to serve as an example of the simplifications possible using a simple class rather than to be held up as the ideal class for all purposes. Many alternative designs, though inevitably similar, would work just as well, perhaps better.[2]

When designing a new class, it is helpful to make some notes about the purpose of the class – a kind of *class manifesto* (apolitically speaking). Here are some brief notes summarising in what circumstances `xlopers` are encountered and describing what the class `cpp_xloper` should do:

A DLL needs to handle `xlopers` when:

- they are supplied to the DLL as arguments to worksheet functions and XLL interface functions and need to be converted before being used within the DLL;
- they need to be created to be passed as arguments in calls to `Excel4()` and `Excel4v()` (see section 8.2 *The Excel4() C API function* on page 171);
- they are returned from calls to `Excel4()` and `Excel4v()` and need to be converted before being used within the DLL;
- They need to be created for return to the worksheet.

The class `cpp_xloper` should (therefore) do the following:

1. It should make the most of C++ class constructors to make the creation and initialisation of `xlopers` as simple and intuitive as possible.
2. It should make use of the class destructor so that all the logic for freeing memory in the appropriate way is in one place.
3. It should make good use of C++ operator overloading to make assignment and extraction of values to and from existing `cpp_xlopers` easy and intuitive.
   a. It should use '=' to assign values (were possible).
   b. It should use unary '&' to obtain the address of the `xloper` it contains in order to look as much like an `xloper` as possible. (This might jar with some people as it carries the risk of making the code deceptive, but it makes the setting up of calls to `Excel4()` easy and identical to calls using `xlopers` directly.)
   c. It should use the `int, bool, double, double *` and `char*` conversion operators so that C-style casts work intuitively.
   d. It should overload the `==` operator to make type and value comparison easy.
4. It should change the `xloper` type and deal with any memory consequences of an assignment of a value to an existing `cpp_xloper`.
5. It should provide a clean way to convert between `xlopers` and supported OLE/COM variants.
6. It should provide a method for obtaining a pointer to a static `xloper` that can be returned to Excel. It should, at the same time, clean up the resources associated with the `cpp_xloper`, and handle any signalling to Excel about memory that still needs to be freed.

---

[2] There is, at the time of writing, a C++ wrapper called XLW developed by Jérôme Lecomte which can be accessed via the Source Forge website at http://xlw.sourceforge.net/. A review of this open source project is beyond the scope of this book, other than to say that it wraps more than just the Excel data structures: it also wraps access to many of the C API functions. It is well worth looking at, if only to see the variety of approaches and resources that can be employed.

The cpp_xloper class (included in the CD ROM) is a fairly thin skin to the xloper, exposing the following types of member functions:

- A number of constructor member functions, one for each of the types of xloper that one regularly needs in this context.
- A number of assignment functions, to change the type or value of an xloper.
- A number of type conversion operator functions that simplify the copying of an xloper's value to a simple C/C++ variable type.
- A number of functions that simplify the getting and setting of values within an xltypeMulti array.
- An overloaded *address of* operator (&) for the address of the xloper, and a function that returns the address of the cpp_xloper object to compensate for the hijacking of '&'.
- Some simple private functions that are self-explanatory.

The class contains some private data members:

- The xloper, m_Op.
- A Boolean, m_RowByRowArray, that determines if xltypeMulti arrays have their elements stored row-by-row or not.
- A Boolean, m_DLLtoFree, that determines if any memory pointed to by the xloper was dynamically allocated by the DLL. (This is set during construction or assignment and referred to during destruction or reassignment.)
- A Boolean, m_XLtoFree, that determines if any memory pointed to by the xloper was dynamically allocated by Excel. (This must be set using the SetExceltoFree() method, as the class has no way of knowing automatically. It is referred to during destruction or reassignment.)

Here is a listing of the header file cpp_xloper.h:

```
#include "xlcall.h"
#include "xloper.h"

class cpp_xloper
{
public:
//-----------------------------------------------------------------------
// constructors
//-----------------------------------------------------------------------
    cpp_xloper();                    // created as xltypeMissing
    cpp_xloper(xloper *p_oper); // contains copy of given xloper
    cpp_xloper(char *text);      // xltypeStr
    cpp_xloper(int w);           // xltypeInt
    cpp_xloper(int w, int min, int max); // xltypeInt (or xltypeMissing)
    cpp_xloper(double d);        // xltypeNum
    cpp_xloper(bool b);          // xltypeBool
    cpp_xloper(WORD e);          // xltypeErr
    cpp_xloper(WORD, WORD, BYTE, BYTE);  // xltypeSRef
    cpp_xloper(char *, WORD, WORD, BYTE, BYTE); // xltypeRef from sheet name
    cpp_xloper(DWORD, WORD, WORD, BYTE, BYTE);  // xltypeRef from sheet ID
    cpp_xloper(VARIANT *pv);     // Takes its type from the VARTYPE
```

```
    // xltypeMulti constructors
    cpp_xloper(WORD rows, WORD cols); // array of undetermined type
    cpp_xloper(WORD rows, WORD cols, double *d_array); // array of xltypeNum
    cpp_xloper(WORD rows, WORD cols, char **str_array); // xltypeStr array
    cpp_xloper(WORD &rows, WORD &cols, xloper *input_oper); // from SRef/Ref
    cpp_xloper(WORD rows, WORD cols, cpp_xloper *init_array);
    cpp_xloper(xl_array *array);

    cpp_xloper(cpp_xloper &source); // Copy constructor

//------------------------------------------------------------------
// destructor
//------------------------------------------------------------------
    ~cpp_xloper();

//------------------------------------------------------------------
// Overloaded operators
//------------------------------------------------------------------
    cpp_xloper &operator=(const cpp_xloper &source);
    void operator=(int);        // xltypeInt
    void operator=(bool b);     // xltypeBool
    void operator=(double);     // xltypeNum
    void operator=(WORD e);     // xltypeErr
    void operator=(char *);     // xltypeStr
    void operator=(xloper *);   // same type as passed-in xloper
    void operator=(VARIANT *);  // same type as passed-in Variant
    void operator=(xl_array *array);
    bool operator==(cpp_xloper &cpp_op2);
    bool operator==(int w);
    bool operator==(bool b);
    bool operator==(double d);
    bool operator==(WORD e);
    bool operator==(char *text);
    bool operator==(xloper *);
    bool operator!=(cpp_xloper &cpp_op2);
    bool operator!=(int w);
    bool operator!=(bool b);
    bool operator!=(double d);
    bool operator!=(WORD e);
    bool operator!=(char *text);
    bool operator!=(xloper *);
    void operator++(void);
    void operator--(void);
    operator int(void);
    operator bool(void);
    operator double(void);
    operator char *(void);
    xloper *operator&() {return &m_Op;}  // return xloper address

//------------------------------------------------------------------
// property get and set functions
//------------------------------------------------------------------
    int  GetType(void);
    void SetType(int new_type);
    bool SetTypeMulti(WORD array_rows, WORD array_cols);
    bool SetCell(WORD rwFirst, WORD rwLast, BYTE colFirst, BYTE colLast);
    bool GetVal(WORD &e);
    bool IsType(int);
    bool IsStr(void)    {return IsType(xltypeStr);}
    bool IsNum(void)    {return IsType(xltypeNum);}
    bool IsBool(void)   {return IsType(xltypeBool);}
```

```
    bool IsInt(void)      {return IsType(xltypeInt);}
    bool IsErr(void)      {return IsType(xltypeErr);}
    bool IsMulti(void)    {return IsType(xltypeMulti);}
    bool IsNil(void)      {return IsType(xltypeNil);}
    bool IsMissing(void){return IsType(xltypeMissing);}
    bool IsRef(void)      {return IsType(xltypeRef | xltypeSRef);}
    bool IsBigData(void);

//-------------------------------------------------------------------
// property get and set functions for xltypeMulti
//-------------------------------------------------------------------
    int  GetArrayElementType(WORD row, WORD column);
    bool GetArraySize(WORD &rows, WORD &cols);
    xloper *GetArrayElement(WORD row, WORD column);

    bool GetArrayElement(WORD row, WORD column, int &w);
    bool GetArrayElement(WORD row, WORD column, bool &b);
    bool GetArrayElement(WORD row, WORD column, double &d);
    bool GetArrayElement(WORD row, WORD column, WORD &e);
    bool GetArrayElement(WORD row, WORD column, char *&text); // deep copy

    bool SetArrayElementType(WORD row, WORD column, int new_type);
    bool SetArrayElement(WORD row, WORD column, int w);
    bool SetArrayElement(WORD row, WORD column, bool b);
    bool SetArrayElement(WORD row, WORD column, double d);
    bool SetArrayElement(WORD row, WORD column, WORD e);
    bool SetArrayElement(WORD row, WORD column, char *text);
    bool SetArrayElement(WORD row, WORD column, xloper *p_source);

    int  GetArrayElementType(DWORD offset);
    bool GetArraySize(DWORD &size);
    xloper *GetArrayElement(DWORD offset);

    bool GetArrayElement(DWORD offset, char *&text); // makes new string
    bool GetArrayElement(DWORD offset, double &d);
    bool GetArrayElement(DWORD offset, int &w);
    bool GetArrayElement(DWORD offset, bool &b);
    bool GetArrayElement(DWORD offset, WORD &e);

    bool SetArrayElementType(DWORD offset, int new_type);
    bool SetArrayElement(DWORD offset, int w);
    bool SetArrayElement(DWORD offset, bool b);
    bool SetArrayElement(DWORD offset, double d);
    bool SetArrayElement(DWORD offset, WORD e);
    bool SetArrayElement(DWORD offset, char *text);
    bool SetArrayElement(DWORD offset, xloper *p_source);

    void InitialiseArray(WORD rows, WORD cols, double *init_data);
    void InitialiseArray(WORD rows, WORD cols, cpp_xloper *init_array);
    bool Transpose(void);

    double *ConvertMultiToDouble(void);

//-------------------------------------------------------------------
// other public functions
//-------------------------------------------------------------------
    void Clear(void);   // Clears the xloper without freeing memory
    void SetExceltoFree(void);  // Tell the destructor to use xlFree
    cpp_xloper *Addr(void) {return this;} // Returns address of cpp_xloper
    xloper *ExtractXloper(bool ExceltoFree = false); // extract xloper
    void Free(bool ExceltoFree = false); // free memory
```

```
    bool ConvertToString(bool ExceltoFree);
    bool AsVariant(VARIANT &var); // Return an equivalent Variant
    xl_array *AsDblArray(void); // Return an xl_array

private:
    xloper m_Op;
    bool m_RowByRowArray;
    bool m_DLLtoFree;
    bool m_XLtoFree;
};
```

A full listing of the body of class code is included on the CD ROM in the example project source file cpp_xloper.cpp. Sections of it are also reproduced below as examples of the low level handling of xlopers and conversion to and from C/C++ types.

6.5   CONVERTING BETWEEN xlopers AND C/C++ DATA TYPES

The need to convert arguments and return values can, in many cases, be avoided by declaring functions as taking C-type arguments and returning C-type values. (How you inform Excel what type of arguments your DLL function expects and what type of return value it outputs is covered in section 8.5 *Registering and un-registering DLL (XLL) functions* on page 182.)

However, conversion from C/C++ types to xlopers *is* necessary when accessing Excel's functionality from within the DLL using the C API. This includes when you want to register your add-in functions. Excel demands that inputs to the interface functions Excel4() and Excel4v() are given as pointers to xlopers. Also, values are returned via xlopers. Fortunately, this conversion is very straightforward in most cases.

If you want to accept input from Excel in the most general form, it is necessary to declare DLL functions as taking xloper * arguments. Unless they are to be passed directly back into Excel via the C API interface, you would then need to convert them. Excel should never pass in a null xloper * pointer even if the argument is missing. The xloper will have the type xltypeMissing instead.

Conversion is also necessary when you want to declare a DLL function as being capable of returning different data types, for example, a string or a number. In this case the function needs to return a pointer to an xloper that is not on the stack, i.e., that will survive the return statement.

The following sections provide a more detailed discussion of the xloper types and give examples of how to convert them to C/C++ types or to create them from C/C++ types. Some of the examples are function methods from the cpp_xloper class.

6.6   CONVERTING BETWEEN xloper TYPES

The cpp_xloper relies on a set of routines for converting from one xloper type to another, as well as to and from native C/C++ types. Many of these routines are reproduced in the examples in section 6.8 below. Of particular importance is the Excel C API function xlCoerce. This function, accessed via the C API interface function Excel4(), attempts to return an `xloper` of a requested type from the type of the passed-in `xloper`. It is covered in detail in section 8.7.3 *Converting one `xloper` type to another: `xlCoerce`* on page 201. In the examples that follow, this function is itself wrapped in a function whose prototype is:

```
bool coerce_xloper(xloper *p_op, xloper &ret_val, int target_type);
```

This attempts to convert any `xloper` to an `xloper` of `target_type`. It returns `false` if unsuccessful and `true` if successful, with the converted value returned via the pass-by-ref argument, `ret_val`. The code for this function is listed in section 8.7.3 on page 201.

6.7   CONVERTING BETWEEN `xlopers` AND VARIANTS

Chapter 3 *Using VBA* discusses the OLE Variant structure and the various types supported by VBA, as well as the more limited subset that Excel passes to VBA functions declared as taking Variant arguments. It is also useful to have a number of conversion routines in an XLL that you also wish to use as interface to VBA, or that you might want to use to access COM. The `cpp_xloper` class has a number of these:

```
cpp_xloper(VARIANT *pv); // Takes its type from the VARTYPE
void operator=(VARIANT *);  // Same type as passed-in Variant
bool AsVariant(VARIANT &var); // Return an equivalent Variant
```

The first two, a constructor and an overloaded assignment operator, rely on the following routine. (The code for the function `array_vt_to_xloper()` is a variation on this function. All the following code is listed in `xloper.cpp` in the example project on the CD ROM.)

```
#include <ole2.h>
#define VT_XL_ERR_OFFSET    2148141008ul

bool vt_to_xloper(xloper &op, VARIANT *pv, bool convert_array)
{
    if(pv->vt & (VT_VECTOR | VT_BYREF))
        return false;

    if(pv->vt & VT_ARRAY)
    {
        if(!convert_array)
            return false;

        return array_vt_to_xloper(op, pv);
    }

    switch(pv->vt)
    {
    case VT_R8:
        op.xltype = xltypeNum;
        op.val.num = pv->dblVal;
        break;
```

```
   case VT_I2:
      op.xltype = xltypeInt;
      op.val.w = pv->iVal;
      break;

   case VT_BOOL:
      op.xltype = xltypeBool;
      op.val._bool = pv->boolVal;
      break;

   case VT_ERROR:
      op.xltype = xltypeErr;
      op.val.err = (unsigned short)(pv->ulVal - VT_XL_ERR_OFFSET);
      break;

   case VT_BSTR:
      op.xltype = xltypeStr;
      op.val.str = vt_bstr_to_xlstring(pv->bstrVal);
      break;

   case VT_CY:
      op.xltype = xltypeNum;
      op.val.num = (double)(pv->cyVal.int64 / 1e4);
      break;

   default: // type not converted
      return false;
   }
   return true;
}
```

The third converts in the other direction and relies on the following routine:

```
bool xloper_to_vt(xloper *p_op, VARIANT &var, bool convert_array)
{
   VariantInit(&var); // type is set to VT_EMPTY

   switch(p_op->xltype)
   {
   case xltypeNum:
      var.vt = VT_R8;
      var.dblVal = p_op->val.num;
      break;

   case xltypeInt:
      var.vt = VT_I2;
      var.iVal = p_op->val.w;
      break;

   case xltypeBool:
      var.vt = VT_BOOL;
      var.boolVal = p_op->val._bool;
      break;

   case xltypeStr:
      var.vt = VT_BSTR;
      var.bstrVal = xlstring_to_vt_bstr(p_op->val.str);
      break;
```

```
    case xltypeErr:
        var.vt = VT_ERROR;
        var.ulVal = VT_XL_ERR_OFFSET + p_op->val.err;
        break;

    case xltypeMulti:
        if(convert_array)
        {
            VARIANT temp_vt;
            SAFEARRAYBOUND bound[2];
            long elt_index[2];

            bound[0].lLbound = bound[1].lLbound = 0;
            bound[0].cElements = p_op->val.array.rows;
            bound[1].cElements = p_op->val.array.columns;

            var.vt = VT_ARRAY | VT_VARIANT; // array of Variants
            var.parray = SafeArrayCreate(VT_VARIANT, 2, bound);

            if(!var.parray)
                return false;

            xloper *p_op_temp = p_op->val.array.lparray;

            for(WORD r = 0; r < p_op->val.array.rows; r++)
            {
                for(WORD c = 0; c < p_op->val.array.columns;)
                {
                // Don't convert array within array
                    xloper_to_vt(p_op_temp++, temp_vt, false);

                    elt_index[0] = r;
                    elt_index[1] = c++;
                    SafeArrayPutElement(var.parray, elt_index, &temp_vt);
                }
            }
            break;
        }
        // else, fall through to default option

    default: // type not converted
        return false;
    }
    return true;
}
```

It is important to note that Variant strings are wide-character OLE BSTRs, in contrast
to the byte-string BSTRs that Excel VBA uses for its String type when exchanging
data with Excel and with a DLL declared as taking a String (in VB)/BSTR (in C/C++)
argument. The following code shows both conversions:

```
// Converts a VT_BSTR wide-char string to a newly allocated C API
// byte-counted string.  Memory returned must be freed by caller.

char *vt_bstr_to_xlstring(BSTR bstr)
{
    if(!bstr)
        return NULL;
```

```
    int len = SysStringLen(bstr);

    if(len > 255)
        len = 255; // truncate

    char *p = (char *)malloc(len + 2);

// VT_BSTR is a wchar_t string, so need to convert to a byte-string
    if(!p || wcstombs(p + 1, bstr, len + 1) < 0)
    {
        free(p);
        return false;
    }

    p[0] = (char)len;
    return p;
}

// Converts a C API byte-counted string to a VT_BSTR wide-char string
// Does not rely on (or assume) that input string is null-terminated.

BSTR xlstring_to_vt_bstr(char *str)
{
    if(!str)
        return NULL;

    wchar_t *p = (wchar_t *)malloc(str[0] * sizeof(wchar_t));

    if(!p || mbstowcs(p, str + 1, str[0]) < 0)
    {
        free(p);
        return NULL;
    }

    BSTR bstr = SysAllocStringLen(p, str[0]);
    free(p);
    return bstr;
}
```

6.8   DETAILED DISCUSSION OF `xloper` TYPES

This section describes in more detail the things you need to know about each `xloper` type to be able to work with it, specifically:

- When you will encounter it.
- When you need to create it.
- How you create an instance of it.
- How you convert it to a C/C++ data type.
- What the memory considerations are.
- How you can avoid using it.

Bear in mind that you may not need to use these structures in those cases where you have declared functions as taking and returning simple C/C++ data types. You only need to use `xlopers` in the following circumstances:[3]

---

[3] You can, of course, avoid using `xlopers` by using a VB interface and variants in many of these cases.

- When implementing the XLL Add-in Manager interface functions that take `xloper *` arguments.
- When receiving arguments of types that are only supported in `xlopers` (cell or range references).
- When receiving arguments that might take different types.
- When receiving arguments that you explicitly DO NOT want Excel to convert before passing them to the DLL.
- Where a function's return type requires the use of `xlopers` (for example, errors or arrays that contain more than just numbers) or might take on more than one data type (a string, a number or an error value).
- When calling into the C API via calls to `Excel4()` or `Excel4v()`.

The code examples that follow use the C `xloper` structure directly in some cases, and the C++ class `cpp_xloper`, described on page 121, in others. Those that use the latter are those where the use of C++ constructors, destructors and operator overloading makes the code far more straightforward: the handling of the elements of the `xloper` and memory are hidden in the class implementation. The majority of the examples that deal with `xltypeMulti`, `xltypeSRef` and `xltypeRef` types only use `cpp_xlopers`.

6.8.1   Freeing `xloper` memory

Some of the code samples below call one or both of the functions `free_xloper()` and `cpp_xloper::Free()` before assigning values to a passed-in `xloper` or `cpp_xloper`. These functions clear any memory that might be associated with the `xloper` according to its type and how the memory was allocated in the first place. The function `free_xloper()`, that deals with `xlopers` and has no knowledge of the `cpp_xloper` class, needs one of two bits in the `xltype` field to be set in order to know how to free memory: `xlbitDLLFree` or `xlbitXLFree`. This must be done in the DLL with some knowledge of how they were originally created. (See Chapter 7 *Memory Management* on page 161 for more details.)

Here is the code for both of these functions:

```
void free_xloper(xloper *p_op, bool use_xlbits)
{
// If created by Excel and the DLL has set this bit, then use Excel
// to free the memory.
    if(use_xlbits && (p_op->xltype & xlbitXLFree))
    {
        p_op->xltype &= ~xlbitXLFree;
        Excel4(xlFree, 0, 1, p_op);
        return;
    }

    WORD dll_free = use_xlbits ? xlbitDLLFree : 0;
    WORD xl_free = use_xlbits ? xlbitXLFree : 0;

    if(p_op->xltype & xltypeMulti)
    {
// First check if elements need to be freed then check if the array
```

```
// itself needs to be freed.
        int limit = p_op->val.array.rows * p_op->val.array.columns;
        xloper *p = p_op->val.array.lparray;

        for(int i = limit; i--; p++)
            if(p->xltype & (xl_free | dll_free))
                free_xloper(p, use_xlbits);

        if(p_op->xltype & dll_free)
            free(p_op->val.array.lparray);
    }
    else if(p_op->xltype == (xltypeStr | dll_free))
    {
        free(p_op->val.str);
    }
    else if(p_op->xltype == (xltypeRef | dll_free))
    {
        free(p_op->val.mref.lpmref);
    }
}
```

```
void cpp_xloper::Free(bool ExceltoFree)   // free mem and initialise
{
    if(ExceltoFree)
        m_XLtoFree = true;

    if(m_XLtoFree)
    {
        Excel4(xlFree, 0, 1, &m_Op);
    }
    else if(m_DLLtoFree)
    {
        free_xloper(&m_Op, false);
    }
// Reset the properties ready for destruction or reuse
    Clear();
}
```

6.8.2   Worksheet (floating point) number: `xltypeNum`

When you will encounter it

This `xloper` type is used by Excel for all numbers passed from worksheets to a DLL, whether floating point or integer. It is also returned by a number of the C API functions.

When you need to create it

A number of Excel's own functions take floating point numbers as arguments, for example, Excel's mathematical worksheet functions. When calling them from within the DLL this data type should be used. Where you are passing an integer argument, you can use the `xltypeInt` type, although there is no advantage in doing this.

Using this kind of `xloper` is the most sensible way to pass numbers back to Excel in those cases where you may also wish to return, say, an Excel error.

How you create an instance of it

The code to populate an `xloper` of this type is:

```
void set_to_double(xloper *p_op, double d)
{
    if(!p_op) return;
    p_op->xltype = xltypeNum;
    p_op->val.num = d;
}
```

Using the `cpp_xloper` class, creation can look like any of these:

```
double x, y, z;
//...
cpp_xloper Oper1(x); // creates an xltypeNum xloper, value = x
cpp_xloper Oper2 = y; // creates an xltypeNum xloper, value = y
cpp_xloper Oper3; // creates an xloper of undefined type

// Change the type of Oper3 to xltypeNum, value = z, using the
// overloaded operator=
Oper3 = z;

// Create xltypeNum=z using copy constructor
cpp_xloper Oper4 = Oper3;
```

The code for the `xltypeNum` constructor is:

```
cpp_xloper::cpp_xloper(double d)
{
    Clear();
    set_to_double(&m_Op, d);
}
```

The code for the overloaded conversion operator '=' is:

```
void cpp_xloper::operator=(double d)
{
    Free();
    set_to_double(&m_Op, d);
}
```

How you convert it to a C/C++ data type

The following code example shows how to access (or convert, if not an `xltypeNum`) the value of the `xloper`:

```
bool coerce_to_double(xloper *p_op, double &d)
{
    if(!p_op)
        return false;

    if(p_op->xltype == xltypeNum)
    {
        d = p_op->val.num;
        return true;
    }
// xloper is not a floating point number type, so try to convert it.
    xloper ret_val;

    if(!coerce_xloper(p_op, ret_val, xltypeNum))
        return false;

    d = ret_val.val.num;
    return true;
}
```

Using the `cpp_xloper` class the conversion would look like this:

```
cpp_xloper Oper;

// Some code that sets Oper's value...

double result = (double)Oper; // use the overloaded cast
```

The code for the overloaded cast operator `(double)` is:

```
cpp_xloper::operator double(void)
{
    double d;

    if(coerce_to_double(&m_Op, d))
        return d;

    return 0.0;
}
```

What the memory considerations are

None (unless the 10 bytes for the `xloper` itself are dynamically allocated), as the `double val.num` is contained entirely within the `xloper`.

How you can avoid using it

Declare functions as taking double arguments and/or returning doubles: Excel will do the necessary conversions.

6.8.3 Byte-counted string: `xltypeStr`

When you will encounter it

This `xloper` type is used by Excel for all text passed from worksheets to a DLL. It is also returned by a number of the C API functions.

When you need to create it

A number of Excel functions take text arguments. Perhaps most importantly, from the point of view of making DLL functions accessible directly from the worksheet, is the function that registers DLL functions. (See section 8.5 *Registering and un-registering DLL (XLL) functions* on page 182.) When calling them from the DLL, this data type should be used. It is also the most sensible way to pass strings back to Excel where you may also sometimes want to return, say, an Excel error.

How you create an instance of it

The code to populate an `xloper` of this type is:

```
void set_to_text(xloper *p_op, char *text)
{
    if(!p_op) return;

    if((p_op->val.str = new_xlstring(text)) == NULL)
        p_op->xltype = xltypeMissing;
    else
        p_op->xltype = xltypeStr;
}
```

The code for `new_xlstring()` is:

```
char *new_xlstring(char *text)
{
    if(!text)        return NULL;
    int len = strlen(text);
    if(len == 0)    return NULL;
    if(len > 255)   len = 255; // truncate

    char *p = (char *)malloc(len + 2);
    memcpy(p + 1, text, len + 1);
    p[0] = (char)len;
    return p;
}
```

Using the `cpp_xloper` class, creation can look like any of these (note that the constructor creates a deep copy of the string, rather than storing a pointer to the initial strings):

```
char *x, *y, *z;
//... Initialise the strings, then...

cpp_xloper Oper1(x); // creates an xltypeStr xloper, value = x
cpp_xloper Oper2 = y; // creates an xltypeStr xloper, value = y
cpp_xloper Oper3; // creates an xloper of undefined type

// Change the type of Oper3 to xltypeStr, value = z, using the
// overloaded operator =
Oper3 = z;

// Create xltypeStr=z using copy constructor
cpp_xloper Oper4 = Oper3;
```

The code for the `xltypeStr` constructor is:

```
cpp_xloper::cpp_xloper(char *text)
{
    Clear();
    set_to_text(&m_Op, text);
    m_DLLtoFree = true;
}
```

Note that in this example it is necessary to set m_DLLtoFree = true to ensure that, at destruction or assignment of a different value, the memory will be freed in the right way.

The code for the overloaded conversion operator '=' is:

```
void cpp_xloper::operator=(char *text)
{
    Free();
    set_to_text(&m_Op, text);
    m_DLLtoFree = true;
}
```

How you convert it to a C/C++ data type

The following code example shows how to get at the string pointed to by the `xloper`. Note that, when making a copy, the code <u>does not</u> assume that a byte-counted string (which might have been created by Excel) is null terminated. This would be an unsafe assumption.

```
bool coerce_to_string(xloper *p_op, char *&text)
{
    char *str;
    xloper ret_val;

    text = 0;

    if(!p_op)
        return false;
```

```
    if(p_op->xltype != xltypeStr)
    {
// xloper is not a string type, so try to convert it.
        if(!coerce_xloper(p_op, ret_val, xltypeStr))
            return false;

        str = ret_val.val.str;
    }
    else if(!(str = p_op->val.str)) // make a working copy of ptr
        return false;

    int len = str[0];

    if((text = (char *)malloc(len + 1)) == NULL) // caller to free
        return false;

    if(len)
        memcpy(text, str + 1, len);

    text[len] = 0; // terminate the copy of the string

// Is the string from which the copy was made was created in a call
// to coerce_xloper above, then need to free it with a call to xlFree
    if(p_op->xltype != xltypeStr)
        Excel4(xlFree, 0, 1, &ret_val);

    return true;
}
```

Using the `cpp_xloper` class the conversion would look like this:

```
// Construct an xltypeStr cpp_xloper. Destructor will clean up memory
// when Oper is no longer required.
    cpp_xloper Oper("Test string");

    char *string_copy = (char *)Oper;

// ... after using the result, free the string memory
    free(string_copy);
```

The code for the overloaded conversion operator (`char *`) is:

```
cpp_xloper::operator char *(void)
{
    char *p;

    if(coerce_to_string(&m_Op, p))
        return p;

    return NULL;
}
```

What the memory considerations are

When Excel passes you an `xltypeStr` it is best to avoid doing anything other than reading it. If you need to modify it, make a copy. When you are allocating memory for strings to be returned to Excel, the returned pointer is forgotten about by Excel once it has copied out the text. Obviously, associated memory cannot be freed by the DLL before returning from the function. This makes returning dynamically allocated strings to Excel as `char *` a bad idea. Returning an `xltypeStr xloper` gives you the ability to instruct Excel to call back into your DLL once it has finished. Then you can release the memory. (This topic is covered in section 7.4 *Getting Excel to call back the DLL to free DLL-allocated memory* on page 166.)

The following example code would leak memory every time it was called with a valid value of `i`.

```
char * __stdcall bad_string_example(short i)
{
    if(i < 1 || i > 26) return NULL;
    char *rtn_string = (char *)malloc(i + 1);
    for(char *p = rtn_string; i; *p++ = 'A' + --i);
    return rtn_string;
}
```

Where an `xloper` points to a *static* byte-counted string, there is nothing to worry about.

How you can avoid using it

Declare functions as taking null-terminated `char *` arguments and/or returning `char *`. Excel will do the necessary conversions, but, <u>beware</u>: returning dynamically allocated strings in this way will result in memory leaks.

6.8.4   Excel Boolean: `xltypeBool`

When you will encounter it

This `xloper` type is used by Excel for all Boolean (`true` or `false`) values passed from worksheets to a DLL. It is also returned by a number of the C API functions.

When you need to create it

A number of Excel's own functions take Boolean arguments, often to trigger non-default behaviour. When calling them from within the DLL using the C API this data type should be used. (Excel will attempt to convert numeric `xltypeNum` or `xltypeInt` arguments to true or false values.) If you want your worksheet function to evaluate to TRUE or FALSE then you have no choice but to use this type.

How you create an instance of it

The code to populate an `xloper` of this type is:

```
void set_to_bool(xloper *p_op, bool b)
{
    if(!p_op) return;
    p_op->xltype = xltypeBool;
    p_op->val._bool = (b ? 1 : 0);
}
```

Using the cpp_xloper class, creation can look like any of these:

```
bool x, y, z;
//...
cpp_xloper Oper1(x); // creates an xltypeBool xloper, value = x
cpp_xloper Oper2 = y; // creates an xltypeBool xloper, value = y
cpp_xloper Oper3; // creates an xloper of undefined type

// Change the type of Oper3 to xltypeBool, value = z, using the
// overloaded operator =
Oper3 = z;

// Create xltypeBool=z using copy constructor
cpp_xloper Oper4 = Oper3;
```

The code for the xltypeBool constructor is:

```
cpp_xloper::cpp_xloper(bool b)
{
    Clear();
    set_to_bool(&m_Op, b);
}
```

The code for the overloaded conversion operator '=' is:

```
void cpp_xloper::operator=(bool b)
{
    Free();
    set_to_bool(&m_Op, b);
}
```

How you convert it to a C/C++ data type

The xloper, being a C structure, does not know about the C++ bool type. Its value is represented within the xloper as integer 1 (TRUE) or 0 (FALSE).

The following code example shows how to access (or convert, if not an xltypeBool) the value of the xloper:

```
bool coerce_to_bool(xloper *p_op, bool &b)
{
    if(!p_op)
        return false;

    if(p_op->xltype == xltypeBool)
    {
        b = (p_op->val._bool != 0);
        return true;
    }
// xloper is not a Boolean number type, so try to convert it.
    xloper ret_val;

    if(!coerce_xloper(p_op, ret_val, xltypeBool))
```

```
        return false;

    b = (ret_val.val._bool != 0);
    return true;
}
```

Using the `cpp_xloper` class the conversion would look like this:

```
    cpp_xloper Oper;

// Some code that sets Oper's value...

    bool result = (bool)Oper;
```

The code for the overloaded conversion operator `(bool)` is:

```
cpp_xloper::operator bool(void)
{
    bool b;

    if(coerce_to_bool(&m_Op, b))
        return b;

    return false;
}
```

What the memory considerations are

None (unless the 10 bytes for the `xloper` itself are dynamically allocated), as the integer `_bool` is contained entirely within the `xloper`.

How you can avoid using it

Declare functions as taking `int` arguments and/or returning `int`s: Excel will do the necessary conversions.

6.8.5   Worksheet error value: `xltypeErr`

When you will encounter it

This `xloper` type is used by Excel for all error values passed from worksheets to a DLL. When you want your DLL code to be called even if one of the inputs evaluates to an error (such as range with invalid references – #REF!), you should declare arguments as `xloper`s. Otherwise Excel will intercept the error and fail the function call before the DLL code is even reached.

This `xloper` type is returned by most of the C API functions when they fail to complete successfully. DLL functions accessed via VB that accept Variant arguments, or arrays of Variants, may need to convert between the Variant representation of Excel errors and the C API error codes. This is discussed in section 3.6.11 *Variant types that Excel can pass to VB functions* on page 59.

When you need to create it

Excel's error codes provide a very well understood way of communicating problems to the worksheet, and are therefore very useful. They have the added benefit of propagating through to dependent cells. It's a good idea to declare fallible worksheet functions as returning `xlopers` so that errors can be returned, in addition to the desired output type.

You might even want to pass an error code into a C API function, although this is unlikely.

How you create an instance of it

An example of code to populate an `xloper` of this type is:

```
void set_to_err(xloper *p_op, WORD e)
{
    if(!p_op) return;

    switch(e)
    {
    case xlerrNull:
    case xlerrDiv0:
    case xlerrValue:
    case xlerrRef:
    case xlerrName:
    case xlerrNum:
    case xlerrNA:
        p_op->xltype = xltypeErr;
        p_op->val.err = e;
        break;

    default:
        p_op->xltype = xltypeMissing; // not a valid error code
    }
}
```

Using the `cpp_xloper` class, creation can look like any of these:

```
WORD x, y, z;
//...
cpp_xloper Oper1(x); // creates an xltypeErr xloper, value = x
cpp_xloper Oper2 = y; // creates an xltypeErr xloper, value = y
cpp_xloper Oper3; // creates an xloper of undefined type

// Change the type of Oper3 to xltypeErr, value = z, using the
// overloaded operator =
Oper3 = z;

// Create xltypeErr=z using copy constructor
cpp_xloper Oper4 = Oper3;
```

The code for the `xltypeErr` constructor is:

```
cpp_xloper::cpp_xloper(WORD e)
{
    Clear();
    set_to_err(&m_Op, e);
}
```

The code for the overloaded conversion operator '=' is:

```
void cpp_xloper::operator=(WORD e)
{
    Free();
    set_to_err(&m_Op, e);
}
```

How you convert it to a C/C++ data type

It is unlikely that you will need to convert an error type to another data type. If you do need the numeric error value, it is obtained from the `err` element of the `xloper`'s `val` union.

What the memory considerations are

None (unless the 10 bytes for the `xloper` itself are dynamically allocated), as the integer `err` is contained entirely within the `xloper`.

How you can avoid using it

If you want to write worksheet functions that can trap and generate errors, you can't.

6.8.6   Excel internal integer: `xltypeInt`

When you will encounter it

This `xloper` type is NEVER passed by Excel from worksheets to a DLL. Some of the C API functions might return this type.

When you need to create it

A number of Excel's own functions take integer arguments and when calling them from within the DLL this data type should be used. (Excel will try to convert the `xltypeNum` type, if that is passed instead.) It can be used to pass integers, within its range, back to Excel, especially in those cases where you might also want to return, say, an Excel error. Again, the `xltypeNum` type can also be used for this and using `xltypeInt` does not deliver any advantage in this case.

How you create an instance of it

The code to populate an `xloper` of this type is:

```
void set_to_int(xloper *p_op, int w)
{
    if(!p_op) return;
    p_op->xltype = xltypeInt;
    p_op->val.w = w;
}
```

Using the `cpp_xloper` class, creation can look like any of these:

```
int x, y, z;
//...
cpp_xloper Oper1(x); // creates an xltypeInt xloper, value = x
cpp_xloper Oper2 = y; // creates an xltypeInt xloper, value = y
cpp_xloper Oper3; // creates an xloper of undefined type

// Change the type of Oper3 to xltypeInt, value = z, using the
// overloaded operator =
Oper3 = z;

// Create xltypeInt=z using copy constructor
cpp_xloper Oper4 = Oper3;
```

The code for the `xltypeInt` constructor is:

```
cpp_xloper::cpp_xloper(int w)
{
    Clear();
    set_to_int(&m_Op, w);
}
```

The code for the overloaded conversion operator '=' is:

```
void cpp_xloper::operator=(int w)
{
    Free();
    set_to_int(&m_Op, w);
}
```

How you convert it into a C/C++ data type

The following code example shows how to access (or convert, if not an `xltypeInt`) the `xloper`:

```
bool coerce_to_int(xloper *p_op, int &w)
{
    if(!p_op)
        return false;
```

```
    if(p_op->xltype == xltypeInt)
    {
        w = p_op->val.w;
        return true;
    }

    if(p_op->xltype == xltypeErr)
    {
        w = p_op->val.err;
        return true;
    }
// xloper is not an integer type, so try to convert it.
    xloper ret_val;

    if(!coerce_xloper(p_op, ret_val, xltypeInt))
        return false;

    w = ret_val.val.w;
    return true;
}
```

Using the `cpp_xloper` class the conversion would look like this:

```
    cpp_xloper Oper;

// Some code that sets Oper's value...

    int result = (int)Oper;
```

The code for the overloaded conversion operator (`int`) is:

```
cpp_xloper::operator int(void)
{
    int i;

    if(coerce_to_int(&m_Op, i))
        return i;

    return 0;
}
```

What the memory considerations are

None (unless the 10 bytes for the `xloper` itself are dynamically allocated), as the integer `w` is contained entirely within the `xloper`.

How you can avoid using it

Declare functions as taking `int` arguments and/or returning `int`s: Excel will do the necessary conversions.

6.8.7 Array (mixed type): `xltypeMulti`

This `xloper` type is used to refer to arrays whose elements may be any one of a number of mixed `xloper` types. The elements of such an array are stored (and read) row-by-row in a continuous block of memory.[4]

There are important distinctions between such an array and an `xloper` that refers to a range of cells on a worksheet:

- The array is not associated with a block of cells on a worksheet.
- The memory for the array elements is pointed to in the `xltypeMulti`. (In range `xlopers` this is not the case. The data contained in the range of cells can only be accessed indirectly, for example, using `xlCoerce`.)
- Some Excel functions accept either range references or arrays as arguments, whereas others will only accept ranges.

An `xltypeMulti` is far more straightforward to work with than the range `xloper` types. Accessing blocks of data passed to the DLL in an `xltypeMulti` is quite easy. Their use is necessary if you want to pass arrays to C API functions where the data is not in any spreadsheet.

When you will encounter it

If a DLL function is registered with Excel as taking an `xloper`, an `xltypeMulti` is only passed to the DLL when the supplied argument is a literal array within the formula, for example, =SUM({1,2,3}). If the function is registered as taking an `oper`, an `xltypeMulti` is passed whenever the function is called with a range *or* a literal array. In this case, Excel handles the conversion from range `xloper` to array `oper` before calling the DLL.

Many of the C API functions return `xltypeMulti` `xlopers`, especially those returning variable length lists, such as a list of sheets in a workbook. (See section 8.9.10 *Information about a workbook*: `xlfGetWorkbook` on page 225 for details of this particular example.)

When you need to create it

A number of Excel's own functions take both array and range arguments. When calling them from within the DLL, an `xltypeMulti` should be used unless the data are on a worksheet. In that case, it is better to use a range `xloper`. (Note that not all C API functions that take ranges will accept arrays: those returning information about a supposedly real collection of cells on a real worksheet will not.)

This `xloper` type provides the best way to return arrays of data that can be of mixed type back to a worksheet. (Note that to return a block of data to a worksheet function, the cell formula must be entered into the worksheet as an array formula.) It can also provide a stepping stone to reading the contents of a worksheet range, being much easier to work with than the `xlopers` that describe ranges `xltypeSRef` and `xltypeRef`. One of the `cpp_xloper` constructors below shows the conversion of these types to `xltypeMulti` using the `xlCoerce` function.

---

[4] Variant arrays passed from VB to a C/C++ DLL store their elements column-by-column. See section 3.7 *Excel ranges, VB arrays, SafeArrays, array Variants* on page 64 for details.

Warning: A range that covers an entire column on a worksheet (e.g., A:A in a cell formula, equivalent to A1:A65536) can, in theory, be passed into a DLL in an xloper of type xltypeSRef or xltypeRef. However, there is a bug. The xloper will be given the rwLast value of 0x3fff instead of 0xffff. Even if this were not the case, coercing a reference that represented an entire column to an xltypeMulti would fail. The rows field in the xltypeMulti, being a WORD that counts from 1, would roll back over to zero. In other words, the xltypeMulti is limited to arrays from ranges with rows from 1 to 65,535 inclusive OR 2 to 65,536 inclusive. You should bear this limitation in mind when coding and documenting your DLL functions.

How you create an instance of it

The cpp_xloper class makes use of a function set_to_xltypeMulti() that populates an xloper as this type. The code for the function set_to_xltypeMulti() is:

```
bool set_to_xltypeMulti(xloper *p_op, WORD rows, WORD cols)
{
    int size = rows * cols;

    if(!p_op || !size || rows == 0xffff || cols > 0x00ff)
        return false;

    p_op->xltype = xltypeMulti;
    p_op->val.array.lparray = (xloper *)malloc(sizeof(xloper)*size);
    p_op->val.array.rows = rows;
    p_op->val.array.columns = cols;
    return true;
}
```

The class cpp_xloper contains four constructors for this xloper type and these are listed below.

The first constructor creates an un-initialised array of the specified size.

```
cpp_xloper::cpp_xloper(WORD rows, WORD cols)
{
    Clear();
    xloper *p_oper;

    if(!set_to_xltypeMulti(&m_Op, rows, cols)
    || !(p_oper = m_Op.val.array.lparray))
        return;

    m_DLLtoFree = true;

    for(int i = rows * cols; i--; p_oper++)
        p_oper->xltype = xltypeMissing; // a safe default
}
```

The second constructor creates an array of xltypeNum xlopers which is initialised using the array of doubles provided.

```
cpp_xloper::cpp_xloper(WORD rows, WORD cols, double *d_array)
{
    Clear();
    xloper *p_oper;

    if(!d_array || !set_to_xltypeMulti(&m_Op, rows, cols)
    || !(p_oper = m_Op.val.array.lparray))
        return;

    m_DLLtoFree = true;

    for(int i = rows * cols; i--; p_oper++)
    {
        p_oper->xltype = xltypeNum;
        p_oper->val.num = *d_array++;
    }
}
```

The third constructor creates an array of `xltypeStr` xlopers which contain deep copies of the strings in the array provided. (The `cpp_xloper` class always creates copies of strings so that there is no ambiguity about whether the strings in a dynamically allocated array should themselves be freed – they will always need to be. See section 5.5.7 *xlAuto-Free* on page 103, and Chapter 7 *Memory management* on page 161 for more details.)

```
cpp_xloper::cpp_xloper(WORD rows, WORD cols, char **str_array)
{
    Clear();
    xloper *p_oper;

    if(!str_array || !set_to_xltypeMulti(&op, rows, cols)
    || !(p_oper = op.val.array.lparray))
        return;

    m_DLLtoFree = true;
    char *p;

    for(int i = rows * cols; i--; p_oper++)
    {
        p = new_xlstring(*str_array++);

        if(p)
        {
            p_oper->xltype = xltypeStr;
            p_oper->val.str = p;
        }
        else
        {
            p_oper->xltype = xltypeMissing;
        }
    }
}
```

The fourth constructor creates an array of `xlopers` from either of the worksheet range types, `xltypeSRef` and `xltypeRef`, leaving the hard work to the `xlCoerce` function.[5] The

---

[5] In fact `xlCoerce` doesn't care what type the input `xloper` is. It will attempt to convert it to an `xltype-Multi` regardless. Even if it is a single cell or, say, numerical value, it will return a 1x1 array. This makes it a very powerful tool.

types of the elements of the resulting array reflect those of the worksheet range originally referred to. The resulting array must only be freed by Excel, either in the DLL via a call to xlFree, or by being returned to Excel with the xlbitXLFree bit set in xltype. (See the destructor code for how the class takes care of this, and Chapter 7 *Memory Management* on page 161.)

```cpp
cpp_xloper::cpp_xloper(WORD &rows, WORD &cols, xloper *input_oper)
{
    Clear();

// Ask Excel to convert the reference to an array (xltypeMulti)
    if(!coerce_xloper(input_oper, op, xltypeMulti))
    {
        rows = cols = 0;
    }
    else
    {
        rows = op.val.array.rows;
        cols = op.val.array.columns;
// Ensure destructor will tell Excel to free memory
        XLtoFree = true;
    }
}
```

The class also contains a number of methods to set elements of an existing array, for example:

```cpp
bool cpp_xloper::SetArrayElement(WORD row, WORD column, char *text)
{
    if(XLtoFree)
        return false;   // Don't assign to an Excel-allocated array

// Get a pointer to the xloper at this (row, column) coordinate
    xloper *p_op = GetArrayElement(row, column);

    if(!p_op)
        return false;

    if(m_DLLtoFree)
    {
        p_op->xltype |= xlbitDLLFree;
        free_xloper(p_op);
    }
    set_to_text(p_op, text);
    return true;
}
```

Creating and initialising static arrays of xlopers is covered in section 6.9 *Initialising xlopers* on page 157. As this section discusses, the easiest way to do this is to create and initialise arrays of cpp_xlopers and use this array to initialise a cpp_xloper of xltypeMulti using either one of the constructor methods or one of the initialisation methods.

How you convert it to a C/C++ data type

The following `cpp_xloper` method converts an `xltypeMulti` array into an array of `doubles`. In doing this, it allocates a block of memory, coerces the elements one-by-one into the array and then returns a pointer to the allocated block. The memory allocated then needs to be freed by the caller once it is no longer required. The code relies on another method that returns a given (row, column) element as a `double` via an argument passed by reference, coercing it to a `double` if required. The class contains similar methods for converting elements of the array to text, integers, Boolean and Excel error values (as integers). There are also methods that use a single *offset* parameter rather than a (row, column) pair – more efficient if accessing all the elements in the array one-by-one.

```
double *cpp_xloper::ConvertMultiToDouble(void)
{
    if(m_Op.xltype != xltypeMulti)
        return NULL;

// Allocate the space for the array of doubles
    int size = m_Op.val.array.rows * m_Op.val.array.columns;
    double *ret_array = (double *)malloc(size * sizeof(double));

    if(!ret_array)
        return NULL;

// Get the cell values one-by-one as doubles and place in the array.
// Store the array row-by-row in memory.
    xloper *p_op = m_Op.val.array.lparray;

    if(!p_op)
    {
        free(ret_array);
        return NULL;
    }

    for(int index = 0; index < size; index++)
        if(!coerce_to_double(p_op++, ret_array[index]))
            ret_array[index] = 0.0;

    return ret_array; // caller must free the memory!
}
```

The class also contains a number of methods that retrieve elements of an array as a particular data type (converted if required and if possible), for example:

```
bool cpp_xloper::GetArrayElement(DWORD offset, double &d)
{
    return coerce_to_double(GetArrayElement(offset), d);
}
```

What the memory considerations are

These `xlopers` contain a pointer to a block of memory. If this points to a static block, or a dynamic block created at DLL initialisation, there is no need to free the memory after use. It's usually easier and makes much more sense, however, to create and destroy the memory as required. Where the `xloper` was created by Excel, say, with a call to `xlCoerce`, the memory must be freed by Excel as outlined in Chapter 7.

Where `xltypeMulti` `xlopers` are being returned to Excel, and where the memory they reference has been dynamically allocated by the DLL or by Excel, the appropriate bit in the `xltype` field must be set to ensure the memory is released. Where the elements of the array themselves have memory allocated for them, they also need to have the appropriate bit set. (See Chapter 7 *Memory Management* on page 161.)

The `cpp_xloper` class always allocates a block of memory for the `xloper` array and sets a Boolean (`m_DLLtoFree`) to `true` to tell the destructor to free it when done.

How you can avoid using it

If you only want to work with arrays of `doubles`, you have the option of using the `xl_array` structure discussed in section 6.2.2 on page 107. If you want to receive/return mixed-value or string arrays from/to a worksheet, or you want to work with C API functions that take or return arrays, then you can't avoid using this type.

6.8.8 Worksheet cell/range reference: `xltypeRef` and `xltypeSRef`

When you will encounter them

These two `xloper` types are used by Excel for all references to single cells and ranges on any sheet in any open workbook. Each type contains references to one or one or more rectangular blocks of cells. The `xltypeSRef` is only capable of referencing a single block of cells on the *current* sheet. The `xltypeRef` type can reference one or more blocks of cells on a specified sheet, which may or may not be the current sheet. For this reason, an `xltypeRef` `xloper` is also known as an *external* reference as it refers to an external sheet, i.e., not the current sheet.

Where a range is passed to a DLL function and is only used as a source of data, it is advisable to convert to an `xltypeMulti` – a much easier type to work with. Arrays of type `xltypeMulti` resulting from conversion from one of these types have their elements stored row-by-row. Where the range is being used as an argument in a call to `Excel4()` it is better to leave it unconverted. Where DLL functions are declared as taking `oper` arguments, Excel will convert range references to `xltypeMulti` or one of the single cell value types (or `xltypeNil` in some cases). (See section 8.5 *Registering and un-registering DLL (XLL) functions* on page 182.)

The C API function `xlfSheetId` returns the internal ID of a worksheet within an `xltypeRef` `xloper`.

When you need to create them

A number of Excel functions take range or array arguments. A few take just ranges. When calling them from within the DLL you need to create one of these types depending on whether you want to access a range on the current sheet or not. (Note that you can use `xltypeRef` to refer explicitly to the current sheet if you prefer not to have to think about whether it is current or not.)

If you want to pass a range reference back to Excel (for use as input to some other worksheet function) you will need to use one of these types depending on the whether the reference is in the context of the current sheet (use xltypeSRef) or some other (use xltypeRef).

How you create an instance of either of them

The first example shows how to populate an xloper of type xltypeSRef. Note that there is no need to specify a worksheet, either by name or by internal ID. Also there's no need to allocate any memory, as all the data members are contained within the xloper's 10 bytes.

```
bool set_to_xltypeSRef(xloper *p_op, WORD rwFirst, WORD rwLast,
           BYTE colFirst, BYTE colLast)
{
    if(!p_op || rwFirst < rwLast || colFirst < colLast)
        return false;

// Create a simple single-cell reference to cell on current sheet
    p_op->xltype = xltypeSRef;
    p_op->val.sref.count = 1;

    xlref &ref = p_op->val.sref.ref; // to simplify code
    ref.rwFirst = rwFirst;
    ref.rwLast = rwLast;
    ref.colFirst = colFirst;
    ref.colLast = colLast;
    return true;
}
```

The second example shows how to populate an xloper of type xltypeRef. This requires that an internal ID for the sheet be provided as a DWORD idSheet. (One of the cpp_xloper constructors listed below shows how to obtain this from a given sheet name using the xlSheetId C API function.) Note that not all of the information carried by an xltypeRef is contained within the 10 bytes of the xloper and, in this example, a small amount of memory is allocated in setting it up. (Another example might have used a static xlmref structure.)

```
bool set_to_xltypeRef(xloper *p_op, DWORD idSheet, WORD rwFirst,
           WORD rwLast, BYTE colFirst, BYTE colLast)
{
    if(!p_op || rwFirst < rwLast || colFirst < colLast)
        return false;

// Allocate memory for the xlmref and set pointer within the xloper
    xlmref *p = (xlmref *)malloc(sizeof(xlmref));

    if(!p)
    {
        p_op->xltype = xltypeMissing;
        return false;
    }
```

```
    p_op->xltype = xltypeRef;
    p_op->val.mref.lpmref = p;
    p_op->val.mref.idSheet = idSheet;
    p_op->val.mref.lpmref->count = 1;

    xlref &ref = p->reftbl[0];// to simplify code
    ref.rwFirst = rwFirst;
    ref.rwLast = rwLast;
    ref.colFirst = colFirst;
    ref.colLast = colLast;
    return true;
}
```

Converting an array of doubles, strings or any other data type *to* an xltypeRef or an xltypeSRef is never a necessary thing to do. If you need to return an array of doubles, integers or strings (mixed or all one type) to Excel via the return value of your DLL function, you should use the xltypeMulti xloper. If you want to set the value of a particular cell that is not the calling cell, then you can use the xlSet function, although this can only be called from a command, not from a worksheet function.

The cpp_xloper class constructor for the xltypeSRef is:

```
cpp_xloper::cpp_xloper(WORD rwFirst, WORD rwLast, BYTE colFirst,
             BYTE colLast)
{
    Clear();
    set_to_xltypeSRef(&m_Op, rwFirst, rwLast, colFirst, colLast);
}
```

The two cpp_xloper class constructors for the xltypeRef are as follows. The first creates a reference on a named sheet. The second creates a reference on a sheet that is specified using its internal sheet ID.

```
cpp_xloper::cpp_xloper(char *sheet_name, WORD rwFirst, WORD rwLast,
             BYTE colFirst, BYTE colLast)
{
    Clear();

// Check the inputs.  No need to check sheet_name, as
// creation of cpp_xloper will set type to xltypeMissing
// if sheet_name is not a valid name.
    if(rwFirst < rwLast || colFirst < colLast)
        return;

// Get the sheetID corresponding to the sheet_name provided. If
// sheet_name is missing, a reference on the active sheet is created.
    cpp_xloper Name(sheet_name);
    cpp_xloper RetOper;

    int xl4 = Excel4(xlSheetId, &RetOper, 1, &Name);
    RetOper.SetExceltoFree();
    DWORD ID = RetOper.m_Op.val.mref.idSheet;

    if(xl4 == xlretSuccess
    && set_to_xltypeRef(&m_Op, ID, rwFirst,rwLast,colFirst,colLast))
```

```
    {
    // created successfully
        m_DLLtoFree = true;
    }
    return;
}
```

Here is the code for the second constructor. It is much simpler than the above, as the constructor does not need to convert the sheet name to an internal ID.

```
cpp_xloper::cpp_xloper(DWORD ID, WORD rwFirst, WORD rwLast,
                        BYTE colFirst, BYTE colLast)
{
    Clear();

    if(rwFirst <= rwLast && colFirst <= colLast
    && set_to_xltypeRef(&m_Op, ID, rwFirst,rwLast,colFirst,colLast))
    {
    // created successfully
        m_DLLtoFree = true;
    }
    return;
}
```

How you convert them to a C/C++ data type

Converting a range reference really means looking up the values from that range. The most straightforward way to do this is to convert the xloper to xltypeMulti. The result can then easily be converted to, say, an array of doubles. (See above discussion of xltypeMulti.) The following example code shows how to do this in a function that sums all the numeric values in a given range, as well as those non-numeric values that can be converted. It uses one of the xltypeMulti constructors to convert the input range (if it can) to an array type. The cpp_xloper member function ConvertMultiTo Double() attempts to convert the array to an array of doubles, coercing the individual elements if required.

```
double __stdcall coerce_and_sum(xloper *input)
{
    WORD rows, cols;
    cpp_xloper Array(rows, cols, input); // converts to xltypeMulti

    if(!Array.IsType(xltypeMulti))
        return 0.0;

// Get an array of doubles
    double *d_array = Array.ConvertMultiToDouble();

    if(!d_array)
        return 0.0;

    double sum = 0.0;
    double *p = d_array;
```

```
    for(unsigned int i = rows * cols; i--;)
        sum += *p++;
// Free the double array
    free(d_array);
    return sum;
}
```

What the memory considerations are

As can be seen from the above code examples, `xltypeRef xlopers` point to a block of memory. If dynamically allocated within the DLL, this needs to be freed when no longer required. (See Chapter 7 *Memory Management* on page 161 for details.) For `xltypeSRef xlopers` there are no memory considerations, as all the data is stored within the `xloper`'s 10 bytes.

How you can avoid using them

If you only want to access values from ranges of cells in a spreadsheet then declaring DLL functions as taking `xloper` arguments but registering them as taking `oper` arguments forces Excel to convert `xltypeSRef` and `xltypeRef xlopers` to one of the value types (or `xltypeNil` in some cases). (See section 8.5 *Registering and un-registering DLL (XLL) functions* on page 182.) However, Excel may not call your code if this conversion fails for some reason, and there is an unnecessary overhead if the argument is only to be passed as an argument to a C API function.

If you only want to access numbers from ranges of cells, then you do have the option of using the `xl_array` data type described in section 6.2.2 on page 107.

If you want to access information about ranges of cells in a spreadsheet, or you want complete flexibility with arguments passed in from Excel, then you cannot avoid their use.

Examples

The first example, `count_used_cells()`, creates a simple reference (`xltypeSRef`) to a range on the sheet from which the function is called. (Note that this will always be the current sheet, but may not be the active sheet.) It then calls the C API function `Excel4(xlfCount,...)`, equivalent to the worksheet function COUNT(), to get the number of cells containing numbers. (The pointer `p_xlErrValue` points to a static `xloper` initialised to #VALUE!. See section 6.3 *Defining constant xlopers* on page 121 for more detail.)

```
xloper * __stdcall count_used_cells(int first_row, int last_row,
                    int first_col, int last_col)
{
    if(first_row > last_row || first_col > last_col)
        return p_xlErrValue;

// Adjust inputs to be zero-counted and cast to WORDs and BYTEs.
    WORD fr = (WORD)(first_row - 1);
```

```
    WORD lr = (WORD)(last_row - 1);
    BYTE fc = (BYTE)(first_col - 1);
    BYTE lc = (BYTE)(last_col - 1);

    cpp_xloper InputRange(fr, lr, fc, lc);
    cpp_xloper RetVal;

    Excel4(xlfCount, &RetVal, 1, &InputRange);
    return RetVal.ExtractXloper(false);
}
```

The second example `count_used_cells2()` does the same as the first except that it creates an external reference (`xltypeRef`) to a range on a specified sheet before calling the C API function. Note that this sheet may not be the one from which the function is called. Note also that a different constructor is used.

```
xloper * __stdcall count_used_cells2(char *sheetname, int first_row,
            int last_row, int first_col, int last_col)
{
    if(first_row > last_row || first_col > last_col)
        return p_xlErrValue;

// Adjust inputs to be zero-counted and cast to WORDs and BYTEs.
    WORD fr = (WORD)(first_row - 1);
    WORD lr = (WORD)(last_row - 1);
    BYTE fc = (BYTE)(first_col - 1);
    BYTE lc = (BYTE)(last_col - 1);

    cpp_xloper InputRange(sheetname, fr, lr, fc, lc);
    cpp_xloper RetVal;

    Excel4(xlfCount, &RetVal, 1, &InputRange);
    return RetVal.ExtractXloper(false);
}
```

6.8.9   Empty worksheet cell: `xltypeNil`

When you will encounter it

The `xltypeNil` xloper will typically turn up in an array of xlopers that has been created from a range reference, where one or more of the cells in the range is completely empty. Many functions ignore nil cells. For example, the worksheet function =AVERAGE() returns the sum of all non-empty numeric cells in the range divided by the number of such cells. If a DLL function is registered with Excel as taking an oper argument and the function is entered on the worksheet with a single-cell reference to an empty cell, then Excel will also pass an xloper of this type. If registered as taking an xloper argument, then the passed-in type would be `xltypeSRef` or `xltypeRef`. (See section 8.5 *Registering and un-registering DLL (XLL) functions* on page 182.)

When you need to create it

There's an obvious contradiction if a worksheet function tries to return an xloper of this type to a single cell: the cell has a formula in it and therefore cannot be empty. Even if the cell is part of an array formula, it's still not empty. If you return an array of xlopers (xltypeMulti) containing xltypeNil elements, they will be converted by Excel to numeric zero values. If you want to return a neutral non-numeric cell in an array, you will need to convert to an empty string. If, however, you want to clear the contents of a cell completely, something that you can only do from a command, you can use the C API function xlSet – see section 8.7.4 on page 203 – and pass an xltypeNil xloper.

How you create an instance of it

The following example shows how to do this in straight C code:

```
xloper op;
op.xltype = xltypeNil;
```

Or...

```
xloper op = {0.0, xltypeNil};
```

The default constructor for the cpp_xloper class initialises its xloper to xltypeNil. The class has a few methods for setting the xloper type later, which can also be used to create an xloper of type xltypeNil. For example:

```
cpp_xloper op; // initialised to xltypeNil

op.SetType(xltypeNil);

// array elements are all initialised to xltypeNil
cpp_xloper array_op((WORD)rows, (WORD)columns);
//...
array_op.SetArrayElementType((WORD)row, (WORD)col, xltypeNil);
array_op.SetArrayElementType((DWORD)offset, xltypeNil);
```

You can also create a pointer to a static structure that looks like an xloper and is initialised to xltypeNil. (See section 6.3 *Defining constant xlopers* on page 121 for more details.)

How you convert it to a C/C++ data type

How you interpret an empty cell is entirely up to your function, whether it is looking for numerical arguments or strings, and so on. If it really matters, you should check your function inputs and interpret it accordingly. Excel will coerce this type to zero if asked to convert to a number, or the empty string if asked to convert to a string. If this is not what you want to happen, you should not coerce xlopers of this type using xlCoerce but write your own conversion instead.

What the memory considerations are

There is no memory associated with this type of xloper.

How you can avoid using it

If you are accepting arrays from worksheet ranges and it matters how you interpret empty cells, or you want to fail your function if the input includes empty cells, then you need to detect this type. If you want to completely clear the contents of cells from a command using xlSet, then you cannot avoid using this type.

6.8.10   Worksheet binary name: `xltypeBigData`

A binary storage name is a named block of unstructured memory associated with a worksheet that an XLL is able to create, read from and write to, and that gets saved with the workbook.

A typical use for such a space would be the creation of a large table of data that you want to store and access in your workbook, which might be too large, too cumbersome or perhaps too public, if stored in worksheet cells. Another use might be to store configuration data for a command that always (and only) acts on the active sheet.

The `xltypeBigData` `xloper` type is used to define and access these blocks of binary data. Section 8.8 *Working with binary names* on page 209 covers binary names in detail.

6.9   INITIALISING `xlopers`

C only allows initialisation of the first member of a union when initialising a static or automatic structure. This pretty much limits `xlopers` to being initialised to floating point numeric values only, given that `double num` is the first declared element of the `val` union of the `xloper` and assigning a type.

For example, the following declarations are all valid:

```
xloper op_pi = {3.14159265358979, xltypeNum};
xloper op_nil = {0.0, xltypeNil};
xloper op_false = {0.0, xltypeBool};
xloper op_missing = {0.0, xltypeMissing};
```

These will compile but will not result in the intended values:

```
xloper op_three = {3, xltypeInt};
xloper op_true = {1, xltypeBool};
```

This will not compile:

```
xloper op_hello = {"\5Hello", xltypeStr};
```

This is very limiting. Ideally, you would want to be able to initialise an `xloper` to any of the types and values that it can represent. In particular, creating static arrays of `xlopers` and initialising them becomes awkward: it is only possible to initialise the type;

something that still has some value in tidying up code. Initialising the value as well as the type is something you might need to do when:

- creating a definition range for a custom dialog box;
- creating a array of fixed values to be placed in a spreadsheet under control of a command or function;
- setting up the values to be passed to Excel when registering new commands or new worksheet functions. (See section 8.5 *Registering and un-registering DLL (XLL) functions* on page 182.)

There are a couple of ways round this limitation. The first is the definition of an `xloper`-like structure that is identical in memory but allows itself to be declared statically and then cast to an `xloper`. This is achieved simply by changing the order of declaration in the union. This approach still has the limitation of only allowing initialisation to one fundamental data type. The following code fragment illustrates this approach:

```
typedef struct
{
    union {char *str; double num;} val; // don't need other types
    WORD xltype;
}
    str_xloper;

str_xloper op_hello = {"\5Hello", xltypeStr};

xloper *pop_hello = (xloper *)&op_hello;
```

The second approach is to create a completely new structure that can be initialised statically to a range of types, but that requires some code to convert it to an `xloper`. One example of this approach would be to redefine the `xloper` structure to include a few simple constructors. Provided the image of the structure in memory was not altered by any amendments, all of the code that used `xlopers` would still work fine.

The C++ class `cpp_xloper` is another example, but one that really harnesses the power of C++. It can be initialised in a far more intuitive way than an `xloper` to any of the data types supported by the `xloper`. Arrays of `cpp_xlopers` can be initialised with bracketed arrays of initialisers of different types: the compiler calls the correct constructor for each type. Once the array of `cpp_xlopers` has been initialised it can be converted into a `cpp_xloper` of type xltypeMulti very easily, as the class contains a member function to do just this. (See sections 6.4 *A C++ class wrapper for the xloper – cpp_xloper* on page 121, and 6.8.7 *Array (mixed type): xltypeMulti* on page 145 for more details.)

The following code initialises a 1-dimensional array of `cpp_xlopers` with values of various types needed to define a simple custom dialog definition table. (Note that the empty string initialises the `cpp_xloper` to type xltypeNil.) The dialog displayed by the command `get_username()` requests a username and password. (See section 8.13 *Working with custom dialog boxes* on page 273 for details of how to construct such a table, and the use of the `xlfDialogBox` function.) The `cpp_xloper` array is then converted into an xltypeMulti xloper (wrapped in a `cpp_xloper`) using the constructor.

```
#define NUM_DIALOG_COLUMNS    7
#define NUM_DIALOG_ROWS       10

cpp_xloper UsernameDlg[NUM_DIALOG_ROWS * NUM_DIALOG_COLUMNS] =
{
    "", "", "", 372, 200, "Logon", "", // Dialog box size
    1, 100, 170, 90, "", "OK", "", // Default OK button
    2, 200, 170, 90, "", "Cancel", "", // Cancel button
    5, 40, 10, "", "", "Please enter your username and password.","",
    14, 40, 35, 290, 100, "", "", // Group box
    5, 50, 53, "", "", "Username", "", // Text
    6, 150, 50, "", "", "", "MyName", // Text edit box
    5, 50, 73, "", "", "Password", "", // Text
    6, 150, 70, "", "", "", "*********", // Text edit box
    13, 50, 110, "", "", "Remember username and password", true,
};

int __stdcall get_username(void)
{
    xloper ret_val;
    int xl4;

    cpp_xloper DialogDef((WORD) NUM_DIALOG_ROWS,
            (WORD)NUM_DIALOG_COLUMNS, UsernameDlg);
    do
    {
        xl4 = Excel4(xlfDialogBox, &ret_val, 1, &DialogDef);

        if(xl4 || (ret_val.xltype == xltypeBool
        && ret_val.val._bool == 0))
            break;

    // Process the input from the dialog by reading
    // the 7th column of the returned array.

    // ... code omitted

        Excel4(xlFree, 0, 1, &ret_val);
        ret_val.xltype = xltypeNil;
    }
    while(1);

    Excel4(xlFree, 0, 1, &ret_val);
    return 1;
}
```

The above approach doubles up the amount of memory used for the strings. (The cpp_xloper makes deep copies of initialisation strings.) This should not be a huge concern, but a more memory-efficient approach would be to use a simple class as follows that only makes shallow copies:

```
// This class is a very simple wrapper for an xloper. The class is
// specifically designed for initialising arrays of static strings
// in a more memory efficient way than with cpp_xlopers. It contains
// NO memory management capabilities and can only represent the same
// simple types supported by an oper.  Member functions limited to
// a set of very simple constructors and an overloaded address-of
// operator.
```

```
class init_xloper
{
public:
    init_xloper()         {op.xltype = xltypeNil;}
    init_xloper(int w)    {op.xltype = xltypeInt; op.val.w = w;}
    init_xloper(double d) {op.xltype = xltypeNum; op.val.num = d;}
    init_xloper(bool b)
    {
        op.xltype = xltypeBool;
        op.val._bool = b ? 1 : 0;
    };
    init_xloper(WORD err) {op.xltype = xltypeErr; op.val.err = err;}
    init_xloper(char *text)
    {
// Expects null-terminated strings.
// Leading byte is overwritten with length of string
        if(*text == 0 || (*text = strlen(text + 1)) == 0)
            op.xltype = xltypeNil;
        else
        {
            op.xltype = xltypeStr;
            op.val.str = text;
        }
    };
    xloper *operator&() {return &op;} // return xloper address
    xloper op;
};
```

6.10   MISSING ARGUMENTS

XLL functions must be called with all arguments provided, except those arguments that have been declared as xlopers or opers. Excel will not call the DLL code until all required arguments have been provided.

Where DLL functions have been declared as taking xloper arguments, Excel will pass an xloper of type xltypeMissing if no argument was provided. If the argument is a single cell reference to an empty cell, this is passed as an xloper of type xltypeRef or xltypeSRef, NOT of type xltypeMissing. However, if the DLL function is declared as taking an oper argument, a reference to an empty cell is passed as type xltypeNil. You will probably want your DLL to treat this as a missing argument in which case the following code is helpful. (Many of the later code examples in this book use this function.)

```
inline bool is_xloper_missing(xloper *p_op)
{
    return !p_op || (p_op->xltype & (xltypeMissing | xltypeNil))!=0;
}
```

Memory Management

7.1 EXCEL STACK SPACE LIMITATIONS

Since Excel 97, there have been about 44 Kbytes normally available to a DLL on a stack that is shared with Excel. (In fact, *it is* Excel's stack; the DLL gets to share it.) Stack space is used when calling functions (to store the arguments and return values) and to create the automatic variables that the called function needs. No stack space is used by function variables declared as `static` or declared outside function code at the module level or by structures whose memory has been allocated dynamically.

This example, of how *not* to do things, uses 8 bytes of stack for the argument, another 8 for the return value, 4 bytes for the integer in the for loop, and a whopping 48,000 bytes for the array – a total of 48,020 bytes. This function would almost certainly result in stack overflow if called from Excel.

```
double stack_hog_example(double arg)
{
    double pig_array[6000];

    pig_array[0] = arg;

    for(int i = 1; i < 6000; i++)
        pig_array[i] = pig_array[i - 1] + 1.0;

    return pig_array[5999];
}
```

To live comfortably within the limited stack space, you only need to follow these simple guidelines:

- Don't pass large structures as arguments to functions. Use pointers or references instead.
- Don't return large structures. Return pointers to static or dynamically allocated memory.
- Don't declare large automatic variable structures in the function code. If you need them, declare them as `static`.
- Don't call functions recursively unless you're sure the depth of recursion will *always* be shallow. Try using a loop instead.

The above code example is easily fixed (at least from the memory point of view) by the use of the `static` keyword in the declaration of `pig_array[]`.

When calling back into Excel using the `Excel4()` function, Excel versions 97 and later check to see if there is enough space for the worst case (in terms of stack space usage) call that could be made. If it thinks there's not enough room, it will fail the function call, even though there might have been enough space for *this* call. Following the above guidelines and being aware of the limited space should mean that you never have to worry about stack space. If you *are* concerned (or just curious) you can find out how much stack space there currently is with a call to Excel's `xlStack` function as the following example shows:

```
double __stdcall get_stack(void)
{
    xloper retval;

    if(xlretSuccess != Excel4(xlStack, &retval, 0))
        return -1.0;

    return (double)(unsigned short)retval.val.w;
}
```

The need to cast the signed integer that xlStack returns to an unsigned integer is a hang-over from the days when Excel provided even less stack space and when the maximum positive value of the signed integer (32,768) was sufficient. Once more stack was made available, the need emerged for the cast to avoid a negative result.

7.2 STATIC ADD-IN MEMORY AND MULTIPLE EXCEL INSTANCES

When multiple instances of Excel run, they share a single copy of the DLL executable code. In Win32 there are no adverse memory consequences of this as each instance of the program using the DLL gets its own memory space allocated for all the static memory defined in the DLL. This means that in a function such as the following the returned value will be the number of times *this* instance of the program has called this function in the DLL.

```
int __stdcall count_calls(void)
{
    static int num_calls = 0;

    return ++num_calls;
}
```

(This was not the case in 16-bit Windows environments and meant a fair amount of fussing around with instance handles, blocks of memory allocated for a given instance, etc).

7.3 GETTING EXCEL TO FREE MEMORY ALLOCATED BY EXCEL

When calling the Excel4() or Excel4v() functions, Excel will sometimes allocate memory for the returned value (an xloper). It will *always* do this if the returned value is a string, for example. In such cases it is the responsibility of the DLL to make sure the memory gets freed. Freeing memory allocated by Excel in this way is done in one of two ways depending on when the memory is no longer needed:

1. Before the DLL returns control to Excel.
2. After the DLL returns control to Excel.

These cases are covered in the next two sub-sections.

Table 7.1 summarises which xloper types will and will not have memory that needs to be freed if returned by Excel4().

Table 7.1 Returned `xlopers` for which Excel allocates memory

Type of `xloper`	Memory allocated if returned by `Excel4()`
`xltypeNum`	No
`xltypeStr`	Yes
`xltypeBool`	No
`xltypeRef`	Yes[1]
`xltypeErr`	No
`xltypeMulti`	Yes
`xltypeMissing`	No
`xltypeNil`	No
`xltypeSRef`	No
`xltypeInt`	No
`xltypeBigData`	No

7.3.1 Freeing `xloper` memory within the DLL call

Excel provides a C API function specifically to allow the DLL to tell Excel to free the memory that it itself allocated and returned in an `xloper` during a call to either `Excel4()` or `Excel4v()`. This function is itself is called using `Excel4()` and is defined as `xlFree` (0x4000).

This function does not return a value and takes the address of the `xloper` associated with the memory that needs to be freed. The function happily accepts `xlopers` that have no allocated memory associated with them, but be warned, NEVER pass an `xloper` with memory that your DLL has allocated: this will cause all sorts of unwanted side effects.

The following code fragment shows an example of `Excel4()` returning a string for which it allocated memory. In general, the second argument in the `Excel4()` is normally a pointer to an `xloper` that would contain the return value of the called function, but since `xlFree` doesn't return a value a null pointer is all that's required in the second call to `Excel4()` in the example.

```
xloper dll_name;

// Get the full path and name of the DLL.
Excel4(xlGetName, &dll_name, 0);

// Do something with the name here, for example...
int len = strlen(dll_name.val.str + 1);

// Get Excel to free the memory that it allocated for the DLL name
Excel4(xlFree, 0, 1, &dll_name);
```

---

[1] The C API function `xlfSheetId` returns this type of `xloper` but does not allocate memory.

If you know *for sure* that the call to Excel4() you are making NEVER returns a type that has memory allocated to it, then you can get away with not calling xlFree on the returned xloper. If you're not sure, calling xlFree won't do any harm.

Warning: Where the type is xltypeMulti it is <u>not</u> necessary to call xlFree for each of the elements, whatever their types. In fact, doing this will confuse and destabilise Excel. Similarly, converting elements of an Excel-generated array to or from an xloper type that has memory associated with it may cause memory problems.

The cpp_xloper class contains a member function, SetExceltoFree(), that sets a flag telling the class to use xlFree to free memory when the destructor is eventually called, or before a new value is assigned. The advantage of this, over using xlopers and xlFree directly, is that calling this method does not free the memory at that point: the method can be called immediately after the memory has been allocated in the call to Excel4(), rather than after its last use. This makes the code much more manageable and leaks much less likely. The following code fragment shows an example of its use. Note that the object Caller is used *after* the call to SetExceltoFree().

```
// Get a reference to the calling cell

    cpp_xloper Caller;

    if(Excel4(xlfCaller, &Caller, 0))
        return p_xlFalse;

// Set a flag to tell the destructor to use xlFree to free memory
    Caller.SetExceltoFree();

// Convert the reference to text with the full
// workbook/current_sheet/range in A1 form

    cpp_xloper GetCellArg(1);
    cpp_xloper RefTextA1;

    Excel4(xlfGetCell, &RefTextA1, 2, &GetCellArg, &Caller);

    RefTextA1.SetExceltoFree();
```

7.3.2 Freeing xloper memory returned by the DLL function

This case arises when the DLL needs to return the xloper, or a pointer to it, to Excel. Excel has no way of knowing that the xloper memory it is being passed was allocated (by itself) during the DLL call, so the DLL function has to tell Excel this fact explicitly so that Excel knows it has to clean up afterwards. The DLL does this by setting the xlbitXLFree bit in the xltype field of the xloper as shown in the following code, which returns the full path and name of the DLL.

```
xloper * __stdcall xloper_memory_example(int trigger)
{
    static xloper dll_name;

    Excel4(xlGetName, &dll_name, 0);

// Excel has allocated memory for the DLL name string which cannot be
// freed until after being returned, so need to set this bit to tell
```

```
// Excel to free it once it has finished with it.
   dll_name.xltype |= xlbitXLFree;

   return &dll_name;
}
```

The cpp_xloper class contains a method for returning a copy of the contained xloper, xloper * ExtractXloper(bool ExceltoFree). This method sets the xlbitXL-Free bit if either the Boolean argument was set to true or a call to cpp_xloper::SetExceltoFree() had been made. (See next section for a listing of the code for ExtractXloper().)

Note: Setting xlbitXLFree on an xloper that is to be used for the return value for a call to Excel4(), prior to the call to Excel4() that allocates it, will have no effect. The correct time to set this bit is:

• after the call that sets its value;
• after it might be passed as an argument to other Excel4() calls;
• before a pointer to it is returned to the worksheet.

The following code will fail to ensure that the string allocated in the call to Excel4() gets freed properly, as the type field of ret_oper is completely overwritten in the call:

```
xloper * __stdcall bad_example1(void)
{
   static xloper ret_oper;
   ret_oper.type |= xlbitXLFree;
   Excel4(xlGetName, &ret_oper, 0);
   return &ret_oper;
}
```

The following code will confuse the call to xlfLen, which will not be able to determine the type of ret_oper correctly.

```
xloper * __stdcall bad_example2(void)
{
   static xloper ret_oper;
   Excel4(xlGetName, &ret_oper, 0);
   ret_oper.type |= xlbitXLFree;

   xloper length;
   Excel4(xlfLen, &length 1, &ret_oper);

   return &ret_oper;
}
```

The following code will work properly.

```
xloper * __stdcall good_example(void)
{
   static xloper ret_oper;
   Excel4(xlGetName, &ret_oper, 0);
```

```
    xloper length;
    Excel4(xlfLen, &length 1, &ret_oper);

    ret_oper.type |= xlbitXLFree;
    return &ret_oper;
}
```

7.4   GETTING EXCEL TO CALL BACK THE DLL TO FREE DLL-ALLOCATED MEMORY

If the DLL returns an `xloper`, or, in fact, a pointer to an `xloper`, Excel copies the values associated with it into the worksheet cell(s) from which it was called and then discards any temporary copies it has made or that were made on the stack for the return value. It does not automatically free any memory that the DLL might have allocated in constructing the `xloper`. If this memory is not freed, however, the DLL will leak memory every time the function is called. To prevent this, the C API provides a way to tell Excel to call back into the DLL once it has finished with the return value, so that the DLL can clean up. The call-back function is one of the required XLL interface functions, `xlAutoFree`. (See section 5.5.7 on page 103 for details.)

It is the responsibility of the DLL programmer to make sure that their implementation of `xlAutoFree` understands the data types that will be passed back to it in this call, and that it knows how to free the memory. For arrays of `xlopers` (`xltypeMulti`), this will, in general, mean freeing the memory associated with each element, and only then freeing the array memory itself. Care should also be taken to ensure that memory is freed in a way that is consistent with the way it was allocated.

The DLL code instructs Excel to call `xlAutoFree` by setting the `xlbitDLLFree` bit in the `xltype` field of the returned `xloper`. The following code shows the creation of an array of `doubles` with random values (set with calls to `Excel4(xlfRand, ...)`), in an `xltypeMulti` `xloper`, and its return to Excel.

```
xloper * __stdcall random_array(int rows, int columns)
{
    int array_size = rows * columns;
    static xloper ret_oper;
    xloper *array;

    if(array_size <= 0)
        return NULL;

    array = (xloper *)malloc(array_size * sizeof(xloper));

    if(array == NULL)
        return NULL;

    for(int i = 0; i < array_size; i++)
        Excel4(xlfRand, array + i, 0);
// Instruct Excel to call back into DLL to free the memory
    ret_oper.xltype = xltypeMulti | xlbitDLLFree;
    ret_oper.val.array.lparray = array;
```

```
        ret_oper.val.array.rows = rows;
        ret_oper.val.array.columns = columns;

        return &ret_oper;
}
```

After returning from this function, the DLL will receive a call to its implementation of xlAutoFree in which the address of the xloper is passed. The code for that function should detect that the type is xltypeMulti and should check that each of the elements themselves do not need to be freed (which they don't in this example). Then it should free the xloper array memory.

The following code does the same thing, but using the cpp_xloper class introduced in section 6.4 on page 121. The code is simplified, but the same things are happening – just hidden within the class.

```
xloper * __stdcall random_array(int rows, int columns)
{
    cpp_xloper array((WORD)rows, (WORD)columns);

    if(!array.IsType(xltypeMulti))
        return NULL;

    DWORD array_size;
    array.GetArraySize(array_size);

    for(DWORD i = 0; i < array_size; i++)
        Excel4(xlfRand, array.GetArrayElement(i), 0);

    return array.ExtractXloper(false);
}
```

The cpp_xloper class contains a method for returning a copy of the contained xloper, xloper *cpp_xloper::ExtractXloper(bool ExceltoFree). Unless the Boolean argument was set to true or a call to cpp_xloper::SetExceltoFree() had been made, this method sets the xlbitDLLFree bit for types where the class had allocated memory. Here is a listing of the code for ExtractXloper().

```
xloper *cpp_xloper::ExtractXloper(bool ExceltoFree)
{
    static xloper ret_val;

    ret_val = m_Op;

    if(ExceltoFree || m_XLtoFree)
    {
        ret_val.xltype |= xlbitXLFree;
    }
    else if(m_DLLtoFree)
    {
        ret_val.xltype |= xlbitDLLFree;

        if(m_Op.xltype & xltypeMulti)
```

```
    {
        int limit = m_Op.val.array.rows * m_Op.val.array.columns;
        xloper *p = m_Op.val.array.lparray;

        for(int i = limit; i--; p++)
            if(p->xltype == xltypeStr |p->xltype == xltypeRef)
                p->xltype |= xlbitDLLFree;
    }
}
// Prevent the destructor from freeing memory by resetting properties
    Clear();
    return &ret_val;
}
```

7.5   RETURNING DATA BY MODIFYING ARGUMENTS IN PLACE

Where you need to return data that would ordinarily need to be stored in dynamically allocated memory, you need to use the techniques described above. However, in some cases you can avoid allocating memory, and the worry of how to free it. This is done by modifying an argument that was passed to your DLL function as a pointer reference – a technique known as modifying in place. Excel accommodates this for a number of argument types, provided that the function is declared and registered in the right way. (See section 8.5.6 *Returning values by modifying arguments in place* on page 189 for details of how to do this.)

There are some limitations. Where the data is a string (a null-terminated char *), Excel allocates enough space for a 255-character string only – not 256! Where the data is an array of doubles of type xl_array (see section 6.2.2 *Excel floating-point array structure: xl_array* on page 107) the returned data can be no bigger than the passed-in array. Arrays of strings cannot be returned in this way.

8

Accessing Excel Functionality
Using the C API

This chapter sets out how to use the C API, and the API's relationship to the Excel 4 macro language. Many of the XLM functions, and their C API counterparts, take multiple arguments and can return a great variety of information, in particular the workspace information functions. It is not the intention of this book to be a reference manual for the XLM language. (The Microsoft XLM help file `Macrofun.hlp` is still freely downloadable from Microsoft at the time of writing.) Instead this chapter aims to provide a description of those aspects of the C API that are most relevant to writing worksheet functions and simple commands. Therefore many of the possible arguments of some of the C API functions are omitted. Also, this chapter is focused on using the C API rather than XLM functions on a macro sheet.

As described in detail in section 8.2 below, the C API is accessed via two functions, `Excel4()` and `Excel4v()`. These functions, and hence C API, can be wrapped up in a number of ways that arguably make its use easier. This book intentionally does not present a wrapped view of the C API, so that its workings are exposed as clearly as possible. C++ wrappers can be envisaged that make implementation of XLLs more straightforward, rapid and the resulting code more easily maintained.[1]

8.1 THE EXCEL 4 MACRO LANGUAGE (XLM)

Excel 4 introduced a macro language, XLM, which was eventually mapped to the C API in Excel 5. Support for XLM and the functionality of the C API remain unchanged up to Excel 2003 (the latest version at the time of writing). The fact that it remains unchanged is clearly a weakness of the C API relative to VBA: VBA has better access to Excel objects and events than the C API. When writing commands to manipulate the Excel environment, life is much easier in VB. The real benefits of using C/C++ DLLs and the C API are realised in worksheet functions. You can have the best of both worlds, of course. VB commands and DLL functions that use the C API are easily interfaced, as described in section 3.6 *Using VBA as an interface to external DLL add-ins* on page 48.

This book is <u>not</u> about writing Excel 4 macro sheets, but some understanding of the syntax of the XLM functions and commands is important when using the C API – the C API mirrors XLM syntax. At a minimum, registering DLL functions requires knowledge of the XLM function REGISTER(). The arguments are identical to those of the C API function `xlfRegister`, one of the enumerated function constants used in calls to `Excel4()` and `Excel4v()`. If you're relying heavily on the C API, then sooner or later you'll need to know what parameters to pass and in what order for one or more of the XLM functions. This chapter covers the aspects of the XLM most relevant to the subject of this book. A Windows help file, `Macrofun.hlp`, downloadable from Microsoft's website,

---

[1] One example, freely available at the time of writing, is the *XLW C++ wrapper* developed by Jérôme Lecomte. This can be accessed at the time of writing via the Source Forge website at xlw.sourceforge.net. A review of this open source project is beyond the scope of this book, but it is well worth looking at, if only to see the variety of approaches and resources that can be employed.

provides a great deal more information than given in this chapter. However it only relates to XLM as used in a macro sheet, and therefore, from a C API point of view, has holes that this chapter aims to fill.

As described below, the `Excel4()` and `Excel4v()` Excel library functions provide access to the Excel 4 macro language and Excel's built-in worksheet functions via enumerated function constants. These are defined in the SDK header file as either `xlfFunctionName` in the case of functions, or `xlcCommandName` in the case of commands. Typically, an Excel function that appears in uppercase on a sheet appears in proper case in the header file. For example, the worksheet function INDEX() is enumerated as `xlfIndex`, and the macro sheet function GET.CELL() becomes `xlfGetCell`. There are also a small number of functions available only to the C API that have no equivalents in the macro language. These are listed in Table 8.1 and described in detail in section 8.7 *Functions defined for the C API only* on page 199.

Table 8.1 C API-only functions

Enumerated constant	Value
xlFree	16384
xlStack	16385
xlCoerce	16386
xlSet	16387
xlSheetId	16388
xlSheetNm	16389
xlAbort	16390
xlGetInst	16391
xlGetHwnd	16392
xlGetName	16393
xlEnableXLMsgs	16394
xlDisableXLMsgs	16395
xlDefineBinaryName	16396
xlGetBinaryName	16397

Note: Some C API functions (starting `xlf-`) are, in fact, commands or command-equivalents. They cannot be called from DLL functions that are called (directly or indirectly) from worksheet cells. However some functions that perform seemingly command-like operations surprisingly *can* be called in this way, for example `xlfWindowTitle` and `xlfAppTitle` which are described below.

8.1.1 Commands, worksheet functions and macro sheet functions

Excel recognises three different categories of function:

1. Commands

2. Macro sheet functions

3. Worksheet functions

Sections 2.8 *Commands versus functions in Excel* on page 19, 3.8 *Commands versus functions in VBA* on page 71 and 8.5.4 *Giving functions macro-sheet function permissions* on page 188 discuss the differences in the way Excel treats these functions and what functions in each category can and cannot do.

8.1.2   Commands that optionally display dialogs – the `xlPrompt` bit

Many Excel commands can optionally invoke dialogs that allow the user to modify inputs or cancel the command. These dialogs will all be familiar to frequent Excel users, so a list of those commands that permit this and those that don't is not given here. The only important points to address here are (1) how to call the command using `Excel4()` to display the dialog, (2) what are the differences in setting up the arguments for the call to the command with and without the dialog being displayed, and (3) what return value to expect if the user cancels the command.

The first point is very straightforward. The enumerated function constant, for example `xlcDefineName`, should be bit-wise or'd with the value `0x1000`, defined as `xlPrompt` in the SDK header file.

On the second point, the arguments supplied pre-populate the fields in the dialog box. Any that are not supplied will result in either blank fields or fields that contain Excel defaults.

Any command function that can be called in this way will return true if successful and false if cancelled or unsuccessful.

For example, the following command calls the `xlcDefineName` function with the dialog displayed.

```
int __stdcall define_new_name(void)
{
// Get the name to be defined from the active cell. First get a
// reference to the active cell.  No need to evaluate it, as call
// to xlcDefineName will try to convert contents of cell to a
// string and use that.

   cpp_xloper Name;
   int xl4 = Excel4(xlfActiveCell, &Name, 0);
   Name.SetExceltoFree();

   if(!xl4 && !Name.IsType(xltypeErr))
       Excel4(xlcDefineName | xlPrompt, 0, 1, &Name);

   return 1;
}
```

8.2   THE `Excel4()` C API FUNCTION

8.2.1   Introduction

Once inside the DLL you will sometimes need or want to call back into Excel to access its functionality. This might be because you want to take advantage of Excel's ability to convert from one data type to another (especially where the input might be one of a number of things that Excel has passed to you as an argument to a function), or because you need to register or un-register a DLL function or free some memory that Excel has allocated. Excel provides two functions that enable you to do all these things, Excel4() and Excel4v(). These are essentially the same function, the first taking a variable argument list, the second fixed but with a variable sized array of arguments that you wish to pass in.

The syntax for Excel4() is:

```
int Excel4(int xlfn, xloper *RetVal, int count, ...);
```

Note that the calling convention is __cdecl in order to support the variable argument list.

Here is a brief overview of the arguments:

Table 8.2 Excel4() arguments

Argument	Meaning	Comments
int xlfn	A number corresponding to a function or command recognised by Excel as part of the C API.	Must be one of the predefined constants defined in the SDK header file xlcall.h
xloper *pRetVal	A pointer to an xloper that will contain the return value of the function xlfn if Excel4() was able to call it. If a return value is not required by the caller, NULL (zero) can be passed.	If Excel4() was unable to call the function, the contents of this are unchanged. Excel allocates memory for certain return types. It is the responsibility of the caller to know when and how to tell Excel to free this memory. (See xlFree and xlbitXLFree.) If a function does not return an argument, for example, xlFree, Excel4() will ignore pRetval.
int count	The number of arguments to xlfn being passed in this call to Excel4().	The maximum value is 30.
xloper *arg1	A pointer to an xlopers containing the arguments for xlfn.	Missing arguments should be passed as xlopers of type xltypeMissing.
...	...	...
xloper *arg30		

The xlfn function being executed will always be one of the following:

- an Excel worksheet function;
- a C API-only function;
- an Excel macro sheet function;
- an Excel macro sheet command function.

These function enumerations are defined in the SDK header file xlcall.h as either xlf- or xlc-prefixed depending on whether they are functions or commands. There are also a number of non-XLM functions available only to the C API, such as xlFree.

The following sections provide more detail.

8.2.2 Excel4() return values

The value that Excel4() returns reflects whether the supplied function (designated by the xlfn argument) was able to be executed or not. If successful Excel4() returns zero (defined as xlretSuccess), **BUT** this does not always mean that the xlfn function executed without error. To determine this you need to check the return value of the xlfn function passed back via the xloper *pRetVal. Where Excel4() returns a non-zero error value (see below for more details) you *do* know that the xlfn function was either not called at all or did not complete.

The return value is always one of the values given in Table 8.3. (Constants in parentheses are defined in the SDK header file xlcall.h.)

Table 8.3 Excel4() return values

Returned value	Meaning
0 (xlretSuccess)	The xlfn function was called successfully, but you need also to check the type and/or value of the return xloper in case the function could not perform the intended task.
1 (xlretAbort)	The function was called as part of a call to a macro that has been halted by the user or the system.
2 (xlretInvXlfn)	The xlfn function is not recognised or not supported or cannot be called in the given context.
4 (xlretInvCount)	The number of arguments supplied is not valid for the specified xlfn function.
8 (xlretInvXloper)	One or more of the passed-in xlopers is not valid.
16 (xlretStackOvfl)	Excel's pre-call stack check indicates a possibility that the stack might overflow. (See section 7.1 *Excel stack space limitations* on page 161.)
32 (xlretFailed)	The xlfn command (not a function) that was being executed failed.

(continued overleaf)

Table 8.3 (*continued*)

Returned value	Meaning
64 (xlretUncalced)	A worksheet function has tried to access data from a cell or range of cells that have not yet been recalculated as part of this workbook recalculation. Macro sheet-equivalent functions and commands are not subject to this restriction and can read uncalculated cell values. (See section 8.1.1 *Commands, worksheet functions and macro sheet functions*, page 170, for details.)

8.2.3 Calling Excel worksheet functions in the DLL using `Excel4()`

Excel exposes all of the built-in worksheet functions through `Excel4()`. Calling a worksheet function via the C API is simply a matter of understanding how to set up the call to `Excel4()` and the number and types of arguments that the worksheet function takes. Arguments are all passed as pointers to `xlopers` so successfully converting from C/C++ types to `xloper` is a necessary part of making a call. (See section 6.5 *Converting between xlopers and C/C++ data types* on page 126.)

The following code examples show how to set up and call `Excel4()` using `xlopers` directly, as well as with the `cpp_xloper` class defined in section 6.4 on page 121. The example function is a fairly useful one: the =MATCH() function, invoked from the DLL by calling `Excel4()` with `xlfMatch`.

Worksheet function syntax: =MATCH(*lookup_value, lookup_array, match_type*)

The following code accepts inputs of exactly the same type as the worksheet function and then sets up the call to the worksheet function via the C API. Of course, there is no value in this other than demonstrating how to use `Excel4()`.

```
xloper * __stdcall Excel4_match(xloper *p_lookup_value,
                    xloper *p_lookup_array, int match_type)
{
    static xloper match_retval = {0, xltypeInt};
    xloper match_type_oper;

// Convert the integer argument into an xloper so that a pointer
// to this can be passed to Excel4()
    match_type_oper.val.w = match_type;

    int xl4 = Excel4(
        xlfMatch,       // 1st arg: the function to be called
        &match_retval,// 2nd arg: ptr to return value
        3,            // 3rd arg: number of subsequent args
        p_lookup_value,    // fn arg1
        p_lookup_array,    // fn arg2
        &match_type_oper);// fn arg3

// Test the return value of Excel4()
    if(xl4 != xlretSuccess)
    {
        match_retval.xltype = xltypeErr;
        match_retval.val.err = xlerrValue;
```

```
    }
    else
    {
// Tell Excel to free up memory that it might have allocated for
// the return value.
        match_retval.xltype |= xlbitXLFree;
    }
    return &match_retval;
}
```

The above example shows how the following steps have been taken:

1. Conversion of arguments to the Excel4() function into xlopers. (Here the integer match_type is converted to an internal integer xloper. It could have been converted to a floating point xloper.)
2. Passing of the correct constant for the function to be called to Excel4(), in this case xlfMatch = 64.
3. Passing of a pointer to an xloper that will hold the return value of the function. (If the function does not return a value, passing NULL or 0 is permitted.)
4. Passing a number telling Excel4() how many subsequent arguments (the arguments for the called function) are being supplied. xlfMatch can take 2 or 3 arguments, but in this case we pass 3.
5. Passing of pointers to the arguments.
6. Collection and testing of the return value of Excel4().

In some cases, you might also want to test the type of the returned xloper to check that the called function completed successfully. In most cases a test of the xltype to see if it is xltypeErr is sufficient. In this case we are returning the xloper directly, so can allow the spreadsheet to deal with any error in the same way that it would after a call to the MATCH() function itself.

Note: If Excel was unable to call the function, say, if the function number was not valid, the return value xloper would be untouched. In some cases it may be safe to assume that Excel4() will not fail and simply test whether the xlfn function that Excel4() was evaluating was successful by testing the xltype of the return value xloper.

Some simplifications to the above code example are possible. The function Excel4_match() need not be declared to take an integer 3rd argument. Instead, it could take another xloper pointer. Also, we can be confident in the setting up of the call to Excel4() that we have chosen the right function constant, that the number of the arguments is good and that we are calling the function at a time and with arguments that are not going to cause a problem. So, there's no need to store and test the return value of Excel4() and the xlfMatch return value can be returned straight away. If xlfMatch returned an error, this will propagate back to the caller in an acceptable way.

The function could therefore be simplified to the following (with comments removed):

```
xloper * __stdcall Excel4_match(xloper *p_lookup_value,
            xloper *p_lookup_array, xloper *p_match_type)
{
    static xloper match_retval;
```

```
Excel4(xlfMatch, &match_retval, 3,
    p_lookup_value, p_lookup_array, p_match_type);

return &match_retval;
}
```

As already mentioned, there is no point in writing a function like this that does exactly what the function in the worksheet does, other than to demonstrate how to call worksheet functions from the DLL. If you want to customise a worksheet function, a cloned function like this is, however, a sensible starting point.

8.2.4   Calling macro sheet functions from the DLL using `Excel4()`

Excel's built-in macro sheet functions typically return some information about the Excel environment or the property of some workbook or cell. These can be extremely useful in an XLL. Two examples are the functions =CALLER() and =GET.CELL() and their C API equivalents `xlfCaller` and `xlfGetCell`. The first takes no arguments and returns a reference to the cell or object from which the function (or command) was called. The second takes a cell reference and an integer value and returns some information. What information depends on the value of the integer argument. Both of the C API functions are covered in more detail later on in this chapter.

The following code fragment shows an example of both functions in action. This function toggles the calling cell between two states, 0 and 1, every time Excel recalculates. (To work as described, the function needs to be declared a volatile function – see section 8.5.5 *Specifying functions as volatile* on page 189.)

```
xloper * __stdcall toggle_caller(void)
{
    xloper Caller;
    xloper GetCell_param;
    static xloper RetVal;

    GetCell_param.xltype = xltypeInt;
    GetCell_param.val.w = 5; // contents of cell as number

    Excel4(xlfCaller, &Caller, 0);
    Excel4(xlfGetCell, &RetVal, 2, &GetCell_param, &Caller);

    if(RetVal.xltype == xltypeNum)
        RetVal.val.num = (RetVal.val.num == 0 ? 1.0 : 0.0);

    Excel4(xlFree, 0, 1, &Caller);
    return &RetVal;
}
```

An alternative method of getting the calling cell's value is to use the C API `xlCoerce` function, also covered in more detail below, to convert the cell reference to the desired data type, in this case a number. The equivalent code written using the `cpp_xloper` class and `xlCoerce` would be:

```
xloper * __stdcall toggle_caller(void)
{
    cpp_xloper Caller;
    Excel4(xlfCaller, &Caller, 0);
    Caller.SetExceltoFree();

    cpp_xloper RetVal;
    cpp_xloper TypeNum(xltypeNum);
    Excel4(xlCoerce, &RetVal, 2, &Caller, &TypeNum);
    RetVal = ((double)RetVal == 0.0) ? 1.0 : 0.0;
    return RetVal.ExtractXloper();
}
```

<u>Circular reference note:</u> In the above example, the function gets information about the calling cell, its value, and then returns a function of it to that same cell. This gives Excel an obvious dilemma: the function depends on itself so there is a circular reference. How Excel deals with this depends on how the `toggle_caller()` was registered. If registered as a worksheet function, the call to `xlfGetCell` will return the error code 2 (`xlretInvXlfn`). Excel considers functions like `xlfGetCell` to be off-limits for normal worksheet functions, getting round this and other problems that can arise. This is the same rejection as you would see if you entered the formula =GET.CELL(5,A1) in a worksheet cell – Excel would display an error dialog saying "That function is not valid". (Such functions were introduced only to be used in Excel macro sheets.) The equivalent code that calls `xlCoerce` would also fail, this time with an error code of 64 (`xlretUncalced`). In this case Excel is complaining that the source cell has not been recalculated. If `toggle_caller()` had been registered as a macro sheet function, Excel is more permissive; the function behaves as you would expect. Section 8.5.4 *Giving functions macro sheet function permissions* on page 188 describes how to do this.

Being able to give your XLL worksheet functions macro sheet function capabilities opens up the possibility of writing some really absurd and useless functions. Some potentially useful ones are also possible, such as the above example, and the following very similar one that simply counts the number of times it is called. In this case, the example uses a trigger argument, and effectively counts the number of times that argument changes.

```
xloper * __stdcall increment_caller(int trigger)
{
    xloper Caller;
    xloper GetCell_param;
    static xloper RetVal;

    GetCell_param.xltype = xltypeInt;
    GetCell_param.val.w = 5; // contents of caller as number

    Excel4(xlfCaller, &Caller, 0);
    Excel4(xlfGetCell, &RetVal, 2, &GetCell_param, &Caller);

    if(RetVal.xltype == xltypeNum)
        RetVal.val.num += 1.0;
```

```
        Excel4(xlFree, 0, 1, &Caller);
        return &RetVal;
}
```

8.2.5   Calling macro sheet commands from the DLL using `Excel4()`

XLM macro sheet commands are entered into macro sheet cells in the same way as worksheet or macro sheet functions. The difference is that they execute command-equivalent actions, for example, closing or opening a workbook. Calling these commands using `Excel4()` is programmatically the same as calling functions, although they only execute successfully if called during the execution of a command. In other words, they are off-limits to worksheet and macro sheet equivalent functions. Sections 8.11 onwards to the end of the chapter contain numerous examples of such calls.

8.3   THE `Excel4v()` C API FUNCTION

The syntax for `Excel4v()` is:

```
    int __stdcall Excel4v(int xlfn, xloper *RetVal, int count,
        xloper *opers[]);
```

which returns the same values as `Excel4()`.

Table 8.4 `Excel4v()` arguments

Argument	Meaning	Comments
`int xlfn`	A number corresponding to a function or command recognised by Excel as part of the C API.	Must be one of the predefined constants defined in the SDK header file `xlcall.h`.
`xloper *RetVal`	A pointer to an `xloper` that will contain the return value of the function `xlfn` if `Excel4v()` was able to call it. If a return value is not required by the caller, NULL (zero) can be passed.	If `Excel4v()` was unable to call the function, the contents of this are unchanged. Excel allocates memory for certain return types. It is the responsibility of the caller to know when and how to tell Excel to free this memory. (See `xlFree` and `xlbitXLFree`.)
`int count`	The number of arguments to `xlfn` being passed in this call to `Excel4v()`.	As with `Excel4()` the maximum value is 30.
`xloper *opers[]`	An array, of at least `count` elements, of *pointers* to `xloper`s containing the arguments for `xlfn`.	

The following example simply provides a worksheet interface to `Excel4v()` allowing the function number and the arguments that are appropriate for that function to be passed in directly from the sheet. This can be an extremely useful tool but also one to be used with great care. This section outlines some of the things this enables you to do, but first here's the code with comments that explain what is going on.

```
xloper * __stdcall XL4(int xlfn, xloper *arg0, xloper *arg1,
            xloper *arg2, xloper *arg3, xloper *arg4,
            xloper *arg5, xloper *arg6, xloper *arg7,
            xloper *arg8, xloper *arg9, xloper *arg10,
            xloper *arg11, xloper *arg12, xloper *arg13,
            xloper *arg14, xloper *arg15, xloper *arg16,
            xloper *arg17, xloper *arg18)
{
   xloper *arg_array[19];
   static xloper ret_xloper;

// Fill in array of pointers to the xloper arguments ready for the
// call to Excel4v()
   arg_array[0] = arg0;
   arg_array[1] = arg1;
   arg_array[2] = arg2;
   arg_array[3] = arg3;
   arg_array[4] = arg4;
   arg_array[5] = arg5;
   arg_array[6] = arg6;
   arg_array[7] = arg7;
   arg_array[8] = arg8;
   arg_array[9] = arg9;
   arg_array[10] = arg10;
   arg_array[11] = arg11;
   arg_array[12] = arg12;
   arg_array[13] = arg13;
   arg_array[14] = arg14;
   arg_array[15] = arg15;
   arg_array[16] = arg16;
   arg_array[17] = arg17;
   arg_array[18] = arg18;

// Find the last non-missing argument
   for(int i = 19; --i >= 0;)
      if(arg_array[i]->xltype != xltypeMissing)
         break;

// Call the function
   int retval = Excel4v(xlfn, &ret_xloper, i + 1, arg_array);

   if(retval != xlretSuccess)
   {
// If the call to Excel4v() failed, return a string explaining why
// and tell Excel to call back into the DLL to free the memory
// about to be allocated for the return string.
      ret_xloper.xltype = xltypeStr | xlbitDLLFree;
      ret_xloper.val.str = new_xlstring(Excel4_err_msg(retval));
   }
   else
   {
// Tell Excel to free up memory that it might have allocated for
```

```
// the return value.
        ret_xloper.xltype |= xlbitXLFree;
    }
    return &ret_xloper;
}
```

The function `Excel4_err_msg()` simply returns a string with an appropriate error message should the call to `Excel4v()` fail, and is listed below. The function `new_xlstring()` creates a byte-counted string from this.

```
char *Excel4_err_msg(int err_num)
{
    switch(err_num)
    {
    case xlretAbort:        return "XL4: macro halted";
    case xlretInvXlfn:      return "XL4: invalid function number";
    case xlretInvCount:     return "XL4: invalid number of args";
    case xlretInvXloper:    return "XL4: invalid oper structure";
    case xlretStackOvfl:    return "XL4: stack overflow";
    case xlretUncalced:     return "XL4: uncalced cell";
    case xlretFailed:       return "XL4: command failed";
    default:                return NULL;
    }
}
```

The function `XL4()` takes 20 arguments (one for the C API function code, and up to 19 function arguments). The Excel worksheet limit for any function is 30 arguments, but the means by which functions are registered (see section 8.5 below) imposes this limit on exported XLL functions.

8.4   WHAT C API FUNCTIONS CAN THE DLL CALL AND WHEN?

The C API was designed to be called from DLL functions that have themselves been called by Excel while executing commands, during worksheet recalculations or during one of the Add-in Manager's calls to one of the `xlAuto-` functions. DLL routines can be called in other ways too: the `DllMain()` function is called by the operating system; VB can call exported DLL functions that have been declared within the VB module; the DLL can set up operating system call-backs, for example, at regular timed intervals; the DLL can create background threads.

Excel is not always ready to receive calls to the `Excel4()` or `Excel4v()` functions. The following table summarises when you can and cannot call these functions safely.

Table 8.5 When it is safe to call the C API

When called	Safe to call?	Additional comments
During a call to the DLL from: • an Excel command, • a user-defined command in a macro sheet, • a user-defined command subroutine in a VB code module, • the Add-in Manager to one of the xlAuto- functions, • an XLL command run using the xlcOnTime C API function.	Yes	In all these cases Excel is running a command, i.e., these are all effectively called as a result of a user action, e.g., starting Excel, loading a workbook, choosing a menu option, etc. All xlf-, xlc- and the C API-only functions are available.
During a call to the DLL from a user-defined VBA worksheet function.	Yes	DLL functions called from VB in this way cannot call macro sheet C API functions such as the workspace information function xlfGetWorkbook.
During a direct call to a macro sheet equivalent function, called as a result of recalculation of a worksheet cell or cells.	Yes	Most of the xlf- functions and the C API-only functions are available. (A number of the xlf- functions are, in fact, command-equivalents and can only be called from commands.) Note: Functions within VB modules that are called as a result of a worksheet recalculation are worksheet function equivalents not macro-sheet equivalents.
During a direct call to a worksheet equivalent function, called as a result of recalculation of a worksheet cell or cells.	Yes	Only worksheet equivalent xlf- functions and the C API-only functions are available. A large number of the xlf- functions are only accessible to macro sheet equivalent functions. Calling these will either result in Excel4() returning xlretFailed.

(continued overleaf)

Table 8.5 (*continued*)

When called	Safe to call?	Additional comments
		Note that some otherwise-permitted `xlf-` functions that attempt to obtain the values of unrecalculated cells will fail, returning `xlretUncalced`, unless called from macro sheet equivalent functions. Functions within VB modules that are called as a result of a worksheet recalculation are subject to the above restrictions.
During a call to a DLL function by the operating system.	No	In both of these cases, calling `Excel4()` or `Excel4v()` will have unpredictable results and may crash or destabilise Excel.
During an execution of a background thread created by the DLL.	No	See section 9.5 *Accessing Excel functionality using COM/OLE* for information about how to call Excel in such cases, including how to get Excel to call into the DLL again in such a way that the C API *is* available.

8.5   REGISTERING AND UN-REGISTERING DLL (XLL) FUNCTIONS

Registering functions is an essential step in making your DLL functions accessible on the worksheet (without going via VB). It is also the means by which you specify what a user sees when they invoke the Paste Function or Add-in Manager dialogs. Functions can be registered from any command at any time, the most sensible place being the `xlAutoOpen` XLL interface function. (See section 5.5 *XLL functions called by the Add-in Manager and Excel* on page 98 for details of when this function is called.)

When your DLL is unloaded, registered functions should, in theory, be un-registered so that Excel knows they are inaccessible – something best done in the `xlAutoClose` XLL interface function. However, a bug in Excel prevents functions from being unregistered properly. This is not a great concern, as it does nothing to destabilise Excel.

Registering functions is equivalent in many ways to declaring DLL functions in VBA. The required minimum information is very similar: the DLL path and file name, the function name as exported, the argument types and the return type. However, Excel allows the DLL to tell it many more things about the function at the same time, such as the calling equivalence of the function (worksheet or macro sheet equivalent), whether or not the function is volatile, as well as providing information for the Add-in Manager and the Paste Function dialog.

8.5.1 The `xlfRegister` function

Overview: Registers and un-registers DLL and XLL commands and functions.

Enumeration value: 149 (x95)

Callable from: Commands only.

Return type: An `xltypeNum` `xloper`.

Arguments: See table below.

Registering and un-registering commands and functions is accomplished with calls to the same function, `xlfRegister`. All arguments can be passed in as byte-counted string `xlopers`, although numerical values can be passed in some cases. Their meaning is given in the following table. To register a worksheet function, at least the first 5 are required. To register a command, at least 6 are needed. (See section 8.6 *Registering and un-registering DLL (XLL) commands* on page 196 for more about commands.)

Table 8.6 `xlfRegister` arguments for registering functions

Argument number	Required or optional	Description
1	Required	The full drive, path and filename of the DLL containing the function.
2	Required	The function name as it is exported. Note: This is case-sensitive.
3	Required	The return type, argument type and calling permission string. (See sections 8.5.3, 8.5.4 and 8.5.5 for details.)
4	Required	The function name as you wish it to appear in the worksheet. Note: This *is* case-sensitive.
5	Required	The argument names as a comma-delimited concatenated string, e.g., `"Arg1,Arg2,Arg3"`. Excel uses this string to work out the number of arguments and to determine the text to show to the left of each of the corresponding text-boxes in the Paste Function dialog.

(continued overleaf)

Table 8.6 (*continued*)

Argument number	Required or optional	Description
6	Optional	The function type: 1 or omitted = Function; 2 = Command.
7	Optional	The Paste Function category in which the function is to be listed. If omitted the function is listed under *User Defined*. (See section 8.5.2 for details.)
8	Optional	*(Not used)*.
9	Optional	The help topic.
10	Optional	A brief description of the function, e.g., `"This function returns the factorial of positive integers less than 20"`. This text is displayed in the Paste Function dialog.
11	Optional	Help for the 1st argument, e.g., `"A positive integer less than 20"`. This text is displayed in the Paste Function dialog when the text box relating to this argument is selected.
12	Optional	Help for the 2nd argument.
...	...	...
30	Optional	Help for the 20th argument.

`Excel4()` and `Excel4v()`'s limit of 30 arguments, through which all these arguments must be passed in order to register the function, imposes the limit of 20 arguments for any DLL function that you wish to export and make available on the worksheet. In practice this is not too much of a problem. If you really need to pass more information than this, combining data into a single array or range argument is the most obvious solution.

Note: A curious Excel bug sometimes causes the truncation of the last 2 characters of the last argument help text in the Paste Function dialog. This can be avoided by padding with a couple of spaces or by passing an extra blank text argument.

Here is an example of code that registers a function using the `cpp_xloper` class to ease creation of the arguments. Note that, in practice, registering functions one by one like this, each with its own registration function, would be extremely cumbersome. Section 8.5.10 *Managing the data needed to register exported functions* on page 191 describes a much more efficient and organised approach.

```
bool register_example(void)
{
    cpp_xloper DllName;
    cpp_xloper FunctionName("exponent_function");
    cpp_xloper TypeText("BB"); // = return a double, take a double
    cpp_xloper Worksheet_function_name("MY_EXP");
    cpp_xloper Arguments("Exponent");
```

```
    cpp_xloper FunctionType(1);
    cpp_xloper Category("My functions");
    cpp_xloper Description("Returns e to the power of Exponent");
    cpp_xloper Arg1Help("Any number such that |n| <= 709");
    cpp_xloper RetVal;

// Get the full path and name of the DLL.
    if(Excel4(xlGetName, &DllName, 0) != xlretSuccess)
        return false;

// Tell destructor to use Excel to free the string memory when done.
    DllName.SetExceltoFree();

    int XL4_ret_val = Excel4(xlfRegister,
        &RetVal,
        11, // number of subsequent arguments
        &DllName,
        &FunctionName,
        &TypeText,
        &WorksheetFunctionName,
        &Arguments,
        &FunctionType,
        &Category,
        p_xlMissing,  // no short-cut
        p_xlMissing,  // no help topic
        &Description,
        &Arg1Help);

    if(XL4_ret_val)
    {
        cpp_xloper Message("Could not register MY_EXP");
        cpp_xloper Type(2); // Dialog box type.

        Excel4(xlcAlert, NULL, 2, &Message, &Type);
        return false;
    }
    return true;
}
```

Warning: It is possible to register the same DLL function twice, giving it a different worksheet name, the 4th argument, in both cases. You might want to do this so that, for example, in one case it is volatile and in the other it is not. Or you might want to register it as taking an `xloper` argument in one case and an `oper` argument in the other. (The following sections discuss how to specify these things.) Excel will not complain if you do this, but it may be unable to distinguish between the two functions, and the desired differentiation might not occur. The simple work-around is to create a wrapper to the function and export both the function and the wrapper.

8.5.2 Specifying which category the function should be listed under

Argument 7 to `xlfRegister` tells Excel which function category to list worksheet functions under in the Paste Function dialog. This can be a number or text corresponding to one of the hard-coded standard categories, or the text of a new category specified by the DLL. If the text given does not exist already, Excel will create a new category with that name. Creating a new category for a given DLL is a good idea, especially where they are to be distributed. It makes it clear which DLL and software provider the functions are associated with.

The standard categories that are visible when viewing the Paste Function dialog from within a worksheet are:

Table 8.7 Standard   worksheet function categories

Number	Text
1	Financial
2	Date & Time
3	Math & Trig
4	Text
5	Logical
6	Lookup & Reference
7	Database
8	Statistical
9	Information
14	User Defined

There are also a number of categories that are only visible when viewing the Paste Function dialog from within a macro sheet. As this book is not about XLM or macro sheets, these are mentioned only for completeness:

Table 8.8 Macro sheet function categories

Number	Text
10	Commands
11	Actions
12	Customising
13	Macro Control

8.5.3   Specifying argument and return types

The string supplied as argument 3 to `xlfRegister` encodes the return type of the function in its first letter and the types of the arguments in its subsequent letters. (In fact it is used to specify more than just this – see sections 8.5.4, 8.5.5 and 8.5.6.) Excel uses these letters to ensure it does the necessary conversions of inputs and return values. Note that Excel has no way to check that the letters used correspond to the function as defined in the DLL code. The `xlfRegister` function will be successful even if they don't match. However, Excel will have problems calling the function, so you need to be sure you've specified these correctly.

The following table shows how the various data types are encoded:

Table 8.9 Registered function argument and return types

Data type	Pass by value	Pass by ref (pointer)	Comments
Boolean	A	L	Implemented as short (0 or 1)
double	B	E	
char *		C, F	Null-terminated string
unsigned char *		D, G	Byte-counted string
unsigned short int	H		Also defined as DWORD
signed short int	I	M	
signed long int	J	N	
struct xl_array		K	See section 6.2.2, page 107
struct oper		P	See section 6.2.6, page 119
struct xloper		R	See section 6.2.3, page 111

If a function uses a pass-by-reference (pointer) type for its return value, you can pass a null pointer as the return value. Microsoft Excel will translate this to the #NUM! error.

Examples

Full explanations of # (indicating a macro sheet equivalent function) and ! (indicating a volatile function) and the leading numeral (indicating the position of an argument to be modified in place as the return value) are given below in sections 8.5.4, 8.5.5 and 8.5.6 respectively.

Table 8.10 Example argument strings for registered functions

Calling specifier (3rd argument to xlfRegister)	Description
BB	Take a double. Return a double.
BJJ	Take two signed long integers. Return a double.
CB	Take a double. Return a null-terminated C string.
1F	Take a null-terminated C string and modify it in-place.

(continued overleaf)

Table 8.10 (*continued*)

Calling specifier (3rd argument to `xlfRegister`)	Description
`1G`	Take a byte-counted string and modify it in-place.
`2BF`	Take a double and a null-terminated C string and modify the string (the 2nd argument) in-place. Function must return `void`.
`FBF`	As above example, except function can return anything: Excel will ignore it.
`CD`	Take a byte-counted string and return a null-terminated C string.
`2EEE`	Take three pointers to `double` and modify the 2nd argument in-place.
`1K`	Take and return a floating-point array structure (see section 6.2.2) by modifying in-place the first and only argument.
`KJJ`	Take two signed long integers. Return a floating-point array structure. (See section 6.2.2.)
`RR`	Take a pointer to `xloper`. Return a pointer to `xloper`.
`J!`	Take no arguments. Return a signed long integer. Function is volatile.
`RJJJJ#`	Take four signed long integers. Return a pointer to `xloper`. Function has macro sheet equivalence and is able to reference uncalculated cells and macro sheet information functions.
`1RR#!`	Take two pointers to `xloper`. Return an `xloper` via the first argument by modifying in place. Function is volatile and has macro sheet equivalence.
`RPP`	Take two pointers to `oper`. Return a pointer to `xloper`.

8.5.4   Giving functions macro sheet function permissions

Excel allows macro sheet functions to do a number of things that ordinary worksheet functions cannot. For example, they are able to access the current value of any cell, whether or not that cell is in need of recalculation. They are also permitted to call a number of workspace information functions that are off-limits to worksheet functions. Effectively, macro sheet functions have a higher permission level than worksheet functions.

When registering DLL functions, (not commands), you tell Excel whether your function should have macro sheet function permissions or not. By default it will not, but is given them by appending a '#' character to the end of the type string, argument 3. For example a function declared as "BB#" (a function that takes a `double` and returns a `double`) will be able to access the value of all uncalculated cells.

Excel forbids the use of built-in macro sheet functions in worksheets. Try entering the formula =Get.Note(A1) in a worksheet – Excel will complain that the function "is not valid". Fortunately, it *does* allow add-in functions declared as macro sheet functions to be called from a worksheet. This opens up the possibility for worksheet functions to access a much wider range of information and functionality.

Note: If a function that is only defined as a worksheet function attempts to reference an uncalculated cell in a call to Excel4(), the call will fail, returning the value xlretUncalced.

8.5.5 Specifying functions as volatile

The concept of volatile functions is explained in section 2.11.3 *Volatile functions* on page 26.

By default, DLL worksheet functions are not volatile. They only recalculate when their precedents change. To make a DLL function volatile it is only necessary to place an exclamation mark '!' at the end of the type string in argument 3. For example a function declared as "BB!" (a function that takes a double and returns a double) will be recalculated every time Excel performs a recalculation.

Be careful about registering functions in this way. Excel not only recalculates volatile functions with every recalculation, but also all their dependents too.

8.5.6 Returning values by modifying arguments in place

Where an argument is passed to a DLL function via a pointer it is possible for the DLL to return its value via this argument – a technique known as modifying in place. This leaves the burden of memory management to Excel. Excel will both allocate the memory for the argument and clean up once it has copied out the returned data. Care must be taken not to expect too much of Excel, however. Strings can only be a maximum of 255 characters in length (the amount of space Excel allocates for these). Where the data is an array of doubles of type xl_array (see section 6.2.2 *Excel floating-point array structure: xl_array* on page 107) the returned data can be no bigger than the passed-in array. Arrays of strings cannot be returned in this way.

Excel also needs fair warning that you intend to do this and only permits one argument (and always the same one) to be used in this way. This is done within the return and argument type string passed as the 3rd argument to xlfRegister. Instead of specifying a return type as the first character, a single digit from 1 to 9 informs Excel that the corresponding argument, counting from 1, is to be used, which must be one of the passed-by-ref types. Functions that Excel expects to return their arguments in this way must be declared as void.

Excel also permits functions that return strings, by modifying either the F or G type, to be declared as returning something other than void. This might be useful if you have a function that returns some modified text both in this way and by returning a pointer. The latter return method enables the function to be called within the calling of another function. For example, a function might be declared as follows:

```
char * __stdcall my_conversion_function(char *input_text)
{
// Modify the input text
    return input_text;
}
```

... and called as follows...

```
int length = strlen(my_conversion_function(input_text));
```

This example could also be registered with Excel with a type string of FF. This instructs Excel to find the first argument that matches the given return type, in this case F, and extract the return value from that. The return value pointer that was placed on the stack by the function is discarded and ignored. When passing the argument to the DLL, Excel allocates a 256 byte buffer, regardless of the length of the passed-in string, so the returned string can be up to 255 characters in length *including* the null termination.

8.5.7 The Paste Function dialog (Function Wizard)

The dialogs shown below illustrate where some of the arguments to xlfRegister end up being displayed.

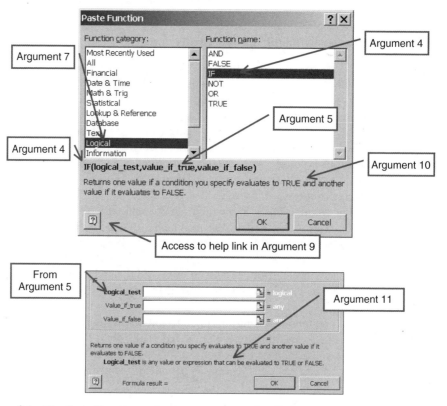

Figure 8.1 The Paste Function and argument construction dialogs

<u>Note:</u> Arguments 11 to 20 cannot be assigned from VB via the COM interface (at time of writing) for user-defined functions or COM DLLs. If parameter names are too long they will work, but they will not display correctly.

8.5.8   Function help parameter to `xlfRegister`

The above screen-shots show where the function help parameter, passed as the 10th argument to `xlfRegister`, is used. Choosing your words well makes a big difference to the ease with which the user can find the right function.

8.5.9   Argument help parameters to `xlfRegister`

As can be seen in the above screen-shot, the dialog that assists with the entry of function arguments displays at the bottom the parameter name (as extracted from the 5th argument passed to `xlfRegister`) in bold, followed by a very useful piece of text explaining something about the parameter. For specialised or complex functions this is a very valuable piece of help to provide the user. It could be as simple as detailing the units in which a number should be input, or the limits within which the function will work properly.

These are provided to the `xlfRegister` function as arguments 11 to 30.

For some reason, these fields are not (currently) exposed via the COM interface and therefore not accessible to VB. At the time of writing, the C API provides the only way to specify these things for user-defined functions.

Note: One of the strange quirks of the `xlfRegister` function, at least as it is exposed via the C API, is a small bug that truncates the very last of these strings (corresponding to the help for the very last argument). It is not serious and easy to work around: Just pad the last string with an extra space or two.

8.5.10   Managing the data needed to register exported functions

One practical issue to grapple with is how best to manage all the data associated with the functions (and commands) you want to export. For every function there are at least 5 and up to 30 arguments to be passed to `xlfRegister`. Deciding how best to initialise them and then pass them is quite important. Getting it right makes adding to or modifying the data easy. Getting it wrong makes your code a mess. It's certainly not worth losing sleep over, but here are some thoughts and suggestions.

The example in section 8.5.1 above showed a function dedicated to registering a single exported function. While you can do this, and call all such functions from your implementation of `xlAutoOpen`, it's error-prone and a lot of work. Not only this but your project will suffer from rapid code inflation. If you are a contract programmer paid per line of code then this is the approach to take.

A better approach is to define all these arguments in one structure, that is then processed by a function that iterates through, registering the functions one-by-one. One simple approach is to set up a 2-dimensional array of pointers to `char *` and then initialise this with the arguments, all as strings. Even where an argument is numeric, representing it as a string is not too inefficient: processing is only done once at the time you register your functions. Excel will happily convert strings to numbers, so there is no need to convert them before passing them as `xlopers` to `xlfRegister`.

The width of the array should be sufficient to store all of the 29 arguments that, together with the DLL name, make up the maximum 30. (You could make the array narrower if you know the maximum number of arguments you'll be declaring.) The length need only be the number of functions being exported. For a DLL that exports 50 functions, the size of the array is only 5,800 bytes plus the size of the static strings – very respectable by today's standards.

One benefit of this approach, apart from its simplicity, is that the strings can all be initialised statically. There's no need to call some function, explicitly or implicitly, to set everything up before calling the function that finally registers the exported functions. Any missing arguments can be left as uninitialised or zero-length strings.

A similar approach would be to use the cpp_xloper class, or a similar wrapper class that contained a few basic constructors. A 2-dimensional array of this class can then be initialised in a very similar way to the char * array mentioned above. You could also take a class-based approach one step further, creating a class and statically instantiating one for each exported function one in your project. The class constructor could also pass a reference of itself to a container class that is then iterated in xlAutoOpen (and xlAutoClose). Whatever your preferred approach, the goal should be ease of addition and deletion of XLL exports, modification of the help text, etc.

Preparing the arguments for the call to xlfRegister is then fairly straightforward. Set up an array of pointers to xlopers and call the function using Excel4v(). This is preferable to using Excel4() as, from function to function, you will be passing a different number of arguments. The advantage of using a wrapper class over a char * array is that converting and preparing the arguments can be made a little simpler.

The following code sample shows the declaration and initialisation of a simple array of strings for the example function in section 8.5.1:

```
#define MAX_EXCEL4_ARGS      30
#define NUM_FUNCS            1

char *FuncExports[NUM_FUNCS][MAX_EXCEL4_ARGS - 1] =
{
    {
        "exponent_function", // function name as exported
        "BB",                // return and argument types
        "MY_EXP",            // function name for Excel use
        "Exponent",          // Argument string (only 1 in this case)
        "1",                 // Function type (1:function, 2:command)
        "My functions",      // Paste Function category
        "", // Short-cut text character (Mac only)
        "", // Help file and topic (omitted in this case)
        "Returns e to the power of Exponent", // Function help text
        "Any number such that |arg1| <= 709 ", // Arg1 help text
    }, // end of data for first function to be registered
};
```

The following code shows a very simple implementation of xlAutoOpen which cycles through the array, registering each function.

```
xloper register_fnID[NUM_FUNCS];

int __stdcall xlAutoOpen(void)
{
    for(int i = 0 ; i < NUM_FUNCS; i++)
```

```
        register_fnID[i] = register_function(i);

    return 1;
}
```

A bug prevents the function (and command) IDs from being used for their intended purpose of un-registering functions. (See the next two sections.) Therefore the above code can be replaced with this:

```
int __stdcall xlAutoOpen(void)
{
    for(int i = 0 ; i < NUM_FUNCS;)
        register_function(i++);

    return 1;
}
```

The function `register_function()` registers the specified function using the above array. The function uses `Excel4v()` since the number of arguments is variable. The code uses the `cpp_xloper` class, described in section 6.4 on page 121, to simplify the handling of `Excel4()` and `Excel4v()` arguments and return values.

```
xloper *register_function(int index)
{
// Array of pointers to xloper that will be passed to Excel4v()
    xloper *ptr_array[MAX_EXCEL4_ARGS];

// Default to this value in case of a problem
    cpp_xloper RetVal((WORD)xlerrValue);

//-----------------------------------------------------------
// Get the full path and name of the DLL.
// Passed as the first argument to xlfRegister, so need
// to set first pointer in array to point to this.
//-----------------------------------------------------------
    cpp_xloper DllName;

    if(Excel4(xlGetName, &DllName, 0) != xlretSuccess)
        return NULL;
    DllName.SetExceltoFree();

    ptr_array[0] = &DllName;
    int num_args = 1;

//-----------------------------------------------------------
// Set up the rest of the array of pointers.
//-----------------------------------------------------------
    cpp_xloper *fn_args = new cpp_xloper[MAX_EXCEL4_ARGS - 1];

    char *p_arg;
    int i = 0, num_args = 1;

    do
    {
```

```
            // get the next string from the char * array
            if((p_arg = FuncExports[fn_index][i]) == NULL)
                break; // that was the last of the arguments for this fn

            // Set the corresponding xlfRegister argument
            fn_args[i] = p_arg; // convert the string to a cpp_xloper
            ptr_array[num_args++] = &(fn_args[i++]); // address of xloper
        }
    while(num_args < MAX_EXCEL4_ARGS);

    if(Excel4v(xlfRegister, &RetVal, num_args, ptr_array)
    || RetVal.IsType(xltypeErr))
    {
        char err[256];
        sprintf(err, "Couldn't register %s", FuncExports[index][0]);
        cpp_xloper ErrMsg(err);
        Excel4(xlcAlert, 0, 1, &ErrMsg);
    }
    delete[] fn_args;

// RetVal type is xltypeErr or xltypeNum, so no need to free
    return RetVal.ExtractXloper(false);
}
```

It would be a simple matter to alter the above code so that arrays of cpp_xlopers, or arrays of look-alike xlopers, are initialised with function information, instead of char * arrays.

8.5.11   Getting and using the function's register ID

In the above section, code example register_function() registers a function and returns a pointer to an xloper. If the function was successful this xloper is of type xltypeNum and contains a unique register ID. This ID is intended to be used in calls to xlfUnregister. However, a bug in Excel prevents this from un-registering functions as intended – see next section.

If you did not record the ID that xlfRegister returned, you can get it at any time using the xlfRegisterId function. This takes 3 arguments:

1. DllName: The name of the DLL as returned by the function xlGetName.
2. FunctionName: The name of the function as exported and passed in the 2nd argument to xlfRegister.
3. ArgRtnTypes: The string that encodes the return and argument types, the calling permission and volatile status of the function, as passed in the 3rd argument to xlfRegister.

The macro sheet functions that take this ID as an argument are:

- xlfUnregister: (See next section.)
- xlfCall: Calls a DLL function. There is no point in calling this function where the caller is in the same DLL, but it does provide a means for inter-DLL calling. (The

macro sheet version of this function, CALL(), used to be available on worksheets. This enabled a spreadsheet with no XLM or VB macros to access *any* DLL's functionality without alerting the user to the potential misuse that this could be put to. This security chasm was closed in version 7.0.)

8.5.12   Un-registering a DLL function

Excel keeps an internal list of the functions that have been registered from a given DLL as well as the number of times each function has been registered. (You can interrogate Excel about the loaded DLL functions using the xlfGetWorkspace, argument 44. See section 8.9.11 *Information about the workspace:* xlfGetWorkspace on page 227 for details.) When registering a function, the xlfRegister function does two things.

1. Increments the count for the registered function.
2. Associates the function's worksheet name, given as the 4th argument to xlfRegister, with the DLL resource.

To un-register a function you therefore have to undo both of these actions in order to restore Excel to the pre-DLL state. The xlfUnregister function, which takes the register ID returned by the call to xlfRegister, decrements the usage count of the function. To disassociate the function's worksheet name, you need to call the xlfSetName function, which usually associates a name with a resource, but without specifying a resource. This clears the existing associated resource – the DLL function. Sadly, a bug in Excel prevents even this two-pronged approach from successfully removing the reference to the function. In practice, not un-registering functions has no grave consequences.

Warning: The C API function xlfUnregister supports another syntax which takes a DLL name, as returned by the function xlfGetName. Called in this way it un-registers *all* that DLL's resources. This syntax also causes Excel to call xlAutoClose(). You will therefore crash Excel with a stack overflow if you call xlfUnregister with this syntax from within xlAutoClose(). You should avoid using this syntax anywhere within the DLL self-referentially.

The following code sample shows a simple implementation of xlAutoClose(), called whenever the DLL is unloaded or the add-in is deselected in the Add-in Manager, and the code for the function it calls, unregister_function(). The example uses the same structures and constant delimitations as in section 8.5.10 above. As stated above, even this will not work as intended, due to an Excel bug. Leaving the body of xlAutoClose() empty in this example will not have grave consequences, although there may be other cleaning up tasks you should be doing here.

```
int __stdcall xlAutoClose(void)
{
    for(int i = 0 ; i < NUM_FUNCS; i++)
        unregister_function(i);

    return 1;
}
```

```
bool unregister_function(int fn_index)
{
// Decrement the usage count for the function using a module-scope
// xloper array containing the function's ID, as returned by
// xlfRegister or xlfRegisterId functions
    Excel4(xlfUnregister, 0, 1, register_ID + fn_index);

// Create a cpp_xloper argument with the name that Excel associates
// with the function
    cpp_xloper xStr(FuncExports[fn_index][2]);

// Undo the association of the name with the resource
    if(Excel4(xlfSetName, 0 , 1, &xStr) != xlretSuccess)
        return false;

    return true;
}
```

As stated already, given the Excel bug, this un-registration function need not be included in your project.

8.6   REGISTERING AND UN-REGISTERING DLL (XLL) COMMANDS

As with functions, XLL commands need to be registered in order to be directly accessible within Excel (without going via VB). As with worksheet functions, the xlfRegister function is used. (See section 8.5 for details of how to call this function.) To register a command, the first 6 arguments to xlfRegister must all be passed.

Table 8.11 xlfRegister arguments for registering commands

Argument number	Required or optional	Description
1	Required	The full drive, path and filename of the DLL containing the function.
2	Required	The command name as it is exported. Note: This is case-sensitive.
3	Required	The return type which should always be "J"
4	Required	The command name as Excel will know how to reference it. Note: This is case-sensitive.
5	Required	The argument names, i.e., an xltypeNil or xltypeMissing xloper, since commands take no arguments.
6	Optional	The function type: 2 = Command.

An exported command will always be of the following form:

```
int __stdcall xll_command(void)
{
    bool all_ok = is_everything_ok();

    if(!all_ok)
        return 0;

    return 1;
}
```

In practice, Excel does not care about the return value, although the above is a good standard to conform to.

As there are always 6 arguments to be passed `xlfRegister` is best called using `Excel4()`, in contrast to functions which are most easily registered by `Excel4v()`. The following code demonstrates how to register Excel commands, requiring only the name of the command as exported in the DLL and the name as Excel will refer to it. The code uses the `cpp_xloper` class, described in section 6.4 on page 121, to simplify the handling of `Excel4()` arguments and return values.

```
xloper *register_command(char *code_name, char *Excel_name)
{
//---------------------------------------------------------
// default to this value in case of a problem
//---------------------------------------------------------
    cpp_xloper RetVal((WORD)xlerrValue);

//---------------------------------------------------------
// Get the full path and name of the DLL.
// Passed as the first argument to xlfRegister, so need
// to set first pointer in array to point to this.
//---------------------------------------------------------
    cpp_xloper DllName;

    if(Excel4(xlGetName, &DllName, 0) != xlretSuccess)
    {
        DllName.Free(true); // don't really need to do this, but...
        return NULL;
    }
    DllName.SetExceltoFree();

//---------------------------------------------------------
// Set up the rest of the arguments.
//---------------------------------------------------------
    cpp_xloper CodeName(code_name);
    cpp_xloper ExcelName(Excel_name);
    cpp_xloper RtnType("J");
    cpp_xloper FnType(2); // Command

    int xl4_retval = Excel4(xlfRegister, &RetVal, 6, &DllName,
        &CodeName, &RtnType, &ExcelName, p_xlNil, &FnType);

    if(xl4_retval != xlretSuccess || RetVal.IsType(xltypeErr))
        display_register_error(code_name, xl4_retval, (int)RetVal);
```

```
// Err or Num: no need to free, but no harm in doing it anyway
   return RetVal.ExtractXloper(true);
}
```

Commands to be exported can simply be described by the two strings that need to be passed to the above function. These strings can be held in a static array that is looped through in the xlAutoOpen function. The following code shows the declaration and initialisation of an array for the example command from section 8.1.2, and a very simple implementation of xlAutoOpen which cycles through the array, registering each command.

```
#define NUM_COMMANDS        1

char *CommandExports[NUM_COMMANDS][2] =
{
// Name in code        Name that Excel uses
   {"define_new_name",   "DefineNewName"},
};

xloper register_cmdID[NUM_COMMANDS];

int __stdcall xlAutoOpen(void)
{
    for(int i = 0 ; i < NUM_COMMANDS; i++)
        register_cmdID[i] = register_command(
            CommandExports[i][0], CommandExports[i][1]);

    return 1;
}
```

A bug prevents the function and command IDs from being used for their intended purpose of unregistering functions. Therefore the above code can be replaced with:

```
int __stdcall xlAutoOpen(void)
{
    for(int i = 0 ; i < NUM_COMMANDS; i++)
        register_command(CommandExports[i][0], CommandExports[i][1]);

    return 1;
}
```

8.6.1 Accessing XLL commands

There are a number of ways to access commands that have been exported and registered as described above.

1. Via custom menus. (See section 8.11 *Working with Excel menus*, page 249.)
2. Via custom toolbars. (See section 8.12 *Working with toolbars*, page 266.)
3. Via a Custom Button on a toolbar. (See below.)
4. Directly via the Macro dialog. (See below.)

5. Via a VB module. (See below.)

6. Via one of the C API event traps. (See section 8.14 *Trapping events*, page 277.)

In addition, there are a number of C API functions that take a command reference (the name of the command as registered with Excel), for example xlfCancelKey.

To assign a command (or macro as Excel often refers to commands) to a custom button, you need to drag a new custom button onto the desired toolbar from the Tools/Customize.../Commands dialog under the Macro category. Still with the customisation dialog showing, right-clicking on the new button shows the properties menu which enables you to specify the appearance of the button and assign the macro (command) to it.

To access the command directly from the Macro dialog, you need simply to type the command's name as registered. The command will not be listed in the list box as Excel treats XLL commands as if they had been defined on a hidden macro sheet, and therefore are themselves hidden.

One limitation of current versions of Excel is the inability to assign XLL commands directly to control objects on a worksheet. You can, however, access an XLL command in any VB module, subject to scope, using the Application.Run ("CmdName") VB statement. If you wish to associate an XLL command with worksheet control, you simply place this statement in the control's VB code.

8.6.2 Breaking execution of an XLL command

The C API provides two functions xlAbort and xlfCancelKey. The first checks for user breaks (the Esc key being pressed in Windows) and is covered in section 8.7.7 *Yielding processor time and checking for user breaks: xlAbort*, on page 206.

The second disables/enables interruption of the currently executing task. If enabled, xlfCancelKey also permits the specification of another command to be run on interruption. This second command is intended to be used to do any necessary cleaning up before control is returned to Excel.

The function takes 2 arguments: (1) a Boolean specifying whether interruption is permitted (true) or not (false), and (2) a command name registered with Excel as a string. If the function is called with the first argument set to true, then the command will be terminated by the user pressing the Esc key. This is the default state when Excel calls a command, so it is not necessary to call this function except, to explicitly disable or re-enable user breaks.

8.7 FUNCTIONS DEFINED FOR THE C API ONLY

8.7.1 Freeing Excel-allocated memory within the DLL: xlFree

Overview: Frees memory allocated by Excel during a call to Excel4()
                   or Excel4v() for the return xloper value. This is only
                   necessary where the returned xloper type involves the
                   allocation of memory by Excel. There are only 3 xloper
                   types that can have memory associated with them in this way,
                   xltypeStr, xltypeRef and xltypeMulti, so it is only

necessary to call `xlFree` if the return type is *or could be* one of these. It is always safe to call this function even if the `xloper` is not one of these types. It is <u>not</u> safe to call this function on an `xloper` that was passed in to the DLL as a function argument from Excel, or that has been initialised by the DLL with either static or dynamic memory.

(See Chapter 7 *Memory management* on page 161 for an explanation of the basic concepts and more examples of the use of `xlFree`.)

Enumeration value:	16384 (x4000)
Callable from:	Commands, worksheet and macro sheet functions.
Return type:	Void.
Arguments:	Takes from 1 to 30 arguments, each of them the address of an `xloper` that was passed to Excel in a call to `Excel4()` or `Excel4v()` to contain the return value.

<u>Warning:</u> Where the type is `xltypeMulti` you do not need to (and must not) call `xlFree` for any of the elements, whatever their types. Doing this will confuse and destabilise Excel.

<u>Note:</u> Where an Excel-allocated `xloper` is being returned (via a pointer) from a DLL function, it is necessary to set the `xlbitXLFree` bit in the `xltype` field to alert Excel to the need to free the memory.

The following example, a command function, gets the full path and file name of the DLL, displays it in a simple alert dialog and then frees the memory that Excel allocated for the string. (Note that only command-equivalent functions can display dialogs.)

```
int __stdcall show_dll_name(void)
{
    xloper dll_name;

    if(Excel4(xlGetName, &dll_name, 0) != xlretSuccess)
        return 0;

    Excel4(xlcAlert, NULL, 1, &dll_name);
    Excel4(xlFree, NULL, 1, &dll_name);
    return 1;
}
```

The equivalent code using the `cpp_xloper` class would be as follows. The call to the member function `SetExceltoFree()` informs the class destructor of the need, ultimately, to call `xlFree` to release the memory. This call is best made immediately after the initialisation by Excel in the call to `Excel4()`. It is not necessary to wait until the `xloper` is no longer being used. This is a less bug-prone approach than the above code, where there's a risk that not all control paths will clean up properly.

```
int __stdcall show_dll_name(void)
{
    cpp_xloper DllName;

    if(Excel4(xlGetName, &DllName, 0) != xlretSuccess)
        return 0;
    DllName.SetExceltoFree();

    Excel4(xlcAlert, NULL, 1, &DllName);
    return 1;
}
```

8.7.2   Getting the available stack space: `xlStack`

Overview: Returns the amount of available space on Excel's stack in bytes.

Enumeration value: 16385 (x4001)

Callable from: Commands, worksheet and macro sheet functions.

Return type: An `xltypeInt` xloper.

Arguments: None.

Stack space in Excel is very limited. (See section 7.1 *Excel stack space limitations* on page 161.) If you are concerned (or just curious) you can find out how much stack space there currently is with a call to Excel's `xlStack` function as the following example shows:

```
double __stdcall get_stack(void)
{
    xloper retval;

    if(xlretSuccess != Excel4(xlStack, &retval, 0))
        return -1.0;

    return (double)(unsigned short)retval.val.w;
}
```

The need to cast the returned signed integer that `xlStack` returns to an unsigned integer is a left-over from the days when Excel provided even less stack space and when the maximum positive value of the signed integer (32,768) was sufficient. Once more stack was made available, the need for the cast emerged to avoid a negative result.

8.7.3   Converting one `xloper` type to another: `xlCoerce`

Overview: Converts an `xloper` from one type to another, where possible.

Enumeration value: 16386 (x4002)

Callable from: Commands, worksheet and macro sheet functions.

Return type: Various depending on 2nd argument.

Arguments: 1: *InputOper*: A pointer to the `xloper` to be converted

2: *TargetType*: (Optional.) An integer `xloper` whose value specifies the type of `xloper` to which the first argument is to be converted. This can be more than one type bit-wise or'd, for example, `xltypeNum | xltypeStr` tells Excel that either one will do.

If the second argument is omitted, the function returns one of the four value types that worksheet cells can contain. This will be the same as the first argument unless it is a range `xloper` (`xltypeSRef` or `xltypeRef`) in which case it returns the *value* of the top-left cell in the range.

This function will not convert from each type to every one of the others. For example, it will not convert error values to other types, or convert a number to a cell reference. Therefore, checking the return value is important. Table 8.12 summarises what conversions are and are not possible for types covered by this book. Note that even for type conversions that *are* possible, the function might fail in some circumstances. For example, you can always convert an `xltypeSRef` to `xltypeRef`, but not always the other way round. (A question mark in the table indicates those conversions that may or may not work depending on the contents of the source `xloper`.)

Table 8.12 `xlCoerce` conversion summary

xltype...	Num	Str	Bool	Ref	Err	Multi	SRef	Int
Num		Y	Y	N	N	Y	N	Y
Str	?		?	?	N	Y	?	?
Bool	Y	Y		N	N	Y	N	Y
Ref	?	Y	?		?	Y	?	?
Err	N	N	N	N		N	N	N
Multi	?	Y	?	N	?		N	?
Nil	Y	Y	Y	N	N	Y	N	Y
SRef	?	Y	?	Y	?	Y		?
Int	Y	Y	Y	N	N	Y	N	

(Column group heading: Conversion to. Row group heading: Conversion from.)

The following example C++ code attempts to convert any `xloper` to an `xloper` of the requested type. It returns `false` if unsuccessful and `true` if successful, returning the converted value returned via the passed-in pointer. Note that the caller of this function must take responsibility for ensuring that any memory allocated by `Excel4()` for the `xloper ret_val` is eventually freed by Excel.

```
bool coerce_xloper(xloper *p_op, xloper &ret_val, int target_type)
{
// Target will contain the information that tells Excel what type to
// convert to.
    xloper target;

    target.xltype = xltypeInt;
    target.val.w = target_type; // can be more than one type

    if(Excel4(xlCoerce, &ret_val, 2, p_op, &target) != xlretSuccess
    || (ret_val.xltype & target_type) == 0)
        return false;

    return true;
}
```

In addition to `xlCoerce` being useful for converting reference `xlopers` to `opers` (by omitting the *TargetType* argument), it is particularly useful for converting multi-celled references to `xltypeMulti` arrays that are much easier to work with. Sections 6.8.7 *Array (mixed type): xltypeMulti* on page 145, and 6.8.8 *Worksheet cell/range reference: xltypeRef and xltypeSRef* on page 150 contain examples of its use in this way.

8.7.4   Setting cell values from a command: `xlSet`

Overview: Sets the values of cells in a worksheet.

Enumeration value: 16387 (x4003)

Callable from: Commands only

Return type: Boolean: true if successful, otherwise false.

Arguments: 1: *TargetRange*: A reference (xltypeSRef or xltypeRef) to the cell(s) to which values are to be assigned.

2: *Value*: (Optional.) A value (xltypeNum, xltypeInt, xltypeStr, xltypeBool, xltypeErr) or array (xltypeMulti) containing the values to be assigned to these cells. A value of type xltypeNil, or an xloper of this type in an array, will cause the relevant cell(s) to be blanked.

If *Value* is omitted, the *TargetRange* is blanked.

For those cases where a command function needs to populate one or more cells on a worksheet with certain fixed values, xlSet provides an efficient means to do this. It can be a particularly useful way to clear cells. (Omission of the second argument has this effect.) Excel does not permit this function to be called from worksheet or macro sheet functions. It would confuse, or at least vastly complicate, its recalculation logic were this not the case.

Excel maps the values to the target cells in the same way that it maps values to arrays generally: a single value will be mapped to all cells in the given range; a single row will be duplicated in all rows; a single column will be duplicated in all columns; a rectangular array will be written once into the top-left corner of the range. If a single row/column is too short for the given range or a rectangular array of values is too small then all cells in the target range not covered will be assigned the #N/A value.

Note: Where xlSet is being used to assign values to a range on a sheet that is not the active sheet, it will fail if the equivalent range on the *active* sheet contains an array formula. This appears to be a bug: Excel seems to be checking the wrong sheet before assigning the values. In failing, Excel displays the alert "You cannot change part of an array".

8.7.5   Getting the internal ID of a named sheet: xlSheetId

Overview:	Every worksheet in every open workbook is assigned an internal DWORD ID by Excel. This ID can be obtained from the text name of the sheet with the function xlSheetId, and can be used in a number of C API functions that require a worksheet ID (rather than a name), and in the construction of xltypeRef xlopers. The ID is returned within the idSheet field of an xltypeRef xloper.
Enumeration value:	16388 (x4004)
Callable from:	Commands, worksheet and macro sheet functions.
Return type:	An xltypeRef xloper if successful, otherwise #VALUE!.
Arguments:	1: *SheetName*: (Optional.) The sheet name as an xloper string in the form [Book1.xls]Sheet1 or simply Sheet1 if the named sheet is within the workbook from which the function is called. If omitted the ID of the *active* sheet is returned.

Note: The returned xltypeRef xloper has the xlmref pointer set to NULL, so there is no need to call xlFree once the ID value has been extracted, although it won't do any harm. If you want to reuse this xloper to construct a valid reference, you will need to allocate memory and assign it to this pointer. Then you can specify which cells on the sheet to reference. (See the example below.)

The following example returns a reference to the cell A1 on the given sheet.

```
xloper * __stdcall get_a1_ref(xloper *sheet_name)
{
    static xloper ret_val;

    Excel4(xlSheetId, &ret_val, 1, sheet_name);

    if(ret_val.xltype == xltypeErr)
        return &ret_val;
// Sheet ID is contained in ret_val.val.mref.idSheet
// Now fill in the other fields to refer to the cell A1
    ret_val.val.mref.lpmref = (xlmref *)malloc(sizeof(xlmref));
    ret_val.val.mref.lpmref->count = 1;
    ret_val.val.mref.lpmref->reftbl[0].rwFirst = 0;
    ret_val.val.mref.lpmref->reftbl[0].rwLast = 0;
    ret_val.val.mref.lpmref->reftbl[0].colFirst = 0;
    ret_val.val.mref.lpmref->reftbl[0].colLast = 0;

// Ensure Excel calls back into the DLL to free the memory
    ret_val.xltype |= xlbitDLLFree;
    return &ret_val;
}
```

Using the `cpp_xloper` class, the same function can be written as follows, constructing an instance of the class that contains the correct `xloper` type, properly initialised:

```
xloper * __stdcall get_a1_ref_cpp(char *sheet_name)
{
    cpp_xloper RetVal(sheet_name, (WORD)0,(WORD)0,(BYTE)0,(BYTE)0);
    return RetVal.ExtractXloper(false);
}
```

8.7.6   Getting a sheet name from its internal ID: `xlSheetNm`

Overview:	Every worksheet in every open workbook is assigned an internal DWORD ID by Excel. This ID can be obtained from the text name of the sheet with the function `xlSheetId` (see above). Conversely, the text name, in the form [Book1.xls]Sheet1, can be obtained from the ID using this function.
Enumeration value:	16389 (x4005)
Callable from:	Commands, worksheet and macro sheet functions.
Return type:	An `xltypeStr` xloper.
Arguments:	1: *SheetID*: The sheet ID contained within the `idSheet` field of an `xltypeRef` xloper.

If ID is zero, the function returns the *current* sheet name. If the argument was an xltypeSRef xloper, which doesn't contain a sheet ID, the function again returns the current sheet name. This means that, in calling this function, it is not necessary to check which type of reference xloper was supplied.

The *SheetID* xloper can have the xlmref pointer field, lpmref, set to NULL. This means that no memory need be allocated in constructing this argument. The argument can also be a reference to a real range, where memory has been allocated. One example use of this function is in finding the named range on a worksheet, if it exists, that corresponds to a given range. The function used for this is xlfGetDef which requires the name of the worksheet in which the name is defined as its second argument.

Warning: If the ID is not valid, Excel can crash! Only use IDs that have been obtained from calls to xlSheetId or from xltypeRef xlopers, and that apply to worksheets that you know are still open.

The following example returns the sheet name given an ID.

```
xloper * __stdcall sheet_name(double ID)
{
    static xloper ret_val;
    xloper ID_ref_oper;

    if(ID < 0)
    {
        ID_ref_oper.xltype = xltypeMissing;
    }
    else
    {
        ID_ref_oper.xltype = xltypeRef;
        ID_ref_oper.val.mref.idSheet = (DWORD)ID;
        ID_ref_oper.val.mref.lpmref = NULL;
    }
    Excel4(xlSheetNm, &ret_val, 1, &ID_ref_oper);
    ret_val.xltype |= xlbitXLFree;
    return &ret_val;
}
```

8.7.7   Yielding processor time and checking for user breaks: xlAbort

Overview: Returns true if the user has attempted to break execution of an XLL command or worksheet function (by pressing Esc in Windows). While checking for an outstanding break, it also yields some time to the operating system to perform other tasks.

If *PreserveBreak* is set to false, the function clears any user break condition it detects and continues with the execution of the command. If set to true or omitted, the function checks to see if the user pressed *break*, but does not clear the break condition. This enables the DLL to detect the same break condition in another part of the code.

Enumeration value: 16390 (x4006)

Callable from: Commands, worksheet and macro sheet functions.

Return type: An `xltypeBool xloper`.

Arguments: 1: *PreserveBreak*: (Optional.) Boolean. Default is true.

User breaks can be disabled/enabled using `xlfCancelKey`, (enumeration 170 decimal), which can take one Boolean argument: true to enable breaks, false to disable them. Section 10.11 *Monte Carlo simulation* on page 376 contains an example of a command that uses both `xlfCancelKey` and `xlAbort`.

As this function can be called from worksheet functions as well as commands, it can be used to end prematurely the execution of very lengthy calculations, as the following example code shows. Note that the break condition is not cleared in this case, so that a single break event can terminate the execution of all instances of all functions that check for this condition. When checking for a break in a command, you would typically clear the break.

```
double __stdcall function_break_example(xloper *arg)
{
    if(arg->xltype != xltypeNum)
        return -1;

    cpp_xloper Break;

    for(long l = (long)arg->val.num; --l;)
    {
// Detect a user break attempt but leave it set so that other
// worksheet functions can also detect it
        Excel4(xlAbort, &Break, 0);

        if((bool)Break)
            break;
    }
    return l;
}
```

8.7.8   Getting Excel's instance handle: `xlGetInst`

This function, enumeration 0x4007, obtains an instance handle for the running instance of Excel that made this call into the DLL. This is useful if there are multiple instances of Excel running and your DLL needs to distinguish between them. This is far less necessary than it used to be under 16-bit Windows, where different instances shared the same DLL memory. The function takes no arguments and returns an `xltypeInt` `xloper` containing the low part of the instance handle.

8.7.9   Getting the handle of the top-level Excel window: `xlGetHwnd`

This function, enumeration 0x4008, obtains Excel's main Window handle. One example of its use is given in section 9.4 *Detecting when a worksheet function is called from the Paste Function dialog (Function Wizard)* on page 294. The function takes no arguments and returns an `xltypeInt` xloper containing the handle. The value returned is a 2-byte `short`, whereas the `HWND` used by the Windows API is a 4-byte `long`. The returned value is therefore the low part of the full handle. The following code shows how to obtain the full handle using the Windows API `EnumWindows()` function.

```
#define CLASS_NAME_BUFFER_SIZE      50

typedef struct
{
    short main_xl_handle;
    HWND full_handle;
}
    get_hwnd_struct;

// The callback function called by Windows for every top-level window
BOOL __stdcall get_hwnd_enum_proc(HWND hwnd, get_hwnd_struct *p_enum)
{
// Check if the low word of the handle matches Excel's
    if(LOWORD((DWORD)hwnd) != p_enum->main_xl_handle)
        return TRUE; // keep iterating

    char class_name[CLASS_NAME_BUFFER_SIZE + 1];
// Ensure that class_name is always null terminated
    class_name[CLASS_NAME_BUFFER_SIZE] = 0;

    GetClassName(hwnd, class_name, CLASS_NAME_BUFFER_SIZE);

// Do a case-insensitive comparison for Excel's main window
// class name
    if(_stricmp(class_name, "xlmain") == 0)
    {
        p_enum->full_handle = hwnd;
        return FALSE;  // Tells Windows to stop iterating
    }
    return TRUE; // Tells Windows to continue iterating
}

HWND get_xl_main_handle(void)
{
    xloper main_xl_handle = {0.0, xltypeNil}; // safe initialisation

    if(Excel4(xlGetHwnd, &main_xl_handle, 0))
        return 0;

    get_hwnd_struct es = {main_xl_handle.val.w, 0};
    EnumWindows((WNDENUMPROC)get_hwnd_enum_proc, (LPARAM)& es);
    return es.full_handle;
}
```

8.7.10   Getting the path and file name of the DLL: `xlGetName`

Overview: It is sometimes necessary to get the path and file name of the DLL that is currently being invoked. The one place this information is *required* is in the registration of XLL functions using `xlfRegister`, where the first argument is exactly this information.

Enumeration value: 16393 (x4009)

Callable from: Commands, worksheet and macro sheet functions.

Return type: An `xltypeStr xloper`.

Arguments: None.

The following code examples show how to call this function using the `cpp_xloper` class or just `xlopers`.

```
char *get_dll_name1(void)
{
    cpp_xloper dll_name;
    int xl4 = Excel4(xlGetName, &dll_name, 0);
    dll_name.SetExceltoFree();

    if(xl4 || !dll_name.IsStr())
        return NULL;

// Return a copy of the string (needs to be freed by the caller)
    return (char *)dll_name;
}
```

```
char *get_dll_name2(void)
{
    xloper dll_name;
    int xl4 = Excel4(xlGetName, &dll_name, 0);

    if(xl4 || dll_name.xltype != xltypeStr)
        return NULL;

// Make a copy of the string (needs to be freed by the caller)
    int len = dll_name.val.str[0];
    char *name = (char *)malloc(len + 1);

    memcpy(name, dll_name.val.str + 1, len);
    name[len] = 0;
    Excel4(xlFree, 0, 1, &dll_name);
    return name;
}
```

8.8   WORKING WITH BINARY NAMES

A binary name is a named block of unstructured memory associated with a worksheet that an XLL is able to create, read from and write to, and that gets saved with the workbook. A typical use for such a space would be the creation of a large table of data that you want to store and access in your workbook, which might be too large, too cumbersome or perhaps too public, if stored in worksheet cells. Another use might be to store configuration data for a command that always (and only) acts on the active sheet.

The `xltypeBigData xloper` type is used to define and access these blocks of binary data together with the C API functions `xlDefineBinaryName` and `xlGetBinaryName`. (The enumeration codes for these functions are 16396/x400c and 16397/x400d respectively.)

Apart from this method of storing data being more memory-efficient, accessing a table of data in the DLL is quicker than accessing the same data from the workbook, even if the table is small and despite Excel providing some fairly efficient ways to do this. This may be a consideration in optimising the performance of certain workbook recalculations. The fact that data get saved automatically with a workbook is clearly an advantage in some circumstances.

However, there are a number of limitations that can make working with these names too much trouble in most cases, given alternative approaches. The problems with binary names are:

- They are associated with the worksheet that was active at the time of creation.
- Data can only be retrieved when the associated worksheet is active.
- Worksheet functions cannot activate a sheet, so that one sheet's binary names cannot be accessed by a function in another sheet.
- Excel (including the C API) provides no straightforward[2] way to interrogate the sheet for all the binary names that are defined in a given (or even the active) sheet.
- If a name is created and then forgotten about, the workbook carries around excess baggage.
- The data is inaccessible except via an add-in using the C API that knows the name of the data in advance.

8.8.1 The `xltypeBigData xloper`

The `xltypeBigData xloper` is used to define, delete and access these blocks of data. To create such a space in the workbook, the `xltypeBigData` is populated with a pointer to the data to be stored and the data length, and passed to Excel in a call to `xlDefineBinaryName`. When the block of binary data needs to be accessed, via a call to `xlGetBinaryName`, the handle to the data is returned to the DLL in an `xltypeBigData xloper`. The DLL then executes a Windows global lock to get a pointer to the data. (This `xloper` type is *only* used in this context and is never passed into the DLL or returned to Excel.) These two C API functions are only accessible via the C API, in common with the functions in section 8.7 above.

This `xloper` type is only used when calling one of these two C API functions. Given its limited uses, it has not been included in the `cpp_xloper` class.

8.8.2 Basic operations with binary names

In general, you need to be able to perform the following basic operations:

- Store a block of data in the active sheet with a given name.
- Retrieve a block of data from the active sheet with a given name.
- Find out if a block with a given name exists on the active sheet.
- Delete a block with a given name from the active sheet.

---

[2] *Straightforward* means using standard Excel or C API functions. Reading the workbook file as a binary file and interpreting the contents directly is one very non-straightforward way.

On top of this, one can easily see the need for some higher-level functions:

- Find out if a block with a given name exists in a workbook.
- Get a list of all the names in a given worksheet.

The first of these latter functions involves changing the active worksheet, something that can only be done from a command, not from a worksheet or macro function. The second is most easily achieved with a higher-level strategy. Possible approaches are:

1. Use a restrictive naming scheme, for example, `Bname1`, `Bname2`, ...
2. Store a list of names using a standard binary name, say, `BnameList`, and build maintenance of this list into your binary name creation and deletion functions. Use this list to find all the names in a sheet.

The second approach is the most sensible, as your add-in will then be able to mirror the functionality of Excel's worksheet ranges. This book does not provide an example as it is assumed that, once the basics of binary names have been explained, any competent programmer could implement such a scheme.

8.8.3   Creating, deleting and overwriting binary names

The following function creates or deletes a binary name according to the given inputs. This function will only work when called from a command or macro sheet function. If the name already exists, the call to `xlDefineBinaryName` is equivalent to deleting and creating anew. This function is easily wrapped in an exportable worksheet function, as shown in the example in section 8.8.5 on page 213 below.

```
int bin_name(char *name, int create, void *data, long len)
{
    if(!name)
        return 0;

    cpp_xloper Name(name);

    if(create)
    {
        if(!data || !len)
            return 0;

        xloper big;

        big.xltype = xltypeBigData;
        big.val.bigdata.h.lpbData = (unsigned char *)data;
        big.val.bigdata.cbData = len;

        if(Excel4(xlDefineBinaryName, 0, 2, &Name, &big))
            return 0;
    }
    else
    {
        Excel4(xlDefineBinaryName, 0, 1, &Name);
    }
    return 1;
}
```

8.8.4   Retrieving binary name data

The following code gets a copy of the data and block size or returns zero if there is an
error. Note that this function hides the data handle and the calls to GlobalLock() and
GlobalUnlock(), and requires the caller to free the pointer to the data when done.
This function is only successful if the name is defined on the active sheet. It can be called
from either a command or a macro sheet equivalent worksheet function. Although the
following function is not exportable as it stands, wrappers can easily be created, say, to
provide access via VB or an Excel worksheet function (see next section).

```cpp
int get_binary_data(char *name, void * &data, long &len)
{
    if(!name)
        return 0;

    cpp_xloper Name(name);
    xloper big;

    if(Excel4(xlGetBinaryName, &big, 1, &Name)
    || big.xltype != xltypeBigData)
        return 0;

    len = big.val.bigdata.cbData;
    if(!(data = malloc(len)))
        return 0;

    void *p = GlobalLock(big.val.bigdata.h.hdata);
    memcpy(data, p, len);
    GlobalUnlock(big.val.bigdata.h.hdata);
    return 1;
}
```

A stripped-down version of the above function can be used to determine if the name
exists on the active sheet. To find out if the name is defined in any sheet in a workbook,
it would be necessary to iterate through all of the sheets, making each sheet active in
turn; something that can only be done by a command function.

```cpp
int __stdcall bin_exists(char *name)
{
    if(!name)
        return 0;

    cpp_xloper Name(name);
    xloper big;

    int x14 = Excel4(xlGetBinaryName, &big, 1, &Name);

    if(x14 || big.xltype != xltypeBigData)
        return 0;

    return 1;
}
```

8.8.5   Example worksheet functions

The following exportable worksheet functions demonstrate the creation, deletion and retrieval of a text string as a binary name in the active sheet. These functions are included in the example project in the source file BigData.cpp and are called in the example worksheet Binary_Name_Example.xls. The functions are registered as "RCP#" and "RC#!" respectively, i.e., both are macro sheet equivalent functions and get_bin_string() is volatile.

```cpp
xloper * __stdcall set_bin_string(char *name, xloper *p_string)
{
    int create = (p_string->xltype == xltypeStr ? 1 : 0);

    if(create)
    {
        long len = p_string->val.str[0] + 1; // Include null
        char *p = p_string->val.str + 1; // Start of string

        if(bin_name(name, create, p, len))
            return p_xlTrue;

        return p_xlErrValue; // couldn't create
    }

    if(bin_name(name, 0, NULL, 0))
        return p_xlErrName; // deleted ok
    else
        return p_xlErrValue; // couldn't delete
}

xloper * __stdcall get_bin_string(char *name)
{
    void *string;
    long len;

    if(get_binary_data(name, string, len))
    {
// Constructor will truncate if too long
        cpp_xloper RetVal((char *)string);
        return RetVal.ExtractXloper();
    }
    return p_xlErrName;
}
```

8.9   WORKSPACE INFORMATION COMMANDS AND FUNCTIONS

This section describes the most relevant capabilities of the following functions:

- xlfAppTitle
- xlfWindowTitle
- xlfActiveCell
- xlfDocuments
- xlfGetCell
- xlfGetDocument
- xlfGetFormula

- xlfGetNote
- xlfGetWindow
- xlfGetWorkbook
- xlfGetWorkspace
- xlfSelection
- xlfWindows
- xlfFormulaConvert
- xlfTextRef
- xlfCaller

Few, if any, details are given of these functions' ability to get information about cell formatting or graphs. The intention is to keep the focus primarily on the creation of worksheet functions. For a full description of these functions you should refer to the XLM macro language help file, Macrofun.hlp, freely downloadable at the time of writing from Microsoft's website.

8.9.1   Setting the application title: xlfAppTitle

Overview:	Attempts to coerce the argument to a string and set this as the application title. Returns true if successful, false if unsuccessful.
	If the argument is omitted, resets the application title to the default value, Microsoft Excel, and returns true.
Enumeration value:	262 (x106)
Callable from:	Commands and macro sheet functions.
Return type:	Boolean.
Arguments:	Application title (optional).

This function is useful if you want to display, say, some progress indicator or other information on the title bar. This information is also shown on the application's start-bar button when minimised.

8.9.2   Setting the document window title: xlfWindowTitle

Overview:	Attempts to coerce the argument to a string and then sets the active document title to this string. Returns true if successful, false if unsuccessful.
	If the argument is omitted, resets the document title to the default value and returns true.
Enumeration value:	263 (x107)
Callable from:	Commands and macro sheet functions.
Return type:	Boolean.
Arguments:	1: (Optional.) Document window title.

8.9.3   Getting a reference to the active cell: `xlfActiveCell`

Overview: Returns a reference to the active cell on the active work sheet,
                      or an error if this could not be obtained.

Enumeration value: 94 (x5e)

Callable from: Commands and macro sheet functions.

Return type: Cell reference `xltypeSRef xloper`.

Arguments: None.

This function is *useful* only in commands, where the action to be performed relates to
the active cell's contents or properties, or where the active cell is to be altered.

Circular Reference Note: If you call this function from a worksheet cell that *is* the
active cell, Excel detects that the call is self-referential and displays a circular reference
alert dialog. This is a good reason not to use this function in this way.

8.9.4   Getting a list of all open Excel documents: `xlfDocuments`

Overview: Returns a row vector containing a list of all open workbook
                      documents, or an error if unsuccessful. If there are no open
                      workbooks, the function returns #NA.

Enumeration value: 93 (x5d)

Callable from: Commands and macro sheet functions.

Return type: A row vector of strings in an `xltypeMulti xloper`.

Arguments: None.

8.9.5   Information about a cell or a range of cells: `xlfGetCell`

Overview: The first argument corresponds to the information you are
                      trying to get, and the second is a reference to the cell or range
                      of cells about which you want to know something. The
                      meaning of the most relevant of the 66 values is given in
                      Table 8.13.

Enumeration value: 185 (xb9)

Callable from: Commands and macro sheet functions.

Return type: Various, depending on the value of the first argument.

Arguments: 1: *ArgNum*: A number from 1 to 66 inclusive.
                      2: *Ref*: A cell reference.

Table 8.13 Selected arguments to `xlfGetCell`

ArgNum	What the function returns
1	Absolute-style reference of the top left cell in reference as text in the [Book1.xls]Sheet1!$A$1 style.
5	The value of the top left cell.
6	The formula in the top left cell in A1 or R1C1 style as determined by workspace settings.
7	The number format of the top left cell.
14	Returns true if the top left cell is locked.
15	Returns true if the top left cell's formula is hidden.
16	Returns 2-column row vector: 1st column: Width of the left column 2nd column: True if the width is the standard width, false if a custom width has been set.
17	Height of top row in points.
32	The name of the workbook and sheet containing the reference in the form [Book1.xls]Sheet1, unless the window contains only a single sheet that has the same name as the workbook without its extension, in which case the form BOOK1.XLS.
41	Returns the formula in the active cell without translation into the language set for the workspace.
46	True if the top left cell has a text note.
48	True if the top left cell contains a formula, false if constant.
49	True if the cell is part of an array formula.
52	If the top left cell is a string constant, the text alignment character ('), otherwise empty text (" ").
53	The top left cell as displayed, converted to text, including formatting numbers and symbols.
62	The name of the workbook and the current sheet in the form [Book1.xls]Sheet1.
66	The workbook name containing the range in the form Book1.xls.

The `Excel4()` function set-up and call would be as shown in the following C/C++ code. This is an example of an exportable function that simply wraps up the call to `xlfGetCell` and returns whatever is returned from that call.

```
xloper * __stdcall get_cell(int arg_num, xloper *p_ref)
{
    xloper arg;
    static xloper ret_xloper;

    arg.xltype = xltypeInt;
    arg.val.w = arg_num;

    Excel4(xlfGetCell, &ret_xloper, 2, &arg1, p_ref);
// Tell Excel to free up memory that it might have allocated for
// the return value.
    ret_xloper.xltype |= xlbitXLFree;

    return &ret_xloper;
}
```

Using the `cpp_xloper` class, the equivalent code would be:

```
xloper * __stdcall get_cell(xloper *pRef, int arg_num)
{
    cpp_xloper Arg(arg_num, 1, 66);
    cpp_xloper RetVal;

    Excel4(xlfGetCell, &RetVal, 2, &Arg, pRef);

    return RetVal.ExtractXloper(true);
}
```

8.9.6 Sheet or workbook information: `xlfGetDocument`

Overview:

The first argument corresponds to the information you are trying to get. The second is the name of a sheet or workbook, depending on the context, about which you want to know something. The meaning of the most useful of these 88 values is given in Table 8.14.[3] If the second argument is omitted, information about the *active* (not the *current*) sheet or workbook is returned.

Name can also be specified as workbook-and-sheet in the form [Book1.xls]Sheet1 where the context allows.

Enumeration value: 188 (xbc)

Callable from: Commands and macro sheet functions.

Return type: Various, depending on the value of the first argument.

Arguments: 1: *ArgNum*: A number from 1 to 88 inclusive.
                       2: *Name*: (Optional.) Sheet or workbook name as text.

---

[3] For values not covered, see the Macro Sheet Function Help included with the Excel SDK.

Table 8.14 Selected arguments to `xlfGetDocument`

ArgNum	What the function returns
1	If *Name* is a sheet name: • If more than one sheet in the *current* workbook, returns the name of the sheet in the form [Book1.xls]Sheet1. • If only one sheet in the *current* workbook, but the name of the workbook is not *Name*, returns the sheet *Name* in the form [Book1.xls]Sheet1 • If only one sheet in the *current* workbook and the workbook and sheet are both called *Name*, returns the name of the workbook in the form Book1.xls • If sheet *Name* does not exist in the *current* workbook, returns #N/A If *Name* is a workbook name: • If more than one sheet in the given workbook, the name of the first sheet in the form [Book1.xls]Sheet1 • If one sheet in the given workbook, and the sheet name is not also *Name*, the name of that sheet in the form [Book1.xls]Sheet1 • If one sheet with the same name as the given workbook, the name of the workbook in the form Book1.xls • If workbook *Name* is not open, returns #N/A If *Name* is omitted: • If more than one sheet in the *active* workbook or the sheet name is not the same as the *active* workbook name, the name of the *active* sheet in the form [Book1.xls]Sheet1. • If one sheet with the same name as the *active* workbook, the name of the workbook in the form Book1.xls (See also *ArgNum* 76 and 88 below, which return the names of the active worksheet and the active workbook respectively.)
2	Path of the directory containing workbook *Name* if it has already been saved, else #N/A
3	A number indicating the type of sheet. If given, *Name* is either a sheet name or a workbook. If omitted the active sheet is assumed. If *Name* is a workbook, the function returns 5 unless the book has only one sheet with the same name as the book, in which case it returns the sheet type. 1 = Worksheet 2 = Chart 3 = Macro sheet 4 = Info window if active 5 = Reserved 6 = Module 7 = Dialog

Table 8.14 (*continued*)

4	True if changes made to the sheet since last saved.
5	True if the sheet is read-only.
6	True if the sheet is password protected.
7	True if cells in the sheet or the series in a chart are protected.
8	True if the workbook windows are protected. (*Name* can be either a sheet name or a workbook. If omitted the active sheet is assumed.)
9	The first used row or 0 if the sheet is empty. (Counts from 1.)
10	The last used row or 0 if the sheet is empty. (Counts from 1.)
11	The first used column or 0 if the sheet is empty. (Counts from 1.)
12	The last used column or 0 if the sheet is empty. (Counts from 1.)
13	The number of windows that the sheet is displayed with.
14	The calculation mode: 1 = Automatic 2 = Automatic except tables 3 = Manual
15, 18, 19, 20	Options dialog box, Calculation tab checkbox settings as either true or false: 15: Returns the Iteration checkbox state 18: Returns the Update Remote References checkbox state 19: Returns the Precision As Displayed checkbox state 20: Returns the 1904 Date System checkbox state
16	Maximum number of iterations.
17	Maximum change between iterations.
33	The state of the Recalculate Before Saving checkbox in the Calculation tab of the Options dialog box.
34	True if the workbook is read-only recommended.
35	True if the workbook is write-reserved.
36	If the workbook has a write-reservation password and it is opened with read/write permission, returns the name of the user who originally saved it with the write-reservation password. If the workbook is opened as read-only, or if a password has not been added, returns the name of the current user.
48	The standard column width setting.

(*continued overleaf*)

Table 8.14 (*continued*)

68	The workbook name without path.
76	The name of the active sheet in the form [Book1.xls]Sheet1
84	The value of the first circular reference on the sheet, or #N/A if none.
87	The position of the given sheet in the workbook. If the workbook name is not given with the sheet name, operates on the *current* workbook. (Includes hidden sheets and counts from 1.)
88	The workbook name in the form Book1

The Excel4() function set-up and call would be as shown in the following C/C++ code example of an exportable function that wraps up the call to xlfGetDocument and returns whatever is returned from that call.

```
xloper * __stdcall get_document(int arg_num, char *sheet_name)
{
    xloper arg1, arg2;
    static xloper ret_xloper;

    if(arg_num < 1 || arg_num > 88)
        return p_xlErrValue;

    arg1.xltype = xltypeInt;
    arg1.val.w = arg_num;

    if(sheet_name)
    {
        arg2.xltype = xltypeStr;
        arg2.val.str = new_xlstring(sheet_name);
    }
    else
        arg2.xltype = xltypeMissing;

    Excel4(xlfGetDocument, &ret_xloper, 2, &arg1, &arg2);
// Tell Excel to free up memory that it might have allocated for
// the return value.
    ret_xloper.xltype |= xlbitXLFree;

    if(sheet_name)
        free(arg2.val.str);

    return &ret_xloper;
}
```

Using the cpp_xloper class, the equivalent code becomes:

```
xloper * __stdcall get_document(int arg_num, char *sheet_name)
{
    cpp_xloper Arg1(arg_num, 1, 88);
```

```
    if(!Arg1.IsType(xltypeInt))
        return p_xlErrValue;

    cpp_xloper Arg2(sheet_name);
    cpp_xloper RetVal;
    Excel4(xlfGetDocument, &RetVal, 2, &Arg1, &Arg2);
    return RetVal.ExtractXloper(true);
}
```

8.9.7   Getting the formula of a cell: `xlfGetFormula`

Overview: Returns the formula, as text, of the top left cell in a given
                        reference. The formula is returned in R1C1 style (see
                        section 2.2, *A1 versus R1C1 cell references* for details).

Enumeration value: 106 (x6a)

Callable from: Commands and macro sheet functions.

Return type: Text or error.

Arguments: *Ref.* A reference `xloper`.

The `Excel4()` function set-up and call would be as shown in the following C/C++
code example of an exportable function that wraps up the call to `xlfGetFormula`. The
function returns the formula as a string.

```
xloper * __stdcall get_formula(xloper *p_ref)
{
    cpp_xloper RetVal;
    Excel4(xlfGetFormula, &RetVal, 1, p_ref);
// Extract and return the xloper, using Excel to free memory
    return RetVal.ExtractXloper(true);
}
```

8.9.8   Getting a cell's comment: `xlfGetNote`

Overview: Returns the text of the comment attached to the top left cell in
                        the given reference. If no comment has been added to the cell,
                        it returns an empty string.

Enumeration value: 191 (xbf)

Callable from: Commands and macro sheet functions.

Return type: Text.

Arguments: *Ref.* A reference `xloper`.

The Excel4() function set-up and call are as shown in the following C/C++ code example of an exportable function that wraps up the call to xlfGetNote. The arguments passed in are a row and column numbers that count from 0. The function creates a reference to a single cell on the *current* sheet and returns the comment as a string.

```
xloper * __stdcall get_note(long row, long column)
{
    xloper Arg;
    static xloper ret_xloper;

// Create a simple single-cell reference to cell on current sheet
    Arg.xltype = xltypeSRef;
    Arg.val.sref.count = 1;

// First row in sheet = row 0
    Arg.val.sref.ref.rwFirst =
    Arg.val.sref.ref.rwLast = (WORD)row;

// First column in sheet = column 0
    Arg.val.sref.ref.colFirst =
    Arg.val.sref.ref.colLast = (BYTE)column;

    int retval = Excel4(xlfGetNote, &ret_xloper, 1, &Arg);

// Tell Excel to free up memory that it might have allocated for
// the return value.
    ret_xloper.xltype |= xlbitXLFree;
    return &ret_xloper;
}
```

The following code is equivalent to the above, but uses the cpp_xloper class.

```
xloper * __stdcall get_note(long row, long column)
{
// Create a simple single-cell reference to cell on current sheet
    cpp_xloper Arg((WORD)row, (WORD)row, (BYTE)column, (BYTE)column);
    cpp_xloper RetVal;
    Excel4(xlfGetNote, &RetVal, 1, &Arg);
    return RetVal.ExtractXloper(true);
}
```

8.9.9 Information about a window: xlfGetWindow

Overview: The function returns information about an open worksheet
                         window.

                         The first argument corresponds to the information you are
                         trying to get. The meaning of the most useful of these 31
                         values is given in Table 8.15.[4]

---

[4] For values not covered, see the Macro Sheet Function Help included with the Excel SDK.

The second is the name of the window about which you want to know something. If omitted, information about the *active* window is returned. (Remember that Excel enables multiple windows to be opened providing views to the same workbook.) The text should be entered in the form it appears in the window title bar, i.e. Book1.xls or Book1.xls:*n* if one of multiple open windows.

Enumeration value:	187 (xbb)
Callable from:	Commands and macro sheet functions.
Return type:	Various, depending on the value of the first argument.
Arguments:	1: *ArgNum*: A number from 1 to 31 inclusive. 2: *WindowName*: (Optional.) Window name as text.

Table 8.15 Selected arguments to `xlfGetWindow`

ArgNum	What the function returns
1	• If more than one sheet in the workbook, returns the name of the active sheet in the form [Book1.xls]Sheet1 • If only one sheet in the workbook with a different name to the workbook, returns the sheet name in the form [Book1.xls]Sheet1 • If one sheet in the workbook, both having the same name, returns the name of the workbook in the form Book1.xls • If a window of that name is not open, returns #VALUE!
2	The number of the window. Always 1 unless there are multiple windows, in which case the number displayed after the colon in the window title.
7	True if hidden.
8	True if formulas are displayed.
9	True if gridlines are displayed.
10	True if row and column headings are displayed.
11	True if zeros are displayed.
20	True if window is maximised.
23	The size of the window: 1 = Restored 2 = Minimised 3 = Maximised
24	True if panes are frozen.

(continued overleaf)

Table 8.15 (*continued*)

ArgNum	What the function returns
25	The magnification of the window as a % of normal size.
26	True if horizontal scrollbars displayed.
27	True if vertical scrollbars displayed.
28	The ratio of horizontal space allotted to workbook tabs versus the horizontal scrollbar. (Default = 1 : 0.6.)
29	True if workbook tabs displayed.
30	The title of the active sheet in the window in the form [Book1.xls]Sheet1
31	The workbook name, in the form Book.xls excluding the read/write status.

The `Excel4()` function set-up and call are as shown in the following C/C++ code example of an exportable function that wraps up the call to `xlfGetWindow` and returns whatever is returned from that call:

```
xloper * __stdcall get_window(int arg_num, char *window_name)
{
    xloper arg1, arg2;
    static xloper ret_xloper;

    if(arg_num < 1 || arg_num > 31)
        return p_xlErrValue;

    arg1.xltype = xltypeInt;
    arg1.val.w = arg_num;

    if(window_name)
    {
        arg2.xltype = xltypeStr;
        arg2.val.str = new_xlstring(window_name);
    }
    else
        arg2.xltype = xltypeMissing;

    Excel4(xlfGetWindow, &ret_xloper, 2, &arg1, &arg2);
// Tell Excel to free up memory that it might have allocated for
// the return value.
    ret_xloper.xltype | = xlbitXLFree;

    if(window_name)
        free(arg2.val.str);

    return &ret_xloper;
}
```

The following code is equivalent to the above, but uses the `cpp_xloper` class.

```
xloper * __stdcall get_window(int arg_num, char *window_name)
{
   cpp_xloper Arg1(arg_num, 1, 31);

   if(!Arg1.IsType(xltypeInt))
      return p_xlErrValue;

   cpp_xloper Arg2(window_name);
   cpp_xloper RetVal;
   Excel4(xlfGetWindow, &RetVal, 2, &Arg1, &Arg2);
   return RetVal.ExtractXloper(true);
}
```

8.9.10   Information about a workbook: `xlfGetWorkbook`

Overview: The function returns information about an open workbook.

The first argument corresponds to the information you are trying to get. The meaning of the most useful of these 38 values is given in Table 8.16.[5]

The second is the name of the workbook about which you want to know something. If omitted information about the *active* workbook is returned.

Enumeration value: 268 (x10c)

Callable from: Commands and macro sheet functions.

Return type: Various, depending on the value of the first argument.

Arguments: 1: *ArgNum*: A number from 1 to 38 inclusive.
                     2: *WorkbookName*: (Optional.) Workbook name as text.

Table 8.16 Selected arguments to `xlfGetWorkbook`

ArgNum	What the function returns
1	A horizontal array of the names of all sheets in the workbook.
3	A horizontal array of the names of workbook's currently selected sheets.
4	The number of sheets in the workbook.
14	True if the workbook structure is protected.

(continued overleaf)

---

[5] For values not covered, see the Macro Sheet Function Help included with the Excel SDK.

Table 8.16 (*continued*)

ArgNum	What the function returns
15	True if the workbook windows are protected.
24	True if changes were made to the workbook since last saved.
33	The title of the workbook as in the Summary Info dialog box.
34	The subject of the workbook as in the Summary Info dialog box.
35	The author of the workbook as in the Summary Info dialog box.
36	The keywords for the workbook as in the Summary Info dialog box.
37	The comment for the workbook as in the Summary Info dialog box.
38	The name of the active worksheet.

The `Excel4()` function set-up and call are as shown in the following C/C++ code example of an exportable function that wraps up the call to `xlfGetWorkbook` and returns whatever is returned from that call:

```
xloper * __stdcall get_workbook(int arg_num, char *book_name)
{
    xloper arg1, arg2;
    static xloper ret_xloper;

    if(arg_num < 1 || arg_num > 38)
        return p_xlErrValue;

    arg1.xltype = xltypeInt;
    arg1.val.w = arg_num;

    if(book_name)
    {
        arg2.xltype = xltypeStr;
        arg2.val.str = new_xlstring(book_name);
    }
    else
        arg2.xltype = xltypeMissing;

    Excel4(xlfGetWorkbook, &ret_xloper, 2, &arg1, &arg2);

// Tell Excel to free up memory that it might have allocated for
// the return value.
    ret_xloper.xltype |= xlbitXLFree;

    if(book_name)
        free(arg2.val.str);

    return &ret_xloper;
}
```

The following code is equivalent to the above, but uses the `cpp_xloper` class.

```
xloper * __stdcall get_workbook(int arg_num, char *book_name)
{
   cpp_xloper Arg1(arg_num, 1, 38);

   if(!Arg1.IsType(xltypeInt))
      return p_xlErrValue;

   cpp_xloper Arg2(book_name);
   cpp_xloper RetVal;
   Excel4(xlfGetWorkbook, &RetVal, 2, &Arg1, &Arg2);
   return RetVal.ExtractXloper(true);
}
```

8.9.11   Information about the workspace: `xlfGetWorkspace`

Overview: The function returns information about the workspace.

                     The argument corresponds to the information you are trying to
                     get. The meaning of the most useful of these 72 values is
                     given in Table 8.17.[6]

Enumeration value: 186 (xba)

Callable from: Commands and macro sheet functions.

Return type: Various, depending on the value of the first argument.

Arguments: *ArgNum*: A number from 1 to 72 inclusive.

Table 8.17 Selected argument to `xlfGetWorkspace`

ArgNum	What the function returns
1	The current environment and version number, e.g., Windows (32-bit) NT 5.00.
2	The Excel version number as a string.
3	If fixed decimals are set, returns the number of decimals, otherwise 0.
4	True if in R1C1 mode.
5	True if scroll bars are displayed. See also `xlfGetWindow` with *ArgNum* = 26 and 27.
6	True if the status bar is displayed.
7	True if the formula bar is displayed.

(continued overleaf)

---

[6] For values not covered, see the Macro Sheet Function Help included with the Excel SDK.

Table 8.17 (*continued*)

ArgNum	What the function returns
8	True if remote DDE requests are enabled.
9	The alternate menu key or #N/A if no alternate menu key is set.
10	The current mode that Excel is in: 0 = Normal 1 = Data Find 2 = Copy 3 = Cut 4 = Data Entry 5 = Unused 6 = Copy and Data Entry 7 = Cut and Data Entry
15	Maximised/minimised state of Excel: 1 = Neither 2 = Minimised 3 = Maximised
16	Kilobytes of free memory.
17	Kilobytes of total memory available to Excel.
20	If a group is present in the workspace, a horizontal array of sheets in the group, otherwise #N/A
21	True if the standard toolbar is displayed.
22	DDE application-specific error code.
23	Full path of the default start-up directory.
24	Full path of the alternate start-up directory, or #N/A if not specified.
25	True if set for relative reference macro recording.
26	Name of user.
27	Name of organisation.
32	The full path of the location of Microsoft Excel.
33	A horizontal array of the names in the Insert... list (accessed from the worksheet tab context menu) in the order they appear. (Note that not all of these are available from the File/New... list.)
34	A horizontal array containing template path and filenames corresponding to the array returned with *ArgNum* = 33. Returns #N/A for built-in document types.

Table 8.17 (*continued*)

ArgNum	What the function returns
36	True if the Allow Cell Drag And Drop check box is selected in the Edit tab of the Options dialog box.
37	A 45-item horizontal array of the items related to country versions and settings. (See next table for details.)
40	True if screen updating is enabled during macro execution.
41	A horizontal array of cell ranges, in R1C1 style, that were previously selected with the Goto command from the Edit menu or macro function equivalent.
44	A three-column array of all currently registered DLL procedures. (See section 8.5, *Registering and un-registering DLL (XLL) functions* for details of the meaning of the data returned in column 3.) **Column 1:** The full path and filename of the DLLs that contains the procedure. **Column 2:** The exported name of the DLL function (which may not be the same as the name as it appears in the worksheet). **Column 3:** String specifying the data type of the return value, the number and type of the arguments, whether volatile or a macro sheet function.
46	True if the Move Selection After Enter checkbox is selected in the Edit tab of the Options dialog box.
48	Pathname of the Excel library subdirectory.
50	True if the full screen mode is on.
51	True if the formula bar is displayed in full screen mode.
52	True if the status bar is displayed in full screen mode.
54	True if the Edit Directly In Cell checkbox is set on the Edit tab in the Options dialog box.
55	True if the Alert Before Overwriting Cells checkbox in the Edit tab on Options dialog box is set.
56	Standard font name in the General tab in the Options dialog box.
57	Standard font size in the General tab in the Options dialog box.
58	True if the Recently Used File List checkbox in the General tab on the Options dialog box is set.
59	True if the Display Old Menus checkbox in the General tab on the Options dialog box is set.

(*continued overleaf*)

Table 8.17 (*continued*)

ArgNum	What the function returns
60	True if the Tip Wizard is enabled.
61	Number of custom list entries in the Custom Lists tab of the Options dialog box.
64	True if the Ask to Update Automatic Links checkbox in the Edit tab of the Options dialog box is set.
65	True if the Cut, Copy, and Sort Objects with Cells checkbox in the Edit tab on the Options dialog box is set.
66	Default number of sheets in a new workbook from the Edit tab on Options dialog box.
67	Default file location from the General tab in the Options dialog box.
68	True if the Show ToolTips checkbox on the Toolbars dialog box is set.
69	True if the Large Buttons checkbox in the Toolbars dialog box is set.
70	True if the Prompt for Summary Info checkbox in the General tab on the Options dialog box is set.
71	True if Excel was opened for in-place object editing (OLE).
72	True if the Color Toolbars checkbox is set in the Toolbars dialog box.

Table 8.18 gives the meaning of the 45 horizontal array elements related to country versions and settings returned by this function with *ArgNum* = 37.

Table 8.18 Country settings returned by `xlfGetWorkspace`

Category	Array index	Description of data returned
Country codes	1	Number corresponding to the country version of Excel.
	2	Number corresponding to the current country setting in the Microsoft Windows Control Panel.
Number separators	3	Decimal separator
	4	1000s separator
	5	List separator
R1C1-style references	6	Row character
	7	Column character

Table 8.18 (*continued*)

Category	Array index	Description of data returned
	8	Lower case row character
	9	Lower case column character
	10	Character used instead of [
	11	Character used instead of]
Array characters	12	Character used instead of {
	13	Character used instead of }
	14	Column separator
	15	Row separator
	16	Alternate array item separator used if the array separator is the same as the decimal separator
Format code symbols	17	Date separator
	18	Time separator
	19	Year symbol
	20	Month symbol
	21	Day symbol
	22	Hour symbol
	23	Minute symbol
	24	Second symbol
	25	Currency symbol
	26	General symbol
Format codes	27	Number of decimal digits used in currency formats
	28	Number indicating the current format for negative currencies where currency is any number and $ represents the currency symbol.
	29	Number of decimal digits used in non-currency formats
	30	Number of characters to use in month names
	31	Number of characters to use in weekday names
	32	Number indicating the date order

(*continued overleaf*)

Table 8.18 (*continued*)

Category	Array index	Description of data returned
Boolean format values	33	True if using 24-hour time, otherwise false for 12-hour time.
	34	True if not displaying functions in English.
	35	True if using the metric system, otherwise false if imperial.
	36	True if a space inserted before currency symbol.
	37	True if currency symbol precedes currency values.
	38	True if minus sign used for negative numbers, otherwise false if parentheses.
	39	True if trailing zeros displayed for zero currency values.
	40	True if leading zeros displayed for zero currency values.
	41	True if leading zero displayed in months where months are displayed as numbers.
	42	True if leading zero shown in days where days are displayed as numbers.
	43	True if using four-digit years, false if two-digit.
	44	True if date order is month-day-year when displaying dates in long form, otherwise false if day-month-year.
	45	True if leading zero shown in the time.

The Excel4() function set-up and call are as shown in the following C/C++ code example of an exportable function that wraps up the call to xlfGetWorkspace and returns whatever is returned from that call:

```
xloper * __stdcall get_workspace(int arg_num)
{
    xloper arg;
    static xloper ret_xloper;

    if(arg_num < 1 || arg_num > 72)
        return p_xlErrValue;
```

```
    arg.xltype = xltypeInt;
    arg.val.w = arg_num;

    Excel4(xlfGetWorkspace, &ret_xloper, 1, &arg);
// Tell Excel to free up memory that it might have allocated for
// the return value.
    ret_xloper.xltype |= xlbitXLFree;
    return &ret_xloper;
}
```

The following code is equivalent to the above, but uses the `cpp_xloper` class.

```
xloper * __stdcall get_workspace(int arg_num)
{
    cpp_xloper Arg(arg_num, 1, 72);

    if(!Arg.IsType(xltypeInt))
        return p_xlErrValue;

    cpp_xloper RetVal;
    Excel4(xlfGetWorkspace, &RetVal, 1, &Arg);
    return RetVal.ExtractXloper(true);
}
```

8.9.12   Information about the selected range or object: `xlfSelection`

Overview: The function returns information about the selected cells or
                     objects in the active sheet. If cells are selected, the function
                     returns the address in the form [Book1]Sheet1!A1:B2. If one or more
                     objects are selected, the function returns a comma-delimited list
                     of the object identifiers, e.g., CommandButton1,CommandButton2,....

Enumeration value: 95 (x5f)

Callable from: Commands and macro sheet functions.

Return type: Text.

Arguments: None.

The `Excel4()` function set-up and call are as shown in the following C/C++ code
example of an exportable function that wraps up the call to `xlfSelection`. Note that a
trigger argument is included in this case to provide a means for the function to be called
from a worksheet.

```
xloper * __stdcall selection(int trigger)
{
    cpp_xloper RetVal;
    Excel4(xlfSelection, &RetVal, 0);
```

```
// Extract & return the xloper. Arg=true to ensure Excel frees memory
    return RetVal.ExtractXloper(true);
}
```

8.9.13   Getting names of open Excel windows: xlfWindows

Overview: The function returns the names of currently open worksheet
                         windows in this instance of Excel. The names are returned in
                         a horizontal array in the form Book1.xls, or Book1.xls:2 if there
                         are multiple windows into the same workbook.

                         The first argument specifies to the type of windows to list:
                         1 or omitted = non-add-in windows only.
                         2 = add-in windows only.
                         3 = all windows.

                         The second is an optional text mask that may contain wildcard
                         characters. If supplied, only names that match are returned.

Enumeration value: 91 (x5b)

Callable from: Commands and macro sheet functions.

Return type: Various, depending on the value of the first argument.

Arguments: 1: *MatchType*: (Optional.) A number from 1 to 3 inclusive.
                         2: *Mask*: (Optional.) Window name mask as text.

The Excel4() function set-up and call are as shown in the following C/C++ code
example of an exportable function that wraps up the call to xlfWindows.

```
xloper * __stdcall xl_windows(int match_type, char *mask)
{
    cpp_xloper Arg1(match_type, 1, 3);
    cpp_xloper Arg2(mask);
    cpp_xloper RetVal;
    Excel4(xlfWindows, &RetVal, 2, &Arg1, &Arg2);
// Extract and return xloper. Arg=true to ensure Excel frees memory
    return RetVal.ExtractXloper(true);
}
```

8.9.14   Converting a range reference: xlfFormulaConvert

Overview: This function converts a text formula's cell or range
                         references to another form depending on its arguments. The
                         formula can be as simple as an equals sign and a cell or range
                         reference, but must always be valid. Conversion can be any
                         mixture of A1 to or from R1C1, or absolute to or from relative.
                         The converted formula is returned as a string.

Enumeration value:	241 (xf1)
Callable from:	Commands and macro sheet functions.
Return type:	Text string.
Arguments:	1: *FormulaStr*. Text string containing the input cell reference.
	2: *FromA1*. Boolean. True if *FormulaStr* uses A1 style references.
	3: *ToA1*: (Optional.) Boolean. True if function is to return a formula using A1 style references. If omitted, the style is the same as the supplied formula.
	4: *ToRefType*: (Optional.) Number from 1 to 4 indicating the absolute/relative type of the returned reference. If omitted, no conversion is done. 1 = row and column absolute, 2 = absolute row only, 3 = absolute column only, 4 = row and column relative.
	5: *RelativeRef*: (Optional.) If required, the cell reference (an xltypeSRef or xltypeRef xloper) which R1C1 style references should be interpreted as being relative to.

The `Excel4()` function set-up and call are as shown in the following C/C++ code example of an exportable function that wraps up the call to `xlfFormulaConvert`. Note that the Boolean arguments are passed to the function as integers and converted in the `cpp_xloper` constructer call. Note also that the 5th argument of the exported function is passed in directly as an `xloper`. This is the only way to prevent Excel converting from the reference to some other data type.

```
xloper * __stdcall formula_convert(char *p_ref, int from_A1,
                int to_A1, int abs_rel_type, xloper *p_rel_ref)
{
    cpp_xloper Arg1(p_ref);
    cpp_xloper Arg4(abs_rel_type, 1, 4);
    cpp_xloper RetVal;

    Excel4(xlfFormulaConvert, &RetVal, 5, &Arg1,
        from_A1 ? p_xlTrue : p_xlFalse,
        to_A1 ? p_xlTrue : p_xlFalse,
        &Arg4, p_rel_ref);

// Extract and return xloper. Arg=true to ensure Excel frees memory
    return RetVal.ExtractXloper(true);
}
```

8.9.15   Converting text to a reference: `xlfTextref`

Overview:	This function converts a text cell reference to an absolute reference `xloper`.
Enumeration value:	147 (x93)

Callable from:	Commands and macro sheet functions.
Return type:	An xltypeRef xloper.
Arguments:	1: *ReferenceStr*: Text string containing the input cell reference
	2: *A1Style*: (Optional.) Boolean. True indicates that the given reference is in A1 style. False or omitted indicates R1C1 style.

The Excel4() function set-up and call are as shown in the following C/C++ code example of an exportable function that wraps up the call to xlfTextref. Note that the Boolean argument is passed as a pointer to a constant xloper.

```
xloper * __stdcall text_ref(char *p_ref, int A1_style)
{
    cpp_xloper Arg1(p_ref);
    cpp_xloper RetVal;
    Excel4(xlfTextref, &RetVal, 2, &Arg1,
            A1_style ? p_xlTrue : p_xlFalse);
// Extract and return xloper. Arg=true to ensure Excel frees memory
    return RetVal.ExtractXloper(true);
}
```

Note: The reference as text must not have a leading '='. For example, the function xlfGetName returns the address of a given named range but includes a leading '=' that should be removed before it can be converted to a range xloper using xlfTextRef.

8.9.16   Converting a reference to text: xlfReftext

Overview:	This function converts a cell reference to a string xloper of the form [Book1.xls]Sheet1! R1C1.
Enumeration value:	146 (x92)
Callable from:	Commands and macro sheet functions.
Return type:	Text string.
Arguments:	1: *Reference*: A reference xloper (xltypeSRef or xltypeRef).
	2: *A1Style*: (Optional.) Boolean. True requests that the returned text is in A1 style. False or omitted requests R1C1 style.

This function is useful when, for example, converting a reference to an R1C1 style string to be passed to the xlfGetDef function, which returns the defined name (if it exists) associated with the original reference. (See section 8.10 *Working with Excel names* on page 239.) This function is used for this purpose in the example project in the code of the xlName class. The function xlfGetCell, argument=1, also returns an address string but only in A1 style.

The `Excel4()` function set-up and call are as shown in the following C/C++ code example of an exportable function that wraps up the call to `xlfReftext`.

```
xloper * __stdcall ref_text(xloper *p_ref, int A1_style)
{
    cpp_xloper Arg2(A1_style != 0);
    cpp_xloper RetVal;
    Excel4(xlfReftext, &RetVal, 2, p_ref, &Arg2);
// Extract and return xloper. Arg=true to ensure Excel frees memory
    return RetVal.ExtractXloper(true);
}
```

8.9.17   Information about the calling cell or object: `xlfCaller`

Overview: Returns information about what originally initiated this call
                        into the DLL. It can be called many times in the same call and
                        will return the same information every time.

Enumeration value: 89 (x59)

Callable from: Commands, worksheet and macro sheet functions.

Return type: Various depending on the how the DLL was called. (See
                        Table 8.19.)

Arguments: None.

Table 8.19 Return types and information for `xlfCaller`

Where the DLL was called from:	What `xlfCaller` returns:
A single cell on a worksheet.	A single-cell `xltypeSRef` or `xltypeRef` `xloper` of that cell.
A multi-cell array formula on a worksheet.	A multi-cell `xltypeSRef` or `xltypeRef` `xloper`.
A command on a menu bar	A horizontal 3-element array: • the command's position number • the menu number • the menu bar number
A command attached to a toolbar	A horizontal 2-element array: • the command's position number • the command bar name
A command attached to a control object	The object's ID
A trapped data entry or double-click event on a worksheet	A single-cell `xltypeSRef` or `xltypeRef` `xloper` of the affected cell or range of cells.
Others	#REF!

Note: `xlfCaller` can sometimes return an `xloper` that has had memory allocated by Excel. When the `xloper` is done with, the memory must be freed by Excel. (See section 7.3, *Getting Excel to free memory allocated by Excel* for details.)

Warning: The DLL can be called by the operating system, for example, `DllMain()` or during a Windows call-back. Calling `xlfCaller` in these contexts is not necessary and may have strange and undesirable consequences.

Note that some of Excel's built-in functions behave differently when called from a single cell or a number of cells in an array formula. This kind of behaviour can be replicated in DLL functions by detecting the type of the caller, and the size if it is a range. (See section 2.6.8 *Conversion of multi-cell range references* on page 14 for more detail.) You can also use the `xlfGetCell` function, with argument 49, to detect if a given cell reference is part of an array.

Apart from the usefulness of this function in determining the type of caller, it plays an important rôle in the naming and tracking of cells that are performing some important task. See section 8.10 immediately below and sections 9.7 to 9.10. It also can play an important role in returning the pre-call value of the calling cell. This can be useful in stopping the propagation of errors as the following simple function demonstrates:

```
xloper * __stdcall CurrentValue(xloper *rtn_input, xloper *rtn_value)
{
    cpp_xloper RetVal;

    if(rtn_input->xltype == xltypeBool && rtn_input->val._bool == 1)
        return rtn_value;

    cpp_xloper Caller;
    Excel4(xlfCaller, &Caller, 0);
    Caller.SetExceltoFree();

    if(!Caller.IsType(xltypeSRef | xltypeRef))
        return NULL;

    Excel4(xlCoerce, &RetVal, 1, &Caller);
    RetVal.SetExceltoFree();

    if(RetVal.IsType(xltypeErr))
        RetVal = 0.0;

    return RetVal.ExtractXloper(false);
}
```

The function takes two optional arguments. The default behaviour of the function is to return the existing value of the cell. (For this to work the function must be registered as a macro sheet equivalent function.) The optional arguments override this and force the return of a supplied value if the first argument is set to true. An example of the use of such a function would be as follows:

```
=IF(OR(ISNA(A1),ISERR(A1)),CurrentValue(B1,C1),A1)
```

Any error that exists in A1 will not be propagated to the result of this formula.

8.10   WORKING WITH EXCEL NAMES

Excel supports the concept of named ranges within sheets. In ordinary Excel use, these are easy to create and access, and aid the formation of easy to read and maintain spreadsheets. The C API provides a number of functions for accessing and managing these names. Excel also supports a type of hidden name that is only accessible within a DLL using the C API. (The latter type has its origins as a private Excel 4 macro sheet name.)

In practice, Excel named ranges are best handled in the DLL with a C++ class. An example of a simple class, xlName, is provided on the CD ROM and discussed in section 9.7 *A C++ Excel name class example, xlName* on page 307. The class supports the reading of values from named ranges, writing values to them using simple data types, as well as creation, deletion and validation. It also assists with the creation of internal names, especially those associated with the calling cell; a very useful technique when dealing with internally held data structures and background tasks.

Before this, sections 8.10.1 to 8.10.8 provide a low-level look at Excel's defined name logic and the C API's name handling capabilities.

8.10.1   Specifying worksheet names and name scope

A defined name in Excel is simply a text string that has an associated definition. The definition can be a constant value (a number, Boolean value or string but not an error value), an array of constant values, or a reference to a range of cells on a worksheet.

Names are associated with either a worksheet (or an Excel 4 macro sheet). The relevance of macro sheets here is only that Excel treats functions in an XLL as if they were on a hidden Macro sheet. Macro sheets and DLLs using the C API, can define worksheet names on a given worksheet but also can create internal (or Macro sheet) names. Both can represent all of the basic Excel data types including range references. From a DLL point of view, it is helpful to think of the two types of names as follows:

1. Worksheet names: defined on a worksheet and persist when the workbook is saved and reloaded.
2. DLL names: defined in a DLL and are only accessible directly by DLLs. Persist only as long as the current Excel session.

Both types of names follow the same naming rules:

- Names can be up to 255 characters in length. (You should use a much shorter length so that worksheet names, when appended to a filename and sheet name, are still well within the 255 character limit for C API compatibility.)
- Names are case-sensitive and can contain the characters 'A' to 'Z', 'a' to 'z', '\' and '_'.
- The numerals 0 to 9, '?' and '.' are permitted except that names cannot begin with these.
- Names cannot contain spaces, tabs, non-printable characters or any of ! " $ % ^ & * ( ) { } [ ] : ; ' @ # ~ < > / | - + = ¬ as well as some other non-alpha and extended ASCII characters, including other currency symbols.

Worksheet names

In general, worksheet names are specified in formulae by the workbook, sheet and name. The most general name specification in a worksheet cell would be of the form

[Book1.xls]Sheet1!Name. Where the use of the name is within the workbook that contains the definition, the filename is not required and its display, including the brackets that contain it, is suppressed. The sheet name and exclamation mark are also not required, and their display suppressed, except when there are two identically named ranges on separate sheets of the same workbook. In this case, they do need to be referred to as, say, Sheet1!Name and Sheet2!Name.

Worksheet names are saved with the workbook and can be used in the sheet in exactly the same way that references are, for example ={*RangeName*} or =SUM(*RangeName*). Where identical names are defined on different sheets in the same workbook, Excel can display some curious behaviour. Ordinarily, cutting and pasting a named range from one sheet to another simply redefines the name's definition to reflect its new location. If a named range with the same name already exists in the paste-to sheet, Excel suppresses the name but does not invalidate or delete it: the pre-existing name masks the added name. Cutting and pasting the (masked) named range to another sheet reveals the name again. The situation can get quite confusing so, in general, it's best not to tempt fate in this way, and to keep range names unique within a workbook.

DLL names

Excel names that are defined as internal to a DLL (see function xlfSetName below for details) cannot be accessed directly in worksheet formulae, unlike worksheet names. They can only be accessed by the C API functions xlfSetName and xlfGetDef in the DLL.

How Excel resolves worksheet and DLL names

The steps Excel takes when interpreting a reference in a worksheet (such as Name) are:

1. Look for a definition of the name on the *current* worksheet.
2. If not found, look for a definition in the *current* workbook.
3. If still not found, return a #NAME? error.

If the name is referred to as Sheet1!Name then Excel looks for the name in the specified sheet in the current workbook and returns #REF! if the sheet does not exist or #NAME? if the name is not defined there.

If the name is referred to as [Book1.xls]Sheet1!Name then Excel looks for the name in the specified sheet in the specified workbook and returns #REF! if the workbook is not open or the sheet does not exist, or returns #NAME? if the name is not defined. If the workbook is closed, the full path name is required as follows (Excel will prompt for the worksheet name on a closed workbook, if omitted.):

```
='C:\Example Folder\[Book1.xls]Sheet1'!Name
```

When accessing a *worksheet* named range from within the DLL using the xlfGetName function (see below), the name must be prefixed by '!' unless the worksheet name is specified. Otherwise Excel will look for the given name in a hidden name-space that is only accessible by DLLs running in this instance of Excel. (See *DLL Names* above.)

8.10.2   Basic operations with Excel names

There are a number of things you might want to do with names. These operations, and the functions that you would use to execute them, are summarised here:

- Find out if a given name is defined and, if so, what its definition is (xlfGetName, not to be confused with xlGetName which returns the name of the DLL).
- Given a reference or value, find out the corresponding defined name if it exists (xlfGetDef).
- Create, define or redefine a name on a worksheet (xlcDefineName).
- Delete a defined name from a given worksheet (xlcDeleteName).
- Create, define or redefine a name in the DLL-space (xlfSetName).
- Delete a defined name from the DLL-space (xlfSetName).
- Get the value(s) corresponding to the defined name (xlfEvaluate).
- Set the value of cells in a given named range (xlfGetName and xlSet).
- Get a list of all defined worksheet names. (xlfNames).

All of these basic operations, except for the last, have been encapsulated in the xlName class in section 9.7. The class also provides simple member functions that inform the caller whether the name is defined and, if so, whether the range reference is still valid.

It is important to remember that Excel names can be valid in the sense that they are defined, but at the same time have invalid range definitions. This can come about when a named cell is deleted by a row or column deletion, a sheet deletion or as a result of a cell cut and paste.

8.10.3   Defining a name on a worksheet: xlcDefineName

Overview:	Defines a name on a worksheet. The name can represent a constant value (which can be a number, Boolean value or string but not an error value), an array of constant values or a reference to one or more cells.
	The function performs the same operation as if the user had selected the menu option Insert/Name/Define... and will, in fact, display the dialog box if used in conjunction with the xlPrompt bit.
Enumeration value:	32829 (x803d)
Callable from:	Commands only.
Return type:	Boolean or error.
Arguments:	1: *Name*: A string satisfying the rules in section 8.10.
	2: *Definition*: (Optional.) One of the following: • A formula (as text using R1C1 style references)

- A constant (as an `xloper` of that type or as text with or without a leading =)
- An array of values. (See note below.)

If *Definition* is omitted, the function defines the name as referring to the currently selected cell(s) on the active worksheet.

Note: There are two ways to specify a literal definition for a name that you wish to define as a constant. For example, a literal array can be passed as a string of the form `"={1,2;3,4}"`, or as an `xloper` of type `xltypeMulti`. The following example commands are equivalent and demonstrate this. Both create a name on the active sheet, so that the formula =SUM(XLL_test_name), if entered anywhere in the active workbook, would return 45.

```
int __stdcall define_name_example_1(void)
{
    cpp_xloper Name("XLL_test_name");
    cpp_xloper Definition("={1,2,3;4,5,6;7,8,9}");

    Excel4(xlcDefineName, 0, 2, &Name, &Definition);
    return 1;
}
```

```
int __stdcall define_name_example_2(void)
{
    double array[9] = {1,2,3,4,5,6,7,8,9};
    cpp_xloper Name("XLL_test_name");
    cpp_xloper Definition(array, 3, 3);

    Excel4(xlcDefineName, 0, 2, &Name, &Definition);
    return 1;
}
```

8.10.4 Defining and deleting a name in the DLL: `xlfSetName`

Overview: Used to define or delete an Excel name that cannot be directly seen or accessed from a worksheet, only from a DLL. The name is created for the current session of Excel only and is defined in a name-space that is shared by all currently Excel-loaded DLLs. This means that such names could be used for inter-DLL communication, for example, to advertise that a DLL is present. Names should be chosen carefully to avoid conflicts or accidental deletions.

Enumeration value: 88 (x58)

Callable from: Commands and macro sheet functions.

Return type:	Boolean true if successful, otherwise #NAME? If the name does not exist or error if it could not be created.
Arguments:	1: *Name*: A string satisfying the rules in section 8.10.

2: *Definition*: (Optional.) One of the following:
- A formula (as text using R1C1 style references)
- A constant (as an `xloper` of that type or as text with or without a leading =)
- An array of values.

If *Definition* is omitted, the function deletes the name.

The most useful application of such a name is to keep track of an instance of a DLL function call from a specific cell, even if the cell is moved. Unlike the function `xlcDefineName` which can only be called from a command, this function can be called from a worksheet function (provided it has been registered as a macro-sheet equivalent function), enabling a function to name its calling cell. Chapter 9 and Chapter 10 both contain example techniques and applications that rely on the DLL being able to do this.

The function `xlfNames` (see section 8.10.8 below) returns a horizontal array of all the worksheet names defined in a specified workbook. Unfortunately, this does not include names created with `xlfSetName`. For this reason, the DLL should maintain an internal list of such names. The example class `xlName`, see section 9.7 below, adds every internal name it creates to a Standard Template Library (STL) container class. The source files `XllNames.cpp` and `XllNames.h` in the example project on the CD ROM contain a full listing of the code for both the `xlName` class and the STL map.

As with the definition of a worksheet name, the *Definition* argument string can be a formula, for example, `"=SQRT(2*PI())"`. When retrieving the value of the name, this formula must be evaluated using the `xlfEvaluate` function before the value can be used. (In this rather simplistic example, it would be better to evaluate first and define the name as the value instead.)

Note: If you want to set the name to be defined as the *value* of a cell reference, rather than the reference itself, it is necessary to obtain that value using either the `xlfDeref` or the `xlCoerce` function before passing it to `xlfSetName`. Passing the reference directly defines the name as the reference instead of the value.

The following code lists a function that creates an internal DLL name, or retrieves its value. If the 4th argument is Boolean and true, the function deletes the name. (The call to `xlfSetName` fails gracefully if the name is not defined.)

```
xloper * __stdcall xll_name(char *name_text, xloper *p_defn,
        xloper *p_as_value), xloper *p_delete)
{
    cpp_xloper Name(name_text); // make a deep copy
    cpp_xloper Defn(p_defn); // make a shallow copy
    cpp_xloper AsValue(p_as_value); // shallow copy
    cpp_xloper Delete(p_delete);
    cpp_xloper RetVal;
    int xl4;

    if(Delete == true)
```

```
    {
        Excel4(xlfSetName, 0, 1, &Name);
// Remove from the DLL's list of internal names.
        clean_xll_name_list();
        return p_xlTrue;
    }

    if(Defn.IsType(xltypeNil | xltypeMissing))
    {
// function is just asking for the name to be evaluated
        Excel4(xlfEvaluate, &RetVal, 1, &Name);
        return RetVal.ExtractXloper(true);
    }

    if(AsValue==true && Defn.IsType(xltypeSRef | xltypeRef))
    {
// Create a name defined as the value of the given reference
        cpp_xloper Val;
        xl4 = Excel4(xlCoerce, &Val, 1, &Defn);
        Val.SetExceltoFree();

        if(xl4 || Val.IsType(xltypeErr))
            return p_xlFalse;

        Excel4(xlfSetName, &RetVal, 2, &Name, &Val);
    }
    else
    {
// Create a name defined as the given reference
        Excel4(xlfSetName, &RetVal, 2, &Name, &Defn);
    }

// Add to DLL's list of internal names.  Done automatically by the
// the xlName constructor
    xlName R(name_text);
    return RetVal.ExtractXloper(true);
}
```

8.10.5 Deleting a worksheet name: `xlcDeleteName`

Overview:	Deletes a defined worksheet name. Once this operation has completed, any cells that reference the deleted name will return the #NAME? error.
	The function performs the same operation as if the user had selected the menu option <u>I</u>nsert/<u>N</u>ame/<u>D</u>efine... and deleted the name in the Define Name dialog.
Enumeration value:	32878 (x806e)
Callable from:	Commands only.
Return type:	Boolean or error.
Arguments:	1: *Name*: A string satisfying the rules in section 8.10.

8.10.6   Getting the definition of a named range: `xlfGetName`

Overview: Returns the definition of a given named range as text. The output of the function depends on where the input range is defined and on whether the range was defined on the *active* sheet.

Enumeration value: 107 (x6b)

Callable from: Commands only.

Return type: Text or an error value.

Arguments: 1: *Name*: A string satisfying the rules in section 8.10. (See table below for examples.)

2: *ReturnedInfo*: A number specifying the type of information to return about the name. If 1 or omitted, returns the name's definition (see following table for details). If 2, returns a Boolean which is true if the scope of the name is limited to the current sheet.

Example

Suppose that three ranges have been defined but with the same name, TestName, in three places as shown in Table 8.20. Suppose also that Book1 is an open workbook containing Sheet1, Sheet2 and Sheet3.

Table 8.20 Example range definitions

Full name	Where defined	Definition
TestName	DLL (see `xlfSetName`)	[Book1.xls]Sheet3!R1C1:R2C2
[Book1.xls]Sheet1!TestName	Book1, Sheet1	[Book1.xls]Sheet1!R2C2:R3C3
[Book1.xls]Sheet2!TestName	Book1, Sheet2	[Book1.xls]Sheet2!R3C3:R4C4

Table 8.21 summarises the values returned by `xlfGetName` in various contexts when the second argument is omitted. (See section 2.2, *A1 versus R1C1 cell references* on page 9 for an explanation of the R1C1 address style.)

Table 8.21 Example `xlfGetName` return values

Name passed as...	The active sheet:	The current sheet:	Value returned
TestName	Any.	Any.	=[Book1.xls]Sheet3!R1C1:R2C2 The definition supplied in the call to `xlfSetName`. This may be a constant value or array, or a worksheet range as in this example.

(*continued overleaf*)

Table 8.21 (*continued*)

Name passed as...	The active sheet:	The current sheet:	Value returned
!TestName	Sheet1	Any.	=R2C2:R3C3
!TestName	Sheet2	Any.	=R3C3:R4C4
!TestName	Sheet3	Any.	=Sheet1!R2C2:R3C3 Name on Sheet2 is masked by name on Sheet1.
!TestName	Any sheet in any other workbook.	Any.	#NAME?
Sheet1!TestName	Sheet1	Any.	=R2C2:R3C3
Sheet1!TestName	Sheet2	Any.	=[Book1.xls]Sheet1!R2C2:R3C3
Sheet1!TestName	Sheet3	Any.	=[Book1.xls]Sheet1!R2C2:R3C3
Sheet1!TestName	Any sheet in any other workbook.	Any sheet in any other workbook.	#NAME?
Sheet1!TestName	Any sheet in any other workbook.	Book1: Sheet1, Sheet2 or Sheet3	=[Book1.xls]Sheet1!R2C2:R3C3
[Book1.xls]Sheet1!TestName	Sheet1	Any.	=R2C2:R3C3
[Book1.xls]Sheet1!TestName	Any other sheet in any workbook.	Any.	=[Book1.xls]Sheet1!R2C2:R3C3

As you can see from the above table, the behaviour of this function, whilst being logical in its own interesting way, is a little confusing. Consequently, it's best to use the most explicit form of the name, as shown at the bottom of the table, to avoid ambiguity or the need to check which is the active sheet before interpreting the result. Where the name is defined within the DLL, its definition is only accessible as shown at the top of Table 8.21. If the name is a worksheet name it must be prefixed with *at least* the '!'.

Where a DLL name was defined as a constant value, even where this is a number, the function returns a string in which the value is prefixed with '='. For example, if the value 1 was assigned, it returns "=1" and if the value "xyz" was assigned it returns ="xyx".

The `Excel4()` function set-up and call are as shown in the following C/C++ code example of an exportable function that wraps up the call to `xlfGetName`.

```
xloper * __stdcall GetName(char *name, xloper *p_info_type)
{
    cpp_xloper Arg1(name);
    cpp_xloper RetVal;

    int retval = Excel4(xlfGetName, &RetVal, 1, &Arg1, p_info_type);

    return RetVal.ExtractXloper(true);
}
```

If the name is defined as a reference to one or more cells, (the most common reason for defining a name), then to convert the text definition returned by `xlfGetName` you need to use `xlfTextRef`, after stripping the leading '=' from the text address. (See section 8.9.15 *Converting text to a reference: xlfTextref* on page 235, and also the `xlName` class code listed on the CD ROM and discussed below.)

8.10.7   Getting the defined name of a range of cells: `xlfGetDef`

Overview:	Returns the defined name of a range of cells (or other nameable object) given the corresponding range as text (or object ID). If no name corresponds to the reference provided, it returns #NAME?.
Enumeration value:	145 (x91)
Callable from:	Commands and macro sheet functions.
Return type:	Text or an error value.
Arguments:	1: *DefinitionText*: A text representation of anything that a name can be assigned to. If a range of cells, then the range address must be expressed in R1C1 form.
	2: *DocumentText*: The name of the sheet in the *current* workbook containing the object or range specified in *DefinitionText*. If omitted the sheet is assumed to be the DLL, i.e., the function returns the internal name if it exists.
	3: *TypeNum*: A number indicating the type of name to find. 1 or omitted will only search for names that are not hidden, 2 only for names that are hidden and 3 for all names.

Where the range name is defined on a worksheet, the first argument should be passed as in the following code fragment, which places the name, if it exists, or #NAME? in `RetVal`:

```
cpp_xloper Address("R1C1"); // Cell A1
cpp_xloper Sheet("Sheet1");
cpp_xloper RetVal;
```

```
Excel4(xlfGetDef, &RetVal, 2, &Address, &Sheet);
RetVal.SetExcelToFree();
```

Where the range name is defined within the DLL, only the first argument should be provided as in the following code fragment:

```
cpp_xloper Address("[Book1.xls]Sheet1!R1C1");
cpp_xloper RetVal;
Excel4(xlfGetDef, &RetVal, 1, &Address);
RetVal.SetExcelToFree();
```

8.10.8   Getting a list of named ranges: `xlfNames`

Overview:

Returns a horizontal array of all the names defined in the specified workbook. (Unfortunately, this function does not return Excel names created within the DLL using `xlfSetName`. For this reason the DLL should maintain an internal list of the hidden DLL names it has created.)

If no names match the criteria, the function returns #N/A.

Enumeration value: 122 (x7a)

Callable from: Commands and macro sheet functions.

Return type: Horizontal array (`xltypeMulti`) of strings (`xltypeStr`).

Arguments:

1: *Workbook/Worksheet*: (Optional.) A string in the form Book1.xls or [Book1.xls]Sheet1. If omitted the *current* workbook is searched.

2: *NameType*: (Optional.) Integer indicating the type of names to select: 1 or omitted = unhidden names, 2 = hidden names, 3 = all names.

3: *Mask*: (Optional.) A wildcard match string. For example "`S*`" will return all names starting with S. (Note: Searches are not case-sensitive). If omitted all names of *NameType* are returned.

Note: This function will not return the names of any binary storage blocks created with the `xlDefineBinaryName` function (see section 8.8 *Working with binary names* on page 209). Nor does it list names defined by a DLL within this session of Excel using `xlfSetName`. The DLL should therefore maintain its own list of such names using, for example, one of the C++ Standard Template Library containers or a simple linked list coded in C.

Where a workbook contains distinct sheets which have duplicate defined names, as in the example in section 8.10.6 on page 245, the function will behave slightly differently depending on whether the first argument is omitted or not. If omitted, the function returns an array of the names in the current workbook with no duplicates. If the workbook is explicitly provided in the first argument, the function returns the array with duplicate names repeated.

8.11   WORKING WITH EXCEL MENUS

Excel displays one menu bar for each sheet type, the most familiar being the default worksheet menu bar which normally contains nine menus:

```
File Edit View Insert Format Tools Data Window Help
```

Customising this and other menu bars, the menus they contain and the commands that the menus contain, enables the DLL to make its own command functions easily accessible. (Remember that commands can perform operations that worksheet functions cannot.) Creating menus using the XLM functions via the C API is fairly easy, as this section aims to show, but complex commands, especially those with complex dialogs and so on, are far better developed in VB. Including a few commands within an XLL can greatly simplify the provision of functionality of a DLL that primarily exists to provide worksheet functions. For example, a command that displays a simple dialog showing DLL version information or that allows configuration of one or more worksheet functions, can make the DLL functionality very much more user-friendly.

The highest level menu object is the menu bar, such as the one shown above, containing one or more menus, e.g. File, with each menu in turn providing access to one or more commands or sub-menus, the latter with its own commands. Excel has a number of built-in menu bars relating to different types of sheet, for example, there is a worksheet menu bar and a chart menu bar. Excel switches automatically between these when the user changes the active sheet.

As well as the add-in developer being able to change existing menu bars, they can also create custom menu bars. The creation of a custom menu bar does not automatically display it – it must be explicitly invoked, replacing the previous menu bar in the process. The display of a custom menu bar also suppresses the automatic switching between menu bars when the sheet type changes. So, unless you deliberately want to restrict the user in what they can do with Excel, it is better to add menus and/or commands to existing menu bars than to use custom bars.

Menus and commands can be accessed with Alt-key sequences. These are defined at the point that the new menu or command is registered with Excel, using an ampersand '&' before the relevant letter in the displayed string. When adding menus or commands care should be taken to avoid conflicts with existing items, especially Excel's built-in menus and commands.

8.11.1   Menu bars and ID numbers and menu and command specifiers

Internally, Excel represents each of the built-in menu bars by an ID number as shown in Table 8.22. Custom menu bars are assigned an ID number outside this range.

Table 8.22 Built-in menu bar IDs

Bar ID number	Built-in menu bar description
1 to 6	*No longer used. These all correspond to versions of Excel 5.0 and earlier.*
7, 8, 9	Short-cut menu groups (see next section)
10	Worksheets (and Excel 4 macro sheets)
11	Chart sheets
12	*No longer used (Excel 4.0 and earlier)*
13 to 35	*Reserved for use by Excel's short-cut menus.*
36 to 50	Returned by `xlfAddBar` when creating custom menu bars.

Each menu bar contains a number of menus which can either be referred to by name (the displayed text) or position number counting from 1 from the left.

Each menu contains a number of lines comprised of the following three types:

- Commands
- Separator lines
- Sub-menus, containing...
  - Commands
  - Separator lines

These lines can be referred to either by name (the displayed text) or position number counting from 1, top to bottom. (Counting includes separator lines.) Where the line is a sub-menu, its sub-commands can also be referred to by name or position number in the same way.

Some of the menu management functions take search strings that can contain wildcards. These strings can be the name of a menu or a menu item. Ampersands, indicating the Alt-key access key, are ignored in these searches. An ellipsis '...' needs to be included if the command contains one. (The ellipsis has no function, but, by convention, indicates that the command will display a dialog box.) Searches are not-case sensitive. Where text is provided in order to create a new menu, the position of any ampersand is important to avoid conflicts with built-in menus.

Note: Built-in menu-bars and menus can change from version to version and, as this section shows, can be altered by add-ins even during an Excel session. Therefore, menus and commands should generally be specified as text rather than by position.

8.11.2   Short-cut (context) menu groups

The short-cut drop-down menus referred to in the above table (Bar ID numbers 7, 8 and 9) are displayed by right-clicking on the relevant object, and are consequently also referred to as context menus. Conceptually, a short-cut menu bar is an invisible menu bar containing a number of invisible short-cut menus, whose drop-down list of commands only becomes visible when you right-click on the associated object. For example, right clicking on a worksheet cell displays a context menu containing the most common cell operations: Cut, Copy, Paste, Paste Special. . . , Insert. . . , Delete. . . , Clear Contents, Insert Comment, Format Cells. . . , Pick From List. . . , Hyperlink. . . .

Commands can be added and deleted in exactly the same way as with menus on visible menu bars, except that instead of being able to specify a menu as either a text argument or position number (see below), the drop-down menu of a specified must be specified by the number shown in Table 8.23:

Table 8.23 Short-cut menus

Worksheet short-cut bar ID	Menu number	Corresponding object description
7	1	Toolbars
	2	Toolbar buttons
	3	*No longer used*
	4	Worksheet cells
	5	Entire column selection
	6	Entire row selection
	7	Workbook tab
	8	Excel 4 Macro sheet cells
	9	Workbook title bar
	10	Desktop (Windows only)
	11, 12, 13, 14	*These menus refer to VB code modules which are no longer supported.*
Non-worksheet object short-cut bar ID	**Menu number**	**Corresponding object description**
8	1	Drawn and imported objects
	2	Buttons on sheets
	3	Text boxes
	4	Dialog sheet
Chart short-cut bar ID	**Menu number**	**Corresponding object description**
9	1	Series
	2	Chart and axis titles
	3	Plot area and walls
	4	Entire chart
	5	Axes
	6	Gridlines
	7	Floor and arrows
	8	Legend

8.11.3   Getting information about a menu bar: `xlfGetBar`

Overview: Provides information about a menu bar.

Enumeration value: 182 (xb6)

Callable from: Commands only.

Return type: Various. (See below.)

Arguments: 1: *MenuID*: The menu bar ID number.
                            2: *Menu*: The menu as either text or position number.
                            3: *MenuPosition*: The command (i.e., menu item) as text or
                               position number.
                            4: *SubMenuPosition*: The sub-command as text or position
                               number.

If all arguments are omitted, the function returns the ID number of the currently displayed menu bar, which can then be used as an argument to other menu-management functions.

Where *MenuID* is given, *Menu* and *MenuPosition* must also be provided, although *MenuPosition* may be passed as `xltypeMissing`.

If *MenuPosition* is zero or `xltypeMissing`, the function returns the position number of the menu on the menu bar (if the menu was specified as text), or as text (if specified by its position number). If the menu is returned as text, it includes the ampersand if there is an Alt-key associated with it. If the menu cannot be found or the position number is not valid, the function returns #N/A.

If *MenuPosition* is specified as a number, the function returns the command in that position as text including any ampersand or ellipsis. If the number corresponds to a command separator line, the returned text is a single dash '-'. If there is no menu item at that position or the menu is not valid the function returns #N/A.

If *MenuPosition* is specified as text, the function returns the position of the command in the menu. If the text provided is a single dash, the function returns the position of the first separator line, and if two dashes "--", the position of the second separator line, and so on. If the specified text cannot be located, the function returns #N/A. (Functions that take the position of a command on a menu or sub-menu also accept text. Two dashes will be treated as equivalent to the position of the second separator.)

In calling the function to obtain command information as described above, *SubMenuPosition* can be omitted.

If *SubMenuPosition* is specified, the first three arguments must also be provided. The argument functions in the same way as when passed only three arguments, except that it returns the position of a command on the sub-menu or the text, depending on whether it was given as text or number. The function returns #N/A if the arguments are not valid. Consequently, a call to this function with *SubMenuPosition* set to 1 will return #N/A if the given menu item is not a sub-menu, giving a fairly easy means of determining which type of menu item is at each position on a menu.

Note: Built-in menu-bars and menus can change from one Excel version to another, and they can be altered by add-ins during an Excel session. Menus and commands should therefore be specified as text rather than by position.

The following example function returns a number specifying whether a menu item is a command, separator line or sub-menu, returning 1, 2 or 3 respectively. It returns 0 if the position is invalid for this menu and −1 if the inputs did not correspond to a valid menu. The menu argument is declared as an integer so that the function will work with short-cut menus that cannot be specified by a text value. The function makes use of the `cpp_xloper` class to simplify the management of the arguments for `Excel4()`. Remember that this function can only be called during execution of a command.

```cpp
int menu_item_type(int bar_ID, xloper *pMenu, int position)
{
    if(position <= 0)
        return -1;

    cpp_xloper BarID(bar_ID);
    cpp_xloper Pos(1);
    cpp_xloper RetVal;

// Check that bar_ID and menu are valid by asking for the
// text of the menu at position 1
    if(Excel4(xlfGetBar, &RetVal, 3, &BarID, pMenu, &Pos)
    || !RetVal.IsType(xltypeStr))
        return -1;

// Get Excel to free the memory before re-use
    RetVal.Free(true);

// Get the text of the menu item at the given position
    Pos = position;

    if(Excel4(xlfGetBar, &RetVal, 3, &BarID, pMenu, &Pos)
    || !RetVal.IsType(xltypeStr))
        return 0;

// Is it a separator line?
    char *p = (char *)RetVal;
    bool is_separator = (*p == '-');
    free(p);
    RetVal.Free(true);

    if(is_separator)
        return 2;

// Is it a command?  Try and get the text of the 1st sub-menu item
    cpp_xloper SubCmd(1);

    if(Excel4(xlfGetBar, &RetVal, 4, &BarID, pMenu, &Pos, &SubCmd)
    || !RetVal.IsType(xltypeStr))
    {
// It's a command
        return 1;
    }
    RetVal.SetExceltoFree();

// It's a sub-menu
    return 3;
}
```

8.11.4   Creating a new menu bar or restoring a default bar: xlfAddBar

Overview: Creates an new user menu bar or restores a built-in menu bar.

If the argument is omitted it creates a new menu bar and returns an ID. This ID is used when adding or deleting menus and commands, displaying it (using xlfShowBar), deleting it and so on. Excel permits up to 15 custom menu bars to be defined. If this limit has already been reached the function will fail with a #VALUE! error.

If the argument is a valid built-in menu bar ID number the function restores the original menu bar, effectively removing any and all customisations: yours and everyone else's. If successful, it returns the ID number of the restored menu bar, otherwise it returns #VALUE!.

Enumeration value: 151 (x97)

Callable from: Commands only.

Return type: Boolean, integer or error.

Arguments: 1: *MenuID*. (Optional.) A menu bar ID number

8.11.5   Adding a menu or sub-menu: xlfAddMenu

Overview: Can be used to add a menu to an existing menu bar with one or more commands, or to add a sub-menu and commands to an existing menu. It can also restore a deleted built-in menu.

Enumeration value: 152 (x98)

Callable from: Commands only.

Return type: Boolean or error.

Arguments: 1: *MenuID*: The menu bar ID number.

2: *MenuRef*: The name of a built-in menu or an array (or reference to a block of cells) containing the menu description (see below for details).

3: *MenuPosition*: (Optional.) Specifies the position of the menu item at which commands described in the menu description are to be placed. This can be a number or the text of an existing menu item. (The nth separator line can be specified by a string of 'n' dashes.)

4: *SubMenuPosition*: (Optional.) Specifies the position on the sub-menu at which commands described in the sub-menu description are to be placed. This can be a number or the text of an existing sub-menu item. (The nth separator line can be specified by a string of 'n' dashes).

If *MenuRef* is simply the name of a built-in menu, the remaining arguments are not required and the function restores the menu to its original default state, returning the position number of the restored menu. To restore it to its original position, you need to specify this in *MenuPosition*, otherwise it is placed at the right of the menu bar.

If not simply the name of a menu, *MenuRef* is an array that describes the menu to be added or extended as shown in Table 8.24.

Table 8.24 Custom menu definition array

Required columns		Optional columns		
Menu text	*(blank)*	*(blank)*	*(blank)*	*(blank)*
Command1 text	*Command1 Name*	*(not used)*	*Status bar text*	*Help reference*
Command2 text	*Command2 Name*	*(not used)*	*Status bar text*	*Help reference*
. . .	. . .	. . .	. . .	. . .

Notes:

- The first two columns and at least two rows are required.
- The second column contains the command name as passed to Excel in the 4th argument to `xlfRegister` or the name of some other command macro VB function.
- If the command is not a recognised name Excel will not complain until the user attempts to run the command, at which point an alert dialog with the message "The macro `'command _name'` cannot be found." is displayed.
- The third column would contain a short-cut key for Macintosh systems and is therefore not used in Windows DLLs.
- The fifth column contains a help reference in the form `HelpFile!TopicNum` where `HelpFile` is a standard Windows help file.
- The third, fourth and fifth columns are all optional.
- This table can be passed to the function as either an `xloper` of type `xltypeMulti` or as a reference to range of cells on a worksheet.

If *MenuPosition* is omitted, commands in the *MenuRef* are placed at the end of the list of existing menu items and the function returns the position number of the first new command.

If argument *SubMenuPosition* is given, the function adds a sub-menu (or adds commands if the sub-menu already exists) to the menu specified by the position in *MenuPosition*. *SubMenuPosition* specifies the position on the sub-menu at which to place the commands. Again, this can be a number or text specifying the line before which the commands will be placed. If *SubMenuPosition* is omitted, then the commands are placed at the end of the menu, not the sub-menu.

Example 1

The following code fragment adds a new menu, with two commands separated by a line, at the right of the worksheet menu bar and records the position number so that it can be modified or deleted. (Note: Referring to the menu by its text "&XLL test" is better as the position number could be altered by other menu changes.)

The code creates an array of strings for the *MenuRef* parameter in an xltypeMulti xloper, as shown in this table, using the cpp_xloper class.

"&XLL test"	""
"&XLL command 1"	"XLL_CMD1"
"-"	""
"X&LL command 2"	"XLL_CMD2"

```
char *menu_txt[8] = {"&XLL test", "", "&XLL command 1", "XLL_CMD1",
          "-", "", "X&LL command 2", "XLL_CMD2"};

cpp_xloper BarNum(10); // the worksheet menu bar
cpp_xloper MenuRef(menu_txt, (WORD)4, (WORD)2); // 4 rows, 2 columns
cpp_xloper RetVal;

int xl4 = Excel4(xlfAddMenu, &RetVal, 2, &BarNum, &MenuRef);

if(xl4 == 0 && !RetVal.IsType(xltypeErr))
   int test_menu_position = (int)RetVal;
```

Example 2

The following code fragment inserts the same new menu as in Example 1, to the immediate left of the Help menu on the worksheet menu bar.

```
char *menu_txt[8] = {"&XLL test", "", "&XLL command 1", "XLL_CMD1",
          "-", "", "X&LL command 2", "XLL_CMD2"};

cpp_xloper BarNum(10); // the worksheet menu bar
cpp_xloper MenuRef(menu_txt, (WORD)4, (WORD)2); // 4 rows, 2 columns
cpp_xloper MenuPos("Help");
cpp_xloper RetVal;

int xl4 = Excel4(xlfAddMenu, &RetVal, 3, &BarNum, &MenuRef, &MenuPos);

if(xl4 == 0 && !RetVal.IsType(xltypeErr))
   int test_menu_position = (int)RetVal;
```

Example 3

The following code fragment inserts the same menu as in Example 1 as a sub-menu just before the Table... command on the Data menu on the worksheet menu bar.

```
char *menu_txt[8] = {"&XLL test", "", "&XLL command 1", "XLL_CMD1",
            "-", "", "X&LL command 2", "XLL_CMD2"};

cpp_xloper BarNum(10); // the worksheet menu bar
cpp_xloper MenuRef(menu_txt, (WORD)4, (WORD)2); // 4 rows, 2 columns
cpp_xloper MenuPos("Data");
cpp_xloper SubMenuPos("Table...");
cpp_xloper RetVal;

int x14 = Excel4(xlfAddMenu, &RetVal, 4, &BarNum, &MenuRef, &MenuPos,
            &SubMenuPos);
```

Example 4

The following code fragment restores the Data menu to the worksheet menu bar in its
default position (just left of the Window menu). This presupposes that the menu was deleted
with the `xlfDeleteMenu` command. Note that the menu will be restored in the same
state in which it was deleted which may not be the Excel's default. (To restore a menu
to its default state use the `xlfAddCommand` function.) Note also that this code assumes
that the Window menu has not itself been deleted.

```
cpp_xloper BarNum(10); // the worksheet menu bar
cpp_xloper MenuRef("Data"); // Just the menu name!
cpp_xloper MenuPos("Window"); // Default posn: left of Window menu
cpp_xloper RetVal;

Excel4(xlfAddMenu, &RetVal, 3, &BarNum, &MenuRef, &MenuPos);
```

8.11.6 Adding a command to a menu: `xlfAddCommand`

Overview: Adds a command to an existing menu or sub-menu, or restores a
                   modified built-in menu to its default state.

Enumeration value: 153 (x99)

Callable from: Commands only.

Return type: Various. (See below.)

Arguments: 1: *MenuID*. (Optional.) A menu bar ID number.

                   2: *Menu*: The name of a menu or its position from the left or its
                      designated number if a short-cut menu.

                   3: *CommandRef*: The ID of a deleted built-in command obtained
                      from the `xlfDeleteCommand` function, or a horizontal
                      array (or range reference) containing the description of the
                      command to be added. (See below for details.)

4: *CommandPosition*: An optional argument specifying the position of the menu item at which the command is to be placed: a number or the text of an existing menu item. (The nth separator line can be specified by a string of *n* dashes.)

5: *SubMenuPosition*: An optional argument specifying the position on the sub-menu at which the command is to be placed. This can be a number or the text of an existing sub-menu item. (The nth separator line can be specified by a string of *n* dashes.)

If *CommandRef* is simply the name of a built-in menu, the remaining arguments are not required and the function restores the menu to its original default state, returning the position number of the restored menu. To restore it to its original position, you need to specify this in *MenuPosition*, otherwise it is placed at the right of the menu bar.

CommandRef is a horizontal array as that describes the menu to be added or extended as shown in Table 8.25.

Table 8.25 Custom command definition array

Required columns		Optional columns		
Command text	*Command1 Name*	*(not used)*	*Status bar text*	*Help reference*

Notes:

- The array is the same as the 2nd (and subsequent) rows in the *MenuRef* array described in the previous section.
- The first two columns are required.
- The second column contains the command name as passed to Excel in the 4th argument to `xlfRegister` or the name of some other command macro of VB function.
- If the command is not a recognised name Excel will not complain until the user attempts to run the command, at which point an alert dialog with the message "The macro '*command_name*' cannot be found." is displayed.
- The third column would contain a short-cut key for Macintosh systems and is therefore not used in Windows DLLs.
- The fifth column contains a help reference in the form `HelpFile!TopicNum` where `HelpFile` is a standard Windows help file.
- The third, fourth and fifth columns are all optional.

If *CommandRef* is simply the text of a previously deleted built-in command on this menu, the command is restored in the position specified by *CommandPosition* and *Sub-CommandPosition*.

If *CommandPosition* is omitted, the command is placed at the end of the menu and the function returns the position number of the added command.

If argument *SubMenuPosition* is given, the function adds the command to the sub-menu at *CommandPosition*. *SubMenuPosition* specifies the position on the sub-menu at which to place the command. Again this can be a number or text specifying the line before which the commands will be placed. If *SubMenuPosition* is zero, the command is placed at the end sub-menu. If omitted, the command is added to the main menu, not the sub-menu.

Example 1

The following code fragment adds a new command to the bottom of the Tools menu. The code creates an array of strings for the *CommandRef* parameter in an xltypeMulti xloper using the cpp_xloper class.

```
char *cmd_txt[2] = {"&XLL command 1", "XLL_CMD1"};

cpp_xloper BarNum(10); // the worksheet menu bar
cpp_xloper Menu("Tools");
cpp_xloper CmdRef(cmd_txt, (WORD)1, (WORD)2); // 1 row, 2 columns

xl4 = Excel4(xlfAddCommand, &RetVal, 3, &BarNum, &Menu, &CmdRef);
```

Example 2

The following code fragment adds a new command before the first separator on the Tools menu.

```
char *cmd_txt[2] = {"&XLL command 1", "XLL_CMD1"};

cpp_xloper BarNum(10); // the worksheet menu bar
cpp_xloper Menu("Tools");
cpp_xloper CmdRef(cmd_txt, (WORD)1, (WORD)2); // 1 row, 2 columns
cpp_xloper CmdPos("-");

Excel4(xlfAddCommand, &RetVal, 4, &BarNum, &Menu, &CmdRef, &CmdPos);
```

Example 3

The following code fragment adds a new command to the end of the Macro sub-menu on the Tools menu.

```
char *cmd_txt[2] = {"&XLL command 1", "XLL_CMD1"};

cpp_xloper BarNum(10); // the worksheet menu bar
cpp_xloper Menu("Tools");
cpp_xloper CmdRef(cmd_txt, (WORD)1, (WORD)2); // 1 row, 2 columns
cpp_xloper CmdPos("Macro");
cpp_xloper SubMenuPos(0);

Excel4(xlfAddCommand, &RetVal, 5, &BarNum, &Menu, &CmdRef, &CmdPos,
                                                      &SubMenuPos);
```

Example 4

The following code fragment adds a new command to the end of the worksheet cells short-cut menu (viewed by right-clicking on any cell).

```
char *cmd_txt[2] = {"&XLL command 1", "XLL_CMD1"};

cpp_xloper BarNum(7); // the worksheet short-cut menu-group
cpp_xloper Menu(4); // the worksheet cells short-cut menu
cpp_xloper CmdRef(cmd_txt, (WORD)1, (WORD)2); // 1 row, 2 columns
cpp_xloper CmdPos(0);

Excel4(xlfAddCommand, &RetVal, 4, &BarNum, &Menu, &CmdRef, &CmdPos);
```

Example 5

The following code fragment restores the deleted Goal Seek ... command on the Tools menu in its default position just above Scenarios....

```
cpp_xloper BarNum(10); // the worksheet menu bar
cpp_xloper Menu("Tools");
cpp_xloper CmdRef("Goal Seek...");
cpp_xloper CmdPos("Scenarios...");

Excel4(xlfAddCommand, &RetVal, 4, &BarNum, &Menu, &CmdRef, &CmdPos);
```

8.11.7   Displaying a custom menu bar: `xlfShowBar`

Overview: Displays a custom menu bar or the default built-in menu for the sheet type.

Enumeration value: 157 (x9d)

Callable from: Commands only.

Return type: Boolean or error.

Arguments: 1: *MenuID*: (Optional.)

When you create a custom menu bar using `xlfAddBar`, it is not automatically displayed. This function takes one optional argument, the menu bar ID number returned by `xlfAddBar`. It replaces the currently displayed menu with the specified one. If the argument is omitted, Excel displays the appropriate built-in menu bar for the active sheet type.

If the menu bar ID corresponds to a built-in menu bar, Excel only allows the DLL to display the appropriate type. For example, you could not display the chart menu bar when a worksheet is active.

Displaying a custom menu bar disables Excel's automatic switching from one menu bar to another when the active sheet type changes. Displaying a built-in menu bar reactivates this feature.

8.11.8   Adding/removing a check mark on a menu command: `xlfCheckCommand`

Overview: Displays or removes a check mark from a custom command.

Enumeration value: 155 (x9b)

Callable from:	Commands only.
Return type:	Boolean or error.
Arguments:	1: *MenuID*: The menu bar ID number.
	2: *Menu*: The menu as text or position number.
	3: *MenuItem*: The command as text or position number.
	4: *DisplayCheck*: A Boolean telling Excel to display a check if true, remove it if false.
	5: *SubMenuItem*: (Optional.) A sub-menu command as text or position number.

The C API provides access to a more limited set of menu features than current versions of Excel provide, and this function reflects this. With Excel 4.0, menus supported the display of a check-mark immediately to the right of the command name as a visual indication that something had been selected or toggled. The typical behaviour of such a command is to toggle the check mark every time the command is run. This function, gives the add-in developer access to this check-mark.

The function returns a Boolean reflecting the value that was set in *DisplayCheck*.

Example 1

The following code fragment toggles a check-mark on the custom command XLL command 1 on the Tools menu.

```
static bool show_check = false;

show_check = !show_check;
cpp_xloper BarNum(10); // the worksheet menu bar
cpp_xloper Menu("Tools");
cpp_xloper Cmd("XLL command 1");
cpp_xloper Check(show_check);

Excel4(xlfCheckCommand, &RetVal, 4, &BarNum, &Menu, &Cmd, &Check);
```

Example 2

The following code fragment toggles a check-mark on the command XLL command 1 on the sub-menu XLL on the Data menu.

```
static bool show_check = false;

show_check = !show_check;
cpp_xloper BarNum(10); // the worksheet menu bar
cpp_xloper Menu("Data");
cpp_xloper Cmd("XLL test");
cpp_xloper Check(show_check);
cpp_xloper SubMenuCmd("XLL command 1");

Excel4(xlfCheckCommand, &RetVal, 5, &BarNum, &Menu, &Cmd, &Check,
                                                &SubMenuCmd);
```

8.11.9   Enabling/disabling a custom command or menu: `xlfEnableCommand`

Overview: Enables or disables (greys-out) custom commands on a menu or sub-menu, or enables or disables the menu itself.

Enumeration value: 154 (x9a)

Callable from: Commands only.

Return type: Boolean or error.

Arguments: 1: *MenuID*: The menu bar ID number.

                         2: *Menu*: The menu as text or position number.

                         3: *MenuItem*: The command as text or position number.

                         4: *Enable*: A Boolean telling Excel to enable if true, disable if false.

                         5: *SubMenuItem*: (Optional.) A sub-menu command as text or position number.

The function returns a Boolean reflecting the *Enable* value.

If *MenuItem* is zero, the function enables or disables the entire menu provided that it is also a custom menu. If *SubMenuItem* is zero and the specified *MenuItem* is a custom sub-menu, the function toggles the state of the entire sub-menu.

Example 1

The following code fragment toggles the state of the command XLL command 1 on the Tools menu.

```
static bool enable = false;

enable = !enable;
cpp_xloper BarNum(10); // the worksheet menu bar
cpp_xloper Menu("Tools");
cpp_xloper Cmd("XLL command 1");
cpp_xloper State(enable);

Excel4(xlfEnableCommand, &RetVal, 4, &BarNum, &Menu, &Cmd, &State);
```

Example 2

The following code fragment toggles the state of the command XLL command 1 on the sub-menu XLL on the Data menu.

```
static bool enable = false;

enable = !enable;
cpp_xloper BarNum(10); // the worksheet menu bar
```

```
cpp_xloper Menu("Data");
cpp_xloper Cmd("XLL test");
cpp_xloper State(enable);
cpp_xloper SubMenuCmd("XLL command 1");

Excel4(xlfEnableCommand, &RetVal, 5, &BarNum, &Menu, &Cmd, &State,
                                                &SubMenuCmd);
```

Example 3

The following code fragment toggles the state of the custom menu XLL test.

```
static bool enable = false;

enable = !enable;
cpp_xloper BarNum(10); // the worksheet menu bar
cpp_xloper Menu("XLL test");
cpp_xloper Cmd(0);
cpp_xloper State(enable);

Excel4(xlfAddCommand, &RetVal, 4, &BarNum, &Menu, &Cmd, &State);
```

Example 4

The following code fragment toggles the state of the sub-menu XLL test on the Data menu.

```
static bool enable = false;

enable = ! enable;
cpp_xloper BarNum(10); // the worksheet menu bar
cpp_xloper Menu("Data");
cpp_xloper Cmd("XLL test");
cpp_xloper State(enable);
cpp_xloper SubMenuCmd(0);

Excel4(xlfEnableCommand, &RetVal, 5, &BarNum, &Menu, &Cmd, &State,
                                                &SubMenuCmd);
```

8.11.10   Changing a menu command name: `xlfRenameCommand`

Overview:	Changes the name of any menu or command, custom or built-in.
Enumeration value:	156 (x9c)
Callable from:	Commands only.
Return type:	Boolean or error.
Arguments:	1: *MenuID*: The menu bar ID number.
	2: *Menu*: The menu as text or position number.
	3: *MenuItem*: The command as text or position number.

4: *NewName*: Text of the new name including any ampersand.

5: *SubMenuItem*: (Optional.) A sub-menu command as text or position number.

Changing the name of a menu or command is a useful thing to do if the command's action is state-dependent and you want to reflect the next action in the command's text. This could be anything from showing a toggle that sets or clears some DLL state, or may be more complex, cycling between many states. Such state-dependent commands are particularly useful for managing background or remote processes.

If *MenuItem* is zero the menu is renamed. If the command could not be found the function returns #VALUE!, otherwise it returns true.

Example

The following code fragment changes the name of the command XLL command 1 on the Tools menu.

```
static bool enable = false;

cpp_xloper BarNum(10); // the worksheet menu bar
cpp_xloper Menu("Tools");
cpp_xloper Cmd("XLL command 1");
cpp_xloper NewText("Ne&w name");

Excel4(xlfRenameCommand, &RetVal, 4, &BarNum, &Menu, &Cmd, &NewText);
```

8.11.11   Deleting a command from a menu: `xlfDeleteCommand`

Overview: Deletes a command or sub-menu from a menu.

Enumeration value: 159 (x9f)

Callable from: Commands only.

Return type: Various. (See below).

Arguments: 1: *MenuID*: The menu bar ID number.

2: *Menu*: The menu as text or position number.

3: *MenuItem*: The command as text or position number.

4: *SubMenuItem*: (Optional.) A sub-menu command as text or position number.

If the command cannot be found the function returns #VALUE!, otherwise it returns true when deleting a custom command or an ID when deleting an Excel command. This ID is a string containing the text of the command including ampersand, that can be used as the *CommandRef* parameter in a call to `xlfAddCommand`.

Note: If the deletion of a command promotes a separator line to the top of the menu, Excel will automatically delete the separator too. If you want to be able to restore a command *and* the separator, you will need to check for this *before* deleting the command.

Note: Remember to store the information needed to be able to restore commands and undo your changes, especially when deleting built-in commands.

Example 1

The following code fragment deletes the command XLL command 1 on the XLL test custom menu. In this case, the function will return a Boolean xloper if successful.

```
cpp_xloper BarNum(10); // the worksheet menu bar
cpp_xloper Menu("XLL test");
cpp_xloper Cmd("&XLL command 1");

Excel4(xlfDeleteCommand, &RetVal, 3, &BarNum, &Menu, &Cmd);
```

Example 2

The following code fragment deletes the command &Print... from the File menu. In this case the function will return a string xloper if successful. This example discards the return value, getting Excel to free any memory allocated for the string using one of the class methods. If the object RetVal is to be reused, this avoids a memory leak.

```
cpp_xloper BarNum(10); // the worksheet menu bar
cpp_xloper Menu("File");
cpp_xloper Cmd("&Print...");

Excel4(xlfDeleteCommand, &RetVal, 3, &BarNum, &Menu, &Cmd);
RetVal.Free(true);//Get Excel to free the memory
```

8.11.12   Deleting a custom menu: xlfDeleteMenu

Overview: Deletes a menu.

Enumeration value: 158 (x9e)

Callable from: Commands only.

Return type: Boolean or error.

Arguments: 1: *MenuID*: The menu bar ID number.

                     2: *Menu*: The menu as text or position number.

                     3: *SubMenuItem*: (Optional.) A sub-menu command as text or position number.

Note: Excel does not permit the deletion of short-cut menus, however, these can be disabled and re-enabled with the xlfEnableCommand function.

If the function cannot find or delete the menu, it returns #VALUE!, otherwise it returns 'true'.

<u>Warning</u>: The action of *SubMenuItem* is intended, according to the XLM reference manuals, to delete the specified sub-menu on the given menu. Instead it deletes the menu itself. Use xlfDeleteCommand to delete a sub-menu.

<u>Note</u>: Remember to store the information needed to restore menus and undo changes, especially when deleting built-in menus. Simply restoring Excel defaults may delete other custom menu items.

Example 1

The following code fragment deletes the <u>D</u>ata menu.

```
cpp_xloper BarNum(10); // the worksheet menu bar
cpp_xloper Menu("Data");
Excel4(xlfDeleteMenu, &RetVal, 2, &BarNum, &Menu);
```

8.11.13   Deleting a custom menu bar: xlfDeleteBar

Overview: Deletes a custom menu bar.

Enumeration value: 200 (xc8)

Callable from: Commands only.

Return type: Boolean or error.

Arguments: 1: *MenuID*: The menu bar ID number returned by the call to xlfAddBar.

If called with an invalid ID the function returns the #VALUE! error.

8.12   WORKING WITH TOOLBARS

Toolbars (also known as command bars) provide the user with a number of graphical controls, typically buttons, that give short-cuts to commands. They can also contain list and text boxes that enable setting of certain object properties quickly.

This section only deals very briefly with the toolbar customising functions of the C API: it is recommended that you use other means to modify command bars if you intend to rely heavily on them. The functions and their argument types are listed and a little detail given, but no code samples. Excel's internal toolbar and tool IDs are not listed.[7] If you want to know them, you can fairly easily extract information about all Excel's toolbars using the xlfGetToolbar and xlfGetTool functions (described briefly below) using the following steps:

1. Get an array of all toolbar IDs as text (both visible and hidden) using the xlfGetToolbar function, passing only the first argument set to 8.

---

[7] For a full listing of tools and toolbar IDs, you should try to get a copy of a *Visual Basic User's Guide* for Excel, which lists them all.

2. For each ID in the returned horizontal array, call `xlfGetToolbar` again with the first argument set to 1 and the second set to the ID, to obtain an array of all the tool IDs on that toolbar.

The above section on customising menu bars provides a relatively easy way to provide access to commands contained within the DLL if you need to.

8.12.1   Getting information about a toolbar: `xlfGetToolbar`

Overview: Gets information about a toolbar.

Enumeration value: 258 (x102)

Callable from: Command and macro sheet functions.

Return type: Various. See Table 8.26 below.

Arguments: 1: *InfoType*: A number from 1 to 10 indicating the type of information to obtain. (See table below.)

                                            2: *BarID*: The name as text or the ID number of a toolbar.

Table 8.26 Information available using `xlfGetToolbar`

InfoType	What the function returns
1	Horizontal array of all tool IDs on the toolbar. (Gaps = zero.)
2	Horizontal position in the docked or floating region.
3	Vertical position in the docked or floating region.
4	Toolbar width in points.
5	Toolbar height in points.
6	Docked at the top (1), left (2), right (3), bottom (4) or floating (5).
7	True if the toolbar is visible.
8	Horizontal array of toolbar IDs, names or numbers, all toolbars.
9	Horizontal array of toolbar IDs, names or numbers, all visible toolbars.
10	True if the toolbar is visible in full-screen mode.

Values of *InfoType* 8 and 9 do not require a *BarID* argument.

8.12.2   Getting information about a tool button on a toolbar: `xlfGetTool`

Overview: Gets information about a tool button on a toolbar.

Enumeration value: 259 (x103)

Callable from: Command and macro sheet functions.

Return type: Various. See Table 8.27 below.

Arguments: 1: *InfoType*: A number from 1 to 9 indicating the type of information to obtain. (See table below.)

                 2: *BarID*: The name as text or the ID number of a toolbar.

                 3: *Position*: The position of the button (or gap) on the toolbar counting from 1 at the left if horizontal, or the top if vertical.

Table 8.27 Information available using `xlfGetTool`

InfoType	What the function returns
1	The button's ID number or zero if a gap at this position.
2	The reference of the macro assigned to the button or #N/A if none assigned.
3	True if the button is down.
4	True if the button is enabled.
5	True if the face on the button is a bitmap, false if a default button face.
6	The help reference of a custom button, or #N/A if built-in.
7	The balloon text reference of a custom button, or #N/A if built-in.
8	The help context string of a custom button.
9	The tip text of a custom button.

8.12.3   Creating a new toolbar: `xlfAddToolbar`

Overview: Creates a custom toolbar.

Enumeration value: 253 (xfd)

Callable from: Commands only.

Arguments: 1: *BarText*: A string that you want to be associated with the new toolbar.

                 2: *ToolRef*: A number specifying a built-in button or an array containing a definition of one or more custom and/or built-in buttons. (See Table 8.28 below.)

Table 8.28 Array of information for adding buttons to a toolbar

Required	Do not provide for built-in tool IDs or zero. Optional for custom tools.							
Tool ID	*Command text*	*Default state is down*	*Default state is enabled*	*Face graphic reference*	*Status text*	*Balloon text*	*Help topic*	*Tip text*
...	...	...	...	...	...	...	...	...

<u>Note:</u> Any arguments omitted from such a range should be passed as `xloper` array elements of `xltypeNil`.

<u>Column notes (from left to right):</u>

1. Can contain the ID of a built-in button, zero to represent a gap or the ID (text name or number between 201 and 231 inclusive) of a custom tool.
2. The name of the DLL command as registered with Excel in the 4th argument of the `xlfRegister` function.
3. A Boolean instructing Excel whether to display the button as depressed by default if true. If omitted or true, the button is up by default.
4. A Boolean determining whether the tool is enabled by default (true) or not (false or omitted).
5. A reference to a defined picture object. If omitted, Excel uses a default face graphic.
6. The text to be displayed in the status bar when the button is pressed.
7. The balloon text for the tool.
8. A reference to a help topic as text of the form HelpFile!TopicNum.
9. The mouse-over text displayed when the mouse is over the button.

8.12.4   Adding buttons to a toolbar: `xlcAddTool`

Overview:	Adds a tool button to a toolbar.
Enumeration value:	33045 (x8115)
Callable from:	Commands only.
Arguments:	1: *BarID*: A number of a built-in toolbar, or the text of a custom toolbar.
	2: *Position*: The position on the toolbar counting from 1 at the left if horizontal, or the top if vertical, at which tools are to be inserted.
	3: *ToolRef*: A number specifying a built-in button or an array containing a definition of one or more custom and/or built-in buttons. (See Table 8.28 above for a detailed description.)

8.12.5   Assigning/removing a command on a tool: `xlcAssignToTool`

Overview:	Gets information about a tool button on a toolbar.
Enumeration value:	33061 (x8125)
Callable from:	Commands only.
Arguments:	1: *BarID*: A number of a built-in toolbar, or the text of a custom toolbar.
	2: *Position*: The position on the toolbar counting from 1 at the left if horizontal, or the top if vertical, at which tools are to be inserted. Can be a built-in or custom button.

3: *Command*: The name of the DLL command as registered with Excel in the 4th argument of the `xlfRegister` function.

If *Command* is omitted, the function removes the existing association between the tool button and the command. If the button is a custom button then Excel prompts the user to assign a command next time the button is pressed by displaying the Assign Macro dialog. The user can manually enter a registered DLL command name to assign another command if they wish. If the button is a built-in tool, the action reverts to the Excel default action.

8.12.6   Enabling/disabling a button on a toolbar: `xlfEnableTool`

Overview:	Enables or disables a tool button on a toolbar.
Enumeration value:	265 (x109)
Callable from:	Commands only.
Arguments:	1: *BarID*: A number of a built-in toolbar, or the text of a custom toolbar.
	2: *Position*: The position on the toolbar counting from 1 at the left if horizontal, or the top if vertical, at which tools are to be inserted. Can be a built-in or custom button.
	3: *Enable*: A Boolean value enabling the button if true or omitted, disabling it if false.

8.12.7   Moving/copying a command between toolbars: `xlcMoveTool`

Overview:	Moves or copies tools between toolbars and resizes drop-down lists on toolbars.
Enumeration value:	33058 (x8122)
Callable from:	Commands only.
Return type:	Various. See table below.
Arguments:	1: *SourceBarID*: A number of a built-in toolbar, or the text of a custom toolbar.
	2: *SourcePosition*: The position on the toolbar counting from 1 at the left if horizontal, or the top if vertical, at which tools are to be inserted. Can be a built-in or custom button.
	3: *TargetBarID*: A number of a built-in toolbar, or the text of a custom toolbar.

     4: *TargetPosition*: The position on the toolbar counting from 1 at the left if horizontal, or the top if vertical, at which tools are to be inserted. Can be a built-in or custom button.

     5: *Copy*: A Boolean value: copy if true, move if false or omitted.

     6: *DropListWidth*: The desired width in points of the drop-down list.

If *TargetBarID* is omitted, the tool is moved within the *SourceBarID* toolbar. If the reason for calling the function is to resize a drop-down list, *Copy* and *TargetPosition* are not required but should be supplied as `xltypeMissing`. If this is not the reason for the call, the *DropListWidth* argument is ignored.

8.12.8   Showing a toolbar button as pressed: `xlfPressTool`

Overview: Depresses or releases a button on a toolbar.

Enumeration value: 266 (x10a)

Callable from: Commands only.

Arguments: 1: *BarID*: A number of a built-in toolbar, or the text of a custom toolbar.

                       2: *Position*: The position on the toolbar counting from 1 at the left if horizontal, or the top if vertical, at which tools are to be inserted. Can be a built-in or custom button.

                       3: *Pressed*: A Boolean value. The button is depressed if true, or normal if false or omitted.

Note: This function will not work on built-in buttons or buttons to which no command has been assigned.

8.12.9   Displaying or hiding a toolbar: `xlcShowToolbar`

Overview: Activates a toolbar.

Enumeration value: 32988 (x80dc)

Callable from: Commands only.

Arguments: 1: *BarID*: A number of a built-in toolbar, or the text of a custom toolbar.

                       2: *IsVisible*: A Boolean value. The toolbar is visible if true, hidden if false.

                       3: *DockPosition*: 1 top; 2 left; 3 right; 4 bottom; 5 floating.

4: *HorizontalPosition*: The distance in points between the left of the toolbar and (1) the left of the docking area if docked, (2) the right of the right-most toolbar in the left docking area if floating.

5: *VerticalPosition*: The distance in points between the top of the toolbar and the top of (1) the docking area if docked, (2) Excel's workspace if floating.

6: *ToolbarWidth*: The width in points. If omitted, the existing width is applied.

7: *Protection*: A number specifying the degree of protection given to the toolbar. (See Table 8.29 below.)

8: *ShowToolTips*: Boolean. Mouse-over ToolTips are displayed if true, not if false.

9: *ShowLargeButtons*: Boolean. Large buttons are displayed if true, not if false.

10: *ShowColourButtons*: Boolean. Toolbar buttons are displayed in colour if true, not if false.

Table 8.29 Toolbar protection parameter values

Protection	Description
0 or omitted	Can be resized, docked, floated and buttons can be added and removed.
1	As 0 except that buttons can not be added or removed.
2	As 1 except that it cannot be resized.
3	As 2 except that it cannot be moved between docked and floating states.
4	As 3 except that it cannot be moved at all.

8.12.10   Resetting a built-in toolbar: `xlfResetToolbar`

Overview: Resets a built-in toolbar.

Enumeration value: 256 (x100)

Callable from: Command and macro sheet functions.

Arguments: 1: *BarID*: The number of a built-in toolbar.

8.12.11   Deleting a button from a toolbar: `xlcDeleteTool`

Overview: Deletes a tool button from a toolbar.

Enumeration value: 33057 (x8121)

Callable from:	Commands only.
Arguments:	1: *BarID*: A number of a built-in toolbar, or the text of a custom toolbar.
	2: *Position*: The position on the toolbar counting from 1 at the left if horizontal, or the top if vertical, at which tools are to be inserted. Can be a built-in or custom button.

8.12.12   Deleting a custom toolbar: `xlfDeleteToolbar`

Overview:	Deletes a custom toolbar.
Enumeration value:	254 (xfe)
Callable from:	Commands and macro sheet functions.
Arguments:	1: *BarName*: The text name of a custom toolbar

8.13   WORKING WITH CUSTOM DIALOG BOXES

IMPORTANT NOTE: The C API only provides access to the dialog capabilities of the Excel 4.0 macro language which are very limited and awkward in comparison to those of VB or MFC. The C API does not support different font sizes, colours, and lacks some control objects: toggle buttons, spinner buttons, scroll bars, among others. Nevertheless, getting input from users, say, to configure a DLL function or to input a username, is something you might decide is most convenient to do using the C API. This section provides a bare-bones description of the relevant functions. You should use an alternative approach for more sophisticated interaction with the user.

8.13.1   Displaying an alert dialog box: `xlcAlert`

Overview:	Displays an alert dialog.
Enumeration value:	32886 (x8076)
Callable from:	Commands only.
Return type:	Boolean. See Table 8.30 below.
Arguments:	1: *Message*: The message text (max length 255 characters: the limit of a byte-counted string).
	2: *AlertType*: An optional number determining the type of alert box. (See table below.)
	3: *HelpReference*: An optional reference of the form HelpFile!TopicNum. If this argument is given, a help button is displayed in the dialog.

Table 8.30 `xlcAlert` dialog types

AlertType	Description	Return value
1	Displays message with an OK and a Cancel button.	True if OK pressed. False if Cancel pressed.
2 or omitted	Displays message with an OK button only and an information icon.	True.
3	Displays message with an OK button only and a warning icon.	True.

8.13.2   Displaying a custom dialog box: `xlfDialogBox`

IMPORTANT NOTE: It is recommended that this function is only used for relatively simple dialogs that need to be completely contained within an XLL add-in.

Overview:	Displays a custom dialog box.
Enumeration value:	161 (xa1)
Callable from:	Commands only.
Return type:	Array (`xltypeMulti`) or Boolean false. See below for details.
Arguments:	1: *DialogRef*: An array containing the data needed to define the dialog box (see Table 8.31), or a Boolean false value to clear a still-displayed dialog that has returned control to the DLL.

Returns a modified *copy* of the original array with values of the elements in the 7th column of the 2nd and subsequent rows and the position of the button pressed to exit the dialog in the 7th column, 1st row. Returns false if the Cancel button was pressed.

Strings within the returned array are *copies* of the original strings or are new strings input by the user. (Remember that these are byte-counted and not, in general, null-terminated). A call to `xlFree` should be used to free the memory of the returned array.

The *DialogRef* table must be seven columns wide and at least two rows high. The contents are interpreted as shown in the Table 8.31.

Table 8.31 Custom dialog definition array

1	2	3	4	5	6	7
[HelpRef] Usually blank, with ref placed in 7th col of help button	Dialog Horizontal position	Dialog Vertical position	Dialog width	Dialog height	Dialog name/title	[Default item position]/Item chosen as trigger
Item number	Horizontal position	Vertical position	Item width	Item height	Item text	Initial value/result
...	...	...	...	...	...	...

Positions are measured in screen units from the top left of the dialog. Screen units correspond to characters in the (fixed-width) system font, where each character is 8 units wide and 12 units high. Note that the font used in a C API dialog is *not* in general fixed-width.

Table 8.32 Custom dialog element item numbers

Item number	Item type	Item number	Item type
1	OK button (default)	13	Check box
2	Cancel button	14	Group box
3	OK button	15	List box
4	Cancel button (default)	16	Linked list box
5	Text	17	Icons
6	Text box	18	Linked file list box
7	Integer box	19	Linked drive and directory box
8	Floating point box	20	Directory text box
9	Formula edit box	21	Drop-down list box
10	Reference edit box	22	Drop-down combo box
11	Radio button group	23	Picture button
12	Radio button	24	Help button

Adding 100 to certain item numbers causes the function to return control to the DLL code when the item is clicked on with the dialog still displayed. This enables the command function to alter the dialog, validate input and so on, before returning for more user interaction. The position of the item number chosen in this way is returned in the 1st row, 7th column of the returned array. This feature does not work with edit boxes (items 6, 7, 8, 9 and 10), group boxes (14), the help button (24), or pictures (23). Adding 200 to any item number, disables (greys-out) the item.

Most of the dialog items are simple and no further explanation is required. For some a little more explanation is helpful.

Text and edit boxes

Vertical alignment of a text label to the text that appears in an edit box is important aesthetically. For edit boxes with the default height (set by leaving the height field blank) this is achieved by setting the vertical position of the text to be that of the edit box+3.

Buttons

Selecting a cancel button (2 or 4) causes the dialog to terminate returning FALSE. Pressing any other button causes the function to return the offset of that button in the definition table in the 7th column, 1st row of the returned array.

Where you just require OK and Cancel buttons, you should use either types 1 and 2 together, or 3 and 4, depending on which default action you want to occur if the user presses enter as soon as the dialog appears.

If item width and/or item height are omitted, the button is given the width and/or height of the previous button in the definition table, or default values if this is the first button in the definition table.

Radio buttons

A group of radio buttons (12) must be preceded immediately by a radio group item (11) and must be uninterrupted by other item types. If the radio group item has no text label the group is not contained within a border. If the height and/or width of the radio group are omitted but text is provided, a border is drawn that surrounds the radio buttons and their labels.

List-boxes

The text supplied in a list box item row should either be a name (DLL-internal or on a worksheet) that resolves to a literal array or range of cells. It can also be a string that looks like a literal array, e.g. "{1,2,3,4,5,\"A\",\"B\",\"C\"}" (where coded in a C source file). List-boxes return the position (counting from 1) of the selected item in the list in the 7th column of the list-box item line. Drop-down list-boxes (21) behave exactly as list boxes (15) except that the list is only displayed when the item is selected.

Linked list-boxes

Linked list-boxes (16), linked file-boxes (18) and drop-down combo-boxes (22) should be preceded immediately by an edit box that can support the data types in the list. The lists themselves are drawn from the text field of the definition row which should be a range name or a string that represents a static array. A linked path box (19) must be preceded immediately by a linked file-box (18).

Drop down combo-boxes return the value selected in the 7th column of the associated edit box and the position (counting from 1) of the selected item in the list in the 7th column of the combo-box item line.

Creating dialogs

The difficulty of manually putting together dialogs, with trial-and-error positioning and sizing of components, cried out for the kind of graphical design interface that Excel 5.0 first introduced and that VBA provides in current versions. (This is one of the reasons for *not* using the C API to create dialogs.)

Given that there may be times where it is more appropriate or convenient to package a simple dialog interface into your XLL, the task is made much easier using an XLM macro sheet to prototype the dialog. The steps are:

1. Open a new Excel workbook.
2. Insert an XLM macro sheet by right-clicking on one of the worksheet tabs and selecting Insert. . ./MS Excel 4.0 Macro.

3. Place a label in cell A1 in the macro sheet, say, DlgTest, and define this as a name for cell A2.
4. Place the formula =DIALOG.BOX(DIALOG_DEFN) in cell A2 – (the range name DIALOG_ DEFN is created in a later step).
5. Place the formula =RETURN() in cell A3.
6. Create a table to contain the definition of the dialog (see above) and name the range DIALOG_DEFN. Do not include a title row in the definition. The location of the table is not important.
7. Via the Insert/Name/Define... dialog, define the name DlgTest as a command and assign a keystroke to it for easy running.

By modifying the contents of your named definition range and executing the command macro, you can fairly easily design simple dialogs that can be recoded in C/C++ within the DLL. (This is still a laborious process compared to the use of graphical design tools such as those that now exist in VB.)

Creating a static initialisation of an array of xlopers in C/C++, to hard-code your table, is complicated by the fact that C only provides a very limited ability to initialise unions, such as val in the xloper. Section 6.9 *Initialising xlopers* on page 157 provides a discussion of this subject and an example of a dialog definition table for a simple username and password dialog.

A more complex example dialog is included in the example project on the CD ROM in the Background.cpp source file. It is used to configure and control a background thread used for lengthy worksheet function execution. The workbook used to design this dialog, XLM_ThreadCfg_Dialog.xls, is included on the CD ROM. It also generates cpp_xloper array initialisation strings that can be cut and paste into a C++ source file.

8.13.3 Restricting user input to dialog boxes: xlcDisableInput

Overview:	Restricts all mouse and keyboard input to the dialog rather than Excel.
Enumeration value:	32908 (x808c)
Callable from:	Commands only.
Return type:	Various. See table below.
Arguments:	1: *Disable*: Boolean. True disables input to Excel, false enables it.

Warning: Commands that call this function passing *true* should call passing *false* before returning control to Excel.

8.14   TRAPPING EVENTS

The C API provides a few simple Excel event traps which can easily be associated with DLL commands. The C API enables the setting of traps within the DLL for only a few of its events, namely:

- data coming in from an external DDE source;
- the user double-clicking on a cell in a worksheet;
- the user entering data into a cell in a worksheet;
- the user pressing a certain key combination;
- the user or the system initiating a recalculation;
- the user selecting a new worksheet window;
- the system clock reaching a specified time.

Excel generates many events that cannot be trapped (directly) by the DLL using the C API. For example, it is not possible to trap a change of selection on the worksheet or, most sadly, the opening or closing of a workbook. The most straightforward, albeit slightly messy, way to have your DLL called when a non-C API event occurs is to set a trap within VBA and use this to call into your DLL. For more details of VB events see section 3.4 *Using VBA to trap Excel events* on page 45. For details of how to call into your DLL from VB, see section 3.6 *Using VBA as an interface to external DLL add-ins* on page 48.

8.14.1   Trapping a DDE data update event: `xlcOnData`

Overview: Instructs Excel to call a specified command whenever DDE data
                         is received for a specified worksheet or from a specified source
                         application. The command is called before Excel performs any
                         recalculation of the worksheet resulting from the new data.

Enumeration value: 32907 (x808b)

Callable from: Commands only.

Arguments: 1: *DataSourceSink*: A string determining either the DDE data
                            source application or the worksheet to which the data is being
                            sent.
                         2: *Command*: The name of the command to be run as passed to
                            Excel in the 4th argument to `xlfRegister` or the name of
                            some other command macro or VB function.

DataSourceSink should be in the format `[Book1.xls]Sheet1` if referring to a worksheet or, if referring to a DDE source application, `SourceApp|DataTopic!DataItem` or `SourceApp|DataTopic` or just `SourceApp|`, where the omission of the later parts of the specifier implies a wildcard. The given command is run whenever data is being sent to the sheet (if specified) or from the source application (if specified).

If the *DataSourceSink* argument is missing <u>and</u> a valid *Command* argument is provided, the given command is run whenever any DDE data is received provided that it is not trapped by a previous, more specific, call to this function.

If *Command* is missing, the function clears the command associated with the *DataSourceSink* argument.

8.14.2 Trapping a double-click event: `xlcOnDoubleclick`

Overview	Instructs Excel to call a specified command whenever the user double-clicks any object in the specified worksheet or chart, overriding any default Excel action.
Enumeration value:	33047 (x8117)
Callable from:	Commands only.
Arguments:	1: *SheetRef*: A string of the format [Book1.xls]Sheet1 specifying the sheet to which the event applies.
	2: *Command*: The name of the command to be run as passed to Excel in the 4th argument to `xlfRegister` or the name of some other command macro or VB function.

If *SheetRef* is missing, the command is run whenever this event occurs on any sheet where the event has not already been trapped by a previous, more specific, call to this function.

If *Command* is missing, the function clears the command associated with this event and sheet.

8.14.3 Trapping a worksheet data entry event: `xlcOnEntry`

Overview:	Instructs Excel to call a specified command whenever the user enters new data into the specified worksheet. The command is called before Excel performs any recalculation of the worksheet resulting from the new data.
Enumeration value:	33048 (x8118)
Callable from:	Commands only.
Arguments:	1: *SheetRef*: A string of the format [Book1.xls]Sheet1 specifying the sheet to which the event applies.
	2: *Command*: The name of the command to be run as passed to Excel in the 4th argument to `xlfRegister` or the name of some other command macro or VB function.

If *SheetRef* is missing, the command is run whenever this event occurs on any sheet where the event has not already been trapped by a previous, more specific, call to this function.

If *Command* is missing, the function clears the command associated with this combination of event and sheet.

The use of other C API functions in the called command may be required to, say, determine which cell was changed. (A call to `xlfActiveCell` will determine this.)

8.14.4   Trapping a keyboard event: `xlcOnKey`

Overview: Instructs Excel to call a specified command whenever the user executes the given keystroke.

Enumeration value: 32936 (x80a8)

Callable from: Commands only.

Arguments: 1: *Keystroke*: A string that describes the keystroke to be trapped. (See Table 8.33 below.)

                         2: *Command*: The name of the command to be run as passed to Excel in the 4th argument to `xlfRegister` or the name of some other command macro or VB function.

If *Keystroke* is missing, the command is run whenever this event occurs on any sheet where the event is not already trapped by a previous, more specific, call to this function.

If *Command* is an empty string (`""`) the keystroke is effectively disabled. If *Command* is missing, the function clears the command associated with this keystroke, or re-enables it if it was disabled in previous call.

The *Keystroke* argument is constructed as follows: *[modifier-key-symbol(s)][key-code]*, for example `+{PGDN}`.

The modifier key symbols are `+` (Shift), `^` (Ctrl) and `%` (Alt) and can be used in any combination or not at all. The key code can be any one of the following:

- Any printable single-key character (e.g. `0` or `;` or `a` or `Z`).
- One of the modifier keys `+`, `^` and `%`, passed within braces, e.g. `{^}`.
- Other keys that do not correspond to a single character, represented within braces as shown in the following table.

Table 8.33 Key codes for `xlcOnKey` keyboard traps

Key	Key-code	Key	Key-code
Backspace	{BACKSPACE} {BS}	Home	{HOME}
Break	{BREAK}	Ins	{INSERT}
Caps Lock	{CAPSLOCK}	Left	{LEFT}
Clear	{CLEAR}	Num lock	{NUMLOCK}
Delete	{DELETE} {DEL}	Page down	{PGDN}
Down	{DOWN}	Page up	{PGUP}
End	{END}	Right	{RIGHT}
Numeric keypad enter	{ENTER}	Scroll lock	{SCROLLLOCK}
Enter	~	Tab	{TAB}
Esc	{ESCAPE} {ESC}	Up	{UP}
Help	{HELP}	Function keys	{Fn}, n=1,2,3...

Note: The trapped keyboard event is based on the physical keys pressed, as mapped for the geographical settings, rather than the character interpreted by the operating system. For this reason, pressing the Caps Lock key is itself a keyboard event. Pressing, say, the A key will always return lowercase a regardless of the Caps Lock state. If you want to trap Ctrl-a you would pass the string "^a". If you pass the string "^A" you will need to press Ctrl-Shift-a on the keyboard even if Caps Lock is set; in other words the strings "^A" and "^+a" are equivalent.

8.14.5 Trapping a recalculation event: `xlcOnRecalc`

Overview:	Instructs Excel to call a specified command whenever Excel *is about to* recalculate the specified worksheet, provided that this recalculation is a result of the user pressing {F9} or the equivalent via Excel's built-in dialogs, or as the result of a change in worksheet data. The command is <u>not</u> called where the recalculation is prompted by another command or macro. Unlike other event traps, there can only be one trap for this event.
Enumeration value:	32995 (x80e3)
Callable from:	Commands only.
Arguments:	1: *SheetRef*: A string of the format `[Book1.xls]Sheet1` specifying the sheet to which the event applies.
	2: *Command*: The name of the command to be run as passed to Excel in the 4th argument to `xlfRegister` or the name of some other command macro or VB function.

If *SheetRef* is missing, the command is run whenever this event occurs on any sheet.

If *Command* is missing, the function clears the command associated with this combination of event and sheet.

8.14.6 Trapping a window selection event: `xlcOnWindow`

Overview:	Instructs Excel to call a specified command whenever Excel is about to switch to the specified worksheet. The command is not called where the switch is the result of actions of another command or macro or as a result of a DDE instruction.
Enumeration value:	32906 (x808a)
Callable from:	Commands only.
Arguments:	1: *WindowRef*: A string of the format [Book1.xls]Sheet1[:*n*] specifying the window to which the event applies.
	2: *Command*: The name of the command to be run as passed to Excel in the 4th argument to `xlfRegister` or the name of some other command macro or VB function.

If *WindowRef* is missing, the command is run whenever this event occurs on any window where the event has not already been trapped by a previous, more specific, call to this function.

If *Command* is missing, the function clears the command associated with this combination of event and window.

8.14.7   Trapping a system clock event: `xlcOnTime`

Overview: Instructs Excel to call a specified command when the system
                         clock reaches a specified time.

Enumeration value: 32916 (x8094)

Callable from: Commands only.

Arguments: 1: *Time*: The time as a serial number.

                         2: *Command*: The name of the command to be run as passed
                            to Excel in the 4th argument to `xlfRegister` or the
                            name of some other command macro or VB function.

                         3: *MaxWaitTime*: (Optional.) The time as a serial number that
                            you want Excel to wait before giving up (if it was not able
                            to call the function at the given time).

                         4: Clear: (Optional.) A Boolean that clears a scheduled trap if
                            false.

This function is covered in more detail in section 9.9.1 *Setting up timed calls to DLL commands:* `xlcOnTime` on page 316.

8.15   MISCELLANEOUS COMMANDS AND FUNCTIONS

8.15.1   Disabling screen updating during command execution: `xlcEcho`

Overview: Disables screen updating during command execution.

Enumeration value: 32909 (x808d)

Callable from: Commands only.

Arguments: 1: *UpdateScreen*: Boolean. If true Excel updates the
                            worksheet screen, if false disables it. If omitted, Excel
                            toggles the state.

Note: Screen updating is automatically re-enabled when a command stops executing.

8.15.2   Displaying text in the status bar: `xlcMessage`

Overview: Displays or clears text on the status bar.

Enumeration value: 32890 (x807a)

Callable from: Commands only.

Arguments: 1: *Display*: Boolean. If true, Excel displays the given message
                          and suppresses Excel's status messages. If false, Excel reverts
                          to displaying the usual Excel status messages.
                          2: *MessageText*: The message to display.

8.15.3   Evaluating a cell formula: `xlfEvaluate`

Overview: Converts a string cell formula to a value. If the conversion fails,
                          returns #VALUE!

Enumeration value: 257 (x101)

Callable from: Commands, macro and worksheet functions.

Arguments: 1: *Formula*: Any string that is syntactically correct. Note that an
                          equals sign at the start of the string is optional.

This function is useful for retrieving the values corresponding to named ranges on a worksheet (see the example in section 8.10), and for evaluating functions that are not available via the C API in cases where the COM interface is also not available. (See section 9.5 *Accessing Excel functionality using COM/OLE Automation* on page 295.)

The following exportable worksheet function demonstrates its use:

```
xloper * __stdcall evaluate(xloper * p_formula)
{
   cpp_xloper RetVal;
   Excel4(xlfEvaluate, &RetVal, 1, p_formula);
   return RetVal.ExtractXloper(true);
}
```


8.16   THE `XLCallVer()` C API FUNCTION

This function returns the version number of the 32-bit library and the C API interface functions contained within it. The following example command, simply displays the version number in a dialog box.

```
int __stdcall xl_call_version(void)
{
    cpp_xloper Version(XLCallVer()); // returns an integer
    Version.ConvertToString(false); // convert integer to string
    Excel4(xlcAlert, 0, 1, &Version); // display the string
    return 1;
}
```

9

Miscellaneous Topics

9.1 TIMING FUNCTION EXECUTION IN VB AND C/C++

Section 9.2 *Relative performance of VB, C/C++: Tests and results* relies on the ability to time the execution of both VB and C/C++ DLL worksheet functions. One fairly obvious strategy for timing how long a function takes to execute in Excel would be to do the following:

(i) Record the start time, T1.
(ii) Call the function.
(iii) Record the end time, T2.
(iv) Calculate the test execution time T2 − T1.

There are a number of problems to overcome, however, before getting Excel to do this and these are:

1. How do I start the test?
2. How do I record the time?
3. How do I make sure that steps (i) to (iii) happen in that order with no delays?
4. What if the granularity of the time I can record is large relative to T2 − T1?

1. How do I start the test?

Starting a test is something the tester has to do, and in Excel there are two ways this can be done: (1) by executing a command, (2) by changing the value of a cell via a cell edit. The second method simplifies the test set-up and provides an easy way to force other cells to be recalculated, using trigger values if necessary.

2. How do I record the time?

The obvious (and wrong) answer might be to use Excel's NOW() function, but this is a volatile function and will be recalculated every time Excel feels the need to update the sheet, destroying the results of the test. The right answer is to use a user-defined function with a trigger argument. This will only be recalculated when the trigger argument changes.[1]

3. How do I make sure that steps (i) to (iii) happen in that order with no delays?

To ensure that the time T1 is recorded in step (i) *before* the cell containing the function is called in step (ii), the time T1 should be used as a trigger argument for the function to

---

[1] There are a number of events that will cause Excel to do an entire rebuild of the calculation dependency tree and/or a complete recalculation of all cells. One example is the insertion or deletion of a row or column.

be tested. This requires that the function being tested is user-defined either in VB or in a C/C++ add-in. Given that these are exactly the things we want to compare, this is not a problem.

Ensuring that the test function is called *immediately* after the time T1 is recorded is a little trickier. We know that Excel will not call the test function before T1 has been evaluated as T1 is an argument to the test function. The problems is that we don't know what Excel might choose to do in the meantime. The solution is to not give Excel any other work to do. Create a very simple sheet and have the initial cell edit that started the test to only be a trigger for this test and no others.

So, for example, you could start the test by editing cell A1, record the time of this edit in B1 using the Get_Time() macro, then set up the function call in C1 and finally record the time that Excel finishes calculating C1 with another call to Get_Time() in D1. The time difference can then be calculated in E1. So, these cells would contain the formulae:

Table 9.1 Example execution timing formulae

Cell	Formula
A1	*No formula, just some value acting as a trigger for the test*
B1	=Get_Time(A1)
C1	=Test_Function(B1, *other arguments*)
D1	=Get_Time(C1)
E1	=D1-B1

The code for the VB function Get_Time() is simply:

```
Function Get_Time(trigger As Double) As Double

    Get_Time = Now

End Function
```

Provided that A1, B1 or C1 have no other dependents, the test should give a fairly good measurement.

4. What if the granularity of the time I can record is large relative to T2 – T1?

Excel reports the system time to a granularity of 1/100 of a second. (Just use the NOW() function with a custom time display format of *[h]:mm:ss.000* and you will see that the third decimal place on the seconds is always zero.) Unfortunately, VB's Now function only provides access to the system time rounded down to the nearest second. (Display the results of the Get_Time() VB macro with the same display format if you need convincing.) The C run-time library function time() only provides access to the system time to the nearest second as well.

Timing things to VB or C run-time granularity may be fine if all you're doing is, say, recording the time-stamp of a piece of data from a live feed – the nearest second would be fine – or if the calculation you want to time was expected to take 30 seconds or more. Where you need to calculate time with a finer granularity, you might think the obvious thing to do would be to access Excel's NOW() function from within VB and improve VB's accuracy by two orders of magnitude. Sadly, this is not one of the functions that VBA has access to.[2]

C/C++ programmers have access to a supposedly higher-granularity way of measuring time than either VB or Excel: the C run-time library function clock(), prototyped in time.h. This returns a clock_t variable. The constant CLOCKS_PER_SEC is defined as 1000 so that clock() appears to provide the means of measuring time to the nearest 1/1,000 of a second. Unfortunately, this is not quite true. The value returned by clock() is in fact incremented approximately once every 10.0144 milliseconds, usually by 10 but sometimes by 11 to catch up. This has the effect of giving a value of time that is reasonably correct when rounded to the nearest 10 milliseconds, i.e., to a 100 of a second: effectively no better than Excel's NOW() function.

Nevertheless, the following example function, get_time_C(), uses clock() wrapped in a DLL function to return this value. The function still has to do some work to do to return a time value consistent with Excel and VB's time format. (An alternative solution is to simply access Excel's NOW() function using xlfNow.) This function can be accessed via VB or exported to Excel as part of an XLL.

```
double __stdcall get_time_C(short trigger)
{
    static bool first_call = true;
    static long initial_100ths;
    static double initial_time;

    if(first_call)
    {
        long T, T_last = current_system_time();

        first_call = false; // do this part only once

// Wait till the second changes, so no fractional second
        while((T = current_system_time()) == T_last);

// Round to the nearest 100th second
        initial_100ths = (clock() + 5) / CLOCKS_PER_100TH_SEC;
        return initial_time = (T / (double)SECS_PER_DAY);
    }
    return initial_time + ((clock() + 5) / CLOCKS_PER_100TH_SEC
                    - initial_100ths) / (SECS_PER_DAY * 100.0);
}
```

---

[2] To see the list of worksheet functions that are accessible from within VBA, type WorksheetFunction. in a VB module. On typing the dot, the editor will display a list.

So now we have a way of measuring time to 1/100 of a second, we still have to address the question of the granularity being large relative to T2 – T1. A spreadsheet user might really be in trouble if every cell takes many hundredths of a second to evaluate. In this section, the goal is to test some elementary operations which should take very much less than 1/100 of a second. Fortunately, the final piece of the puzzle is simple to overcome: have the test function repeat the operation many times. In practice, the best solution is to enclose the test within two nested *for* loops, and pass in limits for each loop as arguments to the test function.

Finally, we are in a position to specify what is required to run the test:

1. A `get_time_C()` worksheet function that takes a trigger argument and returns the time to the nearest 1/100 of a second in an Excel-compatible number format.
2. A wrapper function, that calls the test function in two nested *for* loops, and that takes a trigger argument, an outer-loop limit, an inner-loop limit and whatever other arguments are needed by the test code. (The test function itself performs the test operation within the two nested *for* loops.)
3. One version of the wrapper function written in VB and one written in C/C++ so that a fair comparison can be made.[3]

In order to simplify the test, the number of worksheet cells can be reduced by enclosing the two calls to `get_time_C()` in the test function wrapper. An example VB wrapper function would look like this:

```
Declare Function get_time_C Lib "example.dll" (trigger As Integer) _
    As Double

Function VB_Test_Example(trigger As Variant, _
    Inner_Loops As Integer, Outer_Loops As Integer) As Double

    Dim t As Double
    Dim i As Integer
    Dim j As Integer
    Dim Val As Double

    t = get_time_C(0) ' record the start time
    Val = VB_Test_Function(Inner_Loops, Outer_Loops)
    VB_Test_Example = get_time_C(0) - t

End Function
```

The worksheet formulae for running a test would then be:

Table 9.2 Example single-cell timing formula

Cell	Formula
A1	*No formula, just some value acting as a trigger for the test*
B1	=Test_Function(A1, *other arguments*)

---

[3] The intention is to measure the execution time of the test function only. However, some account should be taken of the relative performance of the wrapper functions as well. As later sections show, this is easy to do and the overhead is not that significant.

The equivalent C code wrapper would look like this:

```
double __stdcall  C_test_example(long trigger, long inner_loops,
                                   long outer_loops)
{
    double t = get_time_C(0);
    double val = C_test_fn(0, inner_loops, outer_loops);
    return get_time_C(0) - t;
}
```

The next section discusses a number of test operations carried out in exactly this way.

9.2 RELATIVE PERFORMANCE OF VB, C/C++: TESTS AND RESULTS

This section applies the above test process to the relative performance of VB and C/C++ code for some fundamental types of operations:

Test 0. No action. Tests the relative performance of the wrappers.
Test 1. Assignment of a constant to an integer.
Test 2. Assignment of a constant to a floating-point double.
Test 3. Copying of the value of one integer to another.
Test 4. Copying of the value of one double to another.
Test 5. Assignment of the result of double multiplication to a double.
Test 6. Assignment of the result of an exp() function call to a double.
Test 7. Evaluation of a degree-4 polynomial.
Test 8. Evaluation of the sum of a 10-element double vector.
Test 9. Allocation and de-allocation of memory for an array of doubles.
Test 10. Call to a trivial sub-routine.
Test 11. String manipulation: summing the character values of a string.

More detail, including source code for all of these in C and VB and the test spreadsheet is provided in the example worksheets and VC project on the CD ROM.

It's important to remember that this kind of test is not 100% scientific: many factors can interfere with the results, such as the operating system or Excel deciding to do some housework behind the scenes. The tests results varied slightly (up to ±5%) each time the tests were run, so they should only be used as a guide to help make the decision about which environment makes most sense.

The tests gave the following results:[4]

---

[4] The tests were carried out on a DELL Inspiron 4100 laptop computer running Windows 2000 Professional version 5.0 (Service Pack 1, build 2195), with a 730 Megahertz Intel Pentium 4 processor and 128 Megabytes of RAM of which about 20 were free at the time the test was run. No other applications were using significant CPU during the tests on the PC which was not connected to a network. The DLL tested was built from the **Release** configuration. The version of Excel was 2000.

Table 9.3 VB function test results

	Test action	Inner loop	Outer loop	Other arguments	Seconds to complete
Test0	No action	1,000	30,000		0.72
Test1	Integer const assignment	1,000	30,000		1.99
Test2	Double const assignment	1,000	30,000		2.40
Test3	Integer variable assignment	1,000	30,000		2.24
Test4	Double variable assignment	1,000	30,000		2.23
Test5	Double const multiplication	1,000	30,000		2.39
Test6	Exp() evaluation and assignment	300	30,000		3.68
Test7	Degree-4 double polynomial evaluation (const coefficients)	100	30,000		0.64
Test8	Sum 10-element double vector	100	30,000		1.46
Test9	Double array allocation test	1	30,000	1,000	1.86
Test10	Simple function call	1,000	30,000		10.70
Test11	Sum of ASCII values of string	100	30,000	abcdefghi	19.16

Table 9.4 C function test results

	Test action	Inner loop	Outer loop	Other arguments	Seconds to complete
Test0	No action	1,000	30,000		0.32
Test1	Integer const assignment	1,000	30,000		0.29
Test2	Double const assignment	1,000	30,000		0.29
Test3	Integer variable assignment	1,000	30,000		0.25
Test4	Double variable assignment	1,000	30,000		0.33
Test5	Double const multiplication	1,000	30,000		0.42

Table 9.4 (*continued*)

	Test action	Inner loop	Outer loop	Other arguments	Seconds to complete
Test6	Exp() evaluation and assignment	300	30,000		3.02
Test7	Degree-4 double polynomial evaluation (const coefficients)	100	30,000		0.06
Test8	Sum 10-element double vector	100	30,000		0.07
Test9	Double array allocation test	1	30,000	1,000	0.85
Test10	Simple function call	1,000	30,000		2.37
Test11	Sum of ASCII values of string	1,000	30,000	abcdefghi	0.62

Table 9.5 Test results comparison

	Test Action	Performance ratio C/C++ : VB
Test0	No action	1 : 2.2
Test1	Integer const assignment	1 : 6.7
Test2	Double const assignment	1 : 8.8
Test3	Integer variable assignment	1 : 7.9
Test4	Double variable assignment	1 : 6.8
Test5	Double const multiplication	1 : 5.6
Test6	Exp() evaluation and assignment	1 : 1.1
Test7	Deg-4 double polynomial evaluation (const coefficients)	1 : 9.5
Test8	Sum of double vector elements (10)	1 : 21.8
Test9	Double array allocation test	1 : 2.1
Test10	Simple function call	1 : 4.5
Test11	Sum of ASCII values of string	1 : 309

Notes:

Test 0

This was a *do nothing* test to measure the difference in wrapper function execution times. Interestingly, as you may have noticed, the do nothing test in C took 10% longer to execute than the test which assigned a constant value to either an integer or a double![5]

---

[5] Despite having looked at the assembler output, the author has no explanation for this. There may be a more rational explanation, but perhaps the compiler and Windows have a collective sense of humour.

Tests 1 to 5

These tests show that C/C++ code is faster by a factor of 6 to 8 for regular variable assignments and simple algebraic operations.

Test 6

In this test, most of the time is being spent calling the VB Exp() or the C exp() library functions, which are roughly as efficient as each other. This reflects the fact that, unsurprisingly, VB can call a compiled Microsoft library function just about as quickly as C can. If you take out the times of Test 0 from scaled-up times for Test 6, the ratio becomes even closer at 1 : 1.002. (It is also interesting to note that the statement v = exp(1.5); executes roughly 45 times slower than v = 1.5; and about 40 times slower than v1 = v2.)

Test 7

In both cases the test code was written so as to use the minimum number of multiplications, as well additions, to evaluate the polynomial. The relatively large ratio indicates partly that VB takes far more time to process all of the symbols in the line, despite being partially pre-compiled. This tends to exaggerate the ratios seen in tests 1 through 5.

Test 8

The same reasoning applies in part to this test as Test 7, i.e., the large number of symbols exaggerate the performance differential. However, it's clear that C/C++ is far more efficient at evaluating array index references than VB.

Test 9

This test compares the relative abilities to dynamically allocate memory in the application's process and freeing it again. Given that well-written code should not be doing this too often, the difference here is not significant.

Test 10

The function called in both cases simply returns its Boolean argument. The ratio here seems to be typical of simple statements and operations.

Test 11

In this test it was difficult to make a *fair* comparison without deliberately restraining C and the powerful low-level string manipulation that it makes possible. The C code makes use of C's powerful pointer arithmetic and null-terminated strings to do the job with typical efficiency. VB, on the other hand, was shackled by its lack of efficient low-level string handling.

9.2.1   Conclusion of test results

VB is very efficient, all things considered. However, C/C++ is typically 5 to 10 times faster for simple operations. If a function needs to do a lot of array manipulation then the ratio could be closer to 15 to 20. If you are considering writing intensive matrix manipulation functions or functions that are evaluating complex algebraic expressions then C/C++ is the best solution. This is especially true if the resulting spreadsheet needs to be able to recalculate in near real-time or is going to be large (or if you're the impatient type).

String manipulation is clearly what C excels at (small e). Some might say that test 11 was an unfair test. Not so. If string manipulation is a large part of what you want to do then don't hesitate to use C or C++. String-intensive activities would include functions that, say, read and analysed all types of cell contents and formulae.

9.3   RELATIVE PERFORMANCE OF C API VERSUS VBA CALLING FROM A WORKSHEET CELL

Apart from the code execution speed of C/C++ versus VB, reviewed in the above section, there is also the difference between the time it takes Excel to call a VBA function, compared to an XLL function registered via the C API. This is easily tested using a simple example function:

In C:

```
double __stdcall C_call_test(double d)
{
    return d;
}
```

In VBA:

```
Function VBA_call_test(d As Double)

    VBA_call_test = d

End Function
```

The example spreadsheets Call Speed Test - C API.xls[6] and Call Speed Test - VBA.xls on the CD ROM contain replications of this formula with one cell depending on the previous in the same pattern across all columns from row 2 down. Cell A1 drives a recalculation of all cells. The former workbook contains just over 1,000,000 copies of the function (one per cell) and the latter just over 50,000. From a crude test (counting the seconds), it can be seen that each C API call is made approximately 20 times faster than a VBA call with the VB editor closed and a staggering 2,000 times faster than a VBA call with the editor open. Given that the code execution ratio is only

---

[6] Care should be taken when opening and running this example test sheet as it is very large, over 41 Mbytes, and could cause Excel severe performance problems if there is insufficient available memory.

about 7:1, most of this disparity clearly comes from the difference in the speed of the calling interface.

When calling an XLL function, Excel only has to look up the function in an internal table to obtain the address, prepare the arguments on the stack, call the function, read the result back from the stack and deposit it in the cell. The looking-up of the function address is optimised: the position in the table is noted, so to speak, at the point the function is entered into the cell. This is a very fast overall operation.

When calling a VBA function, Excel has to do all the work that it previously did, but must use the COM interface to prepare arguments, call the function and retrieve the result. As can be seen, this is an extremely slow operation.

In conclusion, where there are a large number of calls to user-defined functions, the benefit of using the C API becomes even more compelling, especially in applications that need to run in near real time. The very latest versions of Excel and Windows support a more direct access of COM DLLs, whether written in VB or C++, from the worksheet, but there is still a significant calling overhead compared to the directness of the C API.

9.4   DETECTING WHEN A WORKSHEET FUNCTION IS CALLED FROM THE PASTE FUNCTION DIALOG (FUNCTION WIZARD)

For a number of reasons, you may not want one of your worksheet functions to evaluate when the user is entering or editing arguments using the Paste Function dialog, otherwise known as the Function Wizard. The reason might be performance or that the function communicates with some remote process, for example. Detecting that your function is being called from this dialog is fairly straightforward.

The dialog has a class name of the form `bosa_sdm_XLn` where n is the current Excel version. Windows provides an API function, `GetClassName()`, that obtains this name from a Windows handle, an `HWND` variable type. It also provides another function, `EnumWindows()`, that calls a supplied callback function (within your DLL) once for every top-level window that is currently open. The callback function only needs to perform the following steps:

1. Check if the parent of this window is the current version of Excel (in case there are multiple versions running).
2. Get the class name from the handle passed in by Windows.
3. Check if the class name is of the form `bosa_sdm_XLn` (ignoring the Excel version number).

The following C++ code demonstrates how to do this.

```
#define CLASS_NAME_BUFFER_SIZE    50

typedef struct
{
    BOOL is_paste_fn;
    short low_hwnd;
}
    fnwiz_enum_struct;
```

```
// The callback function called by Windows for every top-level window
BOOL __stdcall fnwiz_enum_proc(HWND hwnd, fnwiz_enum_struct *p_enum)
{
// Check if the parent window is Excel
    if(LOWORD((DWORD)GetParent(hwnd)) != p_enum->low_hwnd)
        return TRUE; // keep iterating

    char class_name[CLASS_NAME_BUFFER_SIZE + 1];
// Ensure that class_name is always null terminated
    class_name[CLASS_NAME_BUFFER_SIZE] = 0;

    GetClassName(hwnd, class_name, CLASS_NAME_BUFFER_SIZE);

// Do a case-insensitive comparison for the Paste Function window
// class name with the Excel version number truncated
    if(_strnicmp(class_name, "bosa_sdm_xl", 11) == 0)
    {
        p_enum->is_paste_fn = TRUE;
        return FALSE;  // Tells Windows to stop iterating
    }
    return TRUE; // Tells Windows to continue iterating
}

bool called_from_paste_fn_dlg(void)
{
    xloper hwnd = {0.0, xltypeNil}; // super-safe

    if(Excel4(xlGetHwnd, &hwnd, 0))
// Can't get Excel's main window handle, so assume not
        return false;

    fnwiz_enum_struct es = {FALSE, hwnd.val.w};
    EnumWindows((WNDENUMPROC)fnwiz_enum_proc, (LPARAM)&es);

    return es.is_paste_fn == TRUE;
}
```

Note: There are other times when Excel will call functions with this class active, even though it is not the Function Wizard dialog displayed. One example is during a search and replace that causes Excel to re-enter modified formulae into a worksheet. If your function returns some error value when called from the wizard, the newly changed cells will contain this value and you will need to force a recalculation to flush these errors through.

9.5   ACCESSING EXCEL FUNCTIONALITY USING COM/OLE AUTOMATION USING C++

Full coverage of the COM/OLE Automation and IDispatch interfaces to Excel, as used by VBA, for example, is beyond the scope of this book. One reason for this is that you don't often need to do things that OLE permits and the C API does not when writing high-performance worksheet functions. There are, however, a few situations where COM might be useful or important and this section provides a rudimentary coverage of some of these.

It is important to note that Excel was not designed to allow OLE Automation calls during *normal* calls to either XLL commands or functions. The Microsoft view appears to be that such calls probably won't work, are definitely not safe and are not recommended.

The MSDN Microsoft Knowledge Base Article (KBA) 301443: *Automation Calls to Excel from an XLL May Fail or Return Unexpected Results* explains why. However, many developers' experience is that in certain cases it is safe to call COM, although care is needed. Table 9.6 summarises these cases:

Table 9.6 When it is safe to call Excel's COM interface

Excel's COM interface called from where:	Is it safe?
From an XLL function called directly by Excel	No (see KBA 301443)
From an XLL command called directly by Excel. (This includes the `xlAuto*` interface functions[7] and C API event traps such as `xlcOnTime`.)	KBA 301443 says no. Many developers say yes.
From a Window's call-back to an XLL	No
From an XLL function called via VBA	No
From an XLL command called via VBA	Yes
From a stand-alone application	Yes
From a COM DLL	Yes, subject to the usual distinctions between commands and functions and the associated restrictions.

As an aside, there are a few cases where the C API, accessed via `Excel4()` and `Excel4v()`, is not available even to the XLL. Calling these functions at these times will have unpredictable results and almost certainly cause Excel to crash. The two most important cases where the C API is not available are (1) from a background thread, and (2) when the DLL has been called directly by Windows as a result of, say, a timed call-back request or during calls to `DllMain`. (See sections 8.4 *What C API functions can the DLL call and when* and 9.9 *Multi-tasking, multi-threading and asynchronous calls in DLLs* for more details.)

Where an XLL worksheet function needs to access, say, a new function that was not available when the C API was written, the C API function `xlfEvaluate` should be used, since the COM interface cannot safely be called. (See section 8.15.3 *Evaluating a cell formula: xlfEvaluate* on page 283.)

There are two ways to access Excel's functionality using COM, and these are commonly know as *late binding* and *early* (or *vtable*) *binding*. Without going into too much detail, this section only discusses late binding. This is the method by which a program (or DLL) must interrogate Excel's objects at run-time before it is able to access them. There is an inefficiency associated with this, and the marshalling and conversion of arguments to object method calls, that is largely addressed and removed by early binding. With early binding, the compiler makes use of an object library to remove this inefficiency, and is

---

[7] Note that `xlAutoFree` is an exception: it is a macro-sheet function equivalent, not a command.

not covered here in order to keep this section simple and compiler-independent. However, most of the inefficiency can be removed with the use of static or global variables so that the interrogations need only be done once.

If you want to access COM-exposed Excel methods or properties other than those discussed in the following sections, you can fairly easily get the syntax and names of these from VBA, either by recording a macro or via the VBA Excel help.

As a final note before moving on, this section only shows code examples that work when part of a C++ source module. The syntax for C modules is a little different, and is not described, in the interests of simplicity.

9.5.1   Initialising and un-initialising COM

A number of things need to be initialised when the XLL is activated and then un-initialised when the XLL is deactivated. The following outline and code examples get around many of the inefficiencies of late binding by caching object references and dispatch function IDs (DISPIDs) in global or static variables.

The steps to initialise the interface are:

1. Include the system header <comdef.h> in source files using the COM/OLE interface.
2. Make sure Excel has registered itself in the ROT (Running Object Table).[8]
3. Initialise the COM interface with a call to OleInitialize(NULL).
4. Initialise a CLSID variable with a call to CLSIDFromProgID().
5. Initialise an IUnknown object pointer with a call to GetActiveObject(). If there are two instances of Excel running, GetActiveObject() will return the first.
6. Initialise a global pointer to an IDispatch object for Excel with a call to the QueryInterface() method of the IUnknown object.

The Excel.Application's methods and properties are now available. The most sensible place to call the function that executes these steps is from xlAutoOpen(). The following code shows how these steps can be accomplished:

```
IDispatch *pExcelDisp = NULL; // Global pointer

bool InitExcelOLE(void)
{
    if(pExcelDisp)
        return true; // already initialised

// Make sure Excel is registered in the Running Object Table. Even
// if it already has, telling it to do so again will do no harm.
    HWND hWnd;
    if((hWnd = FindWindow("XLMAIN", 0)) != NULL)
    {
// Sending WM_USER + 18 tells Excel to register itself in the ROT
        SendMessage(hWnd, WM_USER + 18, 0, 0);
    }

// Initialise the COM library for this compartment
```

---

[8] The Microsoft Knowledge Base Articles 147573, 153025 and 138723 provide more background on this topic as well as links to related articles.

```
    OleInitialize(NULL);

    CLSID clsid;
    HRESULT hr;
    char cErr[64];
    IUnknown *pUnk;

    hr = CLSIDFromProgID(L"Excel.Application", &clsid);

    if(FAILED(hr))
    {
// This is unlikely unless you have forgotten to call OleInitialize
        sprintf(cErr, "Error, hr = 0x%08lx", hr);
        MessageBox(NULL, cErr, "CLSIDFromProgID",
                    MB_OK | MB_SETFOREGROUND);
        return false;
    }

    hr = GetActiveObject(clsid, NULL, &pUnk);

    if(FAILED(hr))
    {
// Excel may not have registered itself in the ROT
        sprintf(cErr, "Error, hr = 0x%08lx", hr);
        MessageBox(NULL, cErr, "GetActiveObject",
                    MB_OK | MB_SETFOREGROUND);
        return false;
    }

    hr = pUnk->QueryInterface(IID_IDispatch, (void**)&pExcelDisp);

    if(FAILED(hr))
    {
        sprintf(cErr, "Error, hr = 0x%08lx", hr);
        MessageBox(NULL, cErr, "QueryInterface",
                    MB_OK | MB_SETFOREGROUND);
        return false;
    }
// We no longer need pUnk
    pUnk->Release();

// We have now done everything necessary to be able to access all of
// the methods and properties of the Excel.Application interface.
    return true;
}
```

When the XLL is unloaded the XLL should undo the above steps in the following order:

1. Release the global IDispatch object pointer with a call to its Release() method.
2. Set the global IDispatch object pointer to NULL to ensure that subsequent reactivation of the XLL is not fooled into thinking that the object still exists.
3. Un-initialise the COM interface with a call to OleUninitialize().

The most sensible place to call the function that executes these steps is xlAutoClose(), making sure that this is after any other function calls that might still want to access COM.

The following code shows how these steps can be accomplished:

```
void UninitExcelOLE(void)
{
// Release the IDispatch pointer. This will decrement its RefCount
    pExcelDisp->Release();
    pExcelDisp = NULL; // Good practice
    OleUninitialize();
}
```

Once this is done, the Excel application's methods and properties can fairly straight-forwardly be accessed as demonstrated in the following sections. Note that access to Excel's worksheet functions, for example, requires the getting of the worksheet functions interface, something that is beyond the scope of this book.

9.5.2 Getting Excel to recalculate worksheets using COM

This is achieved using the Calculate method exposed by Excel via the COM interface. Once the above initialisation of the pExcelDisp IDispatch object has taken place, the following code will have the equivalent effect of the user pressing the {F9} key. Note that the call to the GetIDsOfNames() method is executed only once for the Calculate command, greatly speeding up subsequent calls.

```
HRESULT OLE_ExcelCalculate(void)
{
    if(!pExcelDisp)
       return S_FALSE;

    static DISPID dispid = 0;
    DISPPARAMS Params;
    char cErr[64];
    HRESULT hr;

// DISPPARAMS has four members which should all be initialised
    Params.rgdispidNamedArgs = NULL; // Dispatch IDs of named args
    Params.rgvarg = NULL; // Array of arguments
    Params.cArgs = 0; // Number of arguments
    Params.cNamedArgs = 0; // Number of named arguments

// Get the Calculate method's dispid
    if(dispid == 0) // first call to this function
    {
// GetIDsOfNames will only be called once. Dispid is cached since it
// is a static variable. Subsequent calls will be faster.

        wchar_t *ucName = L"Calculate";
        hr = pExcelDisp->GetIDsOfNames(IID_NULL, &ucName, 1,
                 LOCALE_SYSTEM_DEFAULT, &dispid);

        if(FAILED(hr))
        {
// Perhaps VBA command or function does not exist
            sprintf(cErr, "Error, hr = 0x%08lx", hr);
            MessageBox(NULL, cErr, "GetIDsOfNames",
```

```
                   MB_OK | MB_SETFOREGROUND);
               return hr;
          }
     }

// Call the Calculate method
     hr = pExcelDisp->Invoke(dispid, IID_NULL, LOCALE_SYSTEM_DEFAULT,
             DISPATCH_METHOD, &Params, NULL, NULL, NULL);

     if(FAILED(hr))
     {
// Most likely reason to get an error is because of an error in a
// UDF that makes a COM call to Excel or some other automation
// interface
         sprintf(cErr, "Error, hr = 0x%08lx", hr);
         MessageBox(NULL, cErr, "Calculate", MB_OK | MB_SETFOREGROUND);
     }
     return hr; // = S_OK if successful
}
```

Note that calls to `Invoke` do not have to be method calls such as this. `Invoke` is also called for accessor functions that get and/or set Excel properties. For a full explanation of `Invoke`'s syntax, see the Win32 SDK help.

9.5.3 Calling user-defined commands using COM

This is achieved using the Run method exposed by Excel via the COM interface. Once the above initialisation of the `pExcelDisp` `IDispatch` object has taken place, the following code will run any command that takes no arguments and that has been registered with Excel in this session. (The function could, of course, be generalised to accommodate commands that take arguments.) Where the command is within the XLL, the required parameter `cmd_name` should be the same as the 4th argument passed to the `xlfRegister` function, i.e., the name Excel recognises the command rather than the source code name. Note that the call to the `GetIDsOfNames()` method to get the `DISPID` is done only once for the Run command, greatly speeding up subsequent calls.

```
#define MAX_COM_CMD_LEN    512

HRESULT OLE_RunXllCommand(char *cmd_name)
{
    static DISPID dispid = 0;
    VARIANTARG Command;
    DISPPARAMS Params;
    HRESULT hr;
    wchar_t w[MAX_COM_CMD_LEN + 1];
    char cErr[64];
    int cmd_len = strlen(cmd_name);

    if(!pExcelDisp || !cmd_name || !*cmd_name
```

```
    || (cmd_len = strlen(cmd_name)) > MAX_COM_CMD_LEN)
        return S_FALSE;

    try
    {
// Convert the byte string into a wide char string.  A simple C-style
// type cast would not work!
        mbstowcs(w, cmd_name, cmd_len + 1);

        Command.vt = VT_BSTR;
        Command.bstrVal = SysAllocString(w);

        Params.rgdispidNamedArgs = NULL;
        Params.rgvarg = &Command;
        Params.cArgs = 1;
        Params.cNamedArgs = 0;

        if(dispid == 0)
        {
            wchar_t *ucName = L"Run";
            hr = pExcelDisp->GetIDsOfNames(IID_NULL, &ucName, 1,
                LOCALE_SYSTEM_DEFAULT, &dispid);

            if(FAILED(hr))
            {
                sprintf(cErr, "Error, hr = 0x%08lx", hr);
                MessageBox(NULL, cErr, "GetIDsOfNames",
                    MB_OK|MB_SETFOREGROUND);

                SysFreeString(Command.bstrVal);
                return hr;
            }
        }

        hr = pExcelDisp->Invoke(dispid,IID_NULL,LOCALE_SYSTEM_DEFAULT,
                DISPATCH_METHOD, &Params, NULL, NULL, NULL);

        if(FAILED(hr))
        {
            sprintf(cErr, "Error, hr = 0x%08lx", hr);
            MessageBox(NULL, cErr, "Invoke",
                MB_OK | MB_SETFOREGROUND);

            SysFreeString(Command.bstrVal);
            return hr;
        }
        // Success.
    }
    catch(_com_error &ce)
    {
// If COM throws an exception, we end up here. Most probably we will
// get a useful description of the error.

        MessageBoxW(NULL, ce.Description(), L"Run",
            MB_OK | MB_SETFOREGROUND);

// Get and display the error code in case the message wasn't helpful
        hr = ce.Error();
```

```
        sprintf(cErr, "Error, hr = 0x%081x", hr);
        MessageBox(NULL, cErr, "The Error code",
            MB_OK|MB_SETFOREGROUND);
    }
    SysFreeString(Command.bstrVal);
    return hr;
}
```

9.5.4 Calling user-defined functions using COM

This is achieved using the Run method exposed by Excel via the COM interface.

There are some limitations on the exported XLL functions that can be called using COM: the OLE Automation interface for Excel only accepts and returns Variants of types that this interface supports. It is not possible to pass or retrieve Variant equivalents of xloper types xltypeSRef, xltypeSRef, xltypeMissing, xltypeNil or xltypeFlow. Only types xltypeNum, xltypeInt, xltypeBool, xltypeErr and xltypeMulti arrays of these types have Variant equivalents that are supported. Therefore only functions that accept and return these things can be accessed in this way. (The cpp_xloper class contains xloper-VARIANT conversion routines.)

Once the above initialisation of the pExcelDisp IDispatch object has taken place, the following code will run any command that has been registered with Excel in this session. Where the command is within the XLL, the parameter CmdName should be same as the 4th argument passed to the xlfRegister function, i.e. the name Excel recognises the command by rather than the source code name. Note that the call to the GetIDsOfNames() method to get the DISPID is executed only once for the Run command, greatly speeding up subsequent calls.

```
// Run a registered XLL function.  The name of the function is the
// 1st element of ArgArray, and NumArgs is 1 + the number of args
// the XLL function takes.  Function can only take and return
// Variant types that are supported by Excel.

HRESULT OLE_RunXllFunction(VARIANT &RetVal, int NumArgs,
                           VARIANTARG *ArgArray)
{
    if(!pExcelDisp)
        return S_FALSE;

    static DISPID dispid = 0;
    DISPPARAMS Params;
    HRESULT hr;

    Params.cArgs = NumArgs;
    Params.rgvarg = ArgArray;
    Params.cNamedArgs = 0;

    if(dispid == 0)
    {
        wchar_t *ucName = L"Run";
        hr = pExcelDisp->GetIDsOfNames(IID_NULL, &ucName, 1,
            LOCALE_SYSTEM_DEFAULT, &dispid);
```

```
        if(hr != S_OK)
            return hr;
    }

    if(dispid)
    {
        VariantInit(&RetVal);
        hr = pExcelDisp->Invoke(dispid, IID_NULL,
            LOCALE_SYSTEM_DEFAULT, DISPATCH_METHOD, &Params,
            &RetVal, NULL, NULL);
    }
    return hr;
}
```

9.5.5   Calling XLM functions using COM

This can be done using the ExecuteExcel4Macro method. This provides access to less of Excel's current functionality than is available via VBA. However, there may be times where it is simpler to use ExecuteExcel4Macro than COM. For example, you could set a cell's note using the XLM NOTE via ExecuteExcel4Macro, or you could perform the COM equivalent of the following VB code:

```
With Range("A1")
    .AddComment
    .Comment.Visible = False
    .Comment.Text Text:="Test comment."
End With
```

Using late binding, the above VB code is fairly complex to replicate. Using early binding, once set up with a capable compiler, programming in C++ is almost as easy as in VBA.

The syntax of the ExecuteExcel4Macro method is straightforward and can be found using the VBA online help. The C/C++ code to execute the method is easily created by modifying the OLE_RunXllCommand() function above to use this method instead of L"Run".

9.5.6   Calling worksheet functions using COM

When using late binding, worksheet functions are mostly called using the Evaluate method. This enables the evaluation, and therefore the calculation, of anything that can be entered into a worksheet cell. Within VB, worksheet functions can be called more directly, for example, Excel.WorksheetFunction.LogNormDist(...). Using late binding, the interface for WorksheetFunction would have to be obtained and then the dispid of the individual worksheet function. As stated above, using early binding, once set up with a capable compiler, programming in C++ is almost as easy as in VBA.

The following example function evaluates a string expression placing the result in the given Variant, returning S_OK if successful.

```
#define MAX_COM_EXPR_LEN     1024

HRESULT CallVBAEvaluate(char *expr, VARIANT &RetVal)
{
    static DISPID dispid = 0;
    VARIANTARG String;
    DISPPARAMS Params;
    HRESULT hr;
    wchar_t w[MAX_COM_EXPR_LEN + 1];
    char cErr[64];
    int expr_len;

    if(!pExcelDisp || !expr || !*expr
    || (expr_len = strlen(expr)) > MAX_COM_EXPR_LEN)
        return S_FALSE;

    try
    {
        VariantInit(&String);

// Convert the byte string into a wide char string
        mbstowcs(w, expr, expr_len + 1);

        String.vt = VT_BSTR;
        String.bstrVal = SysAllocString(w);

        Params.rgdispidNamedArgs = NULL;
        Params.rgvarg = &String;
        Params.cArgs = 1;
        Params.cNamedArgs = 0;

        if(dispid == 0)
        {
            wchar_t *ucName = L"Evaluate";
            hr = pExcelDisp->GetIDsOfNames(IID_NULL, &ucName, 1,
                LOCALE_SYSTEM_DEFAULT, &dispid);

            if(FAILED(hr))
            {
                sprintf(cErr, "Error, hr = 0x%08lx", hr);
                MessageBox(NULL, cErr, "GetIDsOfNames",
                    MB_OK | MB_SETFOREGROUND);

                SysFreeString(String.bstrVal);
                return hr;
            }
        }

// Initialise the VARIANT that receives the return value, if any.
// If we don't care we can pass NULL to Invoke instead of &RetVal
        VariantInit(&RetVal);

        hr = pExcelDisp->Invoke(dispid,IID_NULL,LOCALE_SYSTEM_DEFAULT,
        DISPATCH_METHOD, &Params, &RetVal, NULL, NULL);

        if(FAILED(hr))
        {
            sprintf(cErr, "Error, hr = 0x%08lx", hr);
            MessageBox(NULL, cErr, "Invoke",
                MB_OK | MB_SETFOREGROUND);
            SysFreeString(String.bstrVal);
            return hr;
```

```
        }
        // Success.
    }
    catch(_com_error &ce)
    {
// If COM throws an exception, we end up here. Most probably we will
// get a useful description of the error.  You can force arrival in
// this block by passing a division by zero in the string

        MessageBoxW(NULL, ce.Description(), L"Evaluate",
            MB_OK | MB_SETFOREGROUND);

// Get and display the error code in case the message wasn't helpful
        hr = ce.Error();

        sprintf(cErr, "Error, hr = 0x%08lx", hr);
        MessageBox(NULL, cErr, "The error code",
            MB_OK | MB_SETFOREGROUND);
    }
    SysFreeString(String.bstrVal);
    return hr;
}
```

9.6   MAINTAINING LARGE DATA STRUCTURES WITHIN THE DLL

Suppose you have a DLL function, call it `UseArray`, that takes as an argument a large array of data or other data structure that has been created by another function in the same DLL, call it `MakeArray`. The most obvious and easiest way of making this array available to `UseArray` would be to return the array from `MakeArray` to a range of worksheet cells, then call `UseArray` with a reference to that range of cells. The work that then gets done each time `MakeArray` is called is as follows:

1. The DLL creates the data structure in a call to `MakeArray`.
2. The DLL creates, populates and returns an array structure that Excel understands. (See sections 6.2.2 *Excel floating-point array structure: `xl_array`* and 6.8.7 *Array (mixed type): `xltypeMulti`*.)
3. Excel copies out the data into the spreadsheet cells from which `MakeArray` was called (as an array formula) and frees the resources (which might involve a call to `xlAutoFree`).
4. Excel recalculates all cells that depend on the returned values, including `UseArray`.
5. Excel passes a reference to the range of cells to `UseArray`.
6. The DLL converts the reference to an array of values.
7. The DLL uses the values.

Despite its simplicity of implementation, there are a number of disadvantages with the above approach:

- `MakeArray` might return a variable-sized array which can only be returned to a block of cells whose size is fixed from edit to edit.
- There is significant overhead in the conversion and hand-over of the data.
- There is significant overhead in keeping large blocks of data in the spreadsheet.

- The data structures are limited in size by the dimensions of the spreadsheet.
- The interim data are in full view of the spreadsheet user; a problem if they are private or confidential.

If the values in the data structure do not need to be viewed or accessed directly from the worksheet, then a far more efficient approach is as follows:

1. DLL creates the data structure in a call to `MakeArray` as a persistent object.
2. DLL creates a text label that it can later associate with the data structure and returns this to Excel.
3. Excel recalculates all cells that depend on the returned label, including `UseArray`.
4. Excel passes the label to `UseArray`.
5. DLL converts the label to some reference to the data structure.
6. DLL uses the original data structure directly.

Even if the structure's data *do* need to be accessed, the DLL can export access functions that can get (and set) values indirectly. (When setting values in this way it is important to remember that Excel will not automatically recalculate the data structure's dependants, and trigger arguments may be required.) These access functions can be made to operate at least as efficiently as Excel's INDEX(), MATCH() or LOOKUP() functions.

This strategy keeps control of the order of calculation of dependant cells on the spreadsheet, with many instances of `UseArray` being able to use the result of a single call to `MakeArray`. It is a good idea to change the label returned in some way after every recalculation, say, by appending a sequence number. (See section 2.11 *Excel recalculation logic*, for a discussion of how Excel recalculates dependants when the precedents have been recalculated and how this is affected by whether the precedent's values change or not.)

To implement this strategy safely, it is necessary to generate a unique label that cannot be confused with the return values of other calls to the same or similar functions. It is also necessary to make sure that there is adequate clearing up of resources in the event that a formula for `MakeArray` gets deleted or overwritten or the workbook gets closed. This creates a need to keep track of those cells from which `MakeArray` has been called. The next section covers the most sensible and robust way to do just this. The added complexity of keeping track of calls, compared with returning the array in question, means that where `MakeArray` returns a small array, or one that will not be used frequently, this strategy is overkill. However, for large, computationally intense calculations, the added efficiency makes it worth the effort. The class discussed in section 9.7 *A C++ Excel name class example,* `xlName`, on page 307, simplifies this effort considerably.

A simpler approach is to return a sequence number, and not worry about keeping track of the calling cell. However, you should only do this when you know that you will only be maintaining the data structure from one cell, in order to avoid many cells trying to set conflicting values. A changing sequence number ensures that dependencies and recalculations are handled properly by Excel, although it can only be used as a trigger, not a reference to the data structure. A function that uses this trigger must be able to find the data structure without being supplied a reference: it must know from the context or from other arguments. This simpler strategy works well where the DLL needs to maintain a table of global or unique data. Calls to `MakeArray` would update the table and return an incremented sequence number. Calls to UseArray would be triggered to recalculate something that depended on the values in the table.

9.7   A C++ EXCEL NAME CLASS EXAMPLE, xlName

This section describes a class that encapsulates the most common named range handling tasks that an add-in is likely to need to do. In particular it facilitates:

- the creation of references to already-defined names;
- the discovery of the defined name corresponding to a given range reference;
- the reading of values from worksheet names (commands and macro sheet functions only);
- the assignment of values to worksheet names (commands only);
- the creation and deletion of worksheet names (commands only);
- the creation and deletion of DLL-internal names (all DLL functions);
- the assignment of an internal name to the calling cell.

It would be possible to build much more functionality into a class than is contained in xlName, but the point here is to highlight the benefit of even a simple wrapper to the C API's name-handling capabilities. A more sophisticated class would, for example, provide some exception handling – a subject deliberately not covered by this book.

The definition of the class follows. (Note that the class uses the cpp_xloper class for two of its data members.) The definition and code are contained in the example project on the CD ROM in the files XllNames.h and XllNames.cpp respectively.

```
class xlName
{
public:
//-------------------------------------------------------------------
// constructors & destructor
//-------------------------------------------------------------------
    xlName():m_Defined(false),m_RefValid(false),m_Worksheet(false){}
    xlName(char *name) {Set(name);} // Reference to existing range
    ~xlName() {Clear();}

// Copy constructor uses operator= function
    xlName(const xlName & source) {*this= source;}

//-------------------------------------------------------------------
// Overloaded operators
//-------------------------------------------------------------------
// Object assignment operator
    xlName& operator =(const xlName& source);

//-------------------------------------------------------------------
// Assignment operators place values in cell(s) that range refers to.
// Cast operators retrieve values or assign nil if range is not valid
// or conversion was not possible.  Casting to char * will return
// dynamically allocated memory that the caller must free.  Casting
// to xloper can also assign memory that caller must free.
//-------------------------------------------------------------------

    void operator=(int);
    void operator=(bool b);
```

```
    void operator=(double);
    void operator=(WORD, e);
    void operator=(char *);
    void operator=(xloper *); // same type as passed-in xloper
    void operator=(VARIANT *); // same type as passed-in Variant
    void operator=(xl_array *array);
    void operator+=(double);
    void operator++(void)  {operator+=(1.0);}
    void operator--(void)  {operator+=(-1.0);}
    operator int(void);
    operator bool(void);
    operator double(void);
    operator char *(void); // DLL-allocated copy, caller must free

    bool IsDefined(void) {return m_Defined;}
    bool IsRefValid(void) {return m_RefValid;}
    bool IsWorksheetName(void) {return m_Worksheet;}
    char *GetDef(void); // get definition (caller must free string)
    char *GetName(void); // returns a copy that the caller must free
    bool GetValues(cpp_xloper &Values); // contents as xltypeMulti
    bool SetValues(cpp_xloper &Values);
    bool NameIs(char *name);
    bool Refresh(void); // refreshes state of name and defn
    bool SetToRef(xloper *, bool internal); // ref's name if exists
    bool SetToCallersName(void); // set to caller's name if it exists
    bool NameCaller(char *name); // create internal name for caller
    bool Set(char *name); // Create a reference to an existing range
    bool Define(xloper *p_definition, bool in_dll);
    bool Define(char *name, xloper *p_definition, bool in_dll);
    void Delete(void); // Delete name and free instance resources
    void Clear(void); // Clear instance memory but don't delete name
    void SetNote(char *text); // Doesn't work - might be C API bug
    char *GetNote(void);

protected:
    bool m_Defined; // Name has been defined
    bool m_RefValid; // Name's definition (if a ref) is valid
    bool m_Worksheet; // Name is worksheet name, not internal to DLL
    cpp_xloper m_RangeRef;
    cpp_xloper m_RangeName;
};
```

Note that the overloaded operator (char *) returns the contents of the named cell as a C string (which needs to be freed by the caller). The function GetName() returns the name of the range as a C string (which also needs to be freed by the caller).

A simple example of the use of this class is the function range_name() which returns the defined name corresponding to the given range reference. This function is also included in the example project on the CD ROM and is registered with Excel as RangeName(). Note that the function is registered with the type string "RRP#!" so that the first argument is passed as a reference rather than being de-referenced to a value, as happens with the second argument.

```
xloper * __stdcall range_name(xloper *p_ref, xloper *p_dll)
{
    xlName R;
```

```
// Are we looking for a worksheet name or a DLL name?
   bool dll = (p_dll->xltype==xltypeBool && p_dll->val._bool != 0);

   if(!R.SetToRef(p_ref, dll))
      return p_xlErrRef;

   char *p = R.GetName();
   cpp_xloper RetVal(p);
   free(p);

   return RetVal.ExtractXloper(false);
}
```

The following section provides other examples of the use of this class as well as listings of some of the code.

9.8   KEEPING TRACK OF THE CALLING CELL OF A DLL FUNCTION

Consider a worksheet function, call it `CreateOne`, which creates a data structure that is unique to the cell from which the function is called. There are a number of things that have to be considered:

- What happens if the user moves the calling cell and Excel recalculates the function? How will the function know that the thing originally created is still to be associated with the cell in its new position, instead of creating a new one for the new cell location?
- What happens if the user clears the formula from the cell? What happens if the user deletes the cell with a column or row deletion or by pasting another cell over it? What happens if the worksheet is deleted or the workbook closed? How will the DLL know how to clean up the resources that the thing was using?

If these questions cannot be addressed properly in your DLL, then you will spring memory leaks (at the very least). The same questions arise where a function is sending some request to a remote process or placing a task on a background thread. The answer to these issues all revolve around an ability to keep track of the calling cell that created the internal object, or remote request, or background task. In general, this needs to be done when:

- The DLL is maintaining large data structures in the DLL (see above section).
- A background thread is used to perform lengthy computations. The DLL needs to know how to return the result to the right cell when next called, bearing in mind the cell may have been moved in the meantime.
- The cell is being used as a means of contributing data, that is only allowed to have one source of updates, to a remote application.
- The cell is being used to create a request for data from a remote application.

Finding out which cell called a worksheet function is done using the C API function `xlfCaller`. However, given that the user can move/delete/overwrite a cell, the cell reference itself cannot be relied upon to be constant from one call to the next. The solution is to name the calling cell, that is, define a name whose definition is the range reference of the calling cell. For a worksheet function to name the calling cell, the name can only be an internal DLL name created using xlfSetName. (Worksheet names can only be created from commands.) The xlfSetName function is used to define a hidden DLL name. As with regular worksheet names, Excel takes care of altering the definition of the name whenever the corresponding cell is moved. Also, the DLL can very straightforwardly check that the definition is still valid (for example, that the cell has not been deleted in a row or column delete) and that it still contains the function for which the name was originally created.

The class discussed in section 9.7 *A C++ Excel name class example,* xlName, on page 307, contains a member function that initialises a class instance to the internal name that corresponds to the calling cell, if it exists, or names it otherwise. Many of the code examples that follow use this class which is provided in the example project on the CD ROM. The sections that immediately follow use the class' member function code to demonstrate the handling of internal names, etc.

9.8.1   Generating a unique name

Generating a valid and unique name for a cell is not too complex and various methods can be devised that will do this. Here's an example:

1. Get the current time as an integer in the form of seconds from some base time.
2. Increment a counter for the number of names created within this second.
3. Create a name that incorporates text representations these two numbers.[9] (This could be a simple 0–9 representation or something more compact if storage space and string comparison speed are concerns.)

The following code shows an example of just such a method:

```
#include <windows.h>
#include <stdio.h>
#include <time.h>

char *make_unique_name(void)
{
    time_t time_t_T;
    static long name_count = 0;
    static unsigned long T_last = 0;

    time(&time_t_T);
    tm tm_T = *localtime(&time_t_T);

// Need an unsigned long to contain max possible value
    unsigned long T = tm_T.tm_sec + 60 * (tm_T.tm_min
        + 60 * (tm_T.tm_hour + 24 * (tm_T.tm_yday
        + 366 * tm_T.tm_year % 100)));

    if(T != T_last)
    {
        T_last = T;
        name_count = 0;
    }

    char buffer[32]; // More than enough space
```

---

[9] The name created must conform to the rules described in section 8.10 *Working with Excel names* on page 239.

```
// Increment name_count so that names created in the current
// second are still unique.  The name_count forms the first
// part of the name.
   int ch_count = sprintf(buffer, "x%ld.", ++name_count);

   int r;
// Represent the time number in base 62 using 0-9, A-Z, a-z.
// Puts the characters most likely to differ at the front
// of the name to optimise name searches and comparisons
   for(;T; T /= 62)
   {
       if((r = T % 62) < 10)
           r += '0';
       else if(r < 36)
           r += 'A' - 10;
       else
           r += 'a' - 36;

       buffer[ch_count++] = r;
   }
   buffer[ch_count] = 0;

// Make a copy of the string and return it
   char *new_name = (char *)malloc(ch_count + 1);
   strcpy(new_name, buffer);
   return new_name; // caller must free the memory
}
```

9.8.2 Obtaining the internal name of the calling cell

The steps for this are:

1. Get a reference to the calling cell using xlfCaller.
2. Convert the reference to a full address specifier complete with workbook and sheet
   name in R1C1 form using xlfReftext.
3. Get the name, if it exists, from the R1C1 reference using xlfGetDef.

The following two pieces of code list two member functions of the xlName class that,
together, perform these steps.

```
bool xlName::SetToCallersName(void)
{
    Clear();

// Get a reference to the calling cell
    cpp_xloper Caller;
    int xl4 = Excel4(xlfCaller, &Caller, 0);
    Caller.SetExceltoFree();

    if(xl4) // if xlfCaller failed
        return false;

    return SetToRef(&Caller, true); // true: look for internal name
}
```

```cpp
bool xlName::SetToRef(xloper *p_ref_oper, bool internal)
{
    Clear();

    if((p_ref_oper->xltype & (xltypeSRef | xltypeRef)) == 0)
        return false;
//-----------------------------------------------------------
// Convert to text of form [Book1.xls]Sheet1!R1C1
//-----------------------------------------------------------
    cpp_xloper RefTextR1C1;
    int xl4 = Excel4(xlfReftext, &RefTextR1C1, 1, p_ref_oper);
    RefTextR1C1.SetExceltoFree();

    if(xl4 || RefTextR1C1.IsType(xltypeErr))
        return false;

//-----------------------------------------------------------
// Get the name, if it exists, otherwise fail.
//
// First look for an internal name (the default if the 2nd
// argument to xlfGetDef is omitted).
//-----------------------------------------------------------
    if(internal)
    {
        xl4 = Excel4(xlfGetDef, &m_RangeName, 1, &RefTextR1C1);
        m_RangeName.SetExceltoFree();

        if(xl4 || !m_RangeName.IsType(xltypeStr))
            return m_Defined = m_RefValid = false;

        m_Worksheet = false;
// If name exists and is internal, add to the list.
// add_name_record() has no effect if already there.
        add_name_record(NULL, *this);
    }
    else
    {
// Extract the sheet name and specify this explicitly
        cpp_xloper SheetName;
        xl4 = Excel4(xlSheetNm, &SheetName, 1, p_ref_oper);
        SheetName.SetExceltoFree();

        if(xl4 || !SheetName.IsType(xltypeStr))
            return m_Defined = m_RefValid = false;

// Truncate RefTextR1C1 at the R1C1 part
        char *p = (char *)RefTextR1C1; // need to free this
        RefTextR1C1 = strchr(p, '!') + 1;
        free(p);

// Truncate SheetName at the sheet name
        p = (char *)SheetName;
        SheetName = strchr(p, ']') + 1;
        free(p);

        xl4 = Excel4(xlfGetDef, &m_RangeName, 2, &RefTextR1C1, &SheetName);
        m_RangeName.SetExceltoFree();

        if(xl4 || !m_RangeName.IsType(xltypeStr))
            return m_Defined = m_RefValid = false;
```

```
        m_Worksheet = true;
    }
    return m_Defined = m_RefValid = true;
}
```

9.8.3 Naming the calling cell

Where internal names are being used, the task is simply one of obtaining a reference to the calling cell and using the function xlfSetName to define a name whose definition is that reference. However, repeated calls to a naïve function that did this would lead to more and more names existing. The first thing to consider is whether the caller already has a name associated with it (see section 9.8.2 above).

Sometimes the reason for naming a cell will be to associate it with a particular function, not just a given cell. Therefore, it may be necessary to look at whether the calling function is the function for which the cell was originally named. If not, the appropriate cleaning up or undoing of the old association should occur where necessary. If the name already exists, and is associated with the calling function, then no action need be taken to rename the cell.

The following code lists the member function of xlName that names the calling cell, if not already named. Note that if the name is specified and a name already exists, it deletes the old name before creating the new one.

```
bool xlName::NameCaller(char *name)
{
//------------------------------------------------------------
// Check if given internal name already exists for this caller
//------------------------------------------------------------
    if(SetToCallersName() && !m_Worksheet)
    {
// If no name specified, then the existing name is what's required
        if(!name || !*name)
            return true;

// Check if name is the same as the specified one
        if(m_RangeName == name)
            return true;

// If not, delete the old name, create a new one.
        Delete();
    }

//------------------------------------------------------------
// If no name provided, create a unique name
//------------------------------------------------------------
    if(!name || !*name)
    {
        name = make_unique_name();
        m_RangeName = name;
        free(name);
    }
    else
    {
        m_RangeName = name;
    }
```

```
    m_Worksheet = false;  // This will be an internal name

//-----------------------------------------------------------
// Get a reference to the calling cell
//-----------------------------------------------------------
    cpp_xloper Caller;
    int xl4 = Excel4(xlfCaller, &Caller, 0);
    Caller.SetExceltoFree();

    if(xl4) // if xlfCaller failed
        return m_Defined = m_RefValid = false;

//-----------------------------------------------------------
// Associate the new internal name with the calling cell(s)
//-----------------------------------------------------------
    cpp_xloper RetVal;
    xl4 = Excel4(xlfSetName, &RetVal, 2, &m_RangeName, &Caller);
    RetVal.SetExceltoFree();

    if(xl4 || RetVal.IsType(xltypeErr))
        return m_Defined = m_RefValid = false;

//-----------------------------------------------------------
// Add the new internal name to the list
//-----------------------------------------------------------
    m_Defined = m_RefValid = true;
    add_name_record(NULL, *this);
    return true;

}
```

The function add_name_record() adds this new internal name to a list that enables management of all such names. (See next section for details.) A simple example of how you would use xlName's ability to do this is the following worksheet function name_me() that assigns an internal name to the calling cell (unless it already has one) and returns the name. (This function has no obvious use other than demonstration.)

```
xloper * __stdcall name_me(int create)
{
   if(called_from_paste_fn_dlg())
      return p_xlErrValue;

// Set the xlName to refer to the calling cell.
   xlName Caller;
   bool name_exists = Caller.SetToCallersName();

   if(create)
   {
      if(!name_exists)
         Caller.NameCaller(NULL);

// Get the defined name.  Need to free this string.
      char *name = Caller.GetName();
      cpp_xloper Name(name);
      free(name);
      return Name.ExtractXloper();
   }
```

```
// Not creating, so deleting
   if(!name_exists)
      return p_xlFalse;

// Delete from Excel's own list of defined names
   Caller.Delete();

// Delete from DLL's list of internal names.  This is a
// slightly inefficient method, especially if a large
// number of internal names are in the list.  A more
// specific method of deleting from list could easily
// be coded.
   clean_xll_name_list();
   return p_xlTrue;
}
```

9.8.4 Internal XLL name housekeeping

The reference associated with an internal XLL name can, for a number of reasons, become invalid or no longer refer to an open workbook. The user may have deleted a row or column containing the original caller, or cut and pasted another cell on top of it. The sheet it was on could have been deleted, or the workbook could have been deleted without ever being saved.

In general Excel is very good at changing the reference when cells are moved, the range expands or contracts, the sheet is renamed or moved, the workbook is saved under a different name, etc. This is one of the main reasons for defining an internal name within the XLL, of course, as the events through which a user can do these things are not easily trapped. Being able to clean up unused or invalid internal names, and associated resources, is clearly very important.

The C API function xlfNames returns an array of worksheet names, but not, unfortunately, internal DLL names. Therefore, it is necessary for the DLL to maintain some kind of container for the internal names it has created, through which it can iterate to perform this housekeeping. For C++ programmers, the most sensible way to do this is using a Standard Template Library (STL) container. (The source file XllNames.cpp in the example project on the CD ROM contains an implementation of an STL map that is used by the xlName class for this purpose.)

The following two steps can be employed to identify whether an internal name is valid and associated reference with a valid:

- Attempt to get the definition reference for the name using the xlfGetName function. If this fails, the name is not valid or has not yet been defined.
- Attempt to convert the reference definition returned by xlfGetName (as text in the form [Book1.xls]Sheet1!R1C1) to a reference using the xlfTextref function. If this fails the reference is not valid.

The following code lists the xlName member function Refresh() that updates the current cell address of a named range and confirms that the name and the reference are (still) valid. This function is called whenever the class needs to be sure that the name still exists and the cell reference is up-to-date.

```
bool xlName::Refresh(void)
{
    m_RangeRef.Free();

//-----------------------------------------------------------
// First check that the name is defined
//-----------------------------------------------------------
    cpp_xloper Defn;
    int xl4 = Excel4(xlfGetName, &Defn, 1, &m_RangeName);
    Defn.SetExceltoFree();

    if(xl4 || !Defn.IsType(xltypeStr))
        return m_Defined = m_RefValid = false;

    m_Defined = true;

//-----------------------------------------------------------
// Now check if the definition is a valid reference
//-----------------------------------------------------------
    char *temp = (char *)Defn; // allocates some memory
    Defn = temp + 1; // remove the leading '='
    free(temp); // free the temporary memory

    xl4 = Excel4(xlfTextref, &m_RangeRef, 2, &Defn, p_xlFalse);
    m_RangeRef.SetExceltoFree();

    m_RefValid = !xl4 && m_RangeRef.IsType(xltypeSRef | xltypeRef);
    return m_RefValid;
}
```

As well as having a way of detecting whether a name is valid, it is necessary to have a strategy for when and/or how often the DLL checks the list of internally defined names. This depends largely on the application. There needs to be a balance between the overhead associated with frequent checking and the benefit of knowing that the list is good.

In some cases you may not be concerned if the list contains old and invalid names. In this case a clean-up function that is invoked (1) as a command, or (2) when a new name is being added or explicitly deleted, would do fine.

In other cases, for example, where you are using a function to contribute some piece of real-time data, it may be imperative that the application informs the recipient within a set time that the source cell has been deleted. In this case, it might be sufficient to set up a trap for a recalculation event using the xlcOnRecalc function that calls such a function. Or it may be necessary to create an automatically repeating command (see sections 9.9.1 and 9.10 for examples of this).

Finally, it is probably a good idea, depending on your application, to delete all the internal names when your XLL is unloaded: calling a function that iterates through the list to do this from xlAutoClose is the most convenient and reliable way. The function delete_all_xll_names() in the example project on the CD ROM does just this.

9.9 MULTI-TASKING, MULTI-THREADING AND ASYNCHRONOUS CALLS IN DLLS

9.9.1 Setting up timed calls to DLL commands: xlcOnTime

There are two readily accessible ways to execute a command at a given point in the future. One is to use VBA Application.OnTime method. The other is to use the C API command xlcOnTime whose enumeration value is 32916 (0x8094). (It is also possible to set up a Windows timed callback from a DLL command or a function. However, a function called back in this way cannot safely use the C API or the COM interface.)

The most accessible of the two is VBA's Application.OnTime which sets up a scheduled call to a user-defined command. The method takes an absolute time argument, but in conjunction with the VB Now function, can be used to set up a relative-time call. Once the specified time is reached, VB uses COM to call the command function. This call will fail if Excel is not in a state where a command can be run.[10]

The C API function is analogous to the VBA method, and both are analogous to the XLM ON.TIME command which takes 4 parameters.

1. The time as a serial number at which the command is to be executed. If the integer (day) part is omitted, the command is run the next time that time occurs, which may be the next day.
2. The name of the command function, as set in the 4th argument to the xlfRegister function.
3. (Optional.) Another time, up until which you would like Excel to wait try executing the command again if it was unable the first time round. If omitted Excel will wait as long as it takes: until the state of Excel is such that it can run the command.
4. (Optional.) A Boolean value that if set to false will cancel a timed call that has not yet been executed.

One key difference between the C API and VBA versions is the third parameter, which tells Excel to execute a command as soon as it can after the specified time. (Excel cannot execute commands when, for example, a user is editing a cell.) Using xlcOnTime, it is Excel itself that calls the command directly. This avoids any subtle problems that VBA might encounter calling the command via COM. A further advantage is that Excel will not make more than one call to the DLL at a time. In other words, the DLL command will not be called at the same time as another command or a worksheet function. This makes the safe management of shared data in the DLL much easier.

The xlcOnTime call returns true if the call was scheduled successfully, otherwise false. (If an attempt was made to cancel a timed callback that did not exist or was already executed, it returns a #VALUE! error.)

Below is some example code showing two inter-dependant commands, on_time_example_cmd() and increment_counter(). Both examples rely heavily on the cpp_xloper class (see section 6.4 *A C++ class wrapper for the xloper – cpp_xloper* on page 118) and the xlName class (see section 9.7 *A C++ Excel name class example, xlName* on page 307).

The command on_time_example_cmd() toggles (enables/disables) repeated timed calls to increment_counter(). The command also toggles a check mark on a menu item associated with the OnTimeExample command in order to inform the user whether the timed calls are running or not.

The command increment_counter() increments the value held in a named worksheet range in the active workbook, Counter, and then sets up the next call to itself using

---

[10] The author has also experienced Excel behaving in an unusual or unexpected way when using this function to set up a command to be run every *n* seconds, say. For this reason, this book recommends using the C API function where robustness is proving hard to achieve.

the `xlcOnTime` command. Note that both commands need to be registered with Excel using the `xlfRegister` command, and that `increment_counter` needs to be registered with the 4th argument as `"IncrementCounter"` in order for Excel to be able to call the command properly.

```
#define SECS_PER_DAY    (60.0 * 60.0 * 24.0)

bool on_time_example_running = false;

int __stdcall increment_counter(void)
{
    if(!on_time_example_running)
        return 0;

   xlName Counter("!Counter");

   ++Counter; // Does nothing if Counter not defined

// Schedule the next call to this command in 10 seconds' time
    cpp_xloper Now;
    Excel4(xlfNow, &Now, 0);
    cpp_xloper ExecTime((double)Now + 10.0 / SECS_PER_DAY);
    cpp_xloper CmdName("IncrementCounter");
    cpp_xloper RetVal;
    int xl4 = Excel4(xlcOnTime, &RetVal, 2, &ExecTime, &CmdName);
    return 1;
}

int __stdcall on_time_example_cmd(void)
{
// Toggle the module-scope Boolean flag and, if now true, start the
// first of the repeated calls to increment_counter()
    if(on_time_example_running = !on_time_example_running)
        increment_counter();

    cpp_xloper BarNum(10); // the worksheet menu bar
    cpp_xloper Menu("&XLL Example");
    cpp_xloper Cmd("OnT&ime example");
    cpp_xloper Status(on_time_example_running);
    Excel4(xlfCheckCommand, 0, 4, &BarNum, &Menu, &Cmd, &Status);
    return 1;
}
```

Note: When Excel executes the timed command it will clear the cut or copy mode state if set. It can be very frustrating for a user if they only have a few seconds to complete a cut and paste within the spreadsheet. Making the enabling/disabling of such repeated calls easily accessible is therefore critically important. This means adding a menu item or toolbar button, or at the very least, a keyboard short-cut, with which to run the equivalent of the `on_time_example_cmd()` command above.

9.9.2   Starting and stopping threads from within a DLL

Setting up threads to perform tasks in the background is straightforward. The following example code contains a few module-scope variables used to store a handle for the background thread and for communication between the thread and a function that would be called by Excel. The function `thread_example()` when called with a non-zero argument from an Excel spreadsheet for the first time, starts up a thread that executes the function `thread_main()`. This example function simply increments a counter with a frequency of the argument in milliseconds. The function `thread_example()` when called subsequently with a non-zero argument returns the incremented counter value. If called with a zero argument, `thread_example()` terminates the thread and deletes the thread object.

```c
#include <windows.h>

bool keep_thread_running = false;
long thread_counter;
HANDLE thread_handle = 0;

//------------------------------------------------------------------
// Thread is defined using a pointer to this function.  Thread
// executes this function and terminates automatically when this
// functions returns.  The void * pointer is interpreted as a pointer
// to long containing the number of milliseconds the thread should
// sleep in each loop in this example.
//------------------------------------------------------------------
DWORD WINAPI thread_main(void *vp)
{
    for(;keep_thread_running;)
    {
// Do whatever work the thread needs to do here:
        thread_counter++;

        if(vp)
            Sleep(*(long *)vp);
        else
            Sleep(100);  // Make life easy for the OS
    }
    return !(STILL_ACTIVE);
}
```

This function `thread_example()` either kills the background thread, sets up or gets the value of `thread_counter`, depending on the value of `activate_ms` and the current state of the thread. It is declared as `__stdcall` so that it can be accessed as a worksheet function.

```c
long __stdcall thread_example(long activate_ms)
{
// Address of thread_param is passed to OS, so needs to persist
    static long thread_param;

// Not used, but pointer to this needs to be passed to CreateThread()
    DWORD thread_ID;

    if(activate_ms)
    {
        if(thread_handle == 0)
        {
            thread_counter = 0;
            keep_thread_running = true;
            thread_param = activate_ms;
            thread_handle = CreateThread(NULL, 0, thread_main,
                    (void *)& thread_param, 0, &thread_ID);
            return 0;
```

```
        }
        return thread_counter;
    }

    if(thread_handle)
    {
// Set flag to tell thread to exit
        keep_thread_running = false;

// Wait for the thread to terminate.
        DWORD code;
        for(;GetExitCodeThread(thread_handle, &code)
                && code == STILL_ACTIVE; Sleep(10));

// Delete the thread object by releasing the handle
        CloseHandle(thread_handle);
        thread_handle = 0;
    }
    return -1;
}
```

The above code makes assumptions that may not be thread-safe. In particular the system could be simultaneously reading (in `thread_example()`) and writing (in `thread_main()`) to the variable `thread_counter`. In practice, in a Win32 environment, the reading and writing of a 32-bit integer will not be split from one slice of execution to another on a single processor machine. Nevertheless, to be really safe, all instructions that read from or write to memory that can be accessed by multiple threads should be contained within *Critical Sections*.

Creating a thread from a worksheet function creates the possibility of leaving a thread running when it is no longer needed, simply by closing the worksheet that contained the formula that created it. A better solution is to create and destroy threads from, say, the `xlAutoOpen()` and `xlAutoClose()` XLL interface functions or some other user command. Section 9.10 *A background task management class and strategy* on page 320 and the associated code on the CD ROM, present a more robust and sophisticated example of managing and using background threads.

9.9.3   Calling the C API from a DLL-created thread

This is not permitted. Excel is not expecting such calls which will fail in a way which might destabilise or crash Excel. This is, of course, unfortunate. It would be nice to be able to access the C API in this way, say, to initiate a recalculation from a background thread when a background task has been completed. One way around this particular limitation is to have the background thread set a flag that a timed command can periodically check, triggering a recalculation, say, if the flag is set. (See section 9.9.1 *Setting up timed calls to DLL commands: `xlcOnTime`* on page 316.)

9.10   A BACKGROUND TASK MANAGEMENT CLASS AND STRATEGY

This section brings together a number of topics, discussed so far. It describes a strategy for managing a background thread, using the C API, that can be used for lengthy worksheet function recalculations. For brevity, worksheet functions that require this approach are referred to in this section as *long tasks*. The reason for wanting to assign long tasks to their own thread is so that the user is not locked-out of Excel while these cells recalculate. On a single-processor machine the total recalculation time will, in general, be worse, albeit imperceptibly, but the difference in usability will be enormous.

To make this work, the key sections that are relied on are:

- Registration custom commands and of volatile macro-sheet equivalent worksheet functions (section 8.5, page 182).
- The use of a repeated timed command call (section 9.9.1, page 316).
- Managing a background thread (section 9.9.2, page 318).
- Working with internal Excel names (section 8.10, page 239).
- Keeping track of the calling cell (section 9.8, page 309).
- Creating custom menu items (section 8.11, page 249).
- Creating a custom dialog box (section 8.13, page 273).

This section discusses the requirements, the design and the function of the various software components needed to make the strategy work.

Both the strategy and the class around which it is centred, are intended simply to illustrate the issues involved. They are not intended to represent the only or best way of achieving this goal. Whatever you do, you should satisfy yourself that your chosen approach is suitable and stable for your particular needs. More sophisticated solutions are certainly possible than that proposed here, but are beyond this book's scope.

9.10.1   Requirements

The high level requirements that drive this example strategy are these:

1. The user must be able to disable/re-enable the background thread from a command.
2. Long task worksheet functions should not, ideally, impose restrictions on the user that ordinary worksheet functions are not limited by.
3. Long task worksheet functions must be given the ability to return intermediate values.
4. A number of different long task functions should be supportable without extra coding other than of the function itself.
5. Changing input values for an in-progress task should cause the existing (old) task to be abandoned as soon as possible and the task to be re-queued with the new parameters.
6. There should be no hard limit to the number of worksheet functions that can be queued.

Other requirements could be envisaged, such as the prioritisation of certain tasks, but for simplicity the above requirements are all that are considered here.

When farming out tasks to threads there are a number of possible approaches:

(a) Create a thread for each task.
(b) Create a thread for each worksheet function.
(c) Create a single thread on which you execute all tasks for all functions.
(d) Create a pool of threads that have tasks assigned according to their availability.

Strategy (a) could very quickly lead to the thread management overhead bringing your machine to a grinding halt, especially where each worksheet cell might get its own thread. Strategy (b) improves on this considerably unless there are, say, dozens of functions. Strategy (d) is perhaps the best approach, but for simplicity of the example strategy (c) is chosen here. Whilst not having all the capabilities of (d), it still touches on all the important issues. It also requires that the code is flexible enough to handle many different functions taking different numbers and types of arguments and returning different values, both intermediate and final. This satisfies requirements (3) and (4) above.

9.10.2   Communication between Excel and a background thread

There are a number of reasons why the foreground thread (Excel, essentially) and the background thread need to communicate with each other. Firstly, there is contention for resources, typically both threads trying to access the same block of memory at the same time. This is addressed with the use of Critical Sections. Secondly, the worksheet functions need to tell the background thread about a new task, or a change to an outstanding task. Getting the worksheet to communicate with the background thread is simple, requiring only that memory contention is handled well. Two flags are used in the example class below that enable the user, via a custom command, to request that the background thread

1. stops processing the current task.
2. stops processing all tasks.

Lastly, the background thread needs to be able to tell Excel that new information is available to the worksheet, in response to which Excel needs to recalculate those functions so that this new information can be acquired. Getting the background thread to tell Excel that something needs to happen requires that Excel polls to see if something needs to be done, say, every n seconds. (Remember that background threads cannot safely call directly into Excel via the C API or COM.) This is achieved here with the use of xlcOnTime embedded in a command associated with the background thread. This command is referred to below as the *polling command*. (See also section 9.9.1 *Setting up timed calls to DLL commands: xlcOnTime* on page 316.)

9.10.3   The software components needed

The list of components required is as follows:

Table 9.7 Software components for a background thread strategy

Component	Notes
TaskList class	• Creates, deletes, suspends and resumes the background thread and the polling command (in foreground) • Handles memory contention between threads using critical sections • Creates and deletes DLL-internal Excel names associated with each caller of a long task function (in foreground). Names are mapped 1-1 to tasks.

Table 9.7 (*continued*)

Component	Notes

	• Maintains a list of tasks and manages the following:
	  ○ Addition of new tasks (in foreground)
	  ○ Modification of existing tasks (in foreground)
	  ○ Deletion of orphaned tasks (in foreground)
	  ○ Execution of a task, and the associated state changes (in background)
	• Provides an interface for information about current tasks and access to configuration parameters

Polling command	• Associated with a given instance of a `TaskList` class • Registered with Excel so that it can be executed via the `xlcOnTime` command • Deletes any invalid names in the list • Initiates Excel recalculation • After recalculation initiates cleaning up of orphaned tasks • Schedules the next call to itself
Control/configuration command(s)	• Accessible to the user via custom menu or toolbar • Provides enable/disable thread function • Provides some task execution information • Provides ability to configure thread settings
Long task interface function	• Registered with Excel as a volatile macro sheet function • Takes `oper` arguments, not `xlopers`[11] • Returns immediately if called from the Function Wizard • Responsible for verification of inputs • Returns immediately if inputs invalid or task list thread is deactivated
Long task main function	• Takes a pointer to a task object/structure and returns a Boolean • Makes no calls, directly or indirectly, to Excel via the C API or COM • Periodically checks the break task flag within the task object/structure while performing its task

One reason for registering a long task interface function as a macro sheet function is to give it the ability to read and return the current value of the calling cell. This may be the required behaviour if the task has not been completed.

9.10.4 Imposing restrictions on the worksheet function

One potential complication is the possibility that a user might enter a number of long task function calls into a single cell. For example, a user might enter the following formula

---

[11] This is a simplifying restriction that ensures that tasks are driven by values not ranges, and simplifies the handling of different functions that take different numbers of arguments of different types.

into a cell:

```
=IF(A1,LONG_TASK(B1),LONG_TASK(B2))
```

Excel's recalculation logic would attempt to recalculate both calls to the function LONG_TASK(). (In this example the user should enter =LONG_TASK(IF(A1,B1,B2)) instead.) In any case, it is not too burdensome to restrict the user to only entering a single long task in a single cell, say. Should you wish to do so, such rules are easily implemented using xlfGetFormula described in section 8.9.7 on page 221. This is one of the things that should be taken care of in the long task interface function. The fact that you might need to do this is one of the reasons for registering it as a macro sheet function.

The example in this section makes no restriction on the way the interface function is used in a cell, although this is a weakness: the user is relied upon only to enter one such function per cell.

9.10.5   Organising the task list

The example in this section uses the following simple structure to represent a task. Note that a more sensible approach would be to use a Standard Template Library (STL) container class. The, some would say, old-fashioned linked list used here could easily be replaced with such a container. The intention is not to propose the best way of coding such things, but simply to lay out a complete approach that can be modified to suit coding preferences and experience.

```
enum {TASK_PENDING = 0, TASK_CURRENT = 1, TASK_READY = 2,
    TASK_UNCLAIMED = 4, TASK_COMPLETE = 8};

typedef struct tag_task
{
    tag_task *prev;   // prev task in list, NULL if this is top
    tag_task *next;   // next task in list, NULL if this is last
    long start_clock; // set by TaskList class
    long end_clock;   // set by TaskList class
    bool break_task;  // if true, processing of this task should end
    short status;     // PENDING,CURRENT,READY,UNCLAIMED,COMPLETE
    char *caller_name; // dll-internal Excel name of caller
    bool (* fn_ptr)(tag_task *);    // passed in function ptr
    xloper fn_ret_val; // used for intermediate and final value
    int num_args;
    xloper arg_array[1]; // 1st in array of args for this task
}
    task;
```

This structure lends itself to either a simple linked list with a head and tail, or a more flexible circular list. For this illustration, the simple list has been chosen. New tasks are added at the tail, and processing of tasks moves from the head down. A decision needs to be made about whether modified tasks are also moved to the end or left where they are. In the former case, the algorithm for deciding which task is next to be processed simply goes to the next in the list. In the latter case, it would need to start looking at the top of the list, just in case a task that had already been completed had subsequently been modified.

The decision made here is that modified tasks are moved to the end of the list. The TaskList class, discussed below and listed in full on the CD ROM, contains three pointers, one to the top of the list, m_pHead, one to the bottom of the list, m_pTail, and one to the task currently being executed, m_pCurrent.

A more sophisticated queuing approach would in general be better, for example, one with a *pending* queue and a *done* queue, or even a queue for each state. The above approach has been chosen in the interests of simplicity.

It is important to analyse how a list of these tasks can be altered and by what thread, background or foreground. The pointers m_pHead and m_pTail will only be modified by the foreground thread (Excel) as it adds, moves or deletes tasks. The m_pCurrent pointer is modified by the background thread as it completes one task and looks for the next one. Therefore, the foreground thread must be extremely careful when accessing the m_pCurrent pointer or assuming it knows what it is, as it can alter from one moment to the next. The foreground can freely read through the list of tasks but must use a critical section when altering a task that is, or could at any moment become, pointed to by m_pCurrent. If it wants to update m_pCurrent's arguments, then it must first break the task so that it is no longer current. If it wants to change the order of tasks in the list, it must enter a critical section to avoid this being done at the same time that the background thread is looking for the next task.

By limiting the scope of the background thread to the value of m_pCurrent, and the task it points to, the class maintains a fairly simple thread-safe design, only needing to use critical sections in a few places.

The strategy assigns a state to a task at each point in its life cycle. Identifying the states, what they mean, and how they change from one to another, is an important part of making any complex multi-threaded strategy work reliably. For more complex projects than this example, it is advisable to use a formal architectural design standard, such as UML, with integral state-transition diagrams. For this example, the simple table of the states below is sufficient.

Table 9.8 Task states and transitions for a background thread strategy

State	Notes
Pending	• The task has been placed on the list and is waiting its turn to be processed. • The foreground thread can delete pending tasks.
Current	• The state is changed from pending to current by the background thread with a critical section • The background thread is processing the task • If the task's execution is interrupted, its state goes back to pending
Ready	• The task has been completed by the background thread which has changed the state from current to ready • The task is ready for the foreground loop to retrieve the result
Unclaimed	• The foreground thread has seen that the task is either ready or complete and has marked it as unclaimed pending recalculation of the workbook(s) • If still unclaimed after a workbook recalculation, the task should be deleted

(continued overleaf)

Table 9.8 (*continued*)

State	Notes
Complete	• The recalculation of the worksheet cell (that originally scheduled the task) changes the state from unclaimed to complete • The task has been processed and the originating cell has been given the final value • A change of inputs will change the status back to pending

The unclaimed state ensures that the foreground thread can clean up any orphaned tasks: those whose originating cells have been deleted, overwritten, or were in worksheets that are now closed. The distinction between ready and unclaimed ensures that tasks completed immediately after a worksheet recalculation don't get mistakenly cleaned up as *unclaimed* before their calling cell has had a chance to retrieve the value.

9.10.6   Creating, deleting, suspending, resuming the thread

In this example, where management of the thread is embedded in a class, the most obvious place to start and finally stop the thread might seem to be the constructor and destructor. It is preferable, in fact, to have more control than this and start the thread with an explicit call to a class member function, ideally from xlAutoOpen. Similarly, it is better to delete the thread in the same way from xlAutoClose.

Threads under Windows can be created in a suspended state. This gives you two choices about how you run your thread: firstly, you can create it in a suspended state and bring it to life later, perhaps only when it has some work to do. Secondly, you can create it in an active state and have the main function that the thread executes loop and sleep until there is something for it to do. Again for simplicity, the second approach has been adopted in this example.

Similarly, when it comes to suspending and resuming threads, there are two Windows calls that will do this. Or you can set some flag in foreground that tells your background loop not to do anything until you reset the flag. The latter approach is simpler and easier to debug, and, more importantly, it also allows the background thread to clean up its current task before becoming inactive. For these reasons, this is the approach chosen here.

9.10.7   The task processing loop

Most of the code involved in making this strategy work is not listed in this book. (It is included on the CD ROM in the source files Background.cpp and Background.h which also call on other code in the example project.) Nevertheless, it is helpful to discuss the logic in this code behind the main function that the thread executes. (When creating the thread, the wrapper function background_thread_main() is passed as an argument together with a pointer to the instance of the TaskList class that is creating the thread.) The loop references three flags, all private class data members, that are used to signal between the fore- and background threads. These are:

• m_ThreadExitFlagSet: Signals that the thread should exit the loop and return, thereby terminating the thread. This is set by the foreground thread in the DeleteTaskThread() member function of the TaskList class.

- m_SuspendAllFlagSet: Signals that the background thread is to stop (suspend) processing tasks after the next task has been completed. This is set by the foreground thread in the SuspendTaskThread() member function of the TaskList class.

- m_ThreadIsRunning: This flag tells both the background and foreground threads whether tasks are being processed or not. It is cleared by the background thread in response to m_SuspendAllFlagSet being set. This gives the foreground thread a way of confirming that the background thread is no longer processing tasks. It is set by the foreground thread in the ResumeTaskThread() member function of the TaskList class.

```
// This is the function that is passed to Windows when creating
// the thread.
DWORD __stdcall background_thread_main(void *vp)
{
    return ((TaskList *)vp)->TaskThreadMain();
}

// This member function executes 'this' instance's tasks.
DWORD TaskList::TaskThreadMain(void)
{
    for(;!m_ThreadExitFlagSet;)
    {
        if(!m_ThreadIsRunning)
        {
// Thread has been put into inactive state
            Sleep(THREAD_INACTIVE_SLEEP_MS);
            continue;
        }

        if(m_SuspendAllFlagSet)
        {
            m_ThreadIsRunning = false;
            m_pCurrent = NULL;
            continue;
        }

// Find next task to be executed. Sets m_pCurrent to
// point to the next task, or to NULL if no more to do.
    GetNextTask();

        if(m_pCurrent)
        {
// Execute the current task and time it. Status == TASK_CURRENT
            m_pCurrent->start_clock = clock();
            if(m_pCurrent->fn_ptr(m_pCurrent))
            {
// Task completed successfully and is ready to be read out
                m_pCurrent->status = TASK_READY;
            }
            else
            {
// Task was broken or failed so need to re-queue it
                m_pCurrent->status = TASK_PENDING;
            }
            m_pCurrent->end_clock = clock();
        }
        else // nothing to do, so have a little rest
```

```
          Sleep(m_ThreadSleepMs);
   }
   return !(STILL_ACTIVE);
}
```

The function `TaskList::GetNextTask()` points `m_pCurrent` to the next task, or sets it to `NULL` if they are all done.

9.10.8   The task interface and main functions

In this example, the only constraint on the interface function is that it is registered as volatile. It is also helpful to register it as a macro-sheet equivalent function which only takes `oper` arguments. Its responsibilities are:

1. To validate arguments and place them into an array of `xlopers`.
2. To call `TaskList::UpdateTask()`.
3. To interpret the returned value of `UpdateTask()` and pass something appropriate back to the calling cell.

The associated function that does the work is constrained, in this case, by the implementation of the `TaskList` class and the `task` structure, to be a function that takes a pointer to a `task` and returns a `bool`. The following code shows an example interface and main function pair. The long task in this case counts from one to the value of its one argument. (This is a useful test function, given its predictable execution time.) Note that `long_task_example_main()` regularly checks the state of the `break_task` flag. It also regularly calls `Sleep(0)`, a very small overhead, in order to make thread management easier for the operating system.

```
// LongTaskExampleMain() executes the task and does the work.
// It is only ever called from the background thread.  It is
// required to check the break_task flag regularly to see if the
// foreground thread needs execution to stop.  It is not required
// that the task populates the return value, fn_ret_val, as it does
// in this case.  It could just wait till the final result is known.
bool long_task_example_main(tag_task *pTask)
{
   long limit;

   if(pTask->arg_array[0].xltype != xltypeNum
   || (limit = (long)pTask->arg_array[0].val.num) < 1)
      return false;

   pTask->fn_ret_val.xltype = xltypeNum;
   pTask->fn_ret_val.val.num = 0;

   for(long i = 1; i <= limit; i++)
   {
      if(i % 1000)
      {
         if(pTask->break_task)
            return false;
```

```
            Sleep(0);
        }
        pTask->fn_ret_val.val.num = (double)i;
    }
    return true;
}
```

The interface function example below shows how the `TaskList` class uses Excel error values to communicate back to the interface function some of the possible states of the task. It is straightforward to make this much richer if required.

```
// LongTaskExampleInterface() is a worksheet function called
// directly by Excel from the foreground thread.  It is only
// required to check arguments and call ExampleTaskList.UpdateTask()
// which returns either an error, or the intermediate or final value
// of the calculation.  UpdateTask() errors can be returned directly
// or, as in this case, the function can return the current
// (previous) value of the calling cell.  This function is registered
// with Excel as a volatile macro sheet function.
xloper * __stdcall LongTaskExampleInterface(xloper *arg)
{
    if(called_from_paste_fn_dlg())
        return p_xlErrNa;

    if(arg->xltype != xltypeNum || arg->val.num < 1)
        return p_xlErrValue;

    xloper arg_array[1]; // only 1 argument in this case
    static xloper ret_val;

// UpdateTask makes deep copies of all the supplied arguments
// so passing in an array of shallow copies is safe.
    arg_array[0] = *arg;

// As there is only one argument in this case, we could instead
// simply pass a pointer to this instead of creating the array
    ret_val = ExampleTaskList.UpdateTask(long_task_example_main,
            arg_array, 1);

    if(ret_val.xltype == xltypeErr)
    {
        switch(ret_val.val.err)
        {
        // the arguments were not valid
        case xlerrValue:
            break;

        // task has never been completed and is now pending or current
        case xlerrNum:
            break;

        // the thread is inactive
        case xlerrNA:
            break;
        }

// Return the existing cell value.
        get_calling_cell_value(ret_val);
```

```
    }
    ret_val.xltype |= xlbitDLLFree; // memory to be freed by the DLL
    return &ret_val;
}
```

9.10.9   The polling command

The polling command only has the following two responsibilities:

- Detect when a recalculation is necessary in order to update the values of volatile long task functions. (In the example code below the recalculation is done on every call into the polling function.)
- Reschedule itself to be called again in a number of seconds determined by a configurable TaskList class data member.

```
int __stdcall long_task_polling_cmd(void)
{
    if(ExampleTaskList.m_BreakPollingCmdFlag)
        return 0; // return without rescheduling next call

// Run through the list of tasks setting TASK_READY tasks to
// TASK_UNCLAIMED. Tasks still unclaimed after recalculation are
// assumed to be orphaned and deleted by DeleteUnclaimedTasks().
    bool need_racalc = ExampleTaskList.SetDoneTasks();

// if(need_racalc) // Commented out in this example
    {
// Cause Excel to recalculate.  This forces all volatile fns to be
// re-evaluated, including the long task functions, which will then
// return the most up-to-date values.  This also causes status of
// tasks to be changed to TASK_COMPLETE from TASK_UNCLAIMED.
        Excel4(xlcCalculateNow, NULL, 0);

// Run through the list of tasks again to clean up unclaimed tasks
        ExampleTaskList.DeleteUnclaimedTasks();
    }

// Reschedule the command to repeat in m_PollingCmdFreqSecs seconds.
    cpp_xloper Now;
    Excel4(xlfNow, &Now, 0);
    cpp_xloper ExecTime((double)Now +
            ExampleTaskList.GetPollingSecs() / SECS_PER_DAY);

// Use command name as given to Excel in xlfRegister 4th arg
    cpp_xloper CmdName("LongTaskPoll"); // as registered with Excel
    cpp_xloper RetVal;

    int xl4 = Excel4(xlcOnTime, &RetVal, 2, &ExecTime, &CmdName);
    RetVal.SetExceltoFree();

    if(xl4 || RetVal.IsType(xltypeErr))
    {
        cpp_xloper ErrMsg("Can't reschedule long task polling cmd");
        Excel4(xlcAlert, 0, 1, &ErrMsg);
    }
    return 1;
}
```

9.10.10   Configuring and controlling the background thread

The `TaskList::CreateTaskThread()` member function creates a thread that is active as far as the OS is concerned, but inactive as far as the handling of background worksheet calculations is concerned. The user, therefore, needs a way to activate and deactivate the thread and the polling command.

As stressed previously, the C API is far from being an ideal way to create dialogs through which the user can interact with your application. In this case, however, it is very convenient to place a dialog within the same body of code as the long task functions. You can avoid using C API dialogs completely by exporting a number of accessor functions and calling them from a VBA dialog.

The example project source file, `Background.cpp`, contains a command function `long_task_config_cmd()`, that displays the following C API dialog that enables the user to control the thread and see some very simple statistics. (See section 8.13 *Working with custom dialog boxes* on page 273.)

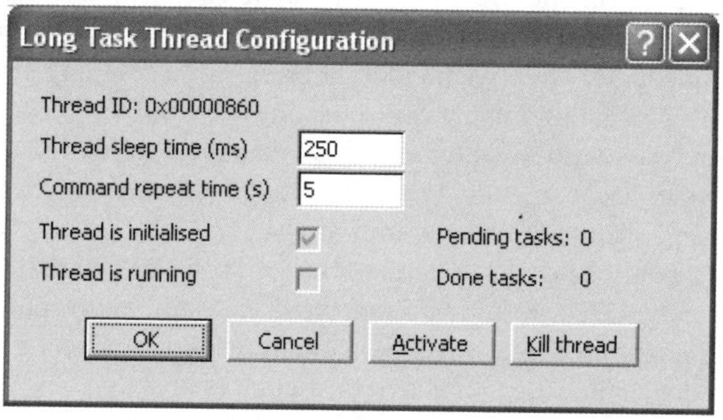

Figure 9.1   Long task thread configuration dialog

This dialog needs to be accessed from either a toolbar or menu. The same source file also contains a command function `long_task_menu_setup()` that, when called for the first time, sets up a menu item on the Tools menu. (A second call removes this menu item.) (The spreadsheet used to design and generate the dialog definition table for this dialog, `XLM_ThreadCfg_Dialog.xls`, is included on the CD ROM.)

9.10.11   Other possible background thread applications and strategies

The strategy and example outlined above lends itself well to certain types of lengthy background calculations. There are other reasons for wanting to run tasks in background, most importantly for communicating with remote applications and servers. Examples of this are beyond the scope of this book, but can be implemented fairly easily as an extension to the above. One key difference in setting up a strategy for communication between worksheet cells and a server is the need to include a *sent/waiting* task state that enables the background thread to move on and send the next task without having to wait for the server to respond to the last. The other key difference is that the background thread, or even an additional thread, must do the job of checking for communication back from the server.

9.11   HOW TO CRASH EXCEL

This section is, of course, about how *not* to crash Excel. Old versions of Excel were not without their problems, some of which were serious enough to cause occasional crashes through no fault of the user. This has caused some to view Excel as an unsafe choice for a front-end application. This is unfair when considering modern versions. Excel, if treated with understanding, can be as robust as any complex system. Third-party add-ins and users' own macros are usually the most likely cause of instability. This brief section aims to expose some of the more common ways that these instabilities arise, so that they can be avoided more easily.

There are a few ways to guarantee a crash in Excel. One is to call the C API when Excel is not expecting it: from a thread created by a DLL or from a call-back function invoked by Windows. Another is to mismanage memory. Most of the following examples involve memory abuse of one kind or another.

If Excel allocated some memory, Excel must free it. If the DLL allocated some memory, the DLL must free it. Using one to free the other's memory will cause a heap error. Over-running the bounds of memory that Excel has set aside for modify-in-place arguments to DLL functions is an equally effective method of bringing Excel to its knees. Over-running the bounds of DLL-allocated memory is also asking for trouble.

Passing `xloper` types with invalid memory pointers to `Excel4()` will cause a crash. Such types are strings (`xltypeStr`), external range references (`xltypeRef`), arrays (`xltypeMulti`) and string elements within arrays.

Memory Excel has allocated in calls to `Excel4()` or `Excel4v()` should be freed with calls to `xlFree`. Leaks resulting from these calls not being made will eventually result in Excel complaining about a lack of system resources. Excel may have difficulty redrawing the screen, saving files, or may crash completely.

Memory can be easily abused within VBA despite VB's lack of pointers. For example, overwriting memory allocated by VB in a call to `String()`, will cause heap errors that may crash Excel.

Great care must be taken where a DLL exposes functions that take data types that are (or contain) pointers to blocks of memory. Two examples of this are strings and `xl_arrays`. (See section 6.2.2 *Excel floating-point array structure: xl_array* on page 107.) The danger arises when the DLL is either fooled into thinking that more memory has been allocated than is the case, say, if the passed-in structure was not properly initialised, or if the DLL is not well behaved in the way it reads or writes to the structure's memory. In the case of the `xl_array`, whenever Excel itself is passing such an argument, it can be trusted. Where this structure has been created in a VB macro by the user's own code, care must be taken. Such dangers can usually be avoided by only exposing functions that take *safe* arguments such as `VARIANT` or `BSTR` strings and `SAFEARRAY`s.

Excel is very vulnerable to stress when it comes close to the limits of its available memory. Creating very large spreadsheets and performing certain operations can crash Excel, or almost as bad, bring it to a virtual grinding halt. Even operations such as copy or delete can have this effect. Memory leaks will eventually stress Excel in this way.

Calls to C API functions that take array arguments, `xlfAddMenu` for example, may crash Excel if the arrays are not properly formed. One way to achieve this is to have the memory allocated for the array to be smaller than required for the specified rows and columns.

There are some basic coding errors that will render Excel useless, although not necessarily crashing it, for example, a loop that might never end because it waits for a condition that might never happen. From the user's perspective, Excel will be dead if control has been passed to a DLL that does this.

A more subtle version of the previous problem can occur when using a background thread and critical sections. Not using critical sections to manage contention for resources is, in itself, dangerous and inadvisable. However, if thread A enters a critical section and then waits for a state to occur set by thread B, *and* if thread B is waiting for thread A to leave the critical section before it can set this state, then both threads effectively freeze each other. Careful design is needed to avoid such deadlocks.

Only slightly better than this are DLL functions, especially worksheet functions, that can take a very large amount of time to complete. Worksheet functions cannot report progress to the user. It is, therefore, extremely important to have an idea of the worst-case execution time of worksheet functions, say, if they are given an enormous range to process. If this worst-case time is unacceptable, from the point of view of Excel appearing to have hung, then you must either check for and limit the size of your inputs or use a background thread and/or remote process. Or your function can check for user breaks (the user pressing Esc in Windows) – see section 8.7.7 on page 206.

Care should be taken with some of the C API functions that request information about or modify Excel objects. For example, xlSheetNm must be passed a valid sheet ID otherwise Excel will crash or become unstable.

Example Add-ins and Financial Applications

Developers are always faced with the need to balance freedoms and constraints when deciding the best way to implement a model. Arguably the most important skill a developer can have is that of being able to choose the most appropriate approach all things considered: Failure can result in code that is cumbersome, or slow, or difficult to maintain or extend, or bug-ridden, or that fails completely to meet a completion time target.

This chapter aims to do two things:

1. Present a few simple worksheet function examples that demonstrate some of the basic considerations, such as argument and return types. For these examples source code is included on the CD ROM in the example project. Sections 10.1 to 10.5 cover these functions.
2. Discuss the development choices available and constraints for a number of financial markets applications. These applications are not fully worked through in the book, and source code is not provided on the CD ROM. Sections 10.6 and beyond cover these functions and applications.

Some of the simple example functions could easily be coded in VB or duplicated with perhaps only a small number of worksheet cells. The point is not to say that these things can only be done in C/C++ or using the C API. If you have decided that you want or need to use C/C++, these examples aim to provide a template or guide.

The most important thing that an add-in developer must get right is the function interface. The choices made as to the types of arguments a function takes, are they required or optional; if optional what the default behaviour is; and so on, are often critical. Much of the discussion in this chapter is on this and similar issues, rather than on one algorithm versus another. The discussion of which algorithm to use, etc., is left to other texts and to the reader whose own experience may very well be more informed and advanced than the author's.

> **Important note:** You should not rely on any of these examples, or the methods they contain, in your own applications without having completely satisfied yourself that they are correct and appropriate for your needs. They are intended only to illustrate how techniques discussed in earlier chapters can be applied.

10.1   STRING FUNCTIONS

Excel has a number of very efficient basic string functions, but string operations can quickly become unnecessarily complex when just using these. Consider, for example, the case where you want to substitute commas for stops (periods) dynamically. This is easily done using Excel's SUBSTITUTE(). However, if you want to simultaneously substitute commas for stops and stops for commas things are more complex. (You could do this in three applications of SUBSTITUTE(), but this is messy.) Writing a function in C that does this is straightforward (see replace_mask() below).

The C and C++ libraries both contain a number of low-level string functions that can easily be given Excel worksheet wrappers or declared and used from VBA. (The latter is a good place to start when optimising VB code.) This section presents a number of example functions, some of which are just wrappers of standard library functions and some of which are not. The code for all of these functions is listed in the Example project on the CD ROM in the source file XllStrings.cpp. When registered with Excel, they are added to the Text category.

Function name	count_char (exported) CountChar (registered with Excel)
Description	Counts the number of occurrences of a given character.
Prototype	short __stdcall count_char(char *text, short ch);
Type string	"ICI"
Notes	Safe to return a short as Excel will only pass a 255-max character string to the function. Function does not need to be volatile and does not access any C API functions that might require it to be registered as a macro sheet equivalent function.

```
short __stdcall count_char(char *text, short ch)
{
    if(!text || ch <= 0 || ch > 255)
        return 0;

    short count = 0;

    while(*text)
        if(*text++ == ch)
            count++;

    return count;
}
```

Function name	replace_mask (exported) ReplaceMask (registered with Excel)
Description	Replaces all occurrences of characters in a search string with *corresponding* characters from a replacement string, or removes all such occurrences if no replacement string is provided.
Prototype	void __stdcall replace_mask(char *text, char *old_chars, xloper *op_new_chars);
Type string	"1CCP"

Notes	Declared as returning void. Return value is the 1st argument modified in place. Third argument is optional and passed as an oper (see page 119) to avoid the need to dereference a range reference.

```c
void __stdcall replace_mask(char *text, char *old_chars, xloper
*op_new_chars)
{
    if(!text || !old_chars)
        return;

    char *p_old, *p;

    if((op_new_chars->xltype & (xltypeMissing | xltypeNil)))
        {
// Remove all occurrences of all characters in old_chars
        for(; *text; text++)
        {
            p_old = old_chars;

            for(;*p_old;)
            {
                if(*text == *p_old++)
                {
                    p = text;
                    do
                    {
                        *p = p[1];
                    }
                    while (*(++p));
                }
            }
        }
        return;
    }

// Substitute all occurrences of old chars with corresponding new
    if(op_new_chars->xltype != xltypeStr
    || (char)strlen(old_chars) != op_new_chars->val.str[0])
        return;

    char *p_new;

    for(; *text; text++)
    {
        p_old = old_chars;
        p_new = op_new_chars->val.str;

        for(; *p_old; p_old++, p_new++)
        {
            if(*text == *p_old)
            {
                *text = *p_new;
                break;
            }
        }
    }
}
```

Function name	reverse_text (exported) Reverse (registered with Excel)
Description	Reverses a string.
Prototype	void __stdcall reverse_text(char *text);
Type string	"1F"
Notes	Declared as returning void. Return value is the 1st argument modified in place. This function is simply a wrapper for the C library function strrev(). This function is useful in the creation of Halton quasi-random number sequences, for example.

```
void __stdcall reverse_text(char *text)
{
    strrev(text);
}
```

Function name	find_first (exported) FindFirst (registered with Excel)
Description	Returns the position of the first occurrence of any character from a search string, or zero if none found.
Prototype	short __stdcall first_inclusive(char *text, char *search_text);
Type string	"ICC"
Notes	Any error in input is reflected with a zero return value, rather than an error type. This function is simply a wrapper for the C library function strpbrk().

```
short __stdcall find_first(char *text, char *search_text)
{
    if(!text || !search_text)
        return 0;

    char *p = strpbrk(text, search_text);

    if(!p)
        return 0;

    return 1 + p - text;
}
```

Function name	find_first_excluded (exported) FindFirstExcl (registered with Excel)
Description	Returns the position of the first occurrence of any character that is <u>not</u> in a search string, or zero if no such character is found.
Prototype	short __stdcall find_first_excluded(char *text, char * search_text);
Type string	"ICC"
Notes	Any error in input is reflected with a zero return value, rather than an error type.

```
short __stdcall find_first_excluded(char *text, char *search_text)
{
    if(!text || !search_text)
        return 0;

    for(char *p = text; *p; p++)
        if(!strchr(search_text, *p))
            return 1 + p - text;

    return 0;
}
```

Function name	find_last (exported) FindLast (registered with Excel)
Description	Returns the position of the last occurrence of a given character, or zero if not found.
Prototype	short __stdcall find_last(char *text, short ch);
Type string	"ICI"
Notes	Any error in input is reflected with a zero return value, rather than an error type. This function is simply a wrapper for the C library function strrchr().

```
short __stdcall find_last(char *text, short ch)
{
    if(!text || ch <= 0 || ch > 255)
        return 0;

    char *p = strrchr(text, (char)ch);
```

```
    if(!p)
        return 0;

    return 1 + p - text;
}
```

Function name	`compare_text` (exported) **CompareText** (registered with Excel)
Description	Compare two strings for equality (return 0), A < B (return -1), A > B (return 1), case sensitive (by default) or not.
Prototype	`xloper * __stdcall compare_text(char *Atext,` `char *Btext, xloper *op_is_case_sensitive);`
Type string	`"RCCP"`
Notes	Any error in input is reflected with an Excel #VALUE! error. Return type does not need to allow for reference `xloper`s. Excel's comparison operators <, > and = are <u>not</u> case-sensitive and Excel's EXACT() function only performs a case-sensitive check for equality. This function is a wrapper for the C library functions `strcmp()` and `stricmp()`.

```
xloper * __stdcall compare_text(char *Atext, char *Btext,
                        xloper *op_is_case_sensitive)
{
    static xloper ret_oper = {0, xltypeNum};

    if(!Atext || !Btext)
        return p_xlErrValue;

// Case-sensitive by default
    bool case_sensitive = (op_is_case_sensitive->xltype == xltypeBool
        && op_is_case_sensitive->val._bool == 1);

    if(!case_sensitive)
        ret_oper.val.num = stricmp(Atext, Btext);
    else
        ret_oper.val.num = strcmp(Atext, Btext);

    return &ret_oper;
}
```

Function name	`compare_nchars` (exported) **CompareNchars** (registered with Excel)
Description	Compare the first n (1 to 255) characters of two strings for equality (return 0), A < B (return -1), A > B (return 1), case sensitive (by default) or not.

Prototype	`xloper * __stdcall compare_nchars(char *Atext, char *Btext, short n_chars, xloper *op_is_case_sensitive);`
Type string	`"RCCIP"`
Notes	Any error in input is reflected with an Excel #VALUE! error. Return type does not need to allow for reference `xlopers`. This function is a wrapper for the C library functions `strncmp()` and `strincmp()`.

```
xloper * __stdcall compare_nchars(char *Atext, char *Btext,
                    short n_chars, xloper *op_is_case_sensitive)
{
    static xloper ret_oper = {0, xltypeNum};

    if(!Atext || !Btext || n_chars <= 0 || n_chars > 255)
        return p_xlErrValue;
// Case-sensitive by default
    bool case_sensitive = (op_is_case_sensitive->xltype == xltypeBool
        && op_is_case_sensitive->val._bool == 1);

    if(!case_sensitive)
        ret_oper.val.num = strnicmp(Atext, Btext, n_chars);
    else
        ret_oper.val.num = strncmp(Atext, Btext, n_chars);

    return &ret_oper;
}
```

Function name	concat (exported) Concat (registered with Excel)
Description	Concatenate the contents of the given range (row-by-row) using the given separator (or comma by default). Returned string length limit is 255 characters by default, but can be set lower. Caller can specify the number of decimal places to use when converting numbers.
Prototype	`xloper * __stdcall concat(xloper *inputs, xloper *p_delim, xloper *p_max_len, xloper *p_num_decs);`
Type string	`"RPPPP"`

```
xloper * __stdcall concat(xloper *inputs, xloper *p_delim,
                    xloper *p_max_len, xloper *p_num_decs)
```

```
{
  cpp_xloper Inputs(inputs);

  if(Inputs.IsType(xltypeMissing | xltypeNil))
     return p_xlErrValue;

  char delim = (p_delim->xltype == xltypeStr) ?
                 p_delim->val.str[1] : ',';
  long max_len = (p_max_len->xltype == xltypeNum) ?
                 (long)p_max_len->val.num : 2551;
  long num_decs = (p_num_decs->xltype == xltypeNum) ?
                 (long)p_num_decs->val.num : -1;
  char *buffer = (char *)calloc(MAX_CONCAT_LENGTH, sizeof(char));
  char *p;
  cpp_xloper Rounding(num_decs);
  long total_length = 0;

  DWORD size;

  Inputs.GetArraySize(size);

  if(size > MAX_CONCAT_CELLS)
     size = MAX_CONCAT_CELLS;

  for(DWORD i = 0; i < size;)
  {
     if(num_decs >= 0 && num_decs < 16
     && Inputs.GetArrayElementType(i) == xltypeNum)
     {
        xloper *p_op = Inputs.GetArrayElement(i);
        Excel4(xlfRound, p_op, 2, p_op, &Rounding);
     }
     Inputs.GetArrayElement(i, p);

     if(p)
     {
        if((total_length += strlen(p)) < MAX_CONCAT_LENGTH)
           strcat(buffer, p);

        free(p);
     }

     if(++i < size)
        buffer[total_length] = delim;

     if(++total_length > max_len)
     {
        buffer[max_len] = 0;
        break;
     }
  }
  cpp_xloper RetVal(buffer);
  free(buffer);
  return RetVal.ExtractXloper(false);
}
```

Function name	parse (exported)
	ParseText (registered with Excel)

Description	Parse the input string using the given separator (or comma by default) and return an array. Caller can request conversion of all fields to numbers, or zero if no conversion possible. Caller can specify a value to be assigned to empty fields (zero by default).
Prototype	`xloper * __stdcall parse(char *input, xloper *p_delim, xloper *p_numeric, xloper *p_empty);`
Type string	`"RCPP"`
Notes	Registered name avoids conflict with the XLM PARSE() function.

```
xloper * __stdcall parse(char *input, xloper *p_delim,
                         xloper *p_numeric, xloper *p_empty)
{
    if(*input == 0)
        return p_xlErrValue;

    cpp_xloper Caller;
    Excel4(xlfCaller, &Caller, 0);
    Caller.SetExceltoFree();

    if(!Caller.IsType(xltypeSRef | xltypeRef))
        return NULL; // return NULL in case was not called by Excel

    char delimiter =
        (p_delim->xltype == xltypeStr && p_delim->val.str[0]) ?
                p_delim->val.str[1] : ',';

    char *p = input;
    WORD count = 1;

    for(;*p;)
        if(*p++ == delimiter)
            ++count;

    cpp_xloper RetVal;

    RetVal.SetTypeMulti(1, count);
// Can't use strtok as it ignores empty fields

    char *p_last = input;
    WORD i = 0;
    double d;

    bool numeric = (p_numeric->xltype == xltypeBool
            && p_numeric->val._bool == 1);
    bool empty_val = (p_empty->xltype != xltypeMissing);

    while(i < count)
    {
        if((p = strchr(p_last, (int)delimiter)))
            *p = 0;

        if((!p && *p_last) || p > p_last)
        {
```

```
            if(numeric)
            {
                d = atof(p_last);
                RetVal.SetArrayElement(0, i, d);
            }
            else
                RetVal.SetArrayElement(0, i, p_last);
        }
        else if(empty_val) // empty field value
        {
            RetVal.SetArrayElement(0, i, p_empty);
        }

        i++;

        if(!p)
            break;

        p_last = p + 1;
    }
    return RetVal.ExtractXloper(false);
}
```

10.2   STATISTICAL FUNCTIONS

As a mathematics professor once told the author (his student), a statistician is someone
with their feet in the fridge, their head in the oven, who thinks on average they are quite
comfortable. This scurrilous remark does no justice at all to what is a vast, complex
and, of course, essential branch of numerical science. Excel provides many functions
that everyday statisticians, actuaries, and so on, will use frequently and be familiar with.
Finance professionals too are heavy users of these built-in capabilities.[1] This section only
aims to provide a few examples of useful functions, or slight improvements on existing
ones, that also demonstrate some of the interface issues discussed in earlier chapters.

Financial markets option pricing relies heavily on the calculation of the cumulative
normal (Gaussian) distribution for a given value of the underlying variable (and its
inverse). Excel provides four built-in functions: NORMDIST(), NORMSDIST(), NORMINV() and
NORMSINV(). One small problem with Excel 2000 is that the inverse functions are not precise inverses. Another is that the range of probabilities for which NORMSINV() works is
not as great as you might wish – see example code below. (Both these problems are fixed
in Excel 2002.) This can lead to accumulated errors in some cases or complete failure.
The function NORMSDIST(X) is accurate to about $\pm 7.3 \times 10^{-8}$ and appears to be based on
the approximation given in Abramowitz and Stegun (1970), section 26.2.17, except that
for $X > 6$ it returns 1 and $X < -8.3$ it returns zero.[2]

There is no Excel function that returns a random sample from the normal distribution.
The compound NORMSINV(RAND()) will provide this, but is volatile and therefore may not
be desirable in all cases. In addition to its volatility, it is not the most efficient way to
calculate such samples.

---

[1] See Jackson and Staunton (2001) for numerous examples of applications of these functions to finance.
[2] Inaccuracies in these functions could cause problems when, say, evaluating probability distribution functions
from certain models.

This section provides a consistent and more accurate alternative to the NORMSDIST() and NORMSINV(), as well as functions (volatile and non-volatile) that return normal samples.

The normal distribution with mean zero and standard deviation of 1 is given by the formula:

$$N(x) = \frac{1}{\sqrt{2\pi}} \int_{-\infty}^{x} e^{-t^2/2} \, dt$$

From this the following Taylor series expansion and iterative scheme can be derived:

$$N(x) = \frac{1}{2} + \frac{1}{\sqrt{2\pi}} \sum_{n=0}^{\infty} t_n$$

$$t_0 = x$$

$$t_n = t_{n-1} \cdot \frac{x^2(2n-1)}{2n(2n+1)}$$

Starting with this, it is straightforward to construct a function that evaluates this series to the limits of machine accuracy, roughly speaking, subject to cumulative errors in the terms of the summation. These cumulative errors mean that, for approximately $|x| > 6$, a different scheme for the tails is needed.

The source code for all these functions in this section is in the module X11Stats.cpp in the example project on the CD ROM. They are registered with Excel under the category Statistical.

Function name	ndist_taylor (exported) NdistTaylor (registered with Excel)
Description	Returns a two-cell row vector containing (1) the value of $N(x)$ calculated using the above Taylor series expansion, and (2) a count of the number of terms used in the summation. For $|x| < 6$ this is accurate roughly to within 10^{-14}.
Prototype	`xloper * __stdcall ndist_taylor(double d);`
Type string	`"RB"`
Notes	Uses the expansion for $|x| < 6$ and the same approximation as Excel (but not Excel's implementation of it) for the tails. The function called is a wrapper to a function that has no knowledge of Excel data types.

```
xloper * __stdcall ndist_taylor(double d)
{
    double retvals[2];
    int iterations;

    retvals[0] = cndist_taylor(d, iterations);
    retvals[1] = iterations;
```

```
    cpp_xloper RetVal((WORD)1, (WORD)2, retvals);
    return RetVal.ExtractXloper();
}

double cndist_taylor(double d, int &iterations)
{
    if(fabs(d) > 6.0)
    {
// Small difference between the cndist() approximation and the real
// thing in the tails, although this might upset some pdf functions,
// where kinks in the gradient create large jumps in the pdf
        iterations = 0;
        return cndist(d);
    }

    double d2 = d * d;
    double last_sum = 0, sum = 1.0;
    double factor = 1.0;
    double k2;

    for(int k = 1; k <= MAX_CNDIST_ITERS; k++)
    {
        k2 = k << 1;
        sum += (factor *= d2 * (1.0 - k2) / k2 / (k2 + 1.0));

        if(last_sum == sum)
            break;

        last_sum = sum;
    }
    iterations = k;
    return 0.5 + sum * d / ROOT_2PI;
}
```

Function name	norm_dist (exported) Ndist (registered with Excel)
Description	Returns the value of $N(x)$ calculated using the same approximation as Excel (but not Excel's implementation of it).
Prototype	`xloper * __stdcall norm_dist(double d);`
Type string	`"BB"`
Notes	NORMSDIST, in Excel 2000 and earlier, rounds down to zero for $x < -8.3$ and up to 1 for $x > 6.15$. The function called is a wrapper to a function that has no knowledge of Excel data types.

```
double __stdcall norm_dist(double d)
{
    return cndist(d);
}
```

```
#define B1          0.31938153
#define B2          -0.356563782
#define B3          1.781477937
#define B4          -1.821255978
#define B5          1.330274429
#define PP          0.2316419
#define ROOT_2PI    2.506628274631

double cndist(double d)
{
    if(d == 0.0) return 0.5;
    double t = 1.0 / (1.0 + PP * fabs(d));
    double e = exp(-0.5 * d * d) / ROOT_2PI;
    double n = ((((B5 * t + B4) * t + B3) * t + B2) * t + B1) * t;
    return (d > 0.0) ? 1.0 - e * n : e * n;
}
```

Function name	norm_dist_inv (exported) NdistInv (registered with Excel)
Description	Returns the inverse of $N(x)$ consistent with the norm_dist().
Prototype	xloper * __stdcall norm_dist_inv(double d);
Type string	"BB"
Notes	Returns the inverse of norm_dist(). Uses a simple solver to return, as far as possible, the exact corresponding value and for this reason may be slower than certain other functions. Code could be easily modified to return the inverse of NORMSDIST() if required.

```
#define NDINV_ITER_LIMIT        50
#define NDINV_EPSILON           1e-12 // How precise do we want to be
#define NDINV_FIRST_NUDGE       1e-7

// How much change in answer from one iteration to the next
#define NDINV_DELTA             1e-10

// Approximate working limits of Excel 2000's NORMSINV() function
#define NORMSINV_LOWER_LIMIT    3.024e-7
#define NORMSINV_UPPER_LIMIT    0.999999

xloper * __stdcall norm_dist_inv(double prob)
{
    if(prob <= 0.0 || prob >= 1.0)
        return p_xlErrNum;

// Get a (pretty) good first approximation using Excel's NORMSINV()
// worksheet function. First check that prob is within NORMSINV's
// working limits

    static xloper op_ret_val;
```

```cpp
    double v1, v2, p1, p2, pdiff, temp;

    op_ret_val.xltype = xltypeNum;

    if(prob < NORMSINV_LOWER_LIMIT)
    {
        v2 = (v1 = -5.0) - NDINV_FIRST_NUDGE;
    }
    else if(prob > NORMSINV_UPPER_LIMIT)
    {
        v2 = (v1 = 5.0) + NDINV_FIRST_NUDGE;
    }
    else
    {
        op_ret_val.val.num = prob;

        Excel4(xlfNormsinv, &op_ret_val, 1, &op_ret_val);

        if(op_ret_val.xltype != xltypeNum)
            return p_xlErrNum; // shouldn't need this here

        v2 = op_ret_val.val.num;
        v1 = v2 - NDINV_FIRST_NUDGE;
    }

// Use a secant method to make the result consistent with the
// cndist() function

    p2 = cndist(v2) - prob;

    if(fabs(p2) <= NDINV_EPSILON)
    {
        op_ret_val.val.num = v2;
        return &op_ret_val; // already close enough
    }

    p1 = cndist(v1) - prob;

    for(short i = NDINV_ITER_LIMIT; --i;)
    {
        if(fabs(p1) <= NDINV_EPSILON || (pdiff = p2 - p1) == 0.0)
        {
// Result is close enough, or need to avoid divide by zero
            op_ret_val.val.num = v1;
            return &op_ret_val;
        }

    temp = v1;
    v1 = (v1 * p2 - v2 * p1) / pdiff;

    if(fabs(v1 - temp) <= NDINV_DELTA) // not much improvement
    {
        op_ret_val.val.num = v1;
        return &op_ret_val;
    }
    v2 = temp;
    p2 = p1;
    p1 = cndist(v1) - prob;
    }
    return p_xlErrValue; // Didn't converge
}
```

Table 10.1 shows a comparison of Excel and the above functions from which it can be seen that Excel 2002 has greatly improved accuracy over 2000.

Table 10.1 Excel's normal distribution accuracy

	Excel 2000	Excel 2002
Cumulative distribution	4	4
NORMSDIST()	0.999968314	0.999968329
NORMSINV()	4.000030458	4
Error (absolute)	3.0458E-05	-3.26814E-11
Ndist()	0.999968314	0.999968314
NdistInv()	3.999999998	4
Error (absolute)	-1.76691E-09	-5.40723E-12

Both the `norm_dist()` and `norm_dist_inv()` functions could easily be made to return results based on any of the algorithms and methods discussed above, including Excel's own worksheet functions, with the addition of an extra *method* parameter. Both functions could even be accommodated in a single function interface.

The next two functions return samples from the normal distribution based on the Box-Muller transform of a standard random variable. (See Clewlow and Strickland, 1998.)

Function name	`nsample_BM_pair` (exported) NsampleBoxMullerPair (registered with Excel)
Description	Takes an array of two uncorrelated random numbers in the range (0, 1] and returns two uncorrelated samples from the normal distribution as a 1×2 or 2×1 array, depending on the shape of the input array.
Prototype	`void __stdcall nsample_BM_pair(xl_array *p_array);`
Type string	`"1K"`
Notes	Makes use of the floating point array structure, `xl_array`, for input and output. (See section 6.2.2 on page 107.) Does not need to manage memory and is therefore fast. Only drawback is the limited error handling: any error in input is reflected with return values of 0.

```
#define TWO_PI    6.28318530717959

void __stdcall nsample_BM_pair(xl_array *p_array)
{
// Max array_size is 0x1000000 = 256 ^ 3
   long array_size = p_array->columns * p_array->rows;
```

```
    if(array_size == 2)
    {
       double r1 = p_array->array[0];
       double r2 = p_array->array[1];

       if(r1 > 0.0 && r1 <= 1.0 && r2 > 0.0 && r2 <= 1.0)
       {
          r1 = sqrt(-2.0 * log(r1));
          r2 *= TWO_PI;
          p_array->array[0] = r1 * cos(r2);
          p_array->array[1] = r1 * sin(r2);
          return;
       }
    }
    memset(p_array->array, 0, array_size * sizeof(double));
}
```

Function name	nsample_BM (exported) NsampleBoxMuller (registered with Excel)
Description	Takes no arguments and returns a sample from the normal distribution. Generates a pair at a time; remembers one and returns the other. Uses Excel's xlfRand C API function, equivalent to the RAND() worksheet function, to generate pseudo-random number inputs for the transformation.
Prototype	`double __stdcall NsampleBoxMuller(void);`
Type string	`"B!"`
Notes	Function takes no arguments and is declared as volatile to ensure it is called whenever the workbook is recalculated.

```
double __stdcall nsample_BM(void)
{
  static double sample_zero;
  static bool loaded = false;

  if(loaded)
  {
     loaded = false;
     return sample_zero;
  }

  loaded = true;

  xloper ret_val;
  Excel4(xlfRand, &ret_val, 0);
  double r1 = ret_val.val.num;

  Excel4(xlfRand, &ret_val, 0);
  double r2 = ret_val.val.num;

  r1 = sqrt(-2.0 * log(r1));
```

```
    r2 * = TWO_PI;

    sample_zero = r1 * cos(r2);
    return r1 * sin(r2);
}
```

Both the above functions perform the same task but in very different ways. The first can take static or volatile inputs and always returns a pair of samples. The second returns a single sample but is volatile. This gives the spreadsheet developer less control than with the first. It would be possible to modify the second so that it took a trigger argument, which would then obviate the need for it to be declared as volatile.

It is a straightforward exercise to generalise the Box-Muller functions above to, optionally, generate samples using the more efficient polar rejection method. (See Clewlow and Strickland (1998) for details.)

10.3   MATRIX FUNCTIONS – EIGENVALUES AND EIGENVECTORS

Excel has a number of useful matrix routines, in particular MMULT(), MINVERSE(), MDETERM(), TRANSPOSE() and SUMPRODUCT(). As well as this, the way that Excel treats range references in array formulae greatly extends its matrix capabilities. Nevertheless, there are a number of matrix operations which, though not as fundamental as these, are valuable for those analysing linear systems. Perhaps the most useful is the calculation of eigenvectors and eigenvalues. The following example function takes a square symmetric (real) N×N matrix and returns an N×(N + 1) array containing the eigenvectors and eigenvalues. The code is contained in the CD ROM and is based on the Jacobi algorithm published in section 11.1 of *Numerical Recipes in C++*. (The code for the Jacobi algorithm itself is omitted from the XllMatrix.cpp source code module in the example project on the CD ROM. However, it can easily be inserted into one of the member functions of the class, d_matrix. See the *read me* file on the CD ROM for details.)

The intention here is not to provide a comprehensive set of functions that will attempt to find the eigenvectors and values of any matrix. As NRC explains very well, this is a complex subject. The intention of this example is to show how to bridge from Excel ranges to C/C++ matrices in a safe and efficient way.

Function name	eigen_system (exported) EigenSystem (registered with Excel)
Description	Takes a square symmetrical range, or array, containing only numbers. Returns a square matrix whose columns are the eigenvectors of the input matrix, with an extra row at the bottom containing the corresponding eigenvalues. Output is sorted in descending size of eigenvalue from left to right.
Prototype	xloper * __stdcall eigen_system(xl_array *);
Type string	"RK"

| Notes | The function takes a pointer to an xl_array rather than, say, an xloper. It uses a matrix class, d_matrix, passing the xl_array data directly to the d_matrix constructor. The function returns a pointer to an xloper, rather than another xl_array, so that errors can be communicated more flexibly. |
| | The routine sets a limit of 100×100 on the input matrix. Excel's own matrix functions have a 60×60 limit. This function is an example of the kind of worksheet function that can take significant time to execute. Some understanding of how the execution time grows with matrix size is important. |

The interface function for this is:

```
xloper * __stdcall eigen_system(xl_array *p_input)
{
    if(called_from_paste_fn_dlg())
        return NULL;

    WORD rows = p_input->rows;
    WORD columns = p_input->columns;

    if(rows < 2 || rows > 100 || rows != columns)
        return p_xlErrValue;

    d_matrix Mat(rows, columns, p_input->array);
    d_matrix Eigenvectors;
    d_vector Eigenvalues;

    if(!Mat.GetEigenvectors(Eigenvectors, Eigenvalues)
    || !Eigenvectors.InsertRow(Eigenvalues, -1))
        return p_xlErrNum;

    cpp_xloper Output(rows + 1, columns, Eigenvectors.data);
    return Output.ExtractXloper();
}
```

Section 10.11 *Monte Carlo simulation* below discusses an Excel and VBA only interface solution. The above function is one that you might want to access directly from VB in this case. The following example code shows a VBA wrapper to the above code. It does not require that the XLL be loaded by the Add-in Manager, but it does require that the C API interface be available, i.e., that the XLL is built and linked with the static xlcall32 library, or is able to detect that it needs to link dynamically with xlcall32.dll. This VBA wrapper is not the most efficient possible, but does demonstrate the use of a number of the conversion routines built into the cpp_xloper class.

```
VARIANT __stdcall VBA_eigen_system(VARIANT *pv)
{
    static VARIANT vt;
```

```
// Convert the passed-in Variant to an xloper within a cpp_xloper
   cpp_xloper Array(pv);

// Convert the xloper to an xl_array of doubles
   xl_array *p_array = Array.AsDblArray();

   if(!p_array)
   {
      xloper_to_vt(p_xlErrValue, vt, false);
      return vt;
   }

// Attempt to convert the array to an xloper xltypeMulti containing
// the required output. Function returns a pointer to a static xloper
   xloper *p_op = eigen_system(p_array);

   free(p_array); // Don't need this anymore

// Re-use the Array cpp_xloper. Assignment operator makes a shallow
// copy and preserves the correct destructor information, i.e.,
// takes note if either xlbitXLFree or xlbitDLLFree are set.
// No need to check if p_op is NULL - assignment operator checks.
   Array = p_op;

// Convert the xloper back to a Variant
   Array.AsVariant(vt);
   return vt;
}
```

Here is an example of the corresponding VBA declaration and usage of this function from VBA:

```
Declare Function VBA_eigen_system Lib "example.xll" _
    (ByRef arg As Variant) As Variant

Function VbaEigenSystem(v As Variant) As Variant

    If IsObject(v) Then
        VbaEigenSystem = VBA_eigen_system(v.Value)
    Else
        VbaEigenSystem = VBA_eigen_system(v)
    End If

End Function
```

10.4 INTERPOLATION FUNCTIONS: LINES, CURVES AND SPLINES

Interpolation is another area where Excel provides very little *native* support. Most people working with data need to interpolate or extrapolate regularly, in at least one dimension. The recalculation time difference between an inefficient interpolation function, such as one that uses VB or numerous worksheet cells, and an efficient one can be significant.

For something fundamental to so many data analysis and modelling applications, the fact that Excel is so short of interpolation functions is very surprising. The *Analysis ToolPak* add-in provides linear and logarithmic estimation functions and a linear prediction function, LINEST(), LOGEST() and FORCAST(), but no, say, INTERP() function. The examples included do not pretend to fill this gap completely, but do provide example implementations of two of the most common types of interpolation:

- Piece-wise linear
- Cubic spline
  - Natural
  - Gradient constrained at one end
  - Gradient constrained at both ends

The assumption is that there exists a table of known x's and known y's, sorted in ascending order of x, and that the user wishes to interpolate/extrapolate some unknown value of y for a given value of x.

In practice, splines have some problems, in common with other polynomial based approaches: Where the y values are naturally bounded but the function has a maximum or minimum near the boundary, the spline may want to put the peak out-of-bounds. A piece-wise linear approach does not have this problem. Another big problem with splines is that the y value at any one point affects all of the curves between all points. This is particularly problematic when dealing with yield curves where the input data may well have sparse patches with less reliable price data. Changing one price can alter parts of the curve that should, intuitively at least, be unaffected.

A simple but practical improvement to the spline function is to add a blend parameter (between 0 and 1) that the returned tabulated 2nd derivatives are scaled by. A value of 0 produces piece-wise linear interpolation. A value of 1, a cubic spline. This blend value can easily be associated with a slider control on a worksheet.

The second problem can be minimised, although not removed, with a sensible choice of the y function (or function of y, depending on your point of view) to be interpolated – something that should always be given careful consideration in any case.

The goal with all of these functions is simplicity and speed. Where very large ranges are involved, the main effort may well be finding the values that surround the value to be interpolated. The example functions use a bisection method to do this. (If successive calls are always related, a more efficient strategy is to start the search in the last known position.)

With cubic spline interpolation, the example opts for a two-stage approach: one function that returns an array of second derivatives of y with respect to x, MakeSpline(), and another that interpolates given the x's, y's and these derivatives, SplineInterp(). The first function allows the user to specify whether the spline is natural or constrained at one or both ends.

The code for these functions is listed on the CD ROM in the source file `Spline.cpp` in the example project, except that code derived from the *Numerical Recipes in C* is omitted for licensing reasons. See the *read me* file on the CD ROM for details.

Function name	make_spline (exported) MakeSpline (registered with Excel)
Description	Takes a two-column input array with the first column being values of x in ascending order, the second being corresponding values of y. Also takes a starting gradient, an end gradient and a mode argument that determines which, if either, of these is used. 0 = neither is used, 1 = the start is defined, 2 = the end is defined, 3 = both are defined. Returns a column of 2nd derivatives of y with respect to x.
Prototype	`xloper * __stdcall make_spline(xl_array *input, double grad_start, double grad_end, int mode);`
Type string	`"RKBBJ"`
Notes	The function returns an `xloper` so that errors can be passed back easily. The input array is passed as an `xl_array` to simplify the code. Excel will not call the function unless it can convert all of the inputs to numbers.

Function name	spline_interp (exported) SplineInterp (registered with Excel)
Description	Takes a three-column input array with the first column being values of x in ascending order, the second being corresponding values of y, the third being 2nd derivatives of y with respect to x. Takes the value of x for which the corresponding value of y is to be found. Takes an optional number between 0 and 1 representing a blend of linear to cubic interpolation.
Prototype	`xloper * __stdcall spline_interp(double x, xl_array *input, xloper *pBlend);`
Type string	`"RBKP"`
Notes	The function returns an `xloper` so that errors can be passed back easily. The input array is passed as an `xl_array` to simplify the code. Excel will not call the function unless it can convert all of the inputs to numbers. The function `spline_interp()` uses a binary search on the first column of the input array, the x's. For this to work, the input must be sorted in ascending order of x. The function does not check that this is true. This is nevertheless a safe assumption if using the output of `make_spline()`, which fails if this is not the case.

Function name	interp (exported) Interp (registered with Excel)
Description	Takes two columns of inputs, the first being values of x in ascending order, the second being corresponding values of y. Takes the value of x for which the corresponding value of y is to be found.
Prototype	`xloper * __stdcall interp(double x, xl_array *xx, xl_array *yy, int dont_extrapolate);`
Type string	`"RBKKJ"`
Notes	The function returns an `xloper` so that error values can be passed back easily. The input is passed as two `xl_arrays`, allowing the range of tabulated x's to be in a separate block from the known y's. Excel will not call the function unless it can convert all of the inputs to numbers. As with the cubic spline above, the function assumes that the x's are in ascending order. The code permits the input ranges/arrays to be either columns or rows but both must be the same. If x is outside the range of the tabulated x's, the function returns either the lowest or highest value of y, i.e., it assumes y is flat. If `dont_extrapolate` is true/non-zero, the function returns #NUM! if x is outside these limits. The function uses a static `xloper` for the return value rather than the `cpp_xloper` class.

The code for this function is as follows:

```
xloper * __stdcall interp(double x, xl_array *yy, xl_array *xx,
                          int dont_extrapolate)
{
// Check that input ranges are same size and shape
    if(yy->columns != xx->columns || yy->rows != xx->rows)
        return p_xlErrValue;

    int low = 0, high, i;
    static xloper ret_val = {0.0, xltypeNum};

// Check that input is either a row or column and get the size
    if(yy->rows == 1)
        high = yy->columns - 1;
    else if(yy->columns == 1)
        high = yy->rows - 1;
    else
        return p_xlErrValue;

    if(high == 0)
    {
        ret_val.val.num = yy->array[0];
        return &ret_val;
    }
```

```
    if(x < xx->array[0]  ||  x > xx->array[high])
    {
        if(dont_extrapolate)
            return p_xlErrNum;
        ret_val.val.num = yy->array[x < xx->array[0] ? 0 : high];
        return &ret_val;
    }

    while(high - low > 1)
    {
        i = (high + low) >> 1;
        if(xx->array[i] > x)
            high = i;
        else
            low = i;
    }

    ret_val.val.num = yy->array[low] +
        (x - xx->array[low]) * (yy->array[high] - yy->array[low])
            / (xx->array[high] - xx->array[low]);

    return &ret_val;
}
```

10.5   LOOKUP AND SEARCH FUNCTIONS

Lookup and search functions, especially those where the input arrays contain strings, are far more efficiently coded in C/C++ than the alternatives. Where you need to use two- or higher-dimensional lookups or searches, or where more complex search or match criteria are needed, on large amounts of data, you should seriously consider using C/C++. The following table briefly outlines the limitations of Excel's own lookup and search functions.

Table 10.2 Excel's lookup and search functions

Function	Limitations
VLOOKUP() HLOOKUP()	Left-most column (top row) needs to be in ascending order for the function to work. Lookup value and returned value need to be in the same single range. Only one lookup value can be matched and only against the left-most column (top row).
LOOKUP()	Form: LOOKUP(Lookup_value,Lookup_vector,Result_vector): left-most column needs to be in ascending order for the function to work. Only one lookup value can be matched.
MATCH()	Only one lookup value can be matched.
COUNTIF() SUMIF()	Only one criterion can be applied

Excel includes a number of database functions which do provide a way around many, if not all, of these limitations, albeit at the expense of more complex workbooks. These functions are also available via the C API.

The primary extension in these examples is to allow for a search on more than one range, so, for example, a value can be retrieved from a row in a table when values of two or more elements in that row match specified search criteria. The function MatchMulti() returns the same kind of information as MATCH() – the offset into the range where the match was found or #N/A if none found – and, if used in conjunction with the INDEX() function, extends VLOOKUP() functionality. The functions SumIfMulti() and CountIfMulti() similarly extend the functions COUNTIF() and SUMIF() respectively.

These functions rely heavily on the `cpp_xloper` class, making the code far cleaner than it would otherwise be if only `xlopers` had been used. There is only a very small performance cost in using the class, but you could re-implement these things using `xlopers` directly if this were a concern. Code for these functions is listed in the example project source file `Lookup.cpp`.

Function name	match_multi (exported) MatchMulti (registered with Excel)
Description	Returns the offset corresponding to the position in one to five search ranges that match the corresponding supplied values. The offset counts from 1 so that it can be used with the INDEX() function to retrieve values from, say, an associated data table. Input search ranges are expected to be either single columns or single rows, and all search ranges must be the same shape and size and have at least 2 elements each. Search ranges do not need to be sorted or all of the same data type. The function looks for exact matches and is case-sensitive when comparing strings. The function returns #VALUE! if inputs are not valid and #N/A if a match cannot be found.

Prototype	`xloper * __stdcall match_multi(`
	 `        xloper *value1, xloper *range1,`
	 `        xloper *value2, xloper *range2,`
	 `        xloper *value3, xloper *range3,`
	 `        xloper *value4, xloper *range4,`
	 `        xloper *value5, xloper *range5);`

Type string	`"RPPPPPPPPPP"`
Notes	Function arguments are declared as `xlopers` but registered as `opers`. This causes Excel to convert range references to `xltypeMulti`, simplifying the type-checking and conversion in the DLL. (If a search range reference is a single cell it will be converted to a single value, rather than an array, and the function will fail.) The function returns an `xloper` so that errors can be returned.

The code for this function is as follows. The function relies heavily on the `cpp_xloper` class to simplify the code, in particular for comparing `xlopers` (the overloaded `!=` operator) and for handling arrays.

```
xloper * __stdcall match_multi(
        xloper *value1, xloper *range1,
        xloper *value2, xloper *range2,
        xloper *value3, xloper *range3,
        xloper *value4, xloper *range4,
        xloper *value5, xloper *range5)
{
// Get the arguments into a more manageable form.
// Arguments are registered as opers so that range references are
// already converted to xltypeMulti.
    cpp_xloper args[5][2] = {{value1, range1}, {value2, range2},
        {value3, range3}, {value4, range4}, {value5, range5}};

// Find the last non-missing value/range pair
    int num_searches = 0;

    do
    {
        if(args[num_searches][0].IsType(xltypeMissing | xltypeErr)
        || !args[num_searches][1].IsType(xltypeMulti))
            break;
    }
    while(++num_searches < 5);

    if(!num_searches)
        return p_xlErrValue;

// Check that all the input arrays are the same shape and size
    WORD rows, columns;
    WORD temp_rows, temp_columns;

    args[0][1].GetArraySize(rows, columns);

// Check that input is either single row or single column
    if(rows != 1 && columns != 1)
        return p_xlErrValue;

    for(int i = 1; i < num_searches; i++)
    {
        args[i][1].GetArraySize(temp_rows, temp_columns);

        if(rows != temp_rows || columns != temp_columns)
            return p_xlErrValue;
    }

    DWORD limit = rows * columns;
    DWORD offset;

// Simple search does not assume search ranges are sorted and
// looks for an exact match
    for(offset = 0; offset < limit; offset++)
    {
        for(i = 0; i < num_searches; i++)
            if(args[i][0] != args[i][1].GetArrayElement(offset))
                break;

        if(i == num_searches) // Match found!
        {
        // Increment the offset as INDEX() counts from 1
            cpp_xloper RetVal((double)(offset + 1));
```

```
            return RetVal.ExtractXloper(false);
        }
    }
    return p_xlErrNa;
}
```

Function name	sum_if_multi (exported) SumIfMulti (registered with Excel)
Description	Returns the sum of all values in a sum range, where corresponding values in up to five search ranges match corresponding search values. Input ranges are expected to be either single columns or single rows, and all search ranges must be the same shape and size and have at least 2 elements each. Search ranges are not required to be sorted or all the same data type. The function looks for exact matches and is case-sensitive when comparing strings. The function returns #VALUE! if inputs are not valid. Values in the sum range are converted to numbers if possible and skipped if not.

Prototype	`xloper * __stdcall sum_if_multi(xloper *sum_range,`
	 `            xloper *value1, xloper *range1,`
	 `            xloper *value2, xloper *range2,`
	 `            xloper *value3, xloper *range3,`
	 `            xloper *value4, xloper *range4,`
	 `            xloper *value5, xloper *range5;`

Type string	`"RPPPPPPPPPPP"`
Notes	Function arguments are declared as xlopers but registered as opers. This causes Excel to convert from references to xltypeMulti xlopers, simplifying the type-checking and conversion that the DLL function needs to do. (If a search range reference is a single cell it will be converted to a single value, rather than an array, and the function will fail.) The function returns an xloper so that errors can be returned.

The code is similar to the code for the function MatchMulti() above.

```
xloper * __stdcall sum_if_multi(xloper *sum_range,
        xloper *value1, xloper *range1,
        xloper *value2, xloper *range2,
        xloper *value3, xloper *range3,
        xloper *value4, xloper *range4,
        xloper *value5, xloper *range5)
{
// Get the arguments into a more manageable form.
// Arguments are registered as opers so that range references are
```

```
// already converted to xltypeMulti.
   cpp_xloper SumRange(sum_range);
   cpp_xloper args[5][2] = {{value1, range1}, {value2, range2},
       {value3, range3}, {value4, range4}, {value5, range5}};

   if(!SumRange.IsType(xltypeMulti))
       return p_xlErrValue;

// Find the last non-missing value/range pair
   int num_searches = 0;

   do
   {
       if(args[num_searches][0].IsType(xltypeMissing | xltypeErr)
       || !args[num_searches][1].IsType(xltypeMulti))
           break;
   }
   while(++num_searches < 5);

   if(!num_searches)
       return p_xlErrValue;

// Check that all the input arrays are the same shape and size
   WORD rows, columns;
   WORD temp_rows, temp_columns;

   SumRange.GetArraySize(rows, columns);

// Check that input is either single row or single column
   if(rows != 1 && columns != 1)
       return p_xlErrValue;

   for(int i = 0; i < num_searches; i++)
   {
       args[i][1].GetArraySize(temp_rows, temp_columns);

       if(rows != temp_rows || columns != temp_columns)
           return p_xlErrValue;
   }

   DWORD limit = rows * columns;
   DWORD offset;
   double temp, sum = 0.0;

// Simple search does not assume first search range is sorted and
// looks for an exact match
   for(offset = 0; offset < limit; offset++)
   {
       for(i = 0; i < num_searches; i++)
           if(args[i][0] != args[i][1].GetArrayElement(offset))
               break;

       if(i == num_searches
       && SumRange.GetArrayElement(offset, temp))
           sum += temp;
   }
   cpp_xloper RetVal(sum);
   return RetVal.ExtractXloper(false);
}
```

Function name	`count_if_multi` (exported) CountIfMulti (registered with Excel)
Description	Counts the number of cases where values in up to five search ranges match corresponding search values. Input ranges are expected to be either single columns or single rows, and all search ranges must be the same shape and size and have at least 2 elements each. Search ranges are not required to be sorted or all the same data type. The function looks for exact matches and is case-sensitive when comparing strings. The function returns #VALUE! if inputs are not valid.

Prototype	`xloper * __stdcall count_if_multi(`
	`        xloper *value1, xloper *range1,`
	`        xloper *value2, xloper *range2,`
	`        xloper *value3, xloper *range3,`
	`        xloper *value4, xloper *range4,`
	`        xloper *value5, xloper *range5);`

Type string	`"RPPPPPPPPPP"`
Notes	Function arguments are declared as `xlopers` but registered as `opers`. This causes Excel to convert from range references to `xltypeMulti` xlopers, simplifying the type checking and conversion that the DLL function needs to do. (If a search range reference is a single cell it will be converted to a single value, rather than an array, and the function will fail.) The function returns an `xloper` so that errors can be returned.

```
xloper * __stdcall count_if_multi(
      xloper *value1, xloper *range1,
      xloper *value2, xloper *range2,
      xloper *value3, xloper *range3,
      xloper *value4, xloper *range4,
      xloper *value5, xloper *range5)
{
// Get the arguments into a more manageable form.
// Arguments are registered as opers so that range references are
// already converted to xltypeMulti.
   cpp_xloper args[5][2] = {{value1, range1}, {value2, range2},
       {value3, range3}, {value4, range4}, {value5, range5}};

// Find the last non-missing value/range pair
   int num_searches = 0;

   do
   {
       if(args[num_searches][0].IsType(xltypeMissing | xltypeErr)
       || !args[num_searches][1].IsType(xltypeMulti))
            break;
   }
```

```
       while(++num_searches < 5);

       if(!num_searches)
           return p_xlErrValue;

   // Check that all the input arrays are the same shape and size
   WORD rows, columns;
   WORD temp_rows, temp_columns;

   args[0][1].GetArraySize(rows, columns);

   // Check that input is either single row or single column
   if(rows != 1 && columns != 1)
       return p_xlErrValue;

   for(int i = 1; i < num_searches; i++)
   {
       args[i][1].GetArraySize(temp_rows, temp_columns);

       if(rows != temp_rows || columns != temp_columns)
           return p_xlErrValue;
   }

   DWORD limit = rows * columns;
   DWORD offset;
   int count = 0;

   // Simple search does not assume first search range is sorted and
   // looks for an exact match
   for(offset = 0; offset < limit; offset++)
   {
       for(i = 0; i < num_searches; i++)
           if(args[i][0]!=args[i][1].GetArrayElement(offset))
               break;

       if(i == num_searches)
           count++;
   }
   cpp_xloper RetVal(count);
   return RetVal.ExtractXloper(false);
}
```

10.6 FINANCIAL MARKETS DATE FUNCTIONS

Financial markets rely on conventions that govern the dates on which certain things happen. For example, there are conventions that determine

- interest payment dates;
- settlement dates for commodity, stock, bond, cash and currency transactions;
- option exercise/expiry dates;
- dates on which price or rate fixings are recorded and published;
- futures contract expiry and settlement dates;
- bond coupon ex-dividend and payment dates;
- the list could go on.

The correct calculation of dates and holidays, and the proper application of day-count and days-in-year conventions are the first things to get right. Pricing and valuation errors caused by just one extra day of interest can be significant in the narrow bid-offer spreads of the professional markets. This section does not attempt to document all conventions in all markets. Instead, it picks a few examples of the kinds of things that need to be done and explores how best to implement functions that do them.

The date functionality of Excel on its own is stretched to do the job of working with these date conventions. The choices for a financial markets application are:

- Use combinations of Excel's worksheet functions.
- Use VB functions.
- Use C/C++ functions from a DLL.
- Use Microsoft or third-party add-ins.

The first choice, while possible, can lead to complex sets of formulae that are difficult to debug and change. They can also produce a spreadsheet that is slow to recalculate, difficult to expand, or that has logic that is difficult for others to follow. VB functions, though accessible, can be slow. Compiled C/C++ code is fast and, if well commented, has none of these problems. An example of the fourth choice is the Analysis ToolPak shipped with Excel which contains a number of bond market date functions, for example, COUPPCD() which returns the previous coupon payment date on a coupon-bearing bond. Performance of third party add-ins may not always be sufficient, especially where these are VBA XLA add-ins.

Market date functions can get a little complex. Take the simple question, 'Given a certain start date for a US dollar interest rate swap, what is the first LIBOR fixing date?'. (This is normally the trade date if the swap is spot-starting, but could be the exercise date if a swaption.) The solution requires knowledge of London bank holidays, US banking holidays, and the convention for spot date calculations for dollars in London. (The spot date is two good London business days forward, unless this falls on a NY holiday in which case the next day that is not a holiday in either centre.) Even in this case, it might be possible that two banks trading a dollar swap in Tokyo might also want to avoid Tokyo banking holidays for spot and settlement dates. Designing function interfaces and function code that balance flexibility with simplicity is part of the programmer's art. It is not possible to say there is a best way, and every set of choices may inevitably have its drawbacks, but choices must be made.

The discussion focuses on the following market date tasks:[3]

1. Given any date, find out if it is a GBD in a given centre or union of centres, returning information about the date if it is not.
2. Given any date, find out if it is the last GBD of the month for a given centre or union of centres.
3. Given any date, adjust it, if it is not a GBD, to the next or previous GDB given a centre or centres and a modification rule (for example, FMBDC).
4. Given a valid business trade (fixing) date, calculate the spot (settlement) date in a given centre or centres for a given transaction type in a given currency or currency pair.

---

[3] The abbreviations GBD (good business day) and FMBDC (following modified business day convention) are used from here on.

5. Given a valid spot (settlement) date, calculate the trade (fixing) date in a given centre or centres for a given transaction type in a given currency or currency pair.

6. Given any date, calculate the GBD that is n (interim) GBDs after (before if $n < 0$), given an interim holiday database and final date holiday database. (Interim holidays only are counted in determining whether n GBDs have elapsed. Final and interim holidays are avoided once n GBDs have elapsed).

7. Given an interest payment date in a regular series, calculate the next date given the frequency of the series, the rollover day-of-month, the holiday centre or centres, according to FMBDC.

8. Given two dates, calculate the fraction of a year or the number of days between them given (i) a day-count/year convention (e.g., Actual/365, Actual/360, 30/360, 30E/360, Actual/Actual), adjusting the dates if necessary to GBDs given a centre or centres, and (ii) a modification rule (for example, FMBDC) and a rollover day-of-month.

9. Given any GBD, calculate a date that is m whole months forward or backward, in a given centre or centres for a given modification rule.

10. Calculate the number of GBDs between two dates given a holiday database.

Many more functions could be added to this list, for example, those relating to futures contract expiries: this is not intended to be an exhaustive list. It can easily be seen that (3), (4) and (5) can all be accomplished by a suitably flexible implementation of (6) assuming that the holiday database(s) reflect all of the centres that are relevant. Less obviously, there are issues with the mapping of trade dates to settlement dates which is not, in general, one-to-one. In some cases two or three consecutive trade dates can map to the same spot date. When $n < 0$, function (6) must therefore provide a means for the user to determine which of the possible trade dates, consistent with the given settlement date, they wish to get – or perhaps a means to get all of them.

The first questions to consider are those relating to holidays. There are three choices:

(i) Generate holidays within the code from algorithms.
(ii) Source holidays externally and store them on the worksheet.
(iii) Source holidays externally and store them in the DLL (or a VB module).

Choice (i) is perhaps the ideal choice but does require the coding and testing of the algorithms which must be capable of adapting to new holidays and rules. For this reason it may not be the most practical. Choice (ii) provides greater flexibility for the date functions, which can simply be passed ranges of holidays, but requires that the holidays are always on an open workbook that uses the data functions. (Holidays can be read from a closed workbook, but this can be quite inefficient.) Choice (iii) is computationally the most efficient. Holidays can be loaded into the DLL with worksheet functions that return, say, a label and sequence number to be passed as an argument to the date functions. (See section 9.6 *Maintaining large data structures within the DLL* on page 305.) The raw holiday input only needs to be verified, sorted and converted once, enabling the most efficient internal coding of an '*is it a holiday?*' routine.

It may be that you want your DLL to load holiday tables from a central source. You may choose to use Excel's ability to access data from external sources, for example, via DDE or VB or by accessing an external database. (See Excel's online help for detail about the external database access and web access choices.) From within the DLL, the choices are use the C API's DDE commands or COM to communicate with another application, or use some other means, perhaps a socket library via one or more background threads. In the interests of simplicity, which correlates highly with reliability, separating the sourcing of holidays from the DLL/XLL that contains the date functions is a good idea.

The following set of tables describe a possible interface for functions (1), (2), (6), (7), (8) and (9). Choice (ii) above is assumed to have been made, i.e., that the holidays are passed in as ranges of dates on the workbook. It is implementation-dependant, and left indeterminate, whether holidays would need to be pre-sorted. The functions all expect that holidays are in a contiguous range in an accessible workbook. Where a function is to use holidays from multiple centres, it is assumed that a combined range of holidays exists on a worksheet.

Dates are passed in as numbers (doubles) and should be interpreted according to the state of the 1904 date system checkbox on the Tools/Options. . ./Calculation dialog. This can be determined within the DLL with a call to xlfGetDocument with *ArgNum* set to 20. (See section 8.9.6 on page 217 for details.) If individual dates were passed in as 16-bit integers (type "I"), the range of dates supported would be too limited.

Optional arguments are prototyped as xlopers, enabling them to be omitted, but registered as opers so that range arguments do not need to be de-referenced. Required arguments may also be prototyped as xlopers for the flexibility that this brings, the assumption being that the function code will fail if a *missing* or *nil* type is passed in. Excel will not call a function if non-xloper arguments cannot be converted to the registered types. All of the functions are prototyped as returning an xloper to provide the greatest flexibility in return type.

Required ranges of holidays are passed in as xl_arrays. Excel will not call the function if the range contains strings that can't be converted to numbers, Booleans or error values. The values of the holidays then needs to be extracted. The cpp_xloper class contains member functions that do just this. (See section 6.4 *A C++ class wrapper for the* xloper – cpp_xloper *on page 121.)

Little or no discussion is made of the body of the functions. It is assumed that any competent programmer could code efficient and safe routines to do the work of testing if a date (truncated to an integer) occurs in a list of holidays, stepping forward one day if it is, and so on.

Conversion of day counts to day-month-year structures is less obvious. The following code shows how this can be done efficiently. Note that the code serialises day-counts using a signed 32-bit integer, ample for storing the maximum Excel date of 31-Dec-9999. However, the simplified leap-year assumption in this code means that the conversion is only valid for dates in the range 1-Jan-1900 to 28-Feb-2100 inclusive.

```
enum {JAN=1,FEB,MAR,APR,MAY,JUN,JUL,AUG,SEP,OCT,NOV,DEC};
int m_days[12] = {0,31,59,90,120,151,181,212,243,273,304,334};

inline int day_count(int day, int month, int year)
{
    return 1 + day + m_days[month - JAN] +
        (month > FEB && !( year & 3))
        + year * 365 + ((year - 1) >> 2);
}

void count_to_date(int count, int &day, int &month, int &year)
{
```

```
    year = (--count << 2) / 1461;
    day = count - year * 365 - ((year - 1) >> 2);

    for(month = JAN; month < MAR; month ++)
    {
        if(m_days[month] >= d)
        {
            day -= m_days[month - 1];
            return;
        }
    }

    if(!(year & 3))
    {
        if(m_days[FEB] == --day)
        {
            day = 29;
            month = FEB;
            return;
        }
    }

    for(;month < DEC; month++)
        if(m_days[month] >= day)
            break;

    day -= m_days[month - 1];
}
```

The above code assumes that the serial day-count is that which Excel stores when using its default 1900 date system.[4] If your application is critically dependent on dates, you should check the status of this setting and convert all incoming and returned dates. The following code samples show how to do this. Note that the exported worksheet function accepts and returns dates as 32-bit integers, type J. Note also that the state of Excel will not change during a single call to a function, but would need to be checked on every call to be super-safe. In practice, this is overkill.

```
bool excel_using_1904_system(void)
{
    cpp_xloper Using1904; // initialised to xltypeNil
    cpp_xloper Arg(20); // initialised to xltypeInt
    Excel4(xlfGetDocument, &Using1904, 1, &Arg);

    if(Using1904.IsBool() && (bool)Using1904)
        return true;

    return false;
}

#define DAYS_1900_TO_1904    1462 // = 1-Jan-1904 in 1900 system
```

---

[4] Excel mistakenly thinks that 1900 was a leap year and therefore the first correct interpretation of a date under this system is 1-Mar-1900 which equates to the value 61.

```
int __stdcall worksheet_date_fn(int input_date)
{
   bool using_1904 = excel_using_1904_system();

   if(using_1904)
      input_date += DAYS_1900_TO_1904;

// Do something with the date
   int result = some_date_fn(input_date);

   if(using_1904)
      result -= DAYS_1900_TO_1904;

   return result;
}
```

Description	Given any date, find out if it is a GBD in a given centre or union of centres, returning either true or false, or information about the date if not a GBD when requested.
Prototype	`xloper * __stdcall is_gbd(double ref_date, xl_array *hols_array, xloper *rtn_string);`
Type string	`"RBKP"`
Notes	Returns a Boolean, a more descriptive string or an error value. The first two arguments are required. The first is the reference date. The second is an array of holidays.
	The third argument is optional and, once coerced to a Boolean, enables the caller to specify a simple true/false return value or, say, a descriptive string. Where the DLL assumes this is Boolean, a blank cell would be interpreted as false, i.e., do not return a string.

Description	Given any date, find out if it is the last GBD of the month for a given centre or union of centres, or obtain the last GBD of the month in which the date falls.
Prototype	`xloper * __stdcall last_gbd(double date, xl_array *hols_array, xloper *rtn_last_gbd);`
Type string	`"RBKP"`
Notes	Returns a Boolean, a date or an error value. The first two arguments are required. The first is the date being tested. The second is an array of holidays.
	The third argument is optional and, once coerced to a Boolean, enables the caller to specify a simple true/false return value or the actual last GBD of the month. Where the DLL assumes this is Boolean, a blank cell would be interpreted as false.

Description	Given any date, calculate the GBD that is n (interim) GBDs after (before if $n < 0$), given an interim holiday database and final date holiday database. (Interim holidays only are counted in determining whether n GBDs have elapsed and final and interim holidays are avoided once n GBDs have elapsed.) If n is zero adjust the date forwards or backwards as instructed if not a GBD. If $n < 0$ and a final holidays database has been provided and a number of dates would map forwards to the same given date, return the latest or all as directed.
Prototype	`xloper * __stdcall adjust_date(double ref_date, short n_gbds, xl_array *interim_hols, xloper *final_hols, xloper *adj_backwards, xloper *rtn_all);`
Type string	`"RBIKPPP"`
Notes	Returns a Boolean, a date, an array of dates or an error value. The first three arguments are required. The first is the date being adjusted. The second is the number of GBDs to adjust the date by. The third is an array of interim holidays. The fourth argument tells the function whether to adjust dates forwards or backwards if $n =$ zero. It is optional, but a default behaviour, in this case, needs to be coded. The fifth argument is optional and, interpreted as a Boolean, instructs the function to return the closest or all of the possible dates when adjusting backwards.

Description	Given an interest payment date in a regular series, calculate the next date given the frequency of the series, the rollover day-of-month, the holiday centre or centres, according to the following modified date convention.
Prototype	`xloper * __stdcall next_rollover(double ref_date, short roll_day, short roll_month, short rolls_pa, xl_array *hols_array, xloper *get_previous);`
Type string	`"RBIIIKP"`
Notes	Returns a date or an error value. All arguments bar the last are required. The rollover day of month (`roll_day`) is a number in the range 1 to 31 inclusive, with 31 being equivalent to an end-end rollover convention. The `roll_month` argument need only be one of the months on which rollovers can occur.

Description	Given two dates, calculate the fraction of a year <u>or</u> the number of days between them given a day-count/year convention (e.g., Actual/365, Actual/360, 30/360, 30E/360, Actual/Actual), adjusting the dates if necessary to GBDs given a centre or centres and a modification rule (for example, FMBDC) and a rollover day-of-month.
Prototype	`xloper * __stdcall date_diff(double date1, double date2, char *basis, xloper *rtn_days_diff, xloper *hols_range, xloper *roll_day, xloper *apply_fmbdc);`
Type string	`"RBBCPPPP"`
Notes	Returns a number of days or fraction of year(s) or an error value. The first three arguments are required. The requirements for the basis strings would be implementation-dependent, with as much flexibility and intelligence as required being built into the function.

The fourth argument is optional and implies that the function returns a year fraction by default. The last three arguments are optional, given that none of them might be required if either the basis does not require GBD correction, or the dates are already known to be GBDs. |

Description	Given any GBD, calculate a date that is *m* whole months forward or backward, in a given centre or centres for a given modification rule.
Prototype	`xloper * __stdcall months_from_date(double ref_date, int months, xl_array *hols_array, xloper *roll_day, xloper *apply_end_end);`
Type string	`"RBJKPP"`
Notes	Returns a date or an error value. The first three arguments are required. The last two arguments are optional. If `roll_day` is omitted, the assumption is that this information would be extracted from `ref_date` subject to whether or not the end-end rule is to be applied.

Description	Calculate the number of GBDs between two dates given a holiday database.
Prototype	`xloper * __stdcall gbds_between_dates(double date1, double date2, xl_array *hols_array);`

Type string	"RBBK"
Notes	Returns an integer or an error value. All arguments are required. An efficient implementation of this function is not complicated. Calculating the number of weekdays and then calculating and subtracting the number of (non-weekend) holidays is the most obvious approach.

10.7 BUILDING AND READING DISCOUNT CURVES

There are many aspects of this subject which are beyond the scope of this book. It is assumed that this is not a new area for readers but for clarity, what is referred to here is the construction of a tabulated function (with an associated interpolation and extrapolation scheme) from which the present value of any future cash-flow can be calculated. (Such curves are often referred to a zero curves, as a point on the curve is equivalent to a zero-coupon bond price.) Curves implicitly contain information about a certain level of credit risk. A curve constructed from government debt instruments will, in general, imply lower interest rates than curves contructed from inter-bank instruments, which are, in turn, lower than those constructed from sub-investment grade corporate bonds.

This section focuses on the issues that any strategy for building such curves needs to address. The assumption is that an application in Excel needs to be able to value future cashflows consistent with a set of market prices of various financial instruments (the input prices). There are several questions to address before deciding how best to implement this in Excel:

• Where do the input prices come from? Are they manually input or sourced from a live feed or a combination of both?
• Are the input prices changing in real-time?
• Does the user's spreadsheet have access to the input prices or is the discount curve constructed centrally? If constructed centrally, how is Excel informed of changes and how does it retrieve the tabulated values and associated information?
• Is the discount curve intended to be a best fit or exact fit to the input prices?
• How is the curve interpolated? What is modelled over time – the instantaneous forward rate, the continuously compounded rate, the discount factor, or something else?
• How is the curve's data structure maintained? Is there a need for many instances of similar curves?
• How is the curve used? What information does the user need to get from the curve?

There is little about building curves that can't be accomplished in an Excel worksheet, although this may become very complex and unwieldy, especially if not supported by an add-in with appropriate date and interpolation functions. The following discussion assumes that this is not a practical approach and that there is a need to create an encapsulated and fast solution. There is nothing about the construction of such curves that can't be done in VBA either: the assumption is that C/C++ has been chosen.

The possibility that the curve is calculated and maintained centrally is not discussed in any detail, although it is worth noting the following two points:

- The remote server would need a means to inform the spreadsheet or the add-in that the curve has changed so that dependent cells can be recalculated. One approach would be for the server to provide a curve sequence number to the worksheet, which can then be used as a trigger argument.
- The server could communicate via a background thread which would initiate recalculation of volatile curve-dependent functions when the curve had changed.

In any case, delays that might arise in communicating with a remote server would make this a strong candidate for use of one or more background threads. It is almost certain that a worksheet would make a large number of references to various parts of a curve, meaning that such a strategy would ideally involve the communication of an entire curve from server to Excel, or to the DLL, to minimise communication overhead.

The discussion that follows focuses on the design of function interfaces that reflect the following assumptions:

1. Input prices are fed into worksheet cells automatically under the control of some external process, causing Excel to recalculate when new data arrive.
2. The user can also manually enter input price data, to augment or override.
3. The user will want to make many references to the same curve.

Assumptions (1) and (2) necessitate that a local copy of the curve be generated. Assumption (3) then dictates that the curve be calculated once and a reference to that curve be used as a trigger to functions that use the curve.

The first issue to address is how to prepare the input data for passing to the curve building function. The most flexible approach is the creation of a table of information in a worksheet along the following lines:

Instrument type	Start date	End date	Price or Rate	Instrument-specific data... (multiple columns)
...	...	...	...	...

The format, size and contents of this table would be governed by the variety of instruments used to construct the curves and by the implementation of the curve builder function. Doing this leads to a very simple interface function when compared to one alternative of, say, an input range for each type of instrument. The addition of new instrument types, with perhaps more columns, can be accommodated with full backwards compatibility – an important consideration. For this discussion, it is assumed that the day basis, coupon amount and frequency, etc., of input instruments are all contained in the *instrument-specific data* columns at the right of the table. (Clearly, there is little to stop the above table being in columns instead of rows. Even where a function is designed to accept row input, use of the TRANSPOSE() function is all that's required.)

Description	Takes a range of input instruments, sorts and verifies the contents as required, creates and constructs a persistent discount curve object associated with the calling cell, based on the type of interpolation or fitting encoded in a *method* argument. Returns a two-cell array of (1) a label containing a sequence number that can be used as a trigger and reference for curve-dependent functions, and (2) a time-of-last-update timestamp.
Prototype	`xloper * __stdcall create_discount_curve(xloper *input_table, xloper *method);`
Type string	`"RPP"`
Notes	Returns an array {label, timestamp} or an error value. The first argument is required but as it is an `xloper`, Excel will always call the function, so that the function will need to check the `xloper` type.
	Returning a timestamp is a good idea when there is a need to know whether a data-feed is still feeding live rates or has been silent for more than a certain threshold time.
	The function needs to record the calling cell and determine if this is the first call or whether a curve has already been built by this caller. (See sections 9.6 on page 305 and 9.8 on page 309.) A strategy for cleaning up disused curves, where an instance of this function has been deleted, also needs to be implemented in the DLL.

Description	Takes a reference to a discount curve returned by a call to `create_discount_curve()` above, and a date, and returns the (interpolated) discount curve value for that date.
Prototype	`xloper * __stdcall get_discount_value(char *curve_ref, double date, xloper *rtn_type);`
Type string	`"RCBP"`
Notes	Returns the discount function or other curve data at the given date, depending on the optional `rtn_type` argument, or an error value.

The above is a minimal set of curve functions. Others can easily be imagined and implemented, such as a function that returns an array of discount values corresponding to an array of input dates, or a function that calculates a forward rate given two dates and a day-basis. Functions that price complex derivatives can be implemented taking only a reference to a curve and to the data that describe the derivative, without the need to retrieve and store all the associated discount points in a spreadsheet.

10.8   BUILDING TREES AND LATTICES

The construction of trees and lattices for pricing complex derivatives raises similar issues to those involved in curve-building. (For simplicity, the term *tree* is used for both trees and lattices.) In both cases decisions need to be made about whether or not to use a remote server. If the decision is to use a server, the same issues arise regarding how to inform dependent cells on the worksheet that the tree has changed, and how to retrieve tree information. (See the above section for a brief discussion of these points.) If the decision is to create the tree locally, then the model of one function that creates the tree and returns a reference for tree-dependent cells to refer to, works just as well for trees as for discount curves.

There is however, a new layer of complexity compared to curve building: whereas an efficient curve-building routine will be quick enough to run in foreground, simple enough to be included in a distributed add-in, and simple enough to have all its inputs available locally in a user's workbook, the same might not be true of a tree. It may be that creating a simple tree might be fine in foreground on a modern fast machine, in which case the creation and reference functions need be no more complex than those for discount curves. However, a tree might be very much more complex to define and create, taking orders of magnitude more time to construct than a discount curve. In this case, the use of background threads becomes important.

Background threads can be used in two ways: (1) to communicate with a remote server that does all the work, or (2) to create and maintain a tree locally as a background task. (Sections 9.9 *Multi-tasking, multi-threading and asynchronous calls in DLLs* on page 316, and 9.10 *A background task management class and strategy* on page 320, cover these topics in detail.) Use of a remote server can be made without the use of background threads, although only if the communication between the two will always be fast enough to be done without slowing the recalculation of Excel unacceptably.

Trees also raise questions about using the worksheet as a tool for relating instances of tree nodes, by having one node to each cell or to a compact group of cells. This then supposes that the relationship between the nodes is set up on the spreadsheet. The flexibility that this provides might be ideal where the structure of the tree is experimental or irregular. However, there are some difficult conceptual barriers to overcome to make this work: tree construction is generally a multi-stage process. Trees that model interest rates might first be calibrated to the current yield curve, as represented by a set of discrete zero-coupon bond prices, then to a stochastic process that the rate is assumed to follow, perhaps represented by a set of market options prices. This may involve forward induction through the tree and backward induction, as well as numerical root-finding or error-minimising processes to match the input data. Excel is unidirectional when it comes to calculations, with a very clear line of dependence going one way only. Some of these things are too complex to leave entirely in the hands of Excel, even if the node objects are held within the DLL. In practice, it is easier to relate nodes to each other in code and have the worksheet functions act as an interface to the entire tree.

10.9   QUASI-RANDOM NUMBER SEQUENCES

Quasi-random sequences aim to reduce the number of samples that must be drawn at random from a given distribution, in order to achieve a certain statistical smoothness; in other words, to avoid clusters that bias the sample. This is particularly useful in Monte Carlo simulation (see section 10.11). A simulation using a sequence of pseudo-random numbers will involve as many trials as are needed to obtain the required degree of accuracy. The use of a predetermined set of quasi-random samples that cover the sample space more evenly, in some sense, reduces the number of trials while preserving the required statistical properties of the entire set.

In practice such sequences can be thought of simply as arrays of numbers of a given size, the size being predetermined by some analysis of the problem or by experiment. Any function or command that uses this information simply needs to read in the array. Where a command is the end-user of the sequence, you can deposit the array in a range of cells on a worksheet and access this, most sensibly, as a named range from the command's code (whether it be C/C++ or VB). Alternatively, you can create the array in a persistent structure in the DLL (or VB module). There is little in the way of performance difference between these choices provided that the code executing the simulation reads the array from a worksheet, if that's where it's kept, once *en bloc* rather than making individual cell references.

There is some appeal to creating such sequences in a worksheet – it allows you to verify the statistical properties easily – the only drawback being if the sequence is so large that it risks the spreadsheet becoming unwieldy or stretches the available memory. Where the sequence is to be used by a DLL function, the same choice of worksheet range or DLL structure is there. Provided that the sequence is not so large as to cause problems, the appeal of being able to see and test the numbers is a powerful one.

If the sequence is to be stored in a persistent structure in the add-in, it is advisable to link its existence to the cell that created it, so that deletion of the cell's contents, or of the cell itself, can be used as a trigger for freeing the resources used. This also enables the return value for the sequence to be passed as a parameter to a worksheet function. (See sections 9.6 *Maintaining large data structures within the DLL* on page 305 and 9.8 *Keeping track of the calling cell of a DLL function* on page 309.)

As far as the creation of sequences is concerned, the functions for this are well documented in a number of places. (Clewlow and Strickland). The creation of large sequences can be time-consuming. This may or may not be a problem for your application as, once created, sequences can be stored and reused. Such sequences are a possible candidate for storage in the worksheet using binary names. (See section 8.8 *Working with binary names* on page 209.) If creation time is a problem, C/C++ makes light work of the task, otherwise VB code might even be sufficient. (Remember that C/C++ with its powerful pointer capabilities, can access arrays much faster than VB.)

10.10   GENERATING CORRELATED RANDOM SAMPLES

When using Monte Carlo simulation (see next section) to model a system that depends on many partially-related variables, it is often necessary to generate vectors of correlated random samples from a normal distribution. These are computed using the (real symmetric) covariance matrix of the correlated variables. Once the eigenvalues have been computed (see section 10.3 on page 351)[5] they can be combined many times with many

---

[5] Note that this relies on code from Numerical Recipes in C omitted from the CD ROM for licensing reasons

sets of normal samples in order to generate the correlated samples. (See Clewlow and Strickland, Chapter 4.)

In practice, therefore, the process needs to be broken down into the following steps:

1. Obtain or create the covariance matrix.
2. Generate the eigenvalues and eigenvectors from the covariance matrix.
3. Generate a vector of uncorrelated normal samples.
4. Transform these into correlated normal samples using the eigenvalues and eigen-vectors.
5. Perform the calculations associated with the Monte Carlo trial.
6. Repeat steps (3) to (5) until the simulation is complete.

The calculation of the correlated samples is essentially one of matrix multiplication. Excel does this fairly efficiently on the worksheet, with only a small overhead of conversion from worksheet range to array of doubles and back again. If the simulation is unacceptably slow, removing this overhead by storing eigenvalues and vectors within the DLL and calculating the correlated samples entirely within the DLL is one possible optimisation.

10.11   MONTE CARLO SIMULATION

Monte Carlo (MC) simulation is a numerical technique used to model complex randomly driven processes. The purpose of this section is to demonstrate ways in which such processes can be implemented in Excel, rather than to present a textbook guide to Monte Carlo techniques.[6]

Simulations are comprised of many thousands of repeated trials and can take a long time to execute. If the user can tolerate Excel being tied up during the simulation, then running it from a VB or an XLL command is a sensible choice. If long simulations need to be hidden within worksheet functions, then the use of background threads becomes necessary. The following sections discuss both of these options.

Each MC trial is driven by one or more random samples from one or more probability distributions. Once the outcome of a single trial is known, the desired quantity can be calculated. This is repeated many times so that an average of the calculated quantity can be derived.

In general, a large number of trials need to be performed to obtain statistically reliable results. This means that MC simulation is usually a time-consuming process. A number of techniques have been developed for the world of financial derivatives that reduce the number of trials required to yield a given statistical accuracy. Two important examples are variance reduction and the use of quasi-random sequences (see above).

Variance reduction techniques aim to find some measure, the control, that is closely correlated to the required result, and for which an exact value can be calculated analytically. With each trial both the control and the result are calculated and difference in

---

[6] There are numerous excellent texts on the subject of Monte Carlo simulation, dealing with issues such as numbers of trials, error estimates and other related topics such as variance reduction. *Numerical Recipes in C* contains an introduction to Monte Carlo methods applied to integration. *Implementing Derivative Models* (Clewlow and Strickland), published by Wiley, contains an excellent introduction of MC to financial instrument pricing.

value recorded. Since the error in the calculation of the control is known at each trial, the average result can be calculated from the control's true value and the average difference between the control and the result. With a well-chosen control, the number of required trials can be reduced dramatically.

The use of quasi-random sequences aims to reduce the amount of clustering in a random series of samples. (See section 10.9 above.) The use of this technique assumes that a decision is made before running the simulation as to how many trials, and therefore samples, are needed. These can be created and stored before the simulation is run. Once generated, they can be used many times of course.

Within Excel, there are a number of ways to tackle MC simulation. The following sub-sections discuss the most sensible of these.

10.11.1   Using Excel and VBA only

A straightforward approach to Monte Carlo simulation is as follows:

1. Set up the calculation of the one-trial result in a single worksheet, as a function of the random samples from the desired distribution(s).
2. Generate the distribution samples using a volatile function (e.g., RAND()).
3. Set up a command macro that recalculates the worksheet as many times as instructed, each time reading the required result from the worksheet, evaluating the average.
4. Deposit the result of the calculation, and perhaps the standard error, in a cell or cells on a worksheet, periodically or at the end of the simulation.

Using Excel and VBA in this way can be very slow. The biggest optimisation is to control screen updating, using the Application.ScreenUpdating = True/False statements, analogous to the C API xlcEcho function, and speeds things up considerably.

The following VB code example shows how this can be accomplished, and is included in the example workbook MCexample1.xls on the CD ROM. The workbook calculates a very simple spread option payoff, MAX(asset_price_1−asset_price_2, 0), using this VB command attached to a button control on the worksheet. The worksheet example assumes that both assets are lognormally distributed and uses an on-sheet Box-Muller transform. The VB command neither knows nor cares about the option being priced nor the pricing method used. A completely different option or model could be placed in the workbook without the need to alter the VB command. (Changing the macro so that it calculates and records more data at each trial would involve some fairly obvious modifications, of course.)

```
Option Explicit

Private Sub CommandButton1_Click()

    Dim trials As Long, max_trials As Long
    Dim dont_do_screen As Long, refresh_count As Long
    Dim payoff As Double, sum_payoff As Double
    Dim sum_sq_payoff As Double, std_dev As Double
    Dim rAvgPayoff As Range, rPayoff As Range, rTrials As Range
    Dim rStdDev As Range, rStdErr As Range
```

```
' Set up error trap in case ranges are not defined
' or calculations fail or ranges contain error values
  On Error GoTo handleCancel

' Set up references to named ranges for optimum access
  Set rAvgPayoff = Range("AvgPayoff")
  Set rPayoff = Range("Payoff")
  Set rTrials = Range("Trials")
  Set rStdDev = Range("StdDev")
  Set rStdErr = Range("StdErr")

  With Application
    .EnableCancelKey = xlErrorHandler 'Esc will exit macro
    .ScreenUpdating = False
    .Calculation = xlCalculationManual
  End With

  max_trials = Range("MaxTrials")

' Macro will refresh the screen every RefreshCount trials
  refresh_count = Range("RefreshCount")
  dont_do_screen = refresh_count

  For trials = 1 To max_trials
    dont_do_screen = dont_do_screen - 1

    Application.Calculate
    payoff = rPayoff
    sum_payoff = sum_payoff + payoff
    sum_sq_payoff = sum_sq_payoff + payoff * payoff

    If dont_do_screen = 0 Then
      std_dev = Sqr(sum_sq_payoff - sum_payoff _
        * sum_payoff / trials) / (trials - 1))

      Application.ScreenUpdating = True
      rAvgPayoff = sum_payoff / trials
      rTrials = trials
      rStdDev = std_dev
      rStdErr = std_dev / Sqr(trials)
      Application.ScreenUpdating = False
      dont_do_screen = refresh_count
    End If
  Next

handleCancel:
  Application.ScreenUpdating = False
  Application.Calculation = xlCalculationAutomatic
End Sub
```

The Application.Calculate = xlAutomatic/xlManual statements control whether or not a whole workbook should be recalculated when a cell changes. (The C API analogue is xlcCalculation with the first argument set to 1 or 3 respectively.) The VB Range().Calculate method allows the more specific calculation of a range of cells. Unfortunately, the C API has no equivalent of this method. Only the functions xlcCalculateNow, which calculates all open workbooks, and xlcCalculateDocument, which calculates the active worksheet, are provided. (See below.)

10.11.2   Using Excel and C/C++ only

If the above approach is sufficient for your needs, then there is little point in making life more complicated. If it is too slow then the following steps should be considered, in this order, until the desired performance has been achieved:

1. Optimise the speed of the worksheet calculations. This might mean wrapping an entire trial calculation in a few C/C++ XLL add-in functions.
2. Port the above command to an exported C/C++ command and associate this with a command button or menu item.
3. If the simulation is simple enough and quick enough, create a (foreground) worksheet function that performs the entire simulation within the XLL so that, to the user, it is just another function that takes arguments and returns a result.
4. If the simulation is too lengthy for (3) use a background thread for a worksheet function that performs the simulation within the XLL. (See section 9.10 *A background task management class and strategy* on page 320.)

Optimisations (3) and (4) are discussed in the next section. If the simulation is too lengthy for (3) and/or too complex for (4), then you are left with optimisations (1) and (2).

For optimisation (1), the goal is to speed up the recalculation of the worksheet. Where multiple correlated variables are being simulated, it is necessary to generate correlated samples in the most efficient way. Once a covariance matrix has been converted to a system of eigenvectors and eigenvalues, this is simply a question of generating samples and using Excel's own (very efficient) matrix multiplication routines. Generation of normal samples using, say, Box-Muller is best done in the XLL. Valuation of the instruments involved in the trial will in many cases be far more efficiently done in the XLL especially where interest rate curves are being simulated and discount curves need to be built with each trial.

For optimisation (2), the C/C++ equivalent of the above VB code is given below. (See sections 8.6 *Registering and un-registering DLL (XLL) commands* on page 196 and 8.6.1 *Accessing XLL commands* on page 198 for details of how to register XLL commands and access them from Excel.) The command monte_carlo_control() runs the simulation, and can be terminated by the user pressing the Esc key. (See section 8.6.2 *Breaking execution of an XLL command* on page 199.)

```
int __stdcall monte_carlo_control(void)
{
    double payoff, sum_payoff = 0.0, sum_sq_payoff = 0.0;
    double std_dev;
    cpp_xloper Break, CalcSetting(3); // Manual recalculation

    Excel4(xlfCancelKey, 0, 1, p_xlTrue); // Enable user breaks
    Excel4(xlfEcho, 0, 1, p_xlFalse); // Disable screen updating
    Excel4(xlcCalculation, 0, 1, &CalcSetting); // Manual

    long trials, max_trials, dont_do_screen, refresh_count;

// Set up references to named ranges which must exist
    xlName MaxTrials("!MaxTrials"), Payoff("!Payoff"),
        AvgPayoff("!AvgPayoff");
```

```
// Set up references to named ranges whose existence is optional
    xlName Trials("!Trials"), StdDev("!StdDev"), StdErr("!StdErr"),
        RefreshCount("!RefreshCount");

    if(!MaxTrials.IsRefValid() || !Payoff.IsRefValid()
    || !AvgPayoff.IsRefValid())
        goto cleanup;

    if(!RefreshCount.IsRefValid())
        refresh_count = 1000;
    else
        refresh_count = (long)(double)RefreshCount;

    dont_do_screen = refresh_count;

    max_trials = (long)(double)MaxTrials;

    for(trials = 1; trials <= max_trials; trials++)
    {
        Excel4(xlcCalculateDocument, 0, 0);

        payoff = (double)Payoff;

        sum_payoff += payoff;
        sum_sq_payoff += payoff * payoff;

        if(!--dont_do_screen)
        {
            std_dev = sqrt(sum_sq_payoff - sum_payoff * sum_payoff
                / trials) / (trials - 1);

            Excel4(xlfEcho, 0, 1, p_xlTrue);

            AvgPayoff = sum_payoff / trials;
            Trials = (double)trials;
            StdDev = std_dev;
            StdErr = std_dev / sqrt((double)trials);

            Excel4(xlfEcho, 0, 1, p_xlFalse);
            dont_do_screen = refresh_count;
// Detect and clear any user break attempt
            Excel4(xlAbort, &Break, 1, p_xlFalse);

            if((bool)Break)
                goto cleanup;
        }
    }
cleanup:
    CalcSetting = 1; // Automatic recalculation
    Excel4(xlfEcho, 0, 1, p_xlTrue);
    Excel4(xlcCalculation, 0, 1, &CalcSetting);
    return 1;
}
```

The above code is listed in MonteCarlo.cpp in the example project on the CD ROM.
Note that the command uses xlcCalculateDocument to recalculate the active sheet
only. If using this function you should be careful to ensure that all the calculations are on
this sheet, otherwise you should use xlcCalculateNow. Note also that the command

does not exit (fail) if named ranges `Trials`, `StdDev` or `StdErr` do not exist on the active sheet, as these are not critical to the simulation.

The above code can easily be modified to remove the recalculation of the payoff from the worksheet entirely: the input values for the simulation can be retrieved from the worksheet, the calculations done entirely within the DLL, and the results deposited as above. The use of the `xlcCalculateDocument` becomes redundant, and the named range `Payoff` becomes write-only. You may still want to disable automatic recalculation so that Excel does not recalculate things that depend on the interim results during the simulation.

When considering a hybrid worksheet-DLL solution, you should be careful not to make the entire trial calculation difficult to understand or modify as a result of being split. It is better to have the entire calculation in one place or the other. It is in general better to use the worksheet, relying heavily on XLL functions for performance if needs be. Bugs in the trial calculations are far more easily found when a single trial can be inspected openly in the worksheet.

10.11.3   Using worksheet functions only

If a family of simulations can be accommodated within a manageable worksheet function interface, there is nothing to prevent the simulation being done entirely in the DLL, i.e., without the use of VB or XLL commands. Where this involves, or can involve, a very lengthy execution time, then use of a background thread is strongly advised. Section 9.10 *A background task management class and strategy* on page 320, describes an approach for this that also enables the function to periodically return interim results before the simulation is complete – something particularly suited to an MC simulation where you might be unsure at the outset how many trials you want to perform.

One drawback of only using functions, is the early ending of the simulation . This is possible with the use of an input parameter that can be used as a flag to background tasks. Worksheet functions that are executed in the foreground cannot communicate interim results back to the worksheet and can only be terminated early through use of the `xlAbort` function.

This approach hides all of the complexity of the MC simulation. One problem is that MC is a technique often used in cases where the calculations are particularly difficult, experimental or non-standard. This suggests that placing the calculations in the worksheet, where they can be inspected, is generally the right approach.

10.12   CALIBRATION

The calibration of models is a very complex and subtle subject, often requiring a deep understanding not only of the model being calibrated but also the background of data – its meaning and reliability; embedded information about market costs, taxation, regulation, inefficiency; etc. – and the purpose to which the model is to be put. This very brief section has nothing to add to the vast pool of professional literature and experience. It does nevertheless aim to make a couple of useful points on this in relation to Excel.

One of the most powerful tools in Excel is the Solver. (See also section 2.10.2 *Goal Seek and Solver Add-in* on page 23.) If used well, very complex calibrations can be performed within an acceptable amount of time, especially if the spreadsheet calculations are optimised. In many cases this will require the use of XLL worksheet functions. It should be noted that worksheet functions that perform long tasks in a background thread (see section 9.10) are not suitable for use with the Solver: the Solver will think that the cells have been recalculated when, in fact, the background thread has simply accepted the task onto its to-do list, but not yet returned a final value.

The most flexible and user-friendly way to harness the Solver is via VBA. The functions that the Solver makes available in VBA are:

- SolverAdd
- SolverChange
- SolverDelete
- SolverFinish
- SolverFinishDialog
- SolverGet
- SolverLoad
- SolverOk
- SolverOkDialog
- SolverOptions
- SolverReset
- SolverSave
- SolverSolve

The full syntax for all of these commands can be found on Microsoft's MSDN web site. Before these can be used, the VBA project needs to have a reference for the Solver add-in. This is simply done via the VB editor Tools/References... dialog.

The example spreadsheet Solver VBA Example.xls on the CD ROM contains a very simple example of a few of these being used to find the square root of a given number. The Solver is invoked automatically from a worksheet-change event trap, and deposits the result in the desired cell without displaying any Solver dialogs.

The VB code is:

```
' For this event trap command macro to run properly, VBA must have a
' reference to the Solver project established. See Tools/
' References...

Private Sub Worksheet_Change(ByVal Target As Range)

    If Target.Address = Range("Input").Address Then
        SolverReset
        SolverOK setCell:=Range("Target"), maxMinVal:=2, _
            byChange:=Range("Output")
        SolverSolve UserFinish:=True ' Don't show a dialog when done
    End If

End Sub
```

Note that the named range Input is simply a trigger for this code to run. In the example spreadsheet it is also an input into the calculation of Target. The Solver will complain if Target does not contain a formula, which, at the very least, should depend on Output. It is a straightforward matter to associate a similar VB sub-routine with a control object, such as a command button, and to create many Solver tasks on a single sheet, something which is fiddly to achieve using Excel's menus alone.

References

Abramowitz M. and Stegun I., 1970, *Handbook of Mathematical Functions with Formulas, Graphs, and Mathematical Tables*, Dover Publications, Inc., Mineola, NY.

Clewlow L. and Strickland C., 1998, *Implementing Derivative Models*, John Wiley & Sons, Chichester.

Jackson M. and Staunton M., 2001, *Advanced Modelling in Finance Using Excel and VBA*, John Wiley & Sons, Chichester.

Kernighan B. and Ritchie D, 1988, *The C Programming Language*, 2nd edn, Prentice Hall, Upper Saddle River, NJ.

Liberty J., *Teach Yourself C++*, 4th edn, Sams Publishing, Indiana.

Microsoft Excel 97 Developer's Kit, 1997, Microsoft Press, Buffalo, NY.

Press W., Teukolsky S., Vetterling W. and Flannery B., 1988, 1992, *Numerical Recipes in C*, Cambridge University Press, Cambridge.

Press W., Teukolsky S., Vetterling W. and Flannery B., 2002, *Numerical Recipes in C++*, Cambridge University Press, Cambridge.

Satir G. and Brown D., 1995, 1996, *C++: The Core Language*, O'Reilly & Associates, Inc.

Stroustrup B., 1991, *The C++ Programming Language*, 2nd edn, Addison-Wesley Publishing Company, Boston, MA.

Web Links and Other Resources

There are many web resources that are useful and relevant to the subject of this book. Some are private, run by interested and enthusiastic individuals. Some are run by consultants both as a public service and as a means of promoting their own services. Many are run by companies who sell relevant software or services; Microsoft being the most important example. Some time spent searching the web with keywords such as *Excel, XLM, XLL*, will quickly yield the majority of these. A review of these sites or the products and services they provide is, of course, completely beyond this book's scope and nothing is said or implied about their content or quality. Here are just a very few examples that were current at the time of writing:

http://www.microsoft.com/downloads/search.asp.

http://www.cppreference.com/index.html

http://www.as-ltd.co.uk/xllplus/default.htm

http://managedxll.net/index.html

http://www.appspro.com

http://www.cpearson.com

http://xcelfiles.homestead.com

The following three links are all discussed in section 1.2 *What tools and resources are required to write add-ins* on page 2:

msdn.microsoft.com/library/default.asp?url=/library/officedev/office97/edkfrnt.htm.

download.microsoft.com/download/platformsdk/sample27/1/NT4/EN-US/Frmwrk32.exe.

download.microsoft.com/download/excel97win/utility4/1/WIN98/EN-US/Macrofun.exe.

Microsoft run a number of Internet newsgroups that provide a useful forum for questions and answers, as well as occasional general announcements from Microsoft technical staff. Here are just three of the many examples:

news://msnews.microsoft.com/microsoft.public.excel

news://msnews.microsoft.com/microsoft.public.excel.sdk

news://msnews.microsoft.com/microsoft.public.excel.programming

The Microsoft Developer Network (MSDN), and the library of Knowledge Base articles accessible through it, are an invaluable source of information about all Microsoft products including Excel, VB and Visual Studio. For example, Knowledge Base article 198477 relates to access violation run-time errors occurring when writing to static strings under debug with the /ZI compiler flag set in certain versions of Visual Studio.[1] There are too many useful and relevant articles to list, but Microsoft's MSDN site at http://msdn.microsoft.com provides a comprehensive search facility.

http://xlw.sourceforge.net
A freely available C++ wrapper developed by Jérôme Lecomte.

Microsoft make available an executable utility called B2C.EXE which converts passages of VB COM Automation code into C++ Automation code, with some limitations. (Search for the executable on the Microsoft download site at the first URL in this section). Resulting code can be cut and pasted into your Visual C++ source code. The utility is also available at the following link:

http://support.microsoft.com/default.aspx?scid=kb;EN-US216388

---

[1] This problem can be encountered when trying to set the length byte on byte-counted static strings.

Index

Index compiled by Terry Halliday

WILEY COPYRIGHT INFORMATION AND TERMS OF USE

CD supplement to *Excel Add-in Development in C/C++, Applications in Finance*

by **Steve Dalton**

ISBN 0-470-02469-0

CD-ROM Copyright © 2004 Eigensys Limited

Published by John Wiley & Sons Ltd, The Atrium, Southern Gate, Chichester, West Sussex, PO19 8SQ. All rights reserved.

All material contained with the accompanying CD product is protected by copyright, whether or not a copyright notice appears on the particular screen where the material is displayed. No part of the material may be reproduced or transmitted in any form or by any means, or stored in a computer for retrieval purposes or otherwise, without written permission from Eigensys, unless this is expressly permitted in a copyright notice or usage statement accompanying the materials. Requests for permission to store or reproduce material for any purpose, or to distribute it on a network, should be emailed to permissions@eigensys.com.

None of the author, Eigensys Ltd or John Wiley & Sons Ltd accept any responsibility or liability for loss or damage occasioned to any person or property through using materials, instructions, methods or ideas contained herein, or acting or refraining from acting as a result of such use. The author, Eigensys and Publisher expressly disclaim all implied warranties, including merchantability or fitness for any particular purpose. There will be no duty on the author, Eigensys or Publisher to correct any errors or defects in the software. The source code and the methods contain are intended solely for example and clarification. It is the responsibility of the user to ensure that whatever software or source code is utilised by him/her is suitable for his/her requirements in all respects.